Seeding the Tradition

Alexander M. Cannon

SEEDING THE TRADITION

Musical Creativity

in Southern Vietnam

Wesleyan University Press   Middletown, Connecticut

Wesleyan University Press
Middletown CT 06459
www.wesleyan.edu/wespress
© 2022 Alexander M. Cannon
All rights reserved
Manufactured in the United States of America
Designed by Mindy Basinger Hill
Typeset in Minion Pro

Library of Congress Cataloging-in-Publication Data
available upon request
Cloth ISBN: 978-0-8195-8079-5
Paperback ISBN: 978-0-8195-8080-1
Ebook ISBN: 978-0-8195-8081-8

5   4   3   2   1

*The Publisher gratefully acknowledges the AMS 75 Publication Awards
for Younger Scholars Fund of the American Musicological Society,
supported in part by the National Endowment for the Humanities and
the Andrew W. Mellon Foundation.*

CONTENTS

MEDIA EXAMPLES

An online reader's companion hosts media referenced throughout the text.
Please navigate to weslpress.org/readers-companions and
use the password [creativity] to gain access.

TRACK 1: "Zen improvisation" performed by Nguyễn Vĩnh Bảo on the đàn tranh (recorded by Nguyễn Vĩnh Bảo, June 19, 2011)

TRACK 2: "Nhạc Miên Nhạc Pháp" performed by Trần Minh Đức on the đàn sến (recorded by the author, June 5, 2009)

TRACK 3: "Ngũ đối hạ" and kèn bóp performed by Thầy Phước Cường and ensemble at the Bửu Sơn Temple, Ho Chi Minh City (recorded by the author, October 23, 2008)

TRACK 4: "Lưu thủy trường" performed by Nguyễn Vĩnh Bảo on the đàn tranh (recorded by Nguyễn Vĩnh Bảo, November 13, 2009)

TRACK 5: "Vọng cổ" performed by Nguyễn Vĩnh Bảo on the đàn kìm and the author on the đàn tranh (recorded by the author, January 15, 2009)

TRACK 6: "Lưu thủy trường qua Phú lục" performed by Trần Minh Đức on the đàn sến (recorded by the author, July 4, 2010)

TRACK 7: *Rao* preceding "Ngũ đối hạ" performed by Nguyễn Vĩnh Bảo on the đàn tranh (recorded by the author, February 19, 2009)

TRACK 8: "Xàng xê" performed by Trần Minh Đức on the đàn sến (recorded by the author, July 4, 2010)

TRACK 9: "Lý con sáo" (no *rao* prelude) performed by Nguyễn Vĩnh Bảo on the đàn tranh (recorded by the author, July 25, 2013)

TRACK 10: "Đảo ngũ cung" performed by Trần Minh Đức on the đàn sến (recorded by the author, June 29, 2010)

TRACK 11: "Tứ đại oán" performed by Nguyễn Vĩnh Bảo on the đàn tranh (recorded by the author, August 5, 2010)

TRACK 12: Lòng bản and kiểu of "Nam Ai" by Huỳnh Khải (recorded by the author, August 14, 2013)

TRACK 13: Excerpt of "Tây thi" performed by Nguyễn Vĩnh Bảo on the đàn kìm (recorded by the author, June 12, 2009)

TRACK 14: "Nam xuân" performed by Nguyễn Vĩnh Bảo on the đàn tranh (recorded by the author, May 6, 2009)

TRACK 15: "Nam xuân" performed by musicians at the Lá Thơm restaurant (recorded by the author, November 5, 2008)

TRACK 16: An excerpt of musicmaking at Ninh Kiều Quán 2 Restaurant featuring Trần Minh Đức, Lê Đình Bích, and friends (recorded by the author, January 6, 2015)

TRACK 17: "Nam xuân" performed by Trần Minh Đức on the đàn sến (recorded by the author, June 24, 2009)

TRACK 18: "Người là Hồ Chí Minh" performed by Thanh Kim on ghi ta phím lõm, Thiện Vũ on đàn kìm, Quốc Tuấn on đàn cò, and singers Thúy Phương and Thái Ngọc Lợi (recorded [very poorly] by the author, June 6, 2010)

TRACK 19: "Trống cơm" rehearsed by the Tiếng Hát Quê Hương Ensemble directed by Phạm Thúy Hoan (recorded by the author, March 8, 2009)

TRACK 20: "Lưu thủy trường" performed by Phạm Thúy Hoan and her students (recorded by the author, August 17, 2013)

TRACK 21: "Ngũ điểm – Bài tạ" performed by Trần Minh Đức and ensemble (recorded by the author, January 6, 2015)

TRACK 22: "Ngũ điểm – Bài tạ" performed by Trần Minh Đức on the đàn sến (recorded by the author, April 16, 2009)

TRACK 23: "Lưu thủy trường" performed by Hải Luận on ghi ta phím lõm, Huỳnh Khải on đàn vĩ cầm, Duy Kim on đàn tranh, and Trường Giang on đàn kìm (recorded by the author, July 16, 2012)

TRACK 24: Vietnamese terms read by Diệp Tử Khôi

TRACK 25: Vietnamese proper names read by Diệp Tử Khôi

TRACK 26: Vietnamese tune titles read by Diệp Tử Khôi

MEDIA EXAMPLES

An online reader's companion hosts media referenced throughout the text.
Please navigate to weslpress.org/readers-companions and
use the password [creativity] to gain access.

TRACK 1: "Zen improvisation" performed by Nguyễn Vĩnh Bảo on the đàn tranh (recorded by Nguyễn Vĩnh Bảo, June 19, 2011)

TRACK 2: "Nhạc Miên Nhạc Pháp" performed by Trần Minh Đức on the đàn sến (recorded by the author, June 5, 2009)

TRACK 3: "Ngũ đối hạ" and kèn bóp performed by Thầy Phước Cường and ensemble at the Bửu Sơn Temple, Ho Chi Minh City (recorded by the author, October 23, 2008)

TRACK 4: "Lưu thủy trường" performed by Nguyễn Vĩnh Bảo on the đàn tranh (recorded by Nguyễn Vĩnh Bảo, November 13, 2009)

TRACK 5: "Vọng cổ" performed by Nguyễn Vĩnh Bảo on the đàn kìm and the author on the đàn tranh (recorded by the author, January 15, 2009)

TRACK 6: "Lưu thủy trường qua Phú lục" performed by Trần Minh Đức on the đàn sến (recorded by the author, July 4, 2010)

TRACK 7: Rao preceding "Ngũ đối hạ" performed by Nguyễn Vĩnh Bảo on the đàn tranh (recorded by the author, February 19, 2009)

TRACK 8: "Xàng xê" performed by Trần Minh Đức on the đàn sến (recorded by the author, July 4, 2010)

TRACK 9: "Lý con sáo" (no rao prelude) performed by Nguyễn Vĩnh Bảo on the đàn tranh (recorded by the author, July 25, 2013)

TRACK 10: "Đảo ngũ cung" performed by Trần Minh Đức on the đàn sến (recorded by the author, June 29, 2010)

TRACK 11: "Tứ đại oán" performed by Nguyễn Vĩnh Bảo on the đàn tranh (recorded by the author, August 5, 2010)

TRACK 12: Lòng bản and kiểu of "Nam Ai" by Huỳnh Khải (recorded by the author, August 14, 2013)

TRACK 13: Excerpt of "Tây thi" performed by Nguyễn Vĩnh Bảo on the đàn kìm (recorded by the author, June 12, 2009)

TRACK 14: "Nam xuân" performed by Nguyễn Vĩnh Bảo on the đàn tranh (recorded by the author, May 6, 2009)

TRACK 15: "Nam xuân" performed by musicians at the Lá Thơm restaurant (recorded by the author, November 5, 2008)

TRACK 16: An excerpt of musicmaking at Ninh Kiều Quán 2 Restaurant featuring Trần Minh Đức, Lê Đình Bích, and friends (recorded by the author, January 6, 2015)

TRACK 17: "Nam xuân" performed by Trần Minh Đức on the đàn sến (recorded by the author, June 24, 2009)

TRACK 18: "Người là Hồ Chí Minh" performed by Thanh Kim on ghi ta phím lõm, Thiện Vũ on đàn kìm, Quốc Tuấn on đàn cò, and singers Thúy Phương and Thái Ngọc Lợi (recorded [very poorly] by the author, June 6, 2010)

TRACK 19: "Trống cơm" rehearsed by the Tiếng Hát Quê Hương Ensemble directed by Phạm Thúy Hoan (recorded by the author, March 8, 2009)

TRACK 20: "Lưu thủy trường" performed by Phạm Thúy Hoan and her students (recorded by the author, August 17, 2013)

TRACK 21: "Ngũ điểm – Bài tạ" performed by Trần Minh Đức and ensemble (recorded by the author, January 6, 2015)

TRACK 22: "Ngũ điểm – Bài tạ" performed by Trần Minh Đức on the đàn sến (recorded by the author, April 16, 2009)

TRACK 23: "Lưu thủy trường" performed by Hải Luận on ghi ta phím lõm, Huỳnh Khải on đàn vĩ cầm, Duy Kim on đàn tranh, and Trường Giang on đàn kìm (recorded by the author, July 16, 2012)

TRACK 24: Vietnamese terms read by Diệp Tử Khôi

TRACK 25: Vietnamese proper names read by Diệp Tử Khôi

TRACK 26: Vietnamese tune titles read by Diệp Tử Khôi

MEDIA EXAMPLES

An online reader's companion hosts media referenced throughout the text.
Please navigate to weslpress.org/readers-companions and
use the password [creativity] to gain access.

TRACK 1: "Zen improvisation" performed by Nguyễn Vĩnh Bảo on the đàn tranh (recorded by Nguyễn Vĩnh Bảo, June 19, 2011)

TRACK 2: "Nhạc Miên Nhạc Pháp" performed by Trần Minh Đức on the đàn sến (recorded by the author, June 5, 2009)

TRACK 3: "Ngũ đối hạ" and kèn bóp performed by Thầy Phước Cường and ensemble at the Bửu Sơn Temple, Ho Chi Minh City (recorded by the author, October 23, 2008)

TRACK 4: "Lưu thủy trường" performed by Nguyễn Vĩnh Bảo on the đàn tranh (recorded by Nguyễn Vĩnh Bảo, November 13, 2009)

TRACK 5: "Vọng cổ" performed by Nguyễn Vĩnh Bảo on the đàn kìm and the author on the đàn tranh (recorded by the author, January 15, 2009)

TRACK 6: "Lưu thủy trường qua Phú lục" performed by Trần Minh Đức on the đàn sến (recorded by the author, July 4, 2010)

TRACK 7: Rao preceding "Ngũ đối hạ" performed by Nguyễn Vĩnh Bảo on the đàn tranh (recorded by the author, February 19, 2009)

TRACK 8: "Xàng xê" performed by Trần Minh Đức on the đàn sến (recorded by the author, July 4, 2010)

TRACK 9: "Lý con sáo" (no rao prelude) performed by Nguyễn Vĩnh Bảo on the đàn tranh (recorded by the author, July 25, 2013)

TRACK 10: "Đảo ngũ cung" performed by Trần Minh Đức on the đàn sến (recorded by the author, June 29, 2010)

TRACK 11: "Tứ đại oán" performed by Nguyễn Vĩnh Bảo on the đàn tranh (recorded by the author, August 5, 2010)

TRACK 12: Lòng bản and kiểu of "Nam Ai" by Huỳnh Khải (recorded by the author, August 14, 2013)

TRACK 13: Excerpt of "Tây thi" performed by Nguyễn Vĩnh Bảo on the đàn kìm (recorded by the author, June 12, 2009)

TRACK 14: "Nam xuân" performed by Nguyễn Vĩnh Bảo on the đàn tranh (recorded by the author, May 6, 2009)

TRACK 15: "Nam xuân" performed by musicians at the Lá Thơm restaurant (recorded by the author, November 5, 2008)

TRACK 16: An excerpt of musicmaking at Ninh Kiều Quán 2 Restaurant featuring Trần Minh Đức, Lê Đình Bích, and friends (recorded by the author, January 6, 2015)

TRACK 17: "Nam xuân" performed by Trần Minh Đức on the đàn sến (recorded by the author, June 24, 2009)

TRACK 18: "Người là Hồ Chí Minh" performed by Thanh Kim on ghi ta phím lõm, Thiện Vũ on đàn kìm, Quốc Tuấn on đàn cò, and singers Thúy Phương and Thái Ngọc Lợi (recorded [very poorly] by the author, June 6, 2010)

TRACK 19: "Trống cơm" rehearsed by the Tiếng Hát Quê Hương Ensemble directed by Phạm Thúy Hoan (recorded by the author, March 8, 2009)

TRACK 20: "Lưu thủy trường" performed by Phạm Thúy Hoan and her students (recorded by the author, August 17, 2013)

TRACK 21: "Ngũ điểm – Bài tạ" performed by Trần Minh Đức and ensemble (recorded by the author, January 6, 2015)

TRACK 22: "Ngũ điểm – Bài tạ" performed by Trần Minh Đức on the đàn sến (recorded by the author, April 16, 2009)

TRACK 23: "Lưu thủy trường" performed by Hải Luận on ghi ta phím lõm, Huỳnh Khải on đàn vĩ cầm, Duy Kim on đàn tranh, and Trường Giang on đàn kìm (recorded by the author, July 16, 2012)

TRACK 24: Vietnamese terms read by Diệp Tử Khôi

TRACK 25: Vietnamese proper names read by Diệp Tử Khôi

TRACK 26: Vietnamese tune titles read by Diệp Tử Khôi

NOTE ON PRONUNCIATION

Many ethnomusicological and anthropological ethnographies start with guides to the pronunciation of terms not found in English or other European languages. I do not find these useful, as one really needs to take language classes or speak with the authors to learn how to pronounce the words correctly. I also am not a linguist. Instead, I offer a brief introduction to the Vietnamese language and include three audio tracks of commonly used terms found in this monograph.

Vietnamese is a syllabic tonal language, and each term written includes an indication of one of six tones (and I include an example in parentheses following the tone): no tone (*song lang*, a wooden clapper played with the foot); rising tone (*nhấn*, a kind of gliding ornament); falling tone (*thầy*, male teacher); slight falling then rising tone (*thủy*, water); rising glottalized tone (*Nguyễn*, a common Vietnamese last name); and short falling glottalized tone (*Việt*, the Vietnamese people). Terms also feature combinations of tones: đờn ca tài tử, the music of talented amateurs under consideration in this study, features the falling tone on the first and third syllables; no tone on the second syllable; and the slight falling then rising tone on the final syllable. It should go without saying that different tones indicate different meanings: *đoàn* is "a music ensemble," while *đoán* is "a guess"; *cô* means "female teacher" or "aunt," while *cổ* means "ancient."

The Vietnamese language also has dialect variety, often divided into the northern, central, and southern dialects. There also are distinctions within these regions. I speak a blend of the Saigon dialect of Ho Chi Minh City and the miền Tây Mekong Delta dialect. My friend, Diệp Tử Khôi, who graciously recorded the tracks listed here, speaks a blend of the Saigon dialect and the south-central dialect of his hometown.

To aid replication of some of the terms found in the text, please listen to the following tracks available on the accompanying website:

- On Track 24, please find the following nouns: (1) cô; (2) đàn bầu; (3) đàn cò; (4) đàn ghi ta phím lõm; (5) đàn kìm; (6) đàn sến; (7) đàn tranh; (8) đàn tùy hứng; (9) điệu Bắc; (10) điệu Hạ; (11) điệu Nam; (12) điệu Oán; (13) đờn ca tài tử; (14) hạt giống; (15) hoa lá cành; (16) kỹ thuật; (17) lòng bản (lồng bản); (18) nhạc dân tộc; (19) phát triển; (20) rao; (21) sáng tạo; (22) song lang; (23) tâm hồn; (24) thầy; (25) Tiếng Hát Quê Hương; (26) tự nhiên; (27) xuất thần.
- On Track 25, please find the following proper names: (1) Nhạc sư Nguyễn Vĩnh Bảo; (2) Nhà giáo ưu tú Phạm Thúy Hoan; (3) Nghệ nhân Trần Minh Đức; (4) Nghệ sĩ ưu tú Huỳnh Khải; (5) Giáo sư Tiến sĩ Trần Văn Khê; (6) Chủ tịch Hồ Chí Minh.
- On Track 26, please find the following tune names: (1) Dạ cổ hoài lang; (2) Lý con sáo; (3) Lưu thủy trường; (4) Nam Ai; (5) Nam Xuân; (6) Ngũ điểm – Bài tạ; (7) Nhạc Miên Nhạc Pháp; (8) Tây thi; (9) Trống cơm; (10) Vọng cổ.

ACKNOWLEDGMENTS

This book would not have been possible without financial and human generosity. At the University of Michigan, I received research funds from the Department of Musicology at the School of Music, Theatre and Dance, the Rackham Graduate School, the International Institute, and the Center for Southeast Asian Studies. A Fulbright Hays Doctoral Dissertation Research Abroad Fellowship from the U.S. Department of Education and the Rackham Graduate School funded my doctoral research. At Western Michigan University, I received a Support for Faculty Scholars Grant and research support from the College of Fine Arts. At the University of Birmingham, I received travel funds for travel to Vietnam to complete the last stages of fieldwork.

Human generosity fills the rest of the acknowledgments. I am extremely grateful for the conversations and encouragement from numerous individuals in the field, academia, and beyond. In Vietnam, I found overwhelming support from established scholars, friends, and kind individuals on the street who all pointed me in a direction when I appeared lost. I thank Nguyễn Thuyết Phong, who introduced me to one of the featured musicians in this book, Nguyễn Vĩnh Bảo, and who provided frequent guidance and clarification on musical practice since 2006; Phạm Ngọc Lanh (d. 2009) who brought me to the rehearsals of Phạm Thúy Hoan, another musician featured prominently here, and introduced me to coffee drinking and conversation on the pavement of the city; Lê Đình Bích for his guidance and for introducing me to Trần Minh Đức, a third musician featured prominently here; and Lê Thị Huyền and her husband Long, who opened their home in Cần Thơ to me, as well as their two children, Bill and Ben, who politely corrected my Vietnamese and kept me entertained when the street flooded during the rainy season. At the University of Social Sciences and Humanities in Ho Chi Minh City, I thank Nguyễn Văn Tiệp and Đặng Thị

Cẩm Tú for their guidance when I was a visiting researcher. I also gained a great deal from informal conversations with Diệp Tử Khôi, Dương Trần Minh Đoàn, Khương Cường, Lê Hồng Sơn, Lê Sĩ Duy, Mai Thanh Sơn, Mai Tuyết Hoa, Anh-Thu Nguyen, Nguyễn Hồng Quân, Nguyễn Thị Hải Phượng, Nguyễn Kim Ửng, Nguyễn Phúc An, Nguyễn Thị Phương Liên, Nguyễn Thái Hòa, Thinh Nguyen, Nguyễn Thúy Uyển, Tina Nguyen, Nguyễn Trương Giang, Nguyễn Văn Hà, Nguyễn Văn Tử, Phan Huy, Trần Quang Hải, Trần Văn Khê (1921–2015), Trương Thành Lâm, and Võ Trường Kỳ. In the United States, I have benefited a great deal from conversations with Cathy Lam, PQ Phan, and Vân-Ánh Võ.

By investigating music in Vietnam, I have the honor of learning from and taking part in interdisciplinary conversations with scholars from Vietnamese Studies and ethnomusicology. I thank my fellow explorers of Vietnamese culture and history for their insights and guidance, including Claudine Ang, Pamela Corey, Sarah Grant, Mariam B. Lam, Marie-Claire Laurent, Khai Thu Nguyen, Martina Nguyen, Phi-Van Nguyen, Thu-hương Nguyễn-võ, Ivan Small, Geoff Stewart, Philip Taylor, and Allen Tran. I continue to learn a great deal from ethnomusicologists Robbie Beahrs, Tara Browner, Raquel Campos, Chen Rong, Saida Daukeyeva, Kiku Day, Byron Dueck, Mercedes Dujunco, Luis-Manuel Garcia, Katherine Hagedorn (1961–2013), Rachel Harris, Hsu Hsin-Wen, Tasaw Lu, Deirdre Morgan, Inna Naroditskaya, Barley Norton, Helen Rees, Shzr Ee Tan, Aja Burrell Wood, and Deborah Wong. I am also thankful for the gracious feedback provided on some of the central arguments in this book by my colleagues at the University of Birmingham, including Amy Brosius, Ben Curry, and Maria Witek, as well as by the anonymous reviewers who gave their time to this project. And although I have deviated a great deal from my doctoral dissertation in these pages, members of my doctoral committee at the University of Michigan still play a significant role in shaping my understanding of research. I therefore thank Judith Becker, Christi-Anne Castro, Fatma Müge Göçek, and especially Joseph Lam.

Close friends and family provide more support that they realize, and a few have lifted my spirits repeatedly over the course of studying and writing about Vietnamese music. Jesse Johnston has served as a guide through ethnomusicology even before I started my PhD training, and is the best conference companion for which one could hope. From delayed flights in Newfoundland to winding alleys in Bangkok, he taught me that some of the closest friends one can make are in one's home discipline. Trần Thị Phương Thảo met me right at the start of my research and has become my closest friend in Vietnam. We've shared our hopes, dreams, and sorrows over her home-cooked meals and trans-Pacific Facebook calls, and she always welcomes me back to what has become my second home in Saigon. Alison DeSimone's support for my work and wellbeing knows no bounds—something she's provided since we first met during a long chat on a swing set as we both completed our PhDs at the University of Michigan. She has showed some of the greatest kindness I've known when I most needed it the most, has visited me in every place I have lived since our time in Ann Arbor, and keeps me positive with gag gifts and an incredible ability to tell a good story. My partner Ko On Chan has proved that despite the horrors of the COVID-19 pandemic, a powerful human connection can blossom at a distance during lockdown, and that leaps of faith in that connection can yield a close, enriching, and lifelong bond. His insights on Daoism in particular helped bring this book to completion, and his keen eye fixed more typos that I care to admit truthfully. Since moving across an ocean to build a life together, he now keeps me well-nourished with divine food and his generous spirit. *Ngo oi nei, my love.* I lastly thank my parents and sister for always keeping their homes open to me, whether in London, Singapore, New York, Williamsburg, San Francisco, or Seattle, and being willing to help me think through a research, teaching, or life problem. (And thanks, also, for the bags of chocolate bits during lockdown. I may not have survived in England without them!)

I conclude by thanking the musicians at the center of this monograph. Trước hết, em xin cảm ơn Nhà giáo ưu tú Phạm Thúy Hoan, Nghệ sĩ ưu tú Huỳnh Khải và nghệ nhân Trần Minh Đức hướng dẫn cho em hiểu rõ hơn về âm nhạc Việt Nam phong phú như thế nào. Con cũng cảm ơn cô Nguyễn Thị Thu Anh, con gái Thầy Vĩnh Bảo và Bà Trâm Anh, mời con vào nhà cô, chăm sóc con, và chia sẽ trên Facebook các hình ảnh, sự ghi âm, bài thư, và bài thơ của Nguyễn Vĩnh Bảo. Mọi người sẽ luôn bên cạnh gia đình Thầy và nhớ tiếng đàn tranh của Thầy. Nguyễn Vĩnh Bảo (1918–2021) passed away just as I completed my revisions, but his music lives on in the enormous archive he left with the music community he worked so hard to create. I hope that this book provides some insight into his wisdom and that all readers learn from his teachings, sounds, and poetry as I have.

Seeding the Tradition

INTRODUCTION

On my first research trip to southern Vietnam in June 2007, I brought my copy of Michel de Certeau's *The Practice of Everyday Life* for some "light reading" on the plane. I soon learned that this reading is not light at all, but between mindless action movies over the Pacific Ocean, I did manage to make my way through the chapter titled "Walking in the City." The opening vignette about the 110th story of the World Trade Center brought back memories of my childhood visits to the buildings, and I found some important warnings for my first research trip to the Socialist Republic of Vietnam. De Certeau writes of the dangerous allure of the perspective at the top—a position of power or a place "lifted out of the city's grasp" and far removed from the everyday (1984, 92). Viewers become "voyeur[s]" and even a "god[s]" from his position, advancing a "fiction of knowledge . . . related to [a] lust to be a viewpoint and nothing more" (92). As the 110th story no longer exists following the terrorist attacks of September 11, 2001, viewers now are immortal gods, peering down on Manhattan from memory—erasing, supplanting, and rewriting whatever seen in the mind's eye to advance their fictions and satiate their lust. As I put away the book before my arrival into Tân Sơn Nhất International Airport (previously Tân Sơn Nhứt Air Base) in Ho Chi Minh City, I considered the many fictions that continued to shape Vietnam today.[1]

I spent the first few days on this trip at the Rex Hotel—a hotel with a rooftop bar known during the Vietnam War for the "Five O'Clock Follies" briefings given to journalists some three decades previous. My father told me of the Rex Hotel, and of the fictions American military officials invented on that rooftop in a desperate attempt to generate support for an unpopular and cruel war. Although my father had not served in the US military, he and my mother were of the generation that watched the war every day on their televisions, wondering if their drafted schoolmates would return home. Many did not, leaving Vietnam permanently etched as a lost conflict in the minds of their generation.

It may seem an old and tired trope for an American writer to start a book about Vietnam with the Vietnam War. Ethnographic writing often starts with the author, however, and I cannot escape the collective memories—or, more accurately, the collective fictions—of Vietnam in the United States. The greatest fiction of American civil discourse—often uncritically exported around the world—propagates an understanding of Vietnam as a war and not a country. A long history of action films, documentaries, and literature advance an agenda to make Vietnam a story about America (Viet Thanh Nguyen 1997). "Vietnam" becomes an index of conflict of various sorts—Americans fighting a faceless enemy; Americans fighting themselves—and the Vietnamese people recede into the background, playing a bit role to American imperialism.

This fiction also overlooks the voices of Vietnamese refugees, including the so-called "boat people" who fled the Vietnamese coast at great personal risk to seek new lives outside of Vietnam after the Vietnam War. The fabric of American culture has permanently changed following their settlement in the United States, although this receives little recognition in multimillion-dollar action films. A flag with three red stripes on a yellow background of the former South Vietnam flies above Vietnamese supermarkets, bakeries, and karaoke parlors in San Jose and Orange County, and *phở* noodle soup is now go-to cold relief from Seattle to New Orleans, Grand Rapids to Newark. The fiction ignores that the United States has become more Vietnamese than Vietnam has become American.

Vietnam is made by its people—how they interact with one another; the sounds and music that they create together. To study this, I took a cue from de Certeau and made walking central to my ethnographic data collection on my research trips from 2007 to 2019. During my time in Ho Chi Minh City, I observed how Saigonese used, changed, and co-opted the spaces of their city. As new skyscrapers and apartment buildings went up, the residents went around. Despite all the changes to the landscape of the city, so much of it, especially the sounds, remained similarly vibrant. The same roosters awoke the city at half past three or four o'clock in the morning; the same vehicular traffic grew from a gentle hum to a roar by six o'clock; the same bread sellers cycled through alleyways with the same recorded greetings; rubbish collectors shouted out their services to residents. Traditional music in the city has also continued. Musicians adapt traditional music to new circumstances while also maintaining past practice to structure future engagement. This constitutes the creativity of the musicians I describe in this book.

I begin with the Vietnam War fiction, then, because this is where most Americans (and others) start; but this is not the past through which one should understand Vietnam. "The War Against America to Save the Country" (*chiến tranh chống Mỹ cứu nước*)—as the "Vietnam War" is known in Vietnamese—devastated the landscape of Vietnam and deeply impacted its people, but it happened at a particular recent point in Vietnam's long history. Only American voyeurs, tourists, and war enthusiasts seem to think the war is all that happened in Vietnam. The past brings about current conditions, certainly, but as my dear friend Phạm Ngọc Lanh told me with some frequency, "The past is behind us." De Certeau's description of New York could even be the same as that of Saigon: the city "has never learned the art of growing old by playing on all its pasts. Its present invents itself, from hour to hour, in the act of throwing away its previous accomplishments and challenging the future" (1984, 91). Saigonese focus on optimism and enthusiasm for change, as do the musicians of traditional music who described their dynamic craft to me.

The knowledge transcribed and evaluated in this ethnography emerges from interactions with musicians, friends, and strangers who guided me through the richness of Vietnamese cultural life. "Văn hóa Việt Nam phong phú lắm" (Vietnamese culture is extraordinarily rich), as more than one stranger has told me upon hearing of my interest in Vietnamese music. The music in this ethnography emerges from what Dylan Robinson has described as "palimpsestous listening," or listening "oriented toward aural traces of history: echoes, whispers, and voices that become audible momentarily, ones that may productively haunt our listening as significantly as ghosts that linger" (2020, 62). These moments of audibility generate recognition, activate memory, and propel the fingers (or voice) in improvised music performance. Indeed, the improvisations I evaluate might be described as chains of these moments: musicians saturate the space with "traces" upon which others draw to congeal sound that communicates knowledge and maintains memory. The conclusions of this ethnography then, too, are cocurated by many voices over time and space. Although I focus on four musicians, many others guide and help me contextualize the creative sounds of southern Vietnam.

MUSIC FOR DIVERSION

My research focuses on the manifestations and uses of creativity in southern Vietnam as understood through improvised practice associated with a genre of music known by two names: *nhạc tài tử Nam bộ* (sometimes *nhạc tài tử*) and *đờn ca tài tử*. *Nhạc* means "music," and *tài tử* has multiple meanings.[2] Translated literally, it means "a talented (*tài*) gentleman (*tử*)." The term is borrowed from the Chinese *caizi* (才子), meaning a scholarly gentleman who composed poetry and had status (Cannon 2016, 148). Some musicians therefore adopt the ethos of the "amateur" figure who has ample free time to play music. Two musicians even described nhạc tài tử to me as high art played in the houses of the wealthy in Saigon and Chợ Lớn (a "Chinatown" area next to Saigon) before 1975 (157). This ultimately leads to translations of the genre name as *la musique dit "des amateurs"* in French (Trần Văn Khê 1962, 98), and "the music of talented amateurs" in English (Nguyễn T. Phong 1998, 483).

The term *tài tử* also has a widely understood figurative and humorous meaning in southern Vietnam. Other musicians understand diversion not as a pastime of the scholarly gentleman but as the habitual practice of the indolent or apathetic. In the Mekong Delta, *tài tử* in spoken language suggests laziness. "That's really *tài tử*" means to do something in a haphazard fashion or without much thought. One friend of mine suggested that not wanting to complete one's homework in favor of sleeping or playing video games is called "tài tử" among close friends (Cannon 2016, 142). Adopting the term for music practice suggests a playful performance atmosphere of joking and ribbing among friends. They played "for their amusement only."[3] In their pursuit of camaraderie, they "diverted" their attention from other matters, leading to a translation of the genre name by Phạm Duy as "music for diversion," or something done as a simple pastime (Pham and Whiteside 1975, 108–9).

Đờn ca tài tử as a term endows the music with a clear sense of southern Vietnamese locality. To *đờn* means "to play an instrument"; its spelling reflects the southern Vietnamese pronunciation of the term *đàn*, which is used in central and northern Vietnam to express the same meaning. To *ca* means "to sing," and vocalists improvise new melodies with new lyrical content or draw on precomposed lyrics either with precomposed or quasi-precomposed melodies. The term as a whole therefore exhibits a southern Vietnamese interest in improvisation, locality, and play.

As I developed an understanding of đờn ca tài tử musicianship over twelve years, I came to recognize how musicians increasingly understood their improvisations as embodying creativity or *sáng tạo*. Creativity is not an uninhibited free-for-all, but a discursive practice in southern Vietnam influenced by Daoism (and to a certain degree Buddhism and Confucianism as part of the *tam giáo*, or three philosophical practices supporting Vietnamese culture). Musicians make subtle changes to past practice by drawing on their emotional states and reflections on everyday life to augment pitch content and add or eliminate ornamentation within certain melodic and rhythmic structures. Musicians refer to this creativity of improvisation in metaphorical terms. These metaphors join the historical with the contemporary and the philosophical with the lived to enable performance conditions negotiated between individual musicians. As Thomas Csordas argues in a different context, "Creativity is to be found not only in one instance or moment but also in the dialectical relations between ritual and social life, between a system of genres and a vocabulary of motives, and between motives and the metaphors generated from them" (1997, 263). Metaphor therefore becomes a structuring mechanism for this fraught navigation in changes in practice (252–55; see also Cook 2006). Đờn ca tài tử musicians draw from their learned knowledge, or the frame (*chân phương*) of practice, and produce melody as the aural equivalent of flowers, leaves, and branches (*hoa lá cành*) in nature. Musicians should not aim to create fast melodies that fill spaces with sound, but should instead use common understandings of modal structures, including vibrato (*rung*), bending (*nhấn*), and other methods of ornamentation, to bring out appropriate emotional sentiment. Musicians can go too far with ornamentation, however, to the point that a song loses its soul (*tâm hồn*) and identity. What are the rules, therefore, that govern creativity and improvisation? With an increasing engagement with global flows of idea, capital, and people in southern Vietnam, have these rules themselves changed to sustain practice?

A methodical account of the musical creativity practiced by musicians of traditional music in southern Vietnam requires two lines of intersecting argumentation. The first focuses on what đờn ca tài tử musicians do in their practice, and the second spotlights discourses of creativity that intersect in southern Vietnamese music. In this monograph, I identify and describe the different forms of creativity in circulation in southern Vietnam and then examine how they impact and are impacted by the practice of đờn ca tài tử. The musicians with whom I interact maintain a primarily Daoist conceptualization of creation long practiced and theorized in Vietnam while adopting strategically from and also reacting to a Western neoliberal model of creativity focused primarily—although not exclusively—on the individual genius.

One of the primary interlocutors of this book, master musician (*nhạc sư*) Nguyễn Vĩnh Bảo, guided me through these understandings, often using subtle changes in terminology to teach me the creativity of his own practice. Beginning in 2007, I studied the *đàn tranh* (a sixteen- or seventeen-stringed zither) and, later, the *đàn kìm* (a moon-shaped lute) with him. He taught me the typical performance practices of what he termed "nhạc tài tử" and explained in great detail the history of nhạc tài tử performance in southern Vietnam, methods of emotional expression on various instruments, and theories of modality. He occasionally referred to the genre as "đờn ca tài tử," especially when speaking with government officials and journalists. (The term became more recognizable in public discourse around 2011 for reasons I describe in Chapter 7.) He appeared more comfortable with "nhạc tài tử," but also started to argue in 2013 that the terms *đờn ca tài tử* and *nhạc tài tử* have little meaning and perhaps "did not exist." To reflect its historical significance, he argued, the music should be called *cổ nhạc* or *nhạc cổ*, meaning "ancient music."[4] A term that has been in circulation since at least the 1960s, *cổ nhạc* indexes a kind of prestige and age—things he believed should be attached to the genre.

Nguyễn Vĩnh Bảo revised his approach in 2014, however, when he told me that đờn ca tài tử originally was "a music without a name."[5] This was a new argument I had not heard advocated by any other musician. When the genre first emerged in the late nineteenth century, he argued, musicians simply riffed in informal settings among friends on older opera and court tunes. They did not put a name to their improvisations, and he sought to return to foregrounding the "play" (*vui chơi*) central to the identification of the music. The appearance of the *nhạc tài tử* or *đờn ca tài tử* monikers, he continued, actually said very little about the genre itself. Musicians played, sung, and improvised to communicate something deeper and more consequential than the genre name designated. They drew on memories of past practice and combined them with the sounds of everyday life to capture the significance of a meeting among friends at a unique time and place. Nguyễn Vĩnh Bảo explained how musicians improvise using the sounds of everyday objects, such as a clock or a spoon falling to the ground, to make the performance more intimate and connect the people in the performance setting.[6] The "playing and singing of cutlery" therefore does not describe this music accurately, as more is happening in the space. A name has a tendency to fix practice when that practice is actually quite fluid. By advocating that the music initially did not have a name—or that it has multiple names—he recaptures an understanding of processes occasionally forgotten.

More than a commentary on genre designation, however, he suggests that the process of creating music is itself without a name. Musicians *do*, and then later find language to describe this action. In a 2019 conversation in his new home in Cao Lãnh, Nguyễn Vĩnh Bảo observed that "when something is no longer interesting to musicians, they change it." He used the term *đổi qua* to indicate both a change (*đổi*) and a passing over or a passing by (*qua*) of the previous practice.[7] As an example, he cited the tune "Dạ cổ hoài lang" ("Listening to the Sound of the Drum at Night, I Think of You") to explain this. The musicians who originally crafted this tune borrowed the happy central Vietnamese song "Hành vân" ("Flying Cloud") and made strategic changes to transform it into a sad tune. Instead of a tune that indexed the landscape and conjured images of clouds passing alongside the mountaintops of the central Vietnamese coastline, "Dạ cổ hoài lang" embodied a sadness typical of other melancholy tunes in the southern Vietnamese tradition.

His example challenges typical narratives about this tune to align it with the genesis narratives of many other traditional tunes. Standard histories of "Dạ cổ hoài lang" suggest that musician Cao Văn Lầu (alias Sáu Lầu) composed the tune sometime between 1918 and 1920 and captured the quintessential southern Vietnamese way of life in this work (Cannon 2012, 146). For this reason, scholars view Sáu Lầu as a kind of founding father of đờn ca tài tử. Rather than invoke the genius trope, Nguyễn Vĩnh Bảo maintains that musicians simply did as they had done for centuries—add ornamentation to certain pitches, add pitches to a melody, and strategically change pitches to make the song more interesting. The tune ultimately became popular when musicians continued to perform and mold it. Crafting a tune evocative of southern Vietnam is typical in his story as creativity without a name.

Nguyễn Vĩnh Bảo's alternative history further asserts difference, specifically between European art music and southern Vietnamese traditional music. During this conversation, Nguyễn Thuyết Phong (with whom I had traveled on this trip to Cao Lãnh in 2019) pressed Nguyễn Vĩnh Bảo to provide evidence of these changes. Nguyễn Vĩnh Bảo responded that "Vietnamese music is *different* than Western music. Western music has compositions . . . [and] the creation of new works. It does not involve the revision of old works. Our ancestors had creations but they did not keep a record of the creation of the works. . . . *Nobody knows who created them."*[8] The process of creating the "work" (*sáng tác*), he indicated, is different than the model imported from Euro-American spheres of musical creation. The "soul" (tâm hồn) of Vietnamese music and identity emerge from this creative process, and any attempt to impose an individual genius genesis model ultimately undermines the Vietnamese soul. In addition, he encourages musicians and his students to embrace the inexactitude of the past and imagine reasons why the tune changed. One might surmise that musicians in the 1910s saw the rapid modernization and reshaping of southern Vietnam (known then as Cochinchina) under French colonial rule and mourned the loss of agency; or it could be that musicians who moved from central to southern Vietnam at the turn of the twentieth century were nostalgic for their home provinces and wanted a tune that embodied both the predecessor and their sadness; or it could be that someone misremembered the "Hành vân" melody and a fellow performer thought the new tune sounded worth replicating. "Nobody knows" encourages improvisation and creativity; this unknowing propels the genre into the future.

The emergence of a name requires explanation, and the meanings of particular terms, such as *tài tử*, introduce a regimentation in opposition to the flexibility and richness of practice. Nguyễn Vĩnh Bảo equated this with a westernization of music practice, where musicians ceased speaking of Vietnamese music in local ways but began to impose foreign understandings. At the same time, musicians continued to teach and perform Vietnamese traditional music in Ho Chi Minh City and throughout the Mekong Delta. Changes occurred and disagreements emerged, but the tradition remained strong. What enables a sustained tradition given the incursions into practice? How do musicians protect the tradition and the meanings that emerge from it? How do musicians talk about or reference this practice? What kinds of new experiments has this practice generated in the twenty-first century?

My encounters and discussions with musicians in Ho Chi Minh City, Cần Thơ, and elsewhere in the Mekong Delta suggest that creativity in southern Vietnam does not necessarily "make new" or revolutionize. Creativity is not always the work of the omnipotent, charismatic individual. Creativity may be extraordinary and shift paradigms, but such conclusions often emerge long after the fact and inaccurately attribute a wide range of creations to one or a few individuals. This has the effect of crowding out important voices. Creativity serves as a weapon of the weak or voiceless. Creativity imbues power; it also overpowers and empowers. The discriminatory and objectifying nature of creativity requires new approaches to ethnomusicology's engagement with the concept and a questioning of what ethnomusicologists have borrowed from antecedent disciplines. Creativity and mastery in the West are both imbued with bias and inflict trauma; continuing to evoke the terms uncritically replicates this discourse. These characterizations may seem radical—or potentially perverse—to some, but I embrace the questioning of long-standing assumptions offered by this line of inquiry.

Previous literature does not have the theoretical nuance to describe these scenes of musical creativity. In ethnomusicology, one finds literature on westernization, modernity, and colonization in rewriting the rules of music performance and practice (Sutton 1991, 174; 2001/2002, 82; 2006, 1; Witzleben 1995, 138). Simplistic characterizations of modernity fracturing traditional practice typically yield a conclusion that change is introduced into an unchanging environment, even when the strict structure of modernization is actually what paralyzed a diverse and dynamic tradition. Vietnamese musicians (and people more generally) are instead empowered social agents capable of maintaining traditional practices alongside effective alliances with international collaborators. Much more can be offered by ethnomusicologists today to combat the ills and delights of creativity.

APPROACHES TO VIETNAMESE PRACTICE

The richness of southern Vietnamese traditional music does not have a significant place in Euro-American ethnomusicology. Recent ethnographies on music in Vietnam by Barley Norton (2009), Lauren Meeker (2013), and Lonán Ó Briain (2018) focus on folk and traditional music in northern Vietnam. Northern Vietnam has a very different cultural makeup compared to southern Vietnam, so the texts provide little insight on other parts of the country, save for descriptions of the implementation of state policy on sound. Details on southern Vietnamese traditional music have appeared in older scholarship by the ethnomusicologists and performers Trần Văn Khê (1962), Phạm Duy (1975), and especially Nguyễn T. Phong (1998). Works by Adelaida Reyes (1999) and Long Bui (2016) impart valuable understandings of southern Vietnamese among Vietnamese refugee communities and those in the Vietnamese diaspora. These descriptions provide snapshots alongside practices originating in other parts of Vietnam.

An effective ethnography of southern Vietnamese music must emerge from the vibrant lived experiences of southern Vietnamese musicians. My study of traditional music started under the stewardship of Nguyễn Vĩnh Bảo in Ho Chi Minh City. Concurrently, I attended rehearsals and performances of the Tiếng Hát Quê Hương (Sounds of the Homeland) music club (*câu lạc bộ*) led by Phạm

Thúy Hoan. I further met and interviewed individuals who consumed and performed traditional music as a hobby, and their insights permeate the pages of this book. I ultimately expanded my work to Cần Thơ, where I studied how to play the three-stringed *đàn sến* (a plum blossom flower lute) with Trần Minh Đức and visited music cafés to sing songs, play music, and observe musical interactions between old friends. During later trips from 2009 to 2019 of anywhere between two and six weeks, I attended performances directed and adjudicated by Huỳnh Khải, who currently serves as Director of the Traditional Music Department at the Ho Chi Minh City Conservatory of Music. I also made visits to Bạc Liêu, Cao Lãnh, and Long Xuyên in the Mekong Delta (see Map 1) to make contact with local musicians—some of whom I met first on Facebook before visiting them—and learn about regional practices of đờn ca tài tử.

I focus on conversations with these individuals and evaluate the tension generated when musicians position themselves vis-à-vis their communities. I lend significant credence to their words, but also interpret the performances I attended and evaluate the positioning of one musician's language against another. One musician is rarely hostile to another, but they find a multitude of ways to critique the practice of others. Indeed, as Thomas Turino (1990) and Kofi Agawu (1992) indicate, one must occasionally listen beyond language to understand practice.

FOUR MUSICIANS

The conclusions drawn in this ethnography emerge primarily from my interactions with four musicians. Each holds a different title that designates a specific niche of practice. All perform đờn ca tài tử and other genres, including the music of *cải lương*—a theatrical genre that emerged in the second and third decades of the twentieth century and told Chinese, Vietnamese, and French stories to the accompaniment of augmented versions of đờn ca tài tử tunes—and *nhạc dân tộc*—a kind of music I translate as "national music" that often involves large ensembles of musicians playing precomposed versions of traditional tunes.

Nguyễn Vĩnh Bảo

Nhạc sư Nguyễn Vĩnh Bảo, who passed away in January 2021, lived in Cao Lãnh in Đồng Tháp Province south of Ho Chi Minh City. Born in 1918 in Mỹ Trà on the northern outskirts of Cao Lãnh, he spent his early years moving between his

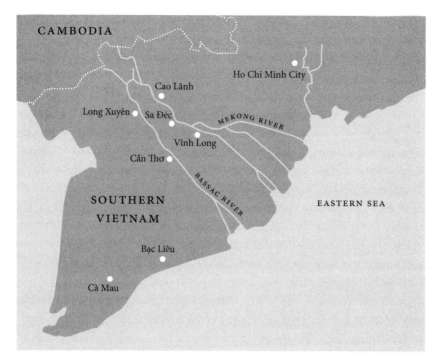

MAP 1 Map of southern Vietnam Ko On Chan, used with permission

hometown, Cambodia (then part of French Indochina), and Saigon, ultimately spending most of his life living and working in Saigon. In addition to his renown as a performer and one of the original professors at the National School of Music (Trường Quốc gia Âm nhạc) in Saigon, Thầy (male teacher) Vĩnh Bảo worked for many years as a luthier and teacher, including for a short period in 1971 and 1972 at Southern Illinois University–Carbondale. He also has held various odd-jobs throughout this life, including as a taxi driver in Saigon.

Nguyễn Thuyết Phong (2006) describes Thầy Vĩnh Bảo as the "last guardian" of the đờn ca tài tử tradition. Thầy Vĩnh Bảo amassed an extensive written and audio archive of đờn ca tài tử, including notation dating from the 1930s, commercial recordings not easily found today, and private recordings of long-dead musicians. He watched đờn ca tài tử expand and contract for much of its life and recalled how musicians molded and shaped works for their own purposes. Even at an advanced age, he continued to communicate with his students and admirers in Vietnamese, French, and English; wrote oftentimes devastatingly sad poetry in French; granted interviews; told jokes on his Facebook page; and performed music with those who visited him. Although he played all of the string instruments of the southern Vietnamese tradition, he most often played the đàn tranh, đàn kìm, and *đàn gáo* (coconut fiddle).[9]

Phạm Thúy Hoan

Nhà giáo ưu tú (Teacher of Merit) Phạm Thúy Hoan lives in Ho Chi Minh City. Born in 1942 in Nam Định Province in northern Vietnam, *Cô* (female teacher) Hoan moved with her family to southern Vietnam at about age ten (HTV 2007). When one of her friends started studying at the newly established National School of Music in Saigon, she visited the school, wandering from room to room. She stopped at the room where instructors taught the đàn tranh, and she felt compelled to listen. The experience was "accidental" but "profound" (HTV 2007). As she pursued her studies at the school, she studied with master musicians Nguyễn Hữu Ba and Nguyễn Vĩnh Bảo, as well as with flutist (of both the *tiêu* and *sáo*) Trần Viết Vấn. In 1962, she met and began studying Vietnamese music history and theory with Trần Văn Khê, who at that time had just completed his doctoral studies in France. Until his death in 2015, the two remained close collaborators.

Phạm Thúy Hoan is an accomplished performer, having received a number of awards for her abilities before 1975, and she also led the *Hoa Sim* National Folk Music Ensemble.[10] She has dedicated much of her career to teaching. From 1962 to 1975, she served as a professor (*giáo sư*) at the National School of Music and Theatrical Arts (Trường Quốc gia Âm nhạc và Kịch nghệ). In 1968, she also taught at the National School of Music in Huế (Trường Quốc gia Âm nhạc Huế). After 1975, she served as a lecturer (*giảng viên*) at the renamed Ho Chi Minh City Conservatory of Music (Nhạc viện Thành phố Hồ Chí Minh) until her retirement in 1997. In 1994, the Ministry of Education and Training bestowed her the honorific title "Teacher of Merit" to recognize her work as a teacher at the Conservatory of Music and director of the ensemble and teaching program Tiếng Hát Quê Hương. Today, she continues to direct the ensemble and compose.

Trần Minh Đức

Nghệ nhân (revered musician) Trần Minh Đức, who goes by the name Hai Đức, lives outside of Cần Thơ City in the Mekong Delta. Born in 1938 in Đồng Phước Village,[11] just south of the city limits in what is now Hậu Giang Province, Hai Đức grew up in a poor household during a period of Vietnamese history defined by occupation and violence. During his youth, he had difficulty finding teachers of traditional music, although he persisted and eventually studied the *ghi ta phím lõm* (a guitar with a scooped fingerboard), đàn kìm, đàn sến, and singing. He did not provide monetary payments for the lessons, but instead worked in some capacity for the teacher. He typically worked in the teacher's home, although in one case, he worked as an oarsman, ferrying the teacher to various appointments. He sometimes studied with the teacher as he rowed, but only, he noted with a smile, if the teacher was sober; for another teacher, he looked after the children of his teacher's female companion during their evening rendezvous.[12] Despite the difficulties of the period, he had opportunities to study with five musicians, including *danh sư* (famous teacher) Sáu Hóa, who gave him voice lessons but was known for his abilities as a performer of the đàn tranh, and Hai Duyên, who taught him the two-stringed đàn sến but was best known for his abilities as a guitar player.

As a musician, Hai Đức defines himself as an amateur—a characterization of which he is very proud—meaning that his primary means of making a living did not involve musical performance. His various occupations took him throughout southern Vietnam and enabled him to not only acquire a knowledge of localized đờn ca tài tử and cải lương traditions but also amass "hundreds" of students.[13] In 2009, he described his primary occupation as "buôn bán đồ la," literally meaning "selling things by yelling." This characterization immediately brings to mind sellers of knickknacks and cigarettes found in Cần Thơ and elsewhere in Vietnam; however, his work has been more successful and lucrative than this. The slightly tongue-in-cheek description simply indicates that he is a self-made entrepreneur and that he has moved around. Nowadays, he largely is retired, but frequently meets his friends for ad hoc performances, accompanies cải lương performances, and occasionally plays for groups of foreign students and academics visiting the local university.

Huỳnh Khải

Nghệ sĩ ưu tú (Artist of Merit) Huỳnh Văn Khải is based in Ho Chi Minh City, although he travels quite frequently across the Mekong Delta and occasionally abroad to teach. Born in 1957, Huỳnh Khải grew up in the Thủ Thừa District of Long An Province, south of present-day Ho Chi Minh City, and started studying the đàn kìm with his father at age eight. He later studied with Võ Văn Khuê and Nguyễn Văn Đời, and ultimately picked up the guitar, đàn sến, *đàn cò* (a two-stringed fiddle), *đàn tỳ bà* (a pear-shaped lute), and *ghi ta Hạ uy* (a Hawaiian lap steel guitar), which is one of his favorite instruments. In 1993, he started teaching at the Ho Chi Minh City Conservatory. He is well known as a pedagogue and a composer; indeed, his compositions are discussed on television programs and are featured in festival performances throughout southern Vietnam. He received a master's degree in 2003 and continues research on methods of studying the đàn kìm for đờn ca tài tử, cải lương, and new composition performance (Sơn Nghĩa 2016). In 2015, the Ministry of Culture, Sports and Tourism bestowed on him the honorific title of "Artist of Merit." Occasionally, he is given the double-barreled title of "Composer and Artist of Merit" (*nhạc sĩ—nghệ sĩ ưu tú*).

Huỳnh Khải is especially adept at generating interest in his craft through performance and social media. He organizes performances across southern Vietnam to continue promoting compatibility between urban structures and rural practices (Cannon 2016, 157–58). Some of his most public performances take place in front of the opera house in Ho Chi Minh City on Saturday mornings throughout the year. He serves as an adjudicator at a weekly radio program for competing đờn ca tài tử musicians from Ho Chi Minh City and surrounding provinces, and is an invited guest to many festival performances throughout the Mekong Delta.

Other Interlocutors

In addition to these four musicians, several friends and connoisseurs appear in these pages: Lê Đình Bích, a university lecturer and musician in Cần Thơ who is close friends with Trần Minh Đức; Lê Hồng Sơn, a flutist and luthier in Ho Chi Minh City; Nguyễn Thuyết Phong, an ethnomusicologist and musician who has published widely on Vietnamese traditional music; friends of Nguyễn Vĩnh Bảo, including Võ Trường Kỳ, a scholar, musician, and government official in Long An Province, and Thầy Phước Cường, a Buddhist monk and musician in Ho Chi Minh City; Phạm Ngọc Lanh, a dearly missed friend who introduced me to Phạm Thúy Hoan and guided many of my early engagements with traditional music in Ho Chi Minh City; and Việt, a pseudonym for a teacher and musician friend of mine in Ho Chi Minh City. Other interlocutors include those with whom I interacted at institutions, and members of student groups. These institutions include media outlets, which propagate certain kinds of knowledge concerning authentic performance practice, and the United Nations Educational, Scientific and Cultural Organization (UNESCO). These institutions shape public perception and certainly promote traditional music, even if some promulgate inaccurate information. The students of music quoted are predominantly working professionals in other fields, including marketing, finance, education, and medicine, who live in the Mekong Delta, Ho Chi Minh City, and in the diaspora. They all interact with some institutional structures and with at least one teacher discussed in this text. All seek interactions with other students through face-to-face contact and through online means, including email and online forums. These meetings generate knowledge based upon that provided by their instructors, and often serve to make that knowledge more flexible and versatile in everchanging supralocal contexts.

CHAPTER SUMMARY

The monograph begins with examinations of creativity in musicological and ethnomusicological literature, and becomes more ethnographic when I introduce descriptions of contemporary practice. If I were to instead mix historical details with contemporary conditions, I would present creativity and đờn ca tài tử as somehow static. Both creativity and traditional music are mutable and very messy (Taruskin 1992, 323). Furthermore, different musicians have different ideas concerning appropriate practice and how that practice relates to history. I therefore frontload background information and history to depict đờn ca tài tử in later chapters as vibrant and alive.

The first two chapters situate creativity in southern Vietnam and in ethnomusicology. Chapter 1 suggests that creativity surfaced in public discourse over the past decade or more in response to particular social and economic events in Vietnam. Imported understandings of a global creativity based on entrepreneurial prowess clashed with local understandings of creation. "Creativity" (sáng tạo) became a common descriptor of musical and artistic excellence, but it did not replicate those imported global models. Creativity became something uniquely Vietnamese as a form of effective mediation between the local and global. Chapter 2 identifies several questionable ways that ethnomusicology has engaged with creativity, and suggests ways in which ethnomusicologists might shift their approach to creativity discourse to reject mastery, engage historical understandings of creativity, and describe creativity as reparative or recuperative. Chapter 3 provides the groundwork for applying these three approaches. I focus on the history of migration to and through southern Vietnam and describe important Daoist concepts that continue to orient creation and creativity in southern Vietnam today.

The next several chapters describe musical practice associated with đờn ca tài tử. Chapter 4 extends a discussion of the concepts explored in the previous chapter to depict how đờn ca tài tử musicians engage with everyday life through improvised music practice. I offer descriptions of the instruments, sounds, emotions, and works found in đờn ca tài tử. Chapter 5 proposes that đờn ca tài tử creativity emerges at the intersection of two primary metaphors: the frame (chân phương) or structures of musical knowledge, and the flower embellishment (hoa lá cành) or spontaneous improvised sound emergent from this frame. Some musicians take these practices further, arguing that the best improvisations generate ecstatic (*xuất thần*) musical practice. Chapter 6 explores the emergence of a competing "development" (*phát triển*) metaphor as a kind of cultural policy that increasingly steers approaches to performance. Chapter 7 examines the visceral reactions some musicians have to the so-called development of traditional music. The metaphor of the "ruin" plays a substantive part of this argument, where musicians label certain performances as corrupted and try to repair the damage done by development. Chapter 8 describes ways in which technology has increasingly played a role in the mediation of creativity experiments practiced by đờn ca tài tử musicians. I describe experiments in various festivals and several television programs that have showcased đờn ca tài tử over the past several years. Although not universally lauded, these performances offer fertile ground for evaluating the approaches to creativity described in the previous chapters. A conclusion then summarizes several findings.

Seeding the Tradition is by no means an exhaustive ethnography on southern Vietnamese traditional music. Although such a book has not yet been written in English, I would risk perpetuating neocolonial representations of the Global South that are still present in ethnomusicology. Invoking authenticity and purity of tradition, these texts fix descriptions of instruments, genres, and other performance practices. Music is much more fluid. Instead, I try to craft an ethnography of musical creativity in southern Vietnam and describe the transformation of a genre of southern Vietnamese traditional music as I have experienced it alongside musicians, consumers, and other observers of cultural practice in Vietnam. I focus on the emergence of forms of creativity discourse about traditional music, and on how ethnomusicologists interact with our discipline—the scholars we cite, the narratives we privilege, and the disciplinary baggage that we desperately need to shed. Ethnomusicology is a discipline in perpetual transition and in flux. I critique previous scholars and know full well that I will be critiqued in time. Transformation needs a starting place, however, and I offer mine to begin.

ONE

Framing Contested Creativities

In June 2018, widespread protests broke out across Vietnam. Protesters holding homemade signs made of A4 paper weaved through intersections and plazas in cities and large towns to air grievances over two bills debated by the Vietnamese National Assembly (*Quốc hội*). The first bill proposed the creation of new Special Economic Zones in Vietnam, which many interpreted as enabling foreign (especially Chinese) companies to build factories under the protection of long-term leases. The legislation exacerbated unease in Vietnam concerning China's increasing development on disputed islands in the Eastern Sea (*Biển Đông*, also South China Sea) and the pollution of Vietnamese waterways and coastlines by foreign companies, including a 2016 incident involving the Formosa Ha Tinh Steel Corporation. The second bill proposed a new cybersecurity law that many feared would further curtail the limited freedoms of expression in the country and lead to more arrests of prominent bloggers spuriously accused of plotting to overthrow the state. The possibility of more environmental pollution and further erosion of personal freedom drove many to take great personal risk so their voices could resonate not only in Vietnam but also to audiences around the world on Facebook, YouTube, and Twitter.

The protests had a number of startling impacts. Local authorities arrested many Vietnamese citizens and deported a Vietnamese American student. One of the two major national newspapers, *Tuổi Trẻ* (*Youth*), was forced to shutter its website for three months for supposedly misprinting a quote from a government official and for allowing another article's comments section to spread alleged falsehoods. For many Vietnamese, these crackdowns opened a new and troubling chapter in the state's relationship with its people.

One month after the protests, I arrived in Ho Chi Minh City for a short period of fieldwork. More than one friend remarked to me privately that these protests were the largest to take place in the city since the student and Buddhist protests in the 1960s. Barbed wire and other crowd-control equipment remained on many street corners in District 1, reminding citizens of the state's authority. When I visited the intersection of Nam Kỳ Khởi Nghĩa and Điện Biên Phủ Streets, where some of the protests occurred, I encountered a new electronic billboard with the following stern warnings:

Người yêu nước là người không vi phạm pháp luật.
People who love the country are those who do not break the law.

Công dân có quyền bày tỏ chính kiến của mình nhưng không vi phạm pháp luật.
The public has the right to express its dissent, but not to break the law.

The government clearly condemned the protests and the rule-breaking behaviors that took place by equating loyalty to the country with obedience to law and order. Those who are loyal to the country are those who dissent without breaking the law. Since Vietnamese law largely prohibits dissent, however, no clear space for dissent actually exists.

Communist Party meetings and conferences also attempted to prevent future protests by identifying their causes. One article in *Sài Gòn Giải Phóng* (*The Liberation of Saigon*), the official organ of the Vietnamese Communist Party in Ho Chi Minh City, directly references the protests in a summary of the 17th Meeting of the Ho Chi Minh City Party Executive Committee's Tenth Congress held from July 4 to July 6, 2018. At this meeting, Municipal Party Secretary for Ho Chi Minh City Nguyễn Thiện Nhân stated: "Something that is very clear is that to prevent protests and violence, we must reassure the people: understand the people, respond to the demands of the people, and do this for them so protest is not needed" (Kiều Phong and Đường Loan 2018).[1]

To my great surprise, Nguyễn Thiện Nhân then suggested that creativity (*sáng tạo*) provided a solution to assuage desires to protest. Put simply, creativity leads to economic development and hence to contentment among the population. The newspaper article offers the following summary.

Trước tiên là báo cáo chuyên đề khơi dậy và phát huy truyền thống sáng tạo để TPHCM phát triển trong giai đoạn 2018–2020. . . . Để thực hiện, đồng chí Nguyễn Thiện Nhân yêu cầu hệ thống lại những bài học sáng tạo của TPHCM từ năm 1975 đến nay; đồng thời tập hợp sáng tạo của thế giới để học hỏi kinh nghiệm. Thông qua đó, khơi dậy sự sáng tạo của mỗi công dân TP, mỗi cán bộ công chức, mỗi kỹ sư, mỗi doanh nghiệp . . . để tới thành một giải pháp đặc thù của TP phát huy sáng tạo để phát triển kinh tế. (2018)

Translation:

> First and foremost, we must spur and promote traditional creativity so that Ho Chi Minh City develops from 2018–2020. . . . To realize this, comrade Nguyễn Thiện Nhân advises a systematization of creativity exercises in Ho Chi Minh City drawn from 1975 to today and, at the same time, combine this with global creativity to gain experience. Through this process, the creativity of every city citizen, every official, every engineer, and every business must be awakened . . . in order to generate a particular solution on promoting creativity in the city and thereby develop the economy.

A "creative city" (*đô thị sáng tạo*), Nguyễn Thiện Nhân argues, is a peaceful and developed one that integrates traditional ideals with contemporary solutions.[2] This strategy must be carefully managed, however, as indicated in the commentary regarding "creativity exercises"; indeed, the inclusion of a time scale suggested that creativity as practiced during the Republic of Vietnam regime before 1975 did not apply to the current context. That said, the municipal party secretary and the official organ of the Communist Party in the city recognized the existence of two different creativity models: an indigenous "traditional" creativity and a global creativity. A combination of both stabilizes the city and enables economic development.

The official English translation of this article, however, makes no mention of the protests. It instead focuses on the comments concerning creativity and emphasizes "growth and economic competitiveness" as the ultimate result of embracing creativity (Kieu Phong and Duong Loan 2018). The article indicates that "Secretary of the HCM City Party Committee Nguyen Thien Nhan asked all committee members to review experiences and lessons on creativity in all fields of Ho Chi Minh City and cities throughout the world to arouse the creativity of every resident, official and business to boost the development of the city" (2018). The English-language article also does not reference "traditional creativity," drawing from experience with creativity from 1975, or the existence of a separate international model of creativity. A suggestion of different types of creativity might appear incongruous with non-Vietnamese readers of the newspaper, who largely understand creativity as being universal.

The differences between the articles in Vietnamese and English point to a rupture between the concept of sáng tạo and "creativity" as applied in Vietnamese society. "Creativity" in its English usage fully aligns with the Western understanding of the term. It is depicted as a net positive good and as something to which everyone should have access in a prospering Ho Chi Minh City. Creativity is aspirational, forward-thinking, and something toward which the population works; it has no external referent and requires no alliances. Creativity expresses rather than suppresses, and its individual character reigns supreme. Sáng tạo, meanwhile, is a powerful discursive device that is both supported by tradition and integrated within Western understandings of creativity. On the one hand, the attachment of "tradition" to the concept facilitates an understanding of sáng tạo as simply creating—or making something—regardless of its novelty. On the other hand, it can equally be understood as innovative and aspirational. Nevertheless, the latter understanding of sáng tạo is not necessarily a net positive good. It also reinforces economic and cultural development, which the government appropriates and deploys to silence dissent and maintain security. "Creativity," then, either in Vietnamese- or English-language understandings, is clearly not a universal concept and is deployed in different ways even in the same cultural context.

This chapter offers a brief snapshot of contemporary southern Vietnam with a focus on the rise of creativity discourse from the start of my fieldwork research in 2007 to the present. I suggest that creativity has emerged as mediated discourse to guide local actors through the proliferation of choice—including artistic choice—in the Vietnamese everyday. In this context, global creativity and local creation come into conflict and generate dynamic ways of engaging in artistic practice. This chapter therefore frames the discussions of đờn ca tài tử creativities contained in the following chapters.

SOUTHERN VIETNAM IN THE TWENTY-FIRST CENTURY

Today, Vietnam exists at a crossroads of global idealism, where foreign direct investment, sprawling indoor shopping centers, television shows like *Anh Chàng Độc Thân* (*The Bachelor Vietnam*), youth-oriented news outlets such as *kenh14. vn*, and social media platforms like Facebook and Instagram grab the attention of Vietnamese audiences, proliferating new epistemologies and imaginative conceptions of everyday life. Street signs advertise study abroad programs in Australia, the United States, and Europe, and a greater diversity of foreign stu-

FIGURE 1.1   A street corner in Ho Chi Minh City with a Tết Lunar New Year poster reading "Celebrating Spring, Celebrating the Party" *photo by the author, January 18, 2009*

dents—including a steady increase in Korean students—attend local universities. Driving down a main thoroughfare in Ho Chi Minh City, Vietnamese pass advertisements for international restaurants, designer retail outlets, and even powdered milk that promises to make their children healthier and stronger. These manifestations of the neoliberal economy seem to contradict previous modes of living and governance in Vietnam, where the state organized all production and dictated consumption. Propaganda and strategic rhetoric, however, merge past policies with present conditions and future dreams: the advertisements for powdered milk and the banners extolling the virtues of Chủ tịch (Chairperson) Hồ Chí Minh and the Đảng (Party) remain ever present in the development of the city (see Figure 1.1).

With more time dedicated to new "modes" of organizing domestic space and temporality, individuals with newfound methods of engaging the imagination have extensive choice (Nguyễn-võ 2008, xxi; see also Jandl 2013). This is especially true in many realms of cultural consumption. In public settings, the music of ABBA, American R&B, K-pop, and Vietnamese pop blare from shops next to advertisements for cải lương performances and concerts for diasporic Vietnamese artists returning to Vietnam after many years abroad.[3] In private and semiprivate settings, young Vietnamese watch the latest American television show or Korean drama on mobile telephones and computers, disengaging the individual from the immediate surrounding. Writing about the television and radio, Jean Baudrillard depicts this type of engagement as a "microprocessing of time, bodies, and pleasure . . . All that remains are miniaturized, concentrated and immediately available effects" (1988, 18). An abundance of choice yields instant gratification; with today's mobile phone technology and fast internet access, the speed of this gratification exceeds that of previous decades. Ideas circulate and dissipate in public as consumers strive for the next technology high (20).

Consumers disengage in this environment of consumption to the extent that difference becomes ignored. In the past, and certainly in the present in many rural areas of Vietnam, observations of something foreign (including myself, the tall, American ethnomusicologist) yield a kind of "spectacle," "stage," or "theatre" (21–22). Even I became increasingly less self-conscious as I walked down streets because my presence, even in locations to which I had never traveled, caused fewer questioning stares or calls of "Hello!" from young children. Without what Baudrillard calls the "symbolic benefit of alienation," all "becomes immediately transparent, visible, exposed in the raw and inexorable light of information and communication" (21–22). With the bombardment of media items from abroad, a kind of "ecstasy of communication" (22) emerges, in which the screen distances the body of the viewer from even the abstraction of value that ultimately enables circulation in the market. "All events, all spaces, all memories are abolished in the sole dimension of information" (24). As a result of condensing all culture and value into one easily accessible and immediately satiable dimension, "space is so saturated, the pressure of all which wants to be heard so strong that I am no longer capable of knowing what I want" (24–25). In this saturated environment, consumers imagine so many possibilities—what to listen to with friends; what to watch with family members—and ultimately prevent a choice from being made.

In theory, the information deluge prevents mobility and change, since no one knows what to desire anymore. Mobility and change continue, however, indicating that something must be propelling the circulation and selection of consumables. Observing the motorbike traffic during rush hour in Ho Chi Minh City serves as an example. Motorbikes fill the streets of these cities to the point where traffic nearly stands still. Traffic continues moving, however, when drivers jump the curb and travel along the sidewalk, make left- and right-hand turns in large groups to block oncoming traffic, drive in the wrong direction down one-way streets to get from one block to another, and dart down alleyways in search of shortcuts. When drivers do need to stop, many take out their mobile phones to look at internet content, take phone calls, or respond to text messages. They are not traveling in two-dimensional circles, as Baudrillard implies, but in increasingly multitemporal and multispatial ways. The "ecstasy of communication" here may lead to gratification, but it is a temporary gratification based on transitory time and space—for the five seconds while driving the wrong way down a one-way street, or the ten seconds that it takes to arrange via text message to meet a friend at a café. They then seek additional gratification, drawing on a storehouse of knowledge of the many multitude of ways of communicating and moving through the city.

Creativity and sáng tạo emerge from and respond to this environment. Immersed in the ecstasy of communication, artists deploy creativity to focus audience attention and offer the best choice for present and future conditions. Musicians, too, find ways to mediate opportunities for effective practice with the state, fellow musicians, and audiences. Negotiating a global perspective in particular allows musicians to imagine themselves as empowered social agents capable of tangible change with long-lasting potential.

Invoking sáng tao in this context reflects a growing and quite recent engagement with creativity in the Vietnamese public sphere. Since 2007, I have heard more individuals and have read more journalists and writers use the term *sáng tạo* to describe the innovation of art, ideas, and even business models. In everyday conversations with friends, even, they label videos seen or music heard as *sáng tạo*, suggesting that having sáng tạo is valuable and consumable. During my visits to the large Fahasa bookstore on Nguyễn Huệ Street in District 1 of Ho Chi Minh City, I have increasingly encountered books on creativity since at least 2013. These include translated versions of Graham Collier's *Art and the Creative Consciousness* (1972) and controversial spiritual leader Osho's *Creativity: Unleashing the Forces Within* (1999).

Sáng tạo has appeared in public marketing as well. As shown in Figure 1.2, the construction site for a new building on Trần Hưng Đạo Street advertises the multiuse space as "the place to be creative." One of my favorite kinds of Trung

FIGURE 1.2 Examples of *sáng tạo* in Vietnamese public discourse *photos by the author*

Nguyên coffee has been marketed since at least 2014 as being "made specifically for creativity."

To put this another way, creativity has become a catchphrase in commercialized settings and a commonly accepted metaphor for aspiration and growth. The building makes new space in downtown Ho Chi Minh City for luxurious dwellings and comfortable workspaces, and the coffee fuels the imaginative exploration of new ideas. "Far from being reactive," Oli Mould describes, creativity "is proactive; it drives society into new worlds of living" (2018, 4). The confluence of value and power ultimately enables monetization of creativity, thereby making it "a distinctly neoliberal trait" (12). This realization leads to the large-scale deployment of creativity to drive economic growth: governments, institutions, and everyday citizens use creativity and related terms such as "entrepreneurship" and "innovation" to judge the value of goods, services, and even personality traits (8).

WHAT IS CREATIVITY?

Recent Euro-American scholarship grounds creativity in a Judeo-Christian religious episteme of original creation as divine. This understanding stems from the first line of the Book of Genesis (originally the Parashat Bereshit in the Hebrew Bible): "In the beginning, God created the heavens and the earth." The Hebrew *bara* (to create) here occurs ex nihilo, and refers only to an ability of the divine (Black 1989, 6). Creativity therefore carries vestiges of this association with the divine: creativity is extraordinary, it makes something new, and it is the work of the individual agent (7; see also Mould 2018, 8). This interpretation did not emerge with the compilation of the Bible, however, but took several centuries to cultivate in Europe. Nicholas Cook explains this transformation, noting in particular the work of sixteenth-century English poet Philip Sidney, who "spoke of God having 'made man in his own likeness,' which included the ability to imagine and create things beyond nature" (2018, 2). Since the Enlightenment, it seems, the Western world has understood creativity as focused on the individual creative genius (Mould 2018, 6).

A temporal dimension of this creativity is equally important. In its translation into Latin from Hebrew, "creativity" became an action of the past with "In principio creavit Deus caelum et terram." "Creavit" is the third-person indicative perfect tense of *creo* (also *creare, creavi,* and *creatum*). The actions of the verb meaning "to produce, to make" therefore have already occurred. Descriptions of creativity maintain this emphasis on the past and, more importantly, the finality or "completeness" imbued in the verb (Pope 2005, 37). Lydia Goehr's evaluation of the "work concept" in music further points to the attachment of the complete work idea to the composer in the eighteenth century. The very survival of music depended on the production of works by individual composers with enduring value (1992, 151–52; see also Mould 2018, 30).

This individual, furthermore, is usually understood as white and male. These associations also developed over time in Europe. If one believes like Sidney that the divine formed humans in his image, one only needs to look at depictions of the divine, such as Michelangelo's *Creazione di Adamo* (1511), for instance, to observe the divine as a white European man. The existence of a nearly all-white male makeup of classical music composers further corroborates the association. Women music composers and music composers of color remain little recognized in the Western art music canon.[4]

These understandings of creativity impact discourse surrounding music composition, performance, and scholarship. First, what is created is complete and final, which leads to the understanding of the "work." Performances of music involve works because they are shaped by complete visions of the author. Scholars study these works because their meanings are complete and can be analyzed.

Second, creation takes place in the past, thereby leading one to seek creativity in the past. Third, what is created is divine, extraordinary, and out of nothing, lending the attribution of "greatness" or "genius" to the creative act. Last, this genius is almost always recognized because the artist is a white man.

Creativity prevents the participation of marginalized groups and sustains the systemic discrimination from which it emerged (Mould 2018, 56–57). If one accepts the description of creativity as a system, as sociologist Mihaly Csikszentmihalyi posits in his classic 1996 text *Creativity: Flow and the Psychology of Discovery and Invention*, then the stability enabled by the system enables these discriminatory practices.[5] "Creativity results from the interaction of a system composed of three elements: a culture that contains symbolic rules, a person who brings novelty into the symbolic domain, and a field of experts who recognize and validate the innovation" (1996, 6).[6] On the surface, this may seem a benign description, but postcolonial studies, ethnic studies, and cultural studies suggest otherwise. The capitalist West builds rules based on colonization, imperialism, and empire, ultimately crowding out the participation of those who did not build the system. When the system requires the participation of the "person," this implies a kind of visibility: those who have greater comparative wealth and access to resources are more likely to be "found" as innovative creative actors. Most important, however, the system of identifying creativity is contingent on the "field of experts," who are more willing to recognize creative acts by those who have similar backgrounds. This ultimately replicates the same kind of standards and prevents participation from those who come from backgrounds outside of the hegemonic white mainstream. People of color and women have a greater difficulty participating, which is why so many so-called individual creative geniuses still are white men.

In a clear sense, then, a study of creativity necessarily requires incorporating voices habitually sidelined by individualism. In the past several years, Euro-American writing has started to recognize the toxic nature of creativity discourse. In a January 2019 article in *The New York Times Magazine*, Jody Rosen wrote a blistering critique of the rise of creativity as a lifestyle and marketing strategy. Creativity offers a route out of the "drudgery" of a nine-to-five career and toward a career of perpetual opportunity, complete agency, and freedom. Embodying an ethos of individual branding, creative workers sell their labor and produce products of bespoke value; however, they do so in cutthroat conditions alongside other workers in increasingly niche markets (see also Pang 2012, 7). Rather than offering freedom from salaried positions, creativity brings about oppressive uncertainty, long hours, and low pay.

Creativity also monetizes intimacy to generate cash flow. Making intimacy to sustain one's career as an artist in the digital and internet ages, Nancy Baym argues, entails a tremendous amount of effort. This precarious and emotional work requires "building relationships," cultivating a "personal brand," and a foregrounding of the self in order to survive in the gig economy (2018, 8). As a strategy, musicians undertake "relational labor," or what Baym defines as "the ongoing, interactive, affective, material, and cognitive work of communicating with people over time to create structures that can support continued work" (19). Musicians try to bridge the distance between themselves and their audiences, but in a contemporary creative industry of "techno-capitalist alienation" (22), they also must differentiate themselves from other musicians to survive. The engagement between artist and audience in the contemporary capitalist age therefore involves the relentless pursuit of intimacy with consumers to survive, during a time when the structures of the system consistently drive a wedge between consumer and producer. The commercialization and industrialization of this process "often becomes a source of inequity, driving a system in which a few—be they elite musicians or, more likely, well-paid executives and computing professionals—profit immensely while most cannot afford to devote their work life to music" (25). This further exacerbates the discriminatory practices as outlined by Mould. If Sisyphus was unsuccessful, so too is the contemporary musician.

Rather than allowing creative workers space and time to build alternative careers, the very actions of work price them out of their markets, and they struggle to make ends meet. This is best understood in supply and demand terms from basic microeconomics. More work generates a larger supply of products, while demand in the niche market remains the same and quite low. When more workers vie for a place in the market, therefore, they drive down the prices of their products through creation. There are too many individuals with too many goods selling to too few consumers.

The focus on the individual creator therefore changes societal understandings of work. Rather than working hard on a particular task or trade, society is taught that one simply needs creativity to be successful. Individuals produce and produce in order to find that product that will help make one's riches. "Our entire productive selves and the relationships we keep are now geared toward producing things, ideas, experiences and services that capitalism can exploit" (Mould 2018, 30). This ultimately leads to a work ethic that disregards communal activity and pursues a singular attempt to get ahead. "The trick of neoliberal creativity then is to convince us that you can only be creative by looking to your own agency; any appeal to wider structures do not matter. Any semblance of the social has collapsed into and onto the individual" (61; see also Toynbee 2017). As a result, Western society focuses on the individual genius as the ultimate driver of the economy, political systems, technology, and culture.[7]

When marketing executives and university brochures sell creativity to the public, then, they offer a sinister revisioning of the world. Placing "creative" in scare quotes, Rosen offers the following rejoinder: "'Creative' puts lipstick—or, more precisely, a pair of Warby Parker eyeglasses and a sleeve tattoo—on a pig. It dresses up a ruptured social compact, the raw deal of the gig economy, as bohemian freedom" (2019). He does not mince words in describing the illusion of contemporary creativity.

Creativity, as it is understood in the neoliberal context, then, is dangerous and destructive. It masks the large-scale restructuring of the economy where individuality is bought and sold. "Creative is not just an attribute," according to Rosen (2019). "It is an identity." The badge of creativity one wears, however, masks the highly manufactured nature of that identity. For Laikwan Pang, individuals no longer are in control of their own identities; these identities are managed by creative industries (2012, 2). The "manipulation" of symbols serves as the currency of cultural industries with the tripartite goals of "entertainment, information and perhaps even enlightenment" (Hesmondhalgh 2013, 6). Power exploits creativity, and for this reason, creativity has quickly become the ideology par excellence of neoliberalism. When one product fails, niche creators immediately begin anew for fear that they will lose their tiny place in the market. In short, they worry they will lose their identities, which is why they try so hard to sustain an ideology of creativity. Must this necessarily be the case? Is identity salvageable from the grips of neoliberal creative practice?

CREATIVITIES AND SHAPING IDENTITY

Creativity cannot operate the same way in the Global South. While understandings of the "work," divine inspiration, and expertise might reorient artists toward Euro-American models, the racism imbued in creativity remains unpalatable. This forms a crack in the creativity doctrine and opens the possibility of reshaping creativity discourse for not only the Global South but also worldwide. Vestiges of Euro-American creativity still remain, but creativity will look and resound differently in the Global South and will have a direct impact on contemporary identity making.

Over the course of my research on traditional music in southern Vietnam, I observed the ways in which musicians negotiated different understandings of sáng tạo in performance. As my Vietnamese interlocutors engaged with musicians across the globe through travel and virtual engagements, they simultaneously reflected on what constitutes the ontological basis of Vietnamese tradition and its place in an increasingly cosmopolitan context. They engaged Euro-American creativity with a clear grounding in Vietnamese local practice, philosophy, and aesthetics. Texts found in the Fahasa bookstore reflect this mediation. Patrick Harris's *The Truth About Creativity* (2009), for example, was translated as *Sự thật về sáng tạo*; however, the editors of the Vietnamese version did not include the original subtitle "Rules Are There to Be Challenged." Musicians and artists do not necessary "challenge" the rules or conventions, as this may constitute a public or dangerous act many wish to avoid. Vietnamese creativity instead unites musicians and connects them to past experiences in collective memory.

Musical creativity in southern Vietnam, then, does not simply replicate the aspirational and developmental creativity of the West, but often returns to previous practices in the face of the increasing marketization of the Vietnamese cultural sphere. Writing for the BBC Vietnamese service on the SEAPHONY orchestra, Phạm Cao Phong (2017) suggests how the director of the ensemble "organized an orchestra of no words but with instruments entirely comprised of the minority peoples of Vietnam, or more precisely the Indigenous peoples of Southeast Asia, to revitalize the creativity of art on the Vietnamese stage, putting an end to the discontinuity and stagnancy of the past eighty years." French colonization, South Vietnamese cultural policy, the American military complex, and an emergent cosmopolitanism gripped and steered certain elements of music production in southern Vietnam from the late nineteenth century and throughout the twentieth and early twenty-first centuries. Creativity, or sáng tạo, repairs and enables a return to Vietnamese roots that had been interrupted by war and imperialism.

The work—or labor, to be more precise—of Vietnamese musicians aligns with descriptions of creativity in Marxism, which offers several ways to rescue creativity and identity from the clutches of those in power. For many twentieth-century Marxists, the subjugation of the worker by the bourgeoisie "mutilate[s] the worker's natural creativity" (Buhle 1986, xii). For C. L. R. James, creativity sits at the center of Hegel's critique of rationalism taken up by Marx. "Contradiction, *not* harmonious increase and decrease, is the creative and moving principle of history" (James [1950] 1986, 117; emphasis in original). More importantly, creativity emerges when the individual fully embraces the societal lessons of the past. "The end toward which mankind is inexorably developing by the constant overcoming of internal antagonisms is . . . self-realization, creativity based upon the incorporation into the individual personality of the whole previous development of humanity" (117). Since the worker is not yet at the end, societies seek advancement in creativity through dialectical materialism. "After the French Revolution," James suggests, "no further progress in thought could be made without holding fast to the principle of creativity and the contradictory process by which this creativity develops" (118). History is written and navigated, therefore, through the creativity of the worker.

Stuart Hall's work on anti-essentialist identities offers a place for creativity to serve as the vanguard of identity making. Hall describes older essentialist identities as working through the "internal antagonisms" described here to move toward a stable essence of ourselves—something he critiques as identity "for a good night's rest" ([1991] 2019, 65). "We are never quite there, but always on our way to it," as the argument goes (64). Anti-essentialism instead suggests that identities are never stabilized. Individuals or community groupings are not "the sole origin or authors of [social] practice"—and can claim no ownership over identity or that "essence" of self—but rely on older generations of practitioners (65). Hall's invocation of the term aligns with Étienne Wenger's description of practice as the "shared historical and social resources, frameworks, and perspectives that can sustain mutual engagement in action" (Wenger 1998, 5). These communities therefore work to solidify tangible, varied, and flexible links between individuals while drawing on resources of the past. This work generates feelings of solidarity and, ultimately, satisfaction (47).[8]

Creativity drives this social practice of forming (and reforming) identity. For Hall, identity produces both narrative and representation to ground lived experience and suggest "things which were not there before" ([1991] 2019, 70, 76). "Identity is not something which is formed outside and then we tell stories about it. It is that which is narrated in one's own self" (70). Creativity emerges at this juncture: practitioners experiment with sounds, artifacts, and ideas that give shape to these narratives and make representations potent.[9]

Creativity remains a hallmark of both neoliberalism and contemporary Marxism, which helps explain its currency in the United States and western Europe, as well as countries governed through Communist ideology. Scholars have observed a "rise of creativity" in China, for instance, where the neoliberal trends of entrepreneurship and originality forcefully guide artistic production in a context ruled by a Communist Party. In a rather superficial engagement with creativity and identity in contemporary China, Shaun Rein (2014) describes the "stages" of China's development from the supposedly noncreative to creative, as if creativity did not exist before the neoliberal turn. Anthropologist Lily Chumley's more nuanced ethnography on *chuangzaoli* (創造力), a concept meaning "creativity," examines the training undertaken by for visual artists for entry into the "creativity industry" in China. In art school, they learn "self-styling," or how to speak about their artwork so their pieces speak for them (2016, 126). Their work needs to move beyond genre, category, and resemblance to other works. This aligns with the neoliberal project of individual agency while also leaving room for audiences' individual interpretations of the work (135). They practice subtle identity formation to produce more creative artistic works.

Individual artists therefore situate themselves within history and community to sustain their engagement with what James called "internal antagonisms" (117). For Pang (2012), who offers a Marxist critique of Chinese cinema, creativity involves "two mutually conditioning dimensions: it is a result of social praxis that demands labor, and it is also a form of textuality that proliferates on its own" (5). This elegant definition incorporates multiple moving parts that often are at odds with one another and captures the unwieldy nature of creativity. Injecting a musical voice into this definition, individual musicians labor together to make music, and audiences listen to and interpret these performances. The improvised melodies, aural interactions between musicians, instruments played in atypical ways, and innovative timbres heard then circulate in societal contexts. They intersect with laboring processes of other musicians who then need to respond, and so on.

Through this work, artists sustain engagement with the past and offer new conceptualizations of identity for the future, as James and Hall offer. These sounds "transgress," drawing again from Pang, "because they build new connections and open new horizons, waiting to be understood and rewritten" (2012, 82). José E. Limón makes a similar argument in his Marxist discussion of the *corrido* and documentation of violence in northern Mexico and southern Texas by *corridistas* at the end of the nineteenth and the beginning of the twentieth centuries. The

conflict depicted "the sedimented ideological traces of older modes of production in conflict with the present or the anticipatory messages of a future mode
of production" (1992, 32). Communities speak through the corrido to interrogate
the violence of the past and present, and anticipate future positive changes.
The performance of the corrido "records" this work and enables future performances to engage with it again (184). The corridista is creative, therefore, when
"record[ing] in repressed symbolic form the traces of [the violent] . . . past and
the anticipations of a utopian future" (184). Creativity in music therefore remains
equally as important to lived experience as the goals of revolution offered by
Marx (via Hall), as described here.

Creativity has an important role to play in the development of society and
the ultimate liberation of its people. In other words, creativity helps build and
shape anti-essentialist identities or, more generally, renovated senses of community within the world. Although the individual provides insight into these
processes, creativity must be understood as a collective social practice. If societies
are to become truly equitable, according to Mould (2018, 60), we must move
away from "the relentless focus on the individual as the key agent of change"
and adopt models of creativity that are communal and destabilizing (15–16).
This book offers an exploration of how Vietnamese musicians undertake this
work in continuing practices of a living tradition of music performance that is
continually on the forefront of societal change.

CONCLUSION

Musical creativity is proactive and generative, and it mediates the global and the
local. This first chapter points to several valuable critiques of the Euro-American
creativity model and provides the contexts in which creativity and sáng tạo operate in southern Vietnam. It is important to note that the pure forms of what I call
a global creativity and a local sáng tạo model do not really exist. Their negotiation
in performance impacts strategies of identity-making in the dynamic spaces of
southern Vietnamese living today.

Musical creativity offers powerful and socially mediated tools of expression.
A study of creativity therefore reveals how musicians sustain and preserve their
stake in Vietnam's future course as they perform within local models of creation
and react to—and occasionally reject—global models of creativity. Vietnamese
musicians therefore offer poignant critique of global or Western models of

creativity; they deemphasize, in particular, the focus on the individual creative genius and the assumed mastery that this individual possesses. Ethnomusicology needs to follow the guidance of these musicians and move past the hegemony and supremacy advanced by the narratives of global creativity.

TWO

Creativity in Ethnomusicology

The evaluation of the creative process is fundamental to the musician's and scholar's craft. One therefore finds the term *creativity* frequently in music studies: important musicians and composers are "creative," so we study them and interview others to understand what they do that is so effective (Hill 2018). Certain scholars replicate the individual genius creativity paradigm described in the previous chapter, while others attempt to draw on observed musical practice to suggest alternative ways of understanding creativity. With its extensive use, the term *creativity* approaches triviality, and scholars like Simon Frith argue that we should dispense with the term entirely (2011, 71). I disagree. The term has potency in Vietnam and in the Global North; indeed, in the negative, nothing raises greater ire than calling a musician "uncreative." More importantly, as I reference later in this chapter, creativity has renewed usage by marginalized groups to redress discrimination.

Studies of creativity in ethnomusicology offer consider insights into local understandings of creative processes and performance. George Dor's (2004) work on the Anlo Ewe *havolu* event locates creativity in a "communal ethos" (26) grounded in local "thought systems" (29). These systems are not necessarily uniform, but they offer nuanced understandings of the many intersections between individual lives and community practices that must support any evaluation of creativity (29–30). Dor identifies "levels of communal creativity" in the creation process (31) and draws on a litany of voices from the region—voices not often heard in the theorization of practice in ethnomusicology. He then extends this discussion to how local actors practice and talk about ownership of musical materials. In so doing, he offers a clear and reproducible template for studying creativity in ethnomusicology that does not privilege Western definitions of the concept.

Ethnomusicologists like Dor mediate between humanistic and social scientific approaches in the study of creativity. They maintain a subject-centered ethnography and investigate the role of the individual in balancing, deploying, and shaping societal knowledge. In this work, ethnomusicologists also must attend to moments of overrun where society or certain power structures overwhelm the individual. These include moments of colonial or imperial resurgence in which notions of individual creative mastery discipline and silence. How the individual works together with others to reclaim power over expression in response to these obstacles should sit at the forefront of future ethnomusicological inquiry, and I try to follow the lead of scholars such as Nancy Baym, Dorinne Kondo, Laudan Nooshin, Laikwan Pang, Julietta Singh, and others who place this kind of advocacy at the center of their work.

In this chapter, I explore ethnomusicology's evaluation of creativity and replication of bias since the discipline's inception. I track the development of creativity studies in ethnomusicology to show how it has—or has not—changed from the early twentieth century to the present. I pinpoint particular works that, like Dor (2004), offer powerful but largely forgotten ways of interrogating creativity in its various forms. I note in particular how these works, often by women scholars and scholars of color, can inform a scholarly investigation of creativity in southern Vietnam. From these works, I propose three approaches that direct the narratives and analytical lenses I use in the rest of the book. I conclude with an example of how these three approaches unite in one of the most powerful studies of creativity in ethnomusicology, authored by Kyra D. Gaunt.

DISCIPLINING CREATIVITY IN ETHNOMUSICOLOGY

My critique begins with a quotation from Alan Merriam, commonly understood as one of the most important early figures in the discipline. For Merriam, ethnomusicologists "study music as a creative cultural activity, including such problems as the sources of musical materials, the standards of excellence in performance, the psychology of music, and the processes of creation" (1960, 110). How ethnomusicologists undertake this study—and how they view creativity—is, however, quite haphazard. In the past and even today, some ethnomusicologists do not engage with the concept at all; some dismiss it due to bias toward nonwhite musicians, and others, who write out of anthropology, understand creativity and the action of creation as mediated through social action. Given the sheer number of voices and the propensity to only highlight voices of more "seminal" ethnomusicologists, it is not surprising that scholars often speak over one another and occasionally regress in their methods by ignoring previous scholarship and reverting to more outdated understandings of the concept.

Proto-ethnomusicological studies did not often engage creativity per se but evaluated individual performance practice to understand larger social categories of music. In her 1910 and 1913 volumes on Chippewa music, Frances Densmore (1973) indicated the names of the singers she recorded alongside transcriptions and written descriptions of tunes. Much of her analysis of the songs of Odjïb'we and others in the second volume, for instance, pointed to the intersections of many moments of a warrior's life and vocal music, but the data presented was mostly descriptive. Alan Lomax ([1962] 1971, 428) continued this kind of work using his cantometrics sheets and the study of cultural intention (1959, 928–30); however, individual or collective creativity was not of primary importance. Although he "had great respect for creativity which, as he clearly realized, can be at its greatest when constrained by even the most conservative and strictly defined traditions," his research assistant Victor Grauer (2005) argued that his cantometrics work sought to "look past the creativity to the traditions beneath it."

Folklorists in the early twentieth century more often engaged with creativity. As Tina Ramnarine argues, however, Constantin Brăiloiu views this work of folklorists as "livel[y]" but ultimately quite "confused" (Ramnarine 2003, 20). Franz Boas examines "originality" in performances of Native American folklore, for instance, and imparts an understanding of the inherent "interdependence of creativity and tradition" (Bronner 1992, 3). Boas's exegesis on style, for instance, observes that despite the rules imposed by previous practice, individual artisans continue to produce different performances from those rules (Boas [1927] 2010, 157). Research evaluates when and how these creative differences emerge.

> We have already seen that the novelty consists generally in the combination of old pattern elements in new ways. Nevertheless, the authors of these designs are convinced that they have created something new. I have information on the attitude of these artists only from the North American Indians. They call designs of this kind "dream designs," and claim that the new pattern actually appeared to them in a dream . . . These is little doubt but that this is merely another term for invention. It expresses a strong power of visualization which manifests itself when the person is alone and at rest, when he can give free play to the imagination. (157–58)

Multisensory practice, play, and imagination intersect to explain creation among these artists. Creativity therefore appears well theorized by local musicians, and Boas suggests a social understanding of creativity in this context; however, Boas also expresses skepticism that they truly created something "new."

Creativity studies stalled after this, as anthropologists and early ethnomusicologists appeared less willing to recognize the role of creation or creative practice.[1] They shared Boas's skepticism. Anthropologist Bronislaw Malinowski does not "account for the speculative and creative aspects of culture" in his scholarship, according to Merriam (1964, 22). In other words, his approach does not include creativity as part of "the basic needs of the human biosocial organism" (23). In music studies, Richard A. Waterman argues that the Yirrkala people of Australia did not "invent . . . or creat[e]" new songs; the songs already existed and simply needed to be "discover[ed]" ([1955] 1971, 168). In classifying Yirrkala songs, Waterman suggests that some "provide an outlet for individual creativity while many may be used simply to conquer personal dysphoria" ([1955] 1971, 168). Later, Merriam maintains that "in nonliterate societies, there is less conscious discussion of techniques and processes of creativity than exists in the West" (1964, 166). Contrary to Boas's earlier conviction that originality and novelty are just as present outside of cosmopolitan centers, Merriam suggests that indigenous theory does not account for this.

Early ethnomusicologists appeared conflicted concerning the location of creation in society. Did creativity exist? If so, was creativity an individualistic or communal endeavor? The response often depended on whether their training and disposition was more humanistic or social scientific.[2] Humanists understood creativity as individual endeavors not always found in "traditional" societies, while social scientists viewed creativity as communal and dispersed in broader society. Merriam notes this distinction in *The Anthropology of Music*. Merriam's mentor Melville J. Herskovits depicts a study of creative output as humanistic, or involved in the study of "man's existence" rather than a study of institutions (Merriam 1964, 22–23). Merriam, too, leans toward the study of creativity as humanistic endeavor; with his contemporaries, they relegate their discussions to "individual human creativity" (1964, 80) or, in Charles Seeger's words, "individual creative initiative, allied probably with exceptional expertness" (1966, 11). Early ethnomusicologists, furthermore, rarely "accept[ed] the theory of communal creation which indicated that the beginning of musical production lurks in the collective creativity of undifferentiated human masses" (Nettl 1954, 81; see also

Wachsmann 1961, 145).[3] Merriam does not dismiss, however, the possibility that creativity could be a social scientific endeavor that emerges from a study of social forces; indeed, Bruno Nettl also points to the importance of "communal recreation" in improvisation, which involves "improvising over a previously existent melody, or changing and varying it" (1954, 82).[4] This seems to imply that the moment of improvisation draws on social convention before generating the tune in performance. Merriam more specifically points to the work of political scientist Carl J. Friedrich, who argues that "creative activities" emerge within societal constructs (Merriam 1964, 23) and therefore exist under the purview of the social sciences and not the humanities.

These debates occurred concurrently with—or perhaps followed—similar debates on the relationship betwen the individual author and social context in studies of other forms of artistic practice. Writing in the 1930s, Mikhail Bakhtin suggests that the analysis of the novel must recognize the reader, whom he occasionally calls the "listener." The speaker—or the composer or performer, for that matter—"orient[s] . . . toward the listener . . . [and] toward a specific conceptual horizon, toward the specific world of the listener" (1981, 282). The text offers material for listeners to consider and combine with their preexisting knowledge; in short, meaning is produced through a listener's mediation. The text, then, "introduces totally new elements into his discourse; it is in this way, after all, that various different points of view, conceptual horizons, systems for providing expressive accents, various social 'languages' come to interact with one another" (282). Creativity emerges when these listeners as a group, rather than the writer, mediate and destabilize meaning following the generation and then dissemination of the text. "Great novelistic images continue to grow and develop even after the moment of their creation; they are capable of being creatively transformed in different eras, far distant from the day and hour of their original birth" (422). In the 1960s, Roland Barthes acknowledges similar understandings of the role of the author. The author does not invent language; the author uses language, and the readers interpret the language used. Once the text is written, the author cedes any notion of control. If the author imposes, then meaning becomes closed and the text dies (1977, 146–48). Scholars later posit artistry and creativity as explicitly social—occasionally without the participation of the artist or composer. Howard Becker indicates more explicitly that "cooperation" of many people ultimately generates the artwork; artists themselves cannot produce the work on their own ([1984] 2008, 1).

Despite clear antecedents in literature that questioned the prowess of the individual, early ethnomusicology often maintained a predilection for the individual creator. In evaluating early ethnomusicological literature, Laudan Nooshin advocates that "creativity" itself disciplined colonial subjects through boundaries and difference (2015, 9). Jason Toynbee calls this an "ideology of creativity" in the West (2017, 38). In the ethnocentric realms of early ethnography, European and American scholars often understood creativity as being built on the prowess of the genius composer operating through divine inspiration (Nooshin 2015, 11–12); even Boas expresses an interest in understanding the "freedom of the creative genius" ([1927] 2010, 156). These ethnographers therefore seek charismatic leaders who practice creativity in apparently the same way as the art music composer. Not finding these leaders, they rarely write of individual musicians (Nooshin 2015, 15–16).[5] Since no individual apparently advances change in practice, they view tradition as static. As late as 1974, Norma McLeod remarks that "there are musical traditions, such as the Hopi, to which no new pieces of music are presently being added" (107). Such a generalization of stationary tradition gives rise to the perception of a difference between noncreative communities and the creative West. Interestingly, McLeod attempts to make the same argument against an ethnocentric view of creation, but in so doing, invokes a lack of "newness" from this same ethnocentric perspective. This kind of logic ultimately supports the colonial and imperialistic project: with change being necessary for survival in an increasingly cosmopolitan and global world, Western ideas help institute change and the possibility of freedom from rigid structures of the past.

Approaches to musical creativity changed when ethnomusicologists started to bridge the divide between the humanistic and social scientific approaches. In these works, ethnomusicologists worked with individuals to understand the role of their practice in wider sociocultural contexts. Leonard Meyer ([1960] 1971) takes part in this work by pivoting creativity into the realm of communication through musical culture. Individual musicians may lead, but they ultimately generate information—including knowledge and understanding—for a community.

Of special relevance to the understanding of individual values is the psychological need for novelty—or, as some have put it, *for information*. Its importance as a basic human drive is implicit in recent studies of creativity, developmental psychology, and stimulus privation. It seems possible that the need for information is in part responsible for the tendency of composers and performers to deviate from established stylistic norms. Or, to put the matter in a different way: exact repetition is dull, clichés are boring, and familiar tasks tedious—without value—because they yield very little information. ([1960] 1971, 275; emphasis added)

In some ways, this returns ethnomusicology to certain understandings of culture advocated by Boas; instead of the creative genius, musicians deviate or follow new paths to generate information about society and encourage new appreciations of value. Nooshin further identifies the work of John Blacking as "position[ing] the socially-situated creative individual at the heart" of the ethnomusicological study (Nooshin 2015, 17).

Like Meyer, Blacking also investigates deviation but uses the more generic "change" to imply an aversion to explicit replication. Many other ethnomusicologists adopt this terminology; for example, as Margaret Kartomi advises, "Where 'borrowing' ends, creative musical change begins" (1981, 229). "Musical change," for Blacking, "must be given a special status in studies of social and cultural change, because music's role as mediator between the nature and the culture in man combines cognitive and affective elements in a unique way" (1977, 5). Blacking focuses here on changes to "musical systems," which involve communities of practitioners, rather than cataloging more individual changes to style as a result of acculturation or the interaction of multiple cultural areas. With the spread of Christianity and European music among the Venda, for example, multiple musical systems and associated processes emerge, which he labels "traditional," "syncretic," and "modern" (2). Despite a maintenance of some forms of difference through categorization, Blacking evaluates the "dynamic" parameters of socially contingent style.

Change also necessarily implied destruction and the crowding out of older, competing musical ideas. Klaus Wachsmann argues that "the acquisition of new musical habits as with the unlearning of previous habits" generates creativity (1961, 144–45). Blacking makes a similar point in his description of "syncretic" South African music used to support the apartheid regime at the expense of Black African musical traditions (1977, 7). This anticipates an important element of creativity theory more generally in the twenty-first century: creativity both generates and destroys (Pang 2012; Cropley et al. 2010).

Following even the interpretive turn of the 1980s, work on creativity remained diffuse and unfocused in ways similar to Brăiloiu's and Ramnarine's assertion. Descriptions of creativity often repeat past work and ultimately argue that what constitutes creativity depends on the perspectives of the creative agent and evaluator. Philip Bohlman's description of folk music in 1988, for example, summarizes previous ethnomusicological assertions concerning the presumed fraught relationship of creativity and tradition.

> The inherent creativity of many folk music traditions represents a vast array of individual attitudes toward the balance of innovation and representation. Some musicians may use the possibilities of creativity as a means of expanding individual poetic license. In contrast, others may take a reactionary stance, recognizing in the processes of creativity a musical territory that violates tradition. Some may use creativity to concentrate audience response on the folk musician, while others successfully diffuse the importance of the individual by consciously sidestepping creativity. (Bohlman 1988, 77)

The insight provided does not appear "new" at this juncture of ethnomusicology's history, as Bohlman advances creativity as a bastion of the individual.

Bohlman does offer an important description of musical creativity as involving some mediation of rigid structure and flexibility in practice. Creativity pinpoints limits and draws "attention to the folk musician's position vis-à-vis those limits" (1988, 77). Ethnomusicologists might view this as a "creative dialectic between text and context" in their studies of musical and cultural change (104–5). Ethnomusicologists interpret and reinterpret musical texts within rapidly shifting social contexts, but these interpretations become messy quickly. The context or "community" of practitioners studied may seem relatively stable to the ethnomusicologist in a particular location; however, the complex systems of practice generated—or what Bohlman calls "canon formation"—preclude clear categorization. Urbanization, modernization, and other realities of the present age propel contexts with greater speed (105); it is not easy for the ethnomusicologist to keep up.

Jonathan Stock (1996) calls attention to shifting conceptualizations of the musical canon in twentieth-century China at the intersection of changing historical circumstance and institutionalization of music culture. In this investigation of "musical creativity," Stock places the individual musician—in this instance, the blind musician Abing—within an examination of larger social developments in musicmaking and meaning-making, or that the "personal, the idiosyncratic, and the exceptional are very much part of the collective, the typical and the ordinary" (1996, 142). This emphasis on the single individual partly reflects the need for the monumental figure to construct national narratives in the People's Republic of

China in the second half of the twentieth century. Furthermore, like Bohlman, Stock finds creativity at the intersection of historical practice and individual contribution to the development of ideology and modernization.

Stock emphasizes the influence of Western understandings of creativity in the creation of stable institutions, including the conservatory, and stable systems designed to shape meaning. This form of creativity makes little room for local and Indigenous creativity models. Stock does describe Abing's approach to music performance as "creative employment" of "small-scale, musical-development techniques" (106)—something Stock describes later as a "creative model" (158)—but does not commit to describing traditional practice as embodying creativity. He instead invokes the "exceptional" ability of Abing and points specifically to the creativity of composition and making establishing "works" to be performed for the new Chinese nation. Notation in particular generates established (and venerated) works of *guoyue* (national music), which imitate the creativity of Western art music compositions (144). It appears, therefore, that Stock upholds the ideological baggage embedded in the concept.

Ethnomusicologists and musicologists further uphold the exceptional by invoking the "novel" as goal of creative acts. Eric Clarke suggests that creativity in performance "arises out of the conjunction of novelty (whether accidental or deliberate) with more slowly evolving norms and traditions" (2012, 20). The musician draws on knowledge to best understand the trajectory of tradition or genre and anticipate, perhaps, what comes next. Juniper Hill puts this in slightly different terms: she understands musical creativity as "using divergent thinking and exercising volition" to produce meaningful music that "does not conform to an entirely predetermined model" (2012, 88). Although not reliant on the "new" per se, value still emerges from this divergence and volition. Rather than looking forward, which Hill seems to imply, I view any study of creativity as equally needing to look back.

PURSUING NEW DIRECTIONS FOR ETHNOMUSICOLOGY

A focus on Vietnamese musical creativity highlights contemporary local practices of traditional music performance and maintenance and suggests the emergence of alternative understandings of creativity that adopt from but also bulwark hegemonic Euro-American models. Scholars on and of the Global South in ethnomusicology and other fields have recently examined the impact of this hegemony. Noriko Manabe (2006) invokes creativity in her evaluation of the messages communicated in innovate rapping schemes in Japan. Laikwan Pang describes *shanzhai* culture in mainland China as a kind of "grassroots creativity" that overturns power structures of consumption and offers "copycat designs of brand-name products, which often introduce something new to cater to the specific needs of potential niche clients" (2012, 1). She offers the example of an enthusiast posting videos on the internet to disseminate knowledge about a particular topic. This is not exactly the same as Kirin Narayan's "everyday creativity," which values noncommercial production and community through communal practice in India (2016, xxi), but both Pang and Narayan advocate locally-emergent creativities as drivers of cultural production. Nooshin (2015) takes Western scholars and musicians to task for the problematic ways they have exported westernized notions of creativity to subjugated and colonized parts of the world. In her work on Iranian classical music, she suggests that the model of individual creative composer and genius undermined the vibrancy of collective mediations of traditional music.

A corpus of recent creativity literature continues to examine the rich intersection of the individual and societal. In the United States, Kay Kaufman Shelemay (2006) investigates how multiple Ethiopian understandings of creativity emerge from local concepts and intersect with external understandings of the concept (306–8); the work of musicians ultimately shapes a community of practitioners (317). In the United Kingdom, Tina Ramnarine (2011, 2018) and contributors to her 2018 edited collection on the orchestra interrogate the impact of history, environment, government policy, and colonial discourse on orchestras around the world, while at the same time highlighting the agency of musicians and institutions in shaping their futures through repertoire selection, sound production, and collaboration. The clashes that occur are inherent in and necessary for creativity (Clarke and Doffman 2017, 16). These clashes are not negative, however, but feature points or moments of play, amusement, agency, and reconciliation. Ramnarine's powerful self-ethnography identifies how the memories held and produced through orchestral interactions have a significant role to play in the decolonizing project (2018, 329–30).

Contemporary work on creativity in ethnomusicology must continue to pinpoint and divest from common creativity narratives. Three approaches are of particular importance and relevance to this project. Ethnomusicologists must undertake more nuanced ethnographic evaluations of individual practice within social contexts and reject mastery as central to this practice. Although resolutely embedded in the present, these creativities simultaneously engage with the past, bringing lost or forgotten histories to the fore for contemporary reuse. In so doing, ethnomusicologists identify forms of creativity distributed throughout a social context rather than collected in the work of a single individual; such an approach recognizes the reparative component of a socialized creativity.

Rejecting Mastery

Creativity, especially as it is understood in Western neoliberal contexts, designates a kind of mastery, which can be equally as dangerous as creativity itself. Despite pronouncements to the contrary, mastery is not, in fact, "harmless, worthwhile, even virtuous" (Singh 2018, 9). As Julietta Singh cogently argues, mastery emerged as an important product and discourse of the Western colonial project. Three characteristics or "qualities" of mastery discourse persist today as vestiges of colonization (and by extension, creativity discourse as well). "Splitting" as small-scale divide-and-conquer, where external powers impose boundaries between subjects that did not previously exist (12–13; see also Nooshin 2015, 9). Splitting leads to "ongoing practices of subordination," where the enforcement of new power dynamics between opposite sides of the boundary, whereby one side inflicts violence or extracts goods from the other (Singh 2018, 13). The use of these practices enforces power over—and even ownership over—time, narrative, and history (14). Here, the colonizer, and later the imperialist, always reaps the rewards of power. "The [colonial] master is envisioned as the winner . . . whose winning comes to be taken for granted in a proleptic narrative account of the world that authorizes future action" (17). The discourses of creativity and even "development" serve as replicating cycles of mastery for those in power.

Creativity and mastery are not objective, but they can objectify. This discourse of objectification has a long history in the West, has been exported elsewhere, and now seemingly lives everywhere. The use of colonial languages serves by way of example (Singh 2018, 84–85). For Indochinese colonial subjects to be accepted, for instance, they mastered French, the language of the colonial oppressor. This served as a kind of splitting of those with a particular kind of "elite" education and those who were forced to desire this education. The colonialists themselves, however, often were monolingual and depended on bi- or trilingual subjects to govern. A version of this continues to this day in Vietnam: I frequently hear European or American academics bemoan the lack of English-language competency among Vietnamese academics, although these Euro-Americans frequently have less-than-fluent competency in Vietnamese. This belief becomes manifest in self-criticism by Vietnamese friends of mine who frequently apologize for their "poor English." My own faults are a different matter: I stumble over my words in my native English language and make many pronunciation and syntax errors in Vietnamese; and yet, my friends laud my English as something to which they aspire and describe my Vietnamese as excellent. As a "foreigner" (*người nước ngoài*), I am perceived as master and therefore as accountable to different rules.

Singh proposes a solution to alienation and discrimination in the form of "dehumanism" of both academic discourse and knowledge maintenance. It is "a practice of recuperation, of stripping away the violent foundations (always structural and ideological) of colonial and neocolonial mastery that continue to render some beings more human than others" (2018, 4). This work produces a subject position free from—or at least at some distance from—the colonial projects that haunt and the imperialist projects that continue to shape everyday lives. The primary method of dehumanism involves what Singh calls "vulnerable reading," or "an open, continuous practice that resists foreclosures by remaining unremittingly susceptible to new world configurations that reading texts—literary, artistic, philosophical, and political—can begin to produce. Vulnerable readings resist disciplinary enclosure, refusing to restrict in advance how and where one might wander through textural engagement" (22). This form of decolonization is not limited to textural analyses, certainly, but also includes evaluates of performance. I therefore look not only to new configurations but also older configurations potentially forgotten in the process of advancing creative practice.

Creativity (sáng tạo) in traditional music exists as the decolonizing force par excellence in contemporary Vietnam, as musicians continually redeploy traditional music to subvert neocolonial, imperialist, and globalist notions of creativity and mastery. At the heart of this effort is the musician's use of metaphor; no one can master something as elusive as metaphor, just as no one can master traditional music. This does not mean, however, that musicians escape neoliberal models of creativity and mastery. Nguyễn Vĩnh Bảo used the title *nhạc sư*, which I and others translate as "master musician," as it designates a highly revered status and some connection to urban and cosmopolitan centers. Nguyễn Vĩnh Bảo spoke several foreign languages including French and English, traveled and was recorded abroad, and was well connected to his students around the world who studied with him over Skype and email. He did not proclaim a mastery of the tradition, but embodied the classification of guardian or steward of the tradition (Nguyễn T. Phong 2006).

Engagement with the past maintains valuable connections to the processes, communities, objects, and bodies that enable creativity. For music educator Pamela Burnard, "the context of musical creativity becomes a source of meaningful representations of objects and actions, representations which are sociohistorical because they emerge from the historical experience of a social group situated in time and space" (2012, 14). An evaluation of history leads to an uncovering of methods of "tacit knowing," which motivates "artistic agency" in composition and performance (Zembylas and Niederauer 2017). The practice and extension of precedent serves as a "mode of becoming" in the present (Clarke, Doffman, and Lim 2013, 659).

Creativity might be understood as a method of bringing something into being, but what is formed is historically contingent, contemporary, and imbued with agency. For Joseph Lam, the creativity of music at the Ming court brought something of the present, including an indication of time, place, thought, and collective participation, into the performance that serves to symbolize and perpetuate a "distinctiveness and purpose" (1998, 12). As long as orthodox practice remains uncontested, participants understand "expressiveness and creative details" (13). They "adjust . . . and interpret . . . the state ritual and music to match their own needs" and "display . . . who they are, what they believe, and what they are doing in particular contexts" (11). Creativity uses past practice for expressing and experiencing the present.

This kind of work advances a kind of knowing of self and knowing of community. Samuel A. Floyd Jr. makes similar observations in several early articles in *Black Music Research Journal*, which he founded in 1980. He advocates the necessity of understanding the African American experience as a way into Black music (1980, 4); the scholar "should . . . unearth, explore, and explain ideas, facts, events, phenomena, and records that have been neglected, forgotten, ignored, falsified, and unknown" (1983, 46). He offers the Black Renaissance, which also is known more widely as the Harlem Renaissance of the 1920s, as an example of an overlooked period of American—not just African American—musical history (1981/1982, 73–74). Ernest Julius Mitchell II later calls this period a "burst of black creativity" (2010, 641). Ignoring and falsifying the impact of Black musicians—borrowing Floyd's appropriate terminology—emerges entirely from racist discourses of creativity that precluded their collective contribution. The ethnomusicologist must work to archive this discovery process to give voice to creative processes; indeed, as Jane Sugarman argues, ethnomusicologists must study how "they, as well as members of the society that they study, have come to 'know' what they 'know'" (1997, 30). Knowing is not simply reflective but also anticipatory. This kind of forward-thinking sits at the heart of creativity work.

Distributed Creativity as Reparative

Many scholars advance the study of collaboration and negotiated decision-making as a primary method to understanding creativity. Eric Clarke and his various collaborators propose the concept of "distributed creativity" to explain the ways that multiple individuals bring diverse perspectives and intentions to music. In an article cowritten with Mark Doffman and composer Liza Lim, they explore the ways that composer, performers, and conductors collaborate within the structures of a particular institutional environment to prepare the première a new work (630). Creative work takes part in an ecosystem, or a system "constituted of objects and processes whose affordances crisscross the physical and the social, the synchronic and the diachronic" (630). As part of coinhabiting this ecosystem, participants become increasingly attuned to one another or "'tuned' by the work" through participation and engagement with the textual content—in this case, a poem—associated with the work (644).

Creativity is not simply a process of the mind, but one of the body and its engagement with environments and other systems. Adam Linson and Eric Clarke (2017) make this point and suggest multiple distributions in performance: embodied distribution, or the ways that various "bodily subsystems" interact to enable music creation; distribution involving the body or "the organism" and an environment in which the body is situated; and, finally, a distribution emergent from the historical and social constructions of instruments, repertories, and other musical materials, as well as those performance practices debated by musicians for generations (55).[6] This work opens a number of possible avenues for understanding the ways in which superstructure impacts musical creativity practiced by the mind and body of the musician, as well as the many routes of resistance through embodied practice (58). In settings where multiple musicians practice, they may "enjoy a unique experience" while maintaining "the feeling of a shared experience" (63). The feeling of community cannot be overestimated in studies of creativity.

The ideals of distribution do not assuage the real possibilities of co-option and dominance of individual figures in the creative process. In other words, the ethnomusicologist must remain attuned to power. Creativity may well involve "inventiveness, interaction, the ability to synthesize new forms of knowledge from diverse sources" (Sarath 2013, 2; see also Csikszentmihalyi 1996, 1); however, creative encounters often involve one-upmanship through inventiveness and collecting knowledge. Alternatively, institutions may invoke certain forms of inventiveness over others toward particular goals. Tina Ramnarine's investigation of "new folk music" in Finland, for example, ties creativity to institutionalization and nation building. "Collective composition as a characteristic of the creative process in folk music is aligned to the homogenizing tendencies of nationalist discourse" (2003, 20–21).

Scholarship particularly outside of ethnomusicology has sought to examine these power dynamics, take back creativity from the clutches of the genius model, and redeploy it as reparative. For this reason, creativity has become a powerful tool for social activism. Both Dorinne Kondo and Nancy Baym extend this work and describe the importance of building alliances as creative action. At this juncture, the labor of musicians and artists builds audiences through emotional connection and a "politics of affiliation" (Kondo 2018, 39). Creativity then emerges when practitioners "experience and reconcile the contradictions of relationships between people and metaphysical deities, one another, and the social institutions that bind and separate" (Baym 2018, 12).

Kondo responds to the discriminatory practices of modern capitalist creativity by foregrounding the collaborative and reparative work for people of color in theater. Creativity provides opportunities for actors, playwrights, and dramaturges to reclaim and shape societal notions of race, as well as generate "hope" (2018, 90). In Kondo's work, Jacques Lacan dovetails with director and actor Anna Deavere Smith to remind readers of the Bakhtinian adage that language belongs to no one; creative usage of language makes the subject (112). This work constitutes "reparative creativity" or the "making" of the racialized subject to heal the "shattering" of the subject following trauma (33). Creativity addresses systemic violence directed toward communities or occurring in theatrical productions where stereotyped Black, Asian, or Indigenous identities serve as foils for white exceptionalism or help generate laughs for primarily white audiences (36). Creativity is always already critical, and serves as "work, practice, method: a site of theory making and political intervention" (7).

Powerful and creative art does not emerge over a few cups of artisanal coffee in Silver Lake or Shoreditch, but requires considerable work by audiences (Kondo 2018, 6). Kondo identifies the work of dramaturges as especially important in this regard, as they labor behind the scenes to bring a critical lens to the artist's output. Kondo describes an oftentimes fraught process of representation and identity making and remaking (132). This work provokes heated arguments and tests the nature of alliances in the determination of what is excluded from the performance and why. Dramaturge and actor mediate disparate subject positions, and allegiances create a "politics of affiliation" or the "discomfort" involved in working towards an amicable solution to a performance problem — or what she later calls "narrative dilemmas" (142) — while "adjudicating passionately held, sometimes incommensurable positions" (138). This "dangerous crossroads," for Kondo, "is our only way to a more equitable society" (138).

Creativity also forgets, and perhaps it is meant to do so. Kondo's descriptions of creativity, critique, and political commentary align quite closely with Dwight Conquergood's theorization of the "three c's" of performance studies, where creativity engages alongside critique and citizenship or "civic struggles for social justice" (2002, 152). Kondo does not cite Conquergood anywhere in her text — a troubling omission, but perhaps an informative one. In the process of repairing, as demonstrated by Kondo's ethnography of the dramaturge, something always is cut, or someone is left out.

A politics of affiliation generates intimacy at this crossroads; indeed, artists rely on creativity to maintain connections across time and distance. For Paul Gilroy, the "formal unity of diverse cultural elements" of the tune "Keep On Moving" by Funki Dreds, he writes, "encapsulate[s] the playful diasporic intimacy that has been a marked feature of transnational black Atlantic creativity" (1993, 16). Kyra D. Gaunt (2006) takes these conclusions concerning play and intimacy further, pinpointing the ways that games practiced by young Black girls inform their musical production and taste later in life. This attention to history constitutes an important component of generating intimacy, building distributive frameworks, and sustaining the agency of creative practitioners.

PLAY AND HISTORY

Ethnomusicology features a number of ethnographies that adopt the approaches that I have advocated here; unfortunately, these are not cited as extensively as they should be. One of the most compelling ethnographies of creativity that brings together these three perspectives on mastery, history, and reparative creativity is Kyra D. Gaunt's 2006 text *The Games Black Girls Play: Learning the Ropes from Double-Dutch to Hip-Hop*. Although a long way from Vietnam, Gaunt forwards the concept of play as being fundamental to creative music practice and identity among the Black communities she studies. Musicians play with history, time, sound, and with each other to advance effective methods of understanding their lived experiences of being in the world. Play ultimately spins wheels of creativity so they turn on their own: play solidifies past practice to make it tangible and simultaneously compel action.

Play has a rich scholastic lineage that suggests that "playing" is not amusement. Play is hard work and therefore features prominently in my ethnography of southern Vietnamese music practice.[7] Play enables the effective growth of the human child (Winnicott [1971] 2005, 72–73) and is fundamental to the development of human communication (Bateson [1972] 2000, 181). Certain "transient constructs" of a human's play bring practice into being and enable the development of "cognitive activity" (Lanzara 2016, 224). The work of play further links one time and place to the next; they are necessarily ephemeral but also grounding. "Transient knowledge . . . helps actors cope with the ambiguities and perceived risks of unfamiliar and threatening situations by establishing provisional 'anchoring' to some features of the situation that can be handled" (224). Anchoring therefore brings elements of the past into the present to ground identity and creativity. Anthropologist Karin Barber calls this "the art of making things stick," or those practices that "transcend time and space" or "provide for the continued generation of novelty in the very act of consolidating tradition" (2007, 28). For Gregory Bateson, play connects the sounds heard and produced to some external condition or "not play" ([1972] 2000, 177–81). Play as creativity then makes similar connections, by suturing the utterance with a larger ideal. As Tina Ramnarine notes in the Finnish folk music context, the "collective creative process is a powerful representative of musical unity that lends itself to the building of an analogous social and political solidarity" (2003, 21). Play then generates a unified and appropriately socialized whole.

These unifying practices resonate with particular forms of power but can become overpowering and impede future play. When this occurs, play takes on a counteracting force that seeks to undermine power structures and reignite creativity. For Conquergood (1989), play emerges out of clearly defined and well-established structures that performers then untangle. Along with poetics, process, and power, play

is linked to improvisation, innovation, experimentation, frame, reflection, agitation, irony, parody, jest, clowning, and carnival. As soon as a world has been made, lines drawn, categories defined, hierarchies erected, then the trick-ster, the archetypal performer, moves in to breach norms, violate taboos, turn everything upside down. By playing with social order, unsettling certainties, the trickster intensifies awareness of the vulnerability of our institutions. The trickster's playful impulse promotes a radical self-questioning critique that yields a deeper self-knowledge, the first step towards transformation. (83)

Since the trickster has very specific cultural connotations—one thinks of Esu-Elgbara in West Africa, Cuba, and elsewhere in the Americas with populations of people of African descent, as Henry Louis Gates Jr. (1988, 5–6) indicates in work on Signifyin(g)—"performer" suffices here to indicate a figure who experiments with power to propose new models of cultural production. The player does not necessarily aim to revolutionize and overturn, but does exploit institutional holes and pinpoint the ways that institutions do not serve certain segments of the population.

With constant reactions and commentary on past practice, musicians play to regroup and recoup power through identified musical anchors. Queer theory also advocates this kind of play. Transgression in music performance suggests new connections between sounds and concepts, and moves away from the rigid straight lines of practice. Creative musicians bring "positively enticing unknow-able political forces into . . . [their] wake, taking risks rather than guarding against them" (Puar 2007, xx). Through this kind of "anticipatory temporality," in Jasbir Puar's terms, musicians do not simply aim to preserve through repetition, but undertake experiments in performance to better negotiate future conditions for audiences and imagine new horizons of expression.

Musicians therefore play to find shared commonalities and alignments be-tween the individual with the social. No one really *controls* play, as suggested by Pang's evaluation of creativity, but it remains firmly rooted in historical practice and experience. Play fosters experimentation and yields unanticipated and un-knowable results. This is the kind of work advocated by Stuart Hall as we march toward anti-essentialism.

Kyra D. Gaunt's Approach

Kyra D. Gaunt's ethnography offers an example of how to effectively examine creativity using the three approaches I describe. She does not foreground "creativ-ity" as a discursive concept as I do, but her work forges a pathway toward more nuanced, reparative, and decolonized evaluations of creativity in ethnomusicology. Her work remains rooted in Black music aesthetics and analysis as a critique of—or, at the very least, commentary on—the stranglehold of white-centered colonialist and imperialist discourse.

Gaunt makes the compelling conclusion that ethnomusicologists ignore the power and communicative abilities of music if they simply investigate those who have "made it" or mastered their craft. Through music, humans learn to navigate their places in the world. "Musical play is a vital environment within which black folks, not just girls, learn to improvise with what it means to be dominant and subordinate in musical and nonmusical ways" (2006, 14). By showing how Black girls play and improvise games on the playground, they build knowledge and understand themselves within the context of power. These are power structures of not only socioeconomic status but also race and gender that are ignored in many studies of Black musicmaking (14).

Musical play engages the past to sustain identity in the present. The "oral-kinetic etudes" practiced by African American girls "function as lessons in black musical style and taste" that stand the test of time (2006, 2). Gaunt notes how these etudes carry multiple types of music practice forward, including improvisation; timbre (also noted by Keyes 2002, 26); "melo-rhythmic essence," a concept defined by Meki Nzewi (1974) as designating melody that has rhythmic qualities and rhythm that has melodic qualities (Gaunt 2006, 31); and methods of organizing time akin to a timeline (33). Members of the Black community pass these etudes to girls—thereby connecting members of the community together—but the etudes also serve as "transient constructs" that "anchor" the girls to the present and as a way through which girls play to propose new uses in the contemporary period. Fundamental music theories of the slide, double-dutch, and other etudes underpin contemporary performance of rap, funk, and other popular music. The play enabled the emergence of these genres to ultimately sustain and shape Black identities into the late twentieth and twenty-first centuries.

Gaunt further foregrounds the distribution of play, showing how Black girls work together to maintain their practice of drawing on what they have learned and including new material. Gaunt discusses several poignant experiences of play, such as an instance in 2000 when she filmed and interacted with a group of girls in Harlem who incorporated the 1980s hit "Candy Girl" by New Edition—a song learned presumably from older relatives—into their chant, handclapping, and dance. She evaluates their work in fine detail and remarks on the ways the girls "revel[led] in the synesthesia of communal memory and musicalized drama that comments on the contemporary and the past, and gives life to a black sense of musical identity" (2006, 75). Many of Gaunt's examples "give life." Following a chapter on the ways that double-dutch has turned into a competition with rules—including the removal of the chant and song from performance—as a way to "police . . . girls' play" (139), Gaunt turns to the Double Dutch Divas, who revitalize double-dutch as adult women. Their work—and Gaunt's—is akin to the reparative work described by Kondo: play, like creativity, gives life to a practice policed. The Divas "reclaimed being girls playing double-dutch" (177; emphasis removed) and made their practice meaningful in new ways.

Kyra D. Gaunt's work on play models how the ethnomusicologist should study creativity, and therein lies the power of her work. Her approaches offer the ethnomusicologist studying a very different context on a different continent various methods of making sense of and giving life to the sounds heard. My interpretation of her work is that creativity through play rejects mastery, reengages history in the present, and uses distributed creativity toward reparative work. These conclusions drive the material—and the approaches I take—to follow.

CONCLUSION

In this chapter, I offer a synthesis of previous discussions of creativity to provide the conceptual framework for the remaining pages of the text. Folklorists and ethnomusicologists have engaged with musical creativity since the early twentieth century. Many of these studies continue to impose Western individualistic understandings of creativity and, by extension, mastery. Other ethnomusicologists like Kyra D. Gaunt offer perspectives that move away from and beyond the fetishization of the master composer/performer dynamic seen in ethnography. I place my ethnography in the latter category.

Creativity is playful and draws extensively from shared experiences and a collective understanding of history. What emerges in performance as being creative maintains this shaping of community, memory, and aspiration. In these situations, creativity often actively works against an alterity produced by whatever mainstream culture of which it is a part. It therefore plays a significant role in repairing social rifts and reclaiming space for expression. Creativity is a tool; it can be misused, but it never can be mastered.

I also suggest that ethnomusicology has a great deal to learn from those who critique creativity. Ethnomusicology, too, replicates biases of Euro-American creativity, blinding the discipline to the extraordinary work of scholars consistently marginalized by "mainstream" ethnomusicology. The women scholars, queer scholars, and scholars of color cited here offer dehumanist and decolonized perspectives that must resound more widely in ethnomusicology. They help the discipline interrogate some of its foundational concepts, including creativity, that we have taken for granted for too long. Their voices have guided me and have shaped how I narrate and evaluate fieldwork experiences. If you, dear reader, find resonance in their words, do not simply take my references as representing even a fraction of their power. Explore the works on your own and raise their voices toward a more equitable and inclusive ethnomusicology.

THREE

The Seed of Creativity in Southern Vietnam

Phong ba bão táp không bằng ngữ pháp Việt Nam
The upheaval of a typhoon does not compare with the complexity
of the Vietnamese language. (A sarcastic Vietnamese proverb)

Vietnamese musicians offer many metaphors to sustain knowledge and craft effective environments for sharing musical ideas, augmenting practice, and making community. Phạm Thúy Hoan, for instance, advocates that teachers plant a *hạt giống* or seed in Vietnamese children that will later sprout an interest in traditional music (Thượng Tùng 2005). She describes how the lullabies and folk songs sung to her by her mother and grandmother planted her seed, which then only germinated with musical experiences later in life (HTV 2007; Cannon 2013, 94–95). All Vietnamese have this seed, she argues, and with proper guidance, this seed cultivates feelings for the *dân tộc* (nation). During weekly rehearsals of her Tiếng Hát Quê Hương (Sounds of the Homeland) Ensemble, therefore, she requires students to sing folk songs to grow and maintain these feelings of national belonging.

Many of her students have quite personal reactions to this strategy. In Cannon (2013, 103–4), I describe how singing folk songs caused one participant in her fifties to reflect on the camaraderie that had emerged between two members of the group who supported opposing sides of the Second Indochina War (another term for the War Against America to Save the Country). Before the Fall of Saigon, she was a young woman largely in agreement with the existence of the Republic of Vietnam, and a man in the group fought for the National Liberation Front (Mặt trận Dân tộc Giải phóng miền Nam Việt Nam) as a guerrilla fighter in the south. They later met through Phạm Thúy Hoan's rehearsals, sang together, and are now friends. Cô Thúy Hoan's efforts helped two former rivals overcome larger social divisions.[1]

When people make music together, they memorialize the event in memory through sound, building bonds outside of spoken language. "Before you play with someone," Nguyễn Vĩnh Bảo indicated in one of my first lessons in 2007, "you must love him. And then, you begin to love his playing."[2] My interactions with Thầy Vĩnh Bảo's family solidified this lesson, as I learned how connecting to other persons makes sound meaningful. Once I started taking lessons regularly in 2008, a ritual led by his wife, Nguyễn Thị Trâm Anh (to whom I referred with the title bà, meaning "grandmother"), emerged. Upon entry into the house, Bà Trâm Anh inquired about my health and family, then she usually cracked a joke about my height. On a handful of occasions, I appeared at the door drenched in perspiration, because I decided to walk to their home in the midday heat. She admonished my idiocy and did not allow me to go into Thầy Vĩnh Bảo's studio until I had washed my face and drank some water.

As interactions with others change, so do the sounds. Through these sounds, one remembers. When Bà Trâm Anh's health deteriorated in 2010, her sons or daughter began to answer the door. Sometimes she sat in the front room and smiled at me as I entered; later, I only heard her cough from her bedroom or from the porch overlooking the alleyway on which the house sat. On one of the last occasions that I saw her before her passing, she whispered, "Je suis malade" (I am ill) as she was carried past me by her sons, her chest rattling with particular gravity as she spoke "malade." The music played by Thầy Vĩnh Bảo that afternoon seemed especially deliberate, resonant, and melancholy. In my recording of our lesson, he played more music than usual, with Bà Trâm Anh's coughs audible in the background. When I listen to the recordings of his music from this time period, whether or not they captured her coughing, I remember my short but meaningful interactions with Bà Trâm Anh, and I understand how traditional music becomes intertwined with specific individuals. Musicians return to these sounds to grieve, console, and remember. Spoken language does not suffice when sound generates clear and durable understandings.

Memories and personal histories align in the narration of these musical experiences. Phạm Thúy Hoan draws on the metaphor of the seed or something planted in the past that requires education and care in the present in order to prosper. Nguyễn Vĩnh Bảo surrounds himself with reminders of the past and often speaks of specific memories that come to mind when he improvises. In both instances, old theories of practice buttress performance decisions in the Vietnamese present. These constitute the seeds of creativity in southern Vietnam that my interlocutors advised I foreground.

This chapter therefore investigates the various "seeds"—those histories, peoples, myths, and philosophies—that help generate and sustain southern Vietnamese traditional music. These seeds germinate a complicated picture, much like the Vietnamese language, as described in the epigraph to this chapter. I frame the chapter as a history lesson to trace the migration of people and ideas into the region and the ways that the particular framing of historical events continues to shape music practice today. I begin with some of the earliest narratives of the Vietnamese people, suggesting several characteristics of the so-called "traditional creativity"—or, more accurately, constituent elements of a theory of music creation—found in southern Vietnam. I then explore the impact of colonization and regime change in Vietnam, as these have significant impacts on how musicians think about creation. I sketch how the emergence of đờn ca tài tử in the late nineteenth and early twentieth centuries suggests ways that musicians approach their performance practice, paying particular attention to how musicians employ Daoist concepts of spontaneity and nonaction in their thinking about inspiration. I finish the chapter with a description of a contemporary performance in Cần Thơ to serve as a springboard to the musical and expressive content described in Chapter 4.

LIVING AND DEBATED VIETNAMESE HISTORY

Historians and cultural scholars frequently debate the extent of Sinitic, Indic, and colonial influence in narratives of the history of southern Vietnam. The narratives and associated practices propagated by musicians in southern Vietnam are especially rich and ripe for interrogation given that the Vietnamese conquered this area, displaced the Khmer and Chăm populations living there, and later absorbed numerous cultural influences from France, the United States, and elsewhere. As musicians consider these influences and inject varying elements from each, music practices change. At the same time, musicians from southern Vietnam use sound to advocate the voice of the diverse population of southern Vietnam within the national sphere, as they frequently view themselves as unequal partners in the creation of the contemporary Vietnamese nation.

Early histories of the lands of contemporary southern Vietnam point to its organization as part of Nokor Phnom (more commonly known by the Chinese-designated term *Funan*) and, later, the Khmer Empire. As a Southeast Asian *mandala* or an area of loosely-aligned Indic states, Funan flourished in what is now the lower Mekong River Delta (Stuart-Fox 1998, 15).[3] By the third century

AD, Funan's major trading city Óc Eo, now an archaeological site in Vietnam's An Giang Province, controlled the earliest international trade route connecting China, Southeast Asia, Europe, and the Middle East (Wolters 1967, 37). After the dissolution of the Funan mandala, the Khmer or Angkor Kingdom emerged and rose to its height from the eleventh to thirteenth centuries. One of the primary trading cities of the kingdom became Prey Nokor—possibly established originally as Baigaur by the Champa Empire (Vo 2011, 1)—which later became Saigon, and then Ho Chi Minh City. Indeed, the Indigenous Khmer Krom (southern Khmer) population, which still inhabits southern Vietnam today, lived in this part of the world well before Vietnamese populations arrived.[4] Vietnamese populations in southern Vietnam therefore are not indigenous to the region but moved slowly from the Red River Delta in present-day northern Vietnam, bringing along their histories and myths which now circulate in southern Vietnamese lands as part of a shared history.

Contemporary Vietnamese scholars invoke "four thousand years of Vietnamese history" in everyday conversation to demonstrate the longevity of the Vietnamese (Việt or Kinh) peoples and their cultures.[5] Many early stories from Vietnamese historical narratives begin with the Lạc Việt period (beginning c. 1000 BC) or the Đông Sơn period (beginning c. 500 BC) in what is now northern Vietnam. This territory came under the direct control of China's Han dynasty in 111 BC. In between the Chinese Tang and Song dynasties in 939 AD, the Vietnamese created an independent ruling dynasty and embarked on a period of relatively uninterrupted self-governance until the mid-nineteenth century. The exception is a brief period between 1407 and 1427 when Đại Việt (Great Việt) came under the rule of the Chinese Ming dynasty. Throughout this period of independence, Vietnamese peoples nevertheless remained well connected to the forms of governance, aesthetic principles, philosophies, and artistic practices that circulated in China.

Following independence, Vietnamese power began to slowly expand southward during a process later termed the *Nam tiến* (southern advancement). By the fifteenth century, the Vietnamese defeated and absorbed lands of the Indic kingdom of Champa in present-day central Vietnam; by the eighteenth century, the part of the Khmer kingdom in present-day southern Vietnam was also under the control of Vietnamese rulers. Much like "manifest destiny" in the United States, Nam tiến suggests that the Vietnamese people were destined to procure and inhabit the land from the border with southern China to the Gulf of Thailand in the south (Ang 2013, 3–4). In the process, they collected musical and other artistic principles from Chăm and Khmer peoples and assimilated them into Vietnamese cultural practice.[6] The Nam tiến narrative also sought to legitimize the presence of Vietnamese peoples in the south, with historians arguing that prior to the arrival of the Vietnamese, the lands were "desolate" and "difficult to access" (Nguyễn Phương Thảo 1994, 8), and the Khmer populations were "scattered" (Sơn Nam [1969] 2006, 361).

Vietnamese peoples now comprise the majority of the population of southern Vietnam. Cultural historians, including those who write about music, have stated that the wealth of Vietnamese cultural value from the north spread to the south during this migration (Võ Trường Kỳ 2014, 13). That said, "the urge for connections with the past," historian K.W. Taylor notes, "is a means of self-affirmation, not a scholarly endeavor" (2013, 2–3). As a result of Nam tiến, Vietnamese inhabitants imprinted their language, myths, histories, and common practices on the region at the expense of its previous inhabitants. The Nam tiến narrative maintains this power and sutures the early emergence of the Vietnamese (Kinh) peoples to the struggle against Chinese domination, the foresight of Vietnamese settlers, the creation of an independent state, as well as the pursuit of new land and resources from the Red River Delta to the Mekong Delta.

Understanding the Nam tiến is imperative when trying to evaluate how artists, historians, and politicians ground southern Vietnamese cultural production. When the Nam tiến narrative emerged in the early twentieth century to establish ways of understanding Vietnamese history (Ang 2013, 3–4), it sought to imprint Vietnamese cultural influence on the lands of the south in an effort to cope with modernization and colonization. Belief and philosophical systems with origins in Chinese lands but with long-standing practice in Vietnamese lands formed the core of music aesthetics in the face of changing and overpowering colonial influences. Even when the surface features changed, the core remained firm. At the same time, southern artistry also incorporated the cultural bounty of the Nam tiến in the form of artistry from the Chăm and Khmer peoples, creating something regionally unique to the south. In the next several sections, I look at the ways in which Daoist belief systems in particular supported the emergence of newer forms of cultural practice, especially đờn ca tài tử.

CHINESE INFLUENCE IN SOUTHERN VIETNAM

Chinese influence looms large in the history of Vietnam, and it plays a significant role in the creation of southern Vietnamese music. These cultural influences came to southern Vietnam during several waves of migration. The Vietnamese who descended along the coastline during the Nam tiến brought many vestiges of Chinese governance and cultural practice. Several groups of immigrants from Fujian and Guangdong in southern China also migrated beginning in the late seventeenth and eighteenth centuries (Li Tana 1998, 34; Phan Trung Nghĩa 2007, 165). These immigrants settled in three regions of contemporary central and southern Vietnam. The first group settled in the area around Huế and Hội An in the mid-seventeenth century. The second group, comprised of approximately three thousand soldiers seeking asylum from the Chinese Qing dynasty, initially arrived in Đà Nẵng in 1679, but moved to the areas near modern-day Biên Hòa, just north of Ho Chi Minh City, and Mỹ Tho, just south of Ho Chi Minh City. The third group arrived at the turn of the eighteenth century in Hà Tiên, a city on the current border of Vietnam and Cambodia (Li Tana 1998, 33). Lastly, many Chinese also moved to Vietnam as traders and settled in ports of exchange, including Chợ Lớn near Saigon (Rigg 2003, 106).

The extent of this influence is still debated. In music scholarship, for example, Nguyễn Đình Lai claims that "Vietnamese music directly derives from Chinese music," and then continues to describe how the instruments, scales and notation also derive from Chinese sources (1956, 11). Nguyen Nang Dac and Nguyen Phung (n.d.) also argue that aesthetics of music in China greatly impacted Vietnamese traditional music. "The honest man in ancient Vietnamese society is versed in music, poetry, painting, and in chess. Music is a sacred art. All musicians who respect [this] will vigorously conform to the edicts of the legendary Chinese Emperor Phục Huy [伏羲, Fu Xi]" (20). These edicts include not playing when there is intense cold, heat, strong winds, wet weather, snow and thunder, as well as while mourning, when the sound of the drum or other instruments troubles the musician, when the musician feels ambitious or dishonest, when the musician does not take care of personal hygiene, and when cologne is not worn. Finally, and perhaps most importantly, one must play in the presence of a knowledgeable audience. These rules make occasional appearances in conversations with musicians. Nguyễn Vĩnh Bảo frequently advocated that troubling or distracting sounds can derail a performance and that connoisseurs should be present in an audience.[7]

The realities of and the narratives regarding Chinese influence are actually more complicated. Trần Văn Khê (1959) penned a strong rebuttal to Nguyễn Đình Lai's 1956 article, stating that "the errors in [that] study of instruments and above all concerning theoretical issues give foreign musicologists the wrong idea concerning Vietnamese traditional music" (Trần Văn Khê 1959, 13). In a longer treatise, Trần Văn Khê (1962) expanded on the multicultural makeup of Vietnamese (including southern Vietnamese) music. He argued that only some instruments used in traditional Vietnamese music, including the đàn tranh zither, originated in China. While this appears plausible given the similarities between the Vietnamese đàn tranh and Chinese *guzheng*, Lê Tuấn Hùng offers a different way of framing Chinese influence. He suggests that the instrument did not develop from the guzheng but from an ancient Southeast Asian bamboo zither (1998, 5–8); he quickly turns to attempts by Vietnamese musicians to embrace Chinese music aesthetics as an antidote to French colonial influence. In the early twentieth century, for instance, Vietnamese musicians incorporated a *hơi Quảng* (from Guangdong) method of performance into đờn ca tài tử performance (20–27; 1991, 4–10). This practice of adopting from abroad to strengthen dimensions of traditional music continues in contemporary Vietnam; however, the seeds of practice remain undeniably planted in a Vietnamese interpretation of much older Chinese practices.

LOCAL CREATIVITY THEORIES

When Vietnamese migrants moved into southern Vietnam, they brought Buddhism, Confucianism, and Daoism, or the *Tam giáo* (three belief systems), with them (Do 2003, 63). In my discussions with musicians, they describe the ways that traditional music intersects with all three belief systems. I use these descriptions to suggest how Sino-Vietnamese notions of creation circulate as the underlying "seeds" of creativity in southern Vietnam today.[8] Following a brief discussion of Buddhism and Confucianism, I focus on Daoist aesthetic influence, as Daoism remains unexplored but vitally important in understanding the sustained practice of đờn ca tài tử.

The Kinh (or Việt) ethnic majority has practiced Buddhism since at least the third century AD (Nguyen T. Phong 2002, 58), and Mahayana Buddhism remains the most widely practiced Buddhist tradition in Vietnam today. Music plays a significant role in ceremonies and rituals, and connections exist between these practices and đờn ca tài tử. Monks train to perform chants and play instruments (bells, gongs, and drums); in ritual settings, however, they do not play the string instruments most often found in đờn ca tài tử (2002, 58; 67). They instead rely on lay musicians to complement ceremonies inside the Buddhist temples with performances of nhạc lễ (ceremonial music performed in temples) and hát bội (classical theater) outside of the temple (64; 68). Buddhist monks do know how to perform with these string instruments, however, and do perform this music in convivial settings much like đờn ca tài tử. In a 2008 conversation with Buddhist monk Thầy Phước Cường at the Chùa Bửu Sơn (Bửu Sơn Temple) in District 5 in Ho Chi Minh City, he noted that he plays not only instrumental nhạc lễ from southern Vietnam but also central Vietnamese ritual music and court music, as well as đờn ca tài tử and even cải lương.[9] He was born into a family of musicians, and thereby was surrounded from a young age by these different genres and musical practices; indeed, his father was an accomplished đàn cò player and his aunt a well-known singer.[10] The types of music inside and outside the temple thereby intersect, offering potential opportunities for the Buddhist influence on the musical, philosophical, and aesthetic practices in nonritual settings of southern Vietnam.

Historical conditions also offer possible intersections between Buddhism and the emergence of đờn ca tài tử. The end of the French colonial period, during which societal conditions also led to the development of đờn ca tài tử, saw a resurgence in popularity in many sects of Buddhism through a proliferation of print media. During the early twentieth century, short publications, often "fragments of sutras important to Zen [Thiền] and Pure Land [Tịnh Độ] practice," circulated in southern Vietnam alongside "commentaries on the sutras, instructional manuals on prayer, or prayers themselves" (McHale 2004, 153). The messages of these publications reached nonliterate Vietnamese—individuals who also performed đờn ca tài tử—by monks who disseminated them orally, even in rural areas (155). Musicians even used the popular đờn ca tài tử and cải lương tune "Vọng cổ" ("Nostalgia for the Past") to spread the Pure Land message of using prayer to "escap[e] . . . from this 'ocean of suffering' (bể khổ)" of the present (166).[11] Zen Buddhism, as a more "learned" form of Buddhism in Vietnam (166) also circulated among đờn ca tài tử musicians. Its impact is seen in Nguyễn Vĩnh Bảo's recordings of improvised preludes called "Zen improvisation." (Listen to **Track 1**.) Nguyễn Thuyết Phong also has a work titled "Thiền" (Zen) on a 1989 cassette released in the United States.

These connections are intriguing, but tenuous, and very little has been written on Buddhist music and aesthetics in Vietnam, save for the work of Nguyễn Thuyết Phong (1982; [1986] 1990; 2002). For instance, he advises that one cannot assume equivalency between Buddhist musical practices throughout Asia, although certain philosophical and aeshtetic practices may have been adopted from Mahayana practices found in China and elsewhere in Asia (2002, 60). For this reason, I avoid applying Buddhist concepts too extensively, except for one or two instances where the concepts help elucidate the meanings of đờn ca tài tử practice. I also refer to the expertise from Thầy Phước Cường, as he is a knowledgeable musician of southern Vietnamese music.

Recent histories of đờn ca tài tử more often focus on the Confucian roots of the genre. Võ Trường Kỳ pinpoints sees the genre's origins in Confucianism because of both the influence of other genres (nhạc lễ and hát bội) with Confucian aesthetics and the performance of đờn ca tài tử in "solemn places" (2015, 66–67). Nguyễn Phúc An investigates the origins of the term *tài tử* in Confucian-influenced literary and historical sources (2019b, 80–89), but suggests that the place of đờn ca tài tử in southern Vietnam — a "new land of promise" (95) — leads to a more "open category" of Confucianism based in understandings of the classic texts but with a more "relaxed character . . . not precisely elegant or humble, not precisely in the realm of the folk or the erudite" (94–95). Musicians simply "must know the rules, understand them, have talent, understand music, and sustain a desire to learn, then they will become a real *tài tử*" (95).

Creativity and creation do not emerge as strongly in these discussions of Buddhism and Confucianism, but given the centrality of creation in Daoism, the philosophy warrants extended consideration. Creativity, along with vitality and longevity, were of central concern to Chinese scholars of Daoism as far back as the fourth century BC (Thrasher 2008, 47). Daoism offers an understanding and ways of interpreting existence. It advocates allowing nature to run its course and observing the way (*đạo* in Vietnamese) in which nature sets its own logic. Chapter Six of the *Tao Te Ching* (*Book of Dao*) by Laozi (老子) offers the following explanation of nature and creation.[12] I include two translations to impart the subtly different meanings of the passage.

The Valley Spirit never dies, and is called Mysterious Female.
The gateway to the Mysterious Female we call the root of creation.
On and on, its energy flows, inexhaustibly.
(Laozi 2005, 9)

The spirit of the valley never dies.
It is called the subtle and profound female.
The gate of the subtle and profound female
Is the root of Heaven and Earth.
It is continuous, and seems to be always existing.
Use it and you will never wear it out.
(Chan 1963, 142)

The valley metaphor offers an image of the symbol V, which of course suggests the uterus and the woman's body. Life, and the "subtle and profound" feminine that creates it, exists within this valley. A stream of water, the source of life and existence, moves through the valley; it connects the opposites of Heaven and Earth. For Wang Chong (王充), "Heaven and Earth are like a furnace. Their work is creation" (Chan 1963, 298). By extension, as long as the stream continues to move, life continues to exist "inexhaustibly" (Laozi 2005, 9). If the stream stops, then life stops. As long as humans practice and continue to make music, therefore, music continues to exist. One need not move within the valley in a linear fashion with a destination in mind; it is more appropriate to appreciate the path and the process. This is creativity at its most fundamental in southern Vietnamese music circles; by moving and playing music, one moves within the valley and experiences creativity of some sort.[13]

Some Vietnamese musicians operate using Daoist metaphors, for example, by connecting musicians with nature and knowledge with action. When musicians improvise together and speak of not wishing to stand out from others in performance, this is a practice of nonaction, or *vô vi* (Chinese *wuwei*, 無為), that draws on the nonaction of nature. Laozi writes, "He does not boast of himself; therefore he is given credit. He does not brag; therefore he can endure for long" (Chan 1963, 151). When musicians speak of being inspired, they practice spontaneity, or *tự nhiên* (Chinese *ziran*, 自然), as action drawn from a knowledge of one's surroundings. These concepts lead musicians to speak of and largely practice a creativity that deemphasizes the impact of individual actions and essentially creates some kind of collective mediation of innerness and outerness.

Spontaneity establishes and maintains connections between knowledge and everyday acts. Musicians connect different realms of experience and close the gap between what they know and what they do; this might also be described as the distinction between one's "implicit" and "explicit" knowledge (Black 1989,

91–92). "The thought is of a potential or implicit knowledge that can only become explicit in actual contact with its materials, to whose changes it must constantly adapt itself," as Alison Harley Black argues (92). In this Daoist conceptualization of spontaneity, humans use direct experiences with one another and with nature to understand the environment around them (30). One establishes a sense of place by engaging with the observable environment and incorporating sights, sounds, and smells of that environment into one's routine and everyday life.

Poetry—and the arts in general—mediates the differences between external and internal realities. In an investigation of the work of poet and philosopher Wang Fuzhi (王夫之, Vietnamese Vương Phu Chu, 1619–1692), Black suggests how Wang's poetry enables ongoing mediation that constitutes expression and creativity. The poems are not fully complete and static but exist as "living entit[ies]" endowed with "power" and "movement"; express human emotions; depict certain "objective properties" mirrored in nature; and strive for spontaneity to express emotion and other components of nature (255–56). The poems foster a dynamic relationship between human emotion and organic growth to create meta-poetic referents outside of the poems, including insights into the poet's mindset at the time of composition (255–56). The key term here is "dynamic": an individual crafted the poems and had highly personal thoughts that cultivated their development. Finally, and importantly, poets must have talent to write truly effective and authentic work. Wang calls this *cai* (才), or "genius." In Vietnamese, this is *tài*, or the third character in đờn ca tài tử (音樂才子), which might be better translated as "talent."

How does one move along this path and keep the stream and practice moving? The writings and operations within a Daoist worldview suggest that the stream continues when upholding a kind of inner virtue, or *đức*. The seed, or hạt giống, then, serves as this inner virtue or "way" (đạo). In Chapter 54, Laozi ruminates on how individuals cultivate inner virtue at different social levels. "Generations honor generations endlessly. Cultivated in the self, virtue is realized; cultivated in the family, virtue overflows; cultivated in the community, virtue increases; cultivated in the state, virtue abounds; cultivated in the world, virtue prevails" (2005, 78). Laozi suggests, in other words, that if everyone cultivates inner virtue, they all follow the stream; inner virtue, then, serves as the bond between peoples. Cultivating the seed, by extension, joins Vietnamese musicians through a connection to this stream. This work is self-replicating as long as the cultivation of the inner seed or virtue takes place: maintain the seed and spontaneously germinate a connection to practice and others.

With the rise of European colonial power, ultimately leading to French control of greater Indochina (including present-day Cambodia, Laos, and Vietnam), previous models of practice encountered alternatives from which many Vietnamese drew. European influence began through Catholic missionary work in the early seventeenth century. Portuguese missionaries were the first to travel to the region, establishing missions in Cochinchina (southern Vietnam) in 1615 and Tonkin (northern Vietnam) in 1626. French missionaries replaced Portuguese ones, and at the beginning of nineteenth century, missionaries were almost entirely French (McLeod 1991, 4–5). In the nineteenth century, however, missionaries and representatives of European powers found themselves unwelcome in Vietnamese lands, so the French sought to solidify control. During the rule of Emperor Tự Đức in 1858, an expeditionary force comprised of French and Spanish troops—the latter based in the Philippines—attacked present-day Đà Nẵng and planned to march to the royal court in Huế. This attack was unsuccessful, so they moved southward and attacked the southern coastal town of Vũng Tàu, close to Saigon, eventually taking control of parts of southern Vietnam (43–44). With the Treaty of 1862, Catholicism could be practiced freely in the Vietnamese lands and the French government had direct control over three southern provinces of Cochinchina (Gia Định, Định Tường and Biên Hòa). In 1867, the French took control of three additional provinces, thereby controlling all *lục tỉnh* (six provinces, also *Nam kỳ lục tỉnh*) (54–55). By 1884, Tonkin and Annam (central Vietnam) became protectorates of the French government, meaning that local laws governed the population—although they were still subject to approval by French authorities. Meanwhile, Cochinchina remained under direct control where French law prevailed (Nguyễn Thê Anh 1985, 147–48).[14]

Colonial Musical Practices

During the colonial era, French administrators, musicians, composers, music critics, and others imported and disseminated performance practice and many artifacts. They also constructed various educational and performance institutions in French Indochina. Tô Vũ, Chí Vũ, and Thụy Loan point to the kinds of music that French officials introduced to Vietnamese audiences, including music played by Vietnamese in military bands; music to accompany dances such as the tango and foxtrot, heard in tea houses and hotels; French songs taught to Vietnamese schoolchildren; and music used to attract Vietnamese audiences to the cinema (1977, 80–90). There even existed a short-lived music conservatory in Hanoi, the Conservatoire d'Extrême-Orient, which taught European instruments (such as the flute, piano, violin, and cello), Western harmony (*hòa âm*), and Western solfège (*môn xướng âm*) to French, Vietnamese, and Lao students (85–87). This educational model later had an impact on the organization of music schools in Hanoi, Saigon, and Huế after 1954.

In the 1920s, intellectuals and urban Vietnamese started to incorporate Vietnamese aesthetics into French music; for example, they sang Vietnamese translations of French lyrics with accompaniment on the Spanish guitar, ukulele, mandolin, violin, and banjo. This became known as *bài ta theo điệu Tây*, or *lời ta theo điệu Tây*, meaning "our songs with Western accompaniment" (Tô Vũ, Chí Vũ, and Thụy Loan 1977, 89–90; see also Gibbs 2003/2004). "Điệu" here means "fashion, manner, song, or type of song" and also can designate "mode" (Nguyễn T. Phong 1998, 455). Vietnamese musicians therefore approximated equal tempered pitch in performances of these tunes (Tô Vũ, Chí Vũ, and Thụy Loan 1977, 89–90). Jason Gibbs notes that musicians disseminated these tunes orally (2003/2004, 69–70); indeed, French songs from this time live on: Tino Rossi's hit "C'est à Capri" continues to be played in Cần Thơ as "Nhạc Miên Nhạc Pháp" ("Khmer Music, French Music"). (Listen to **Track 2**.) Vietnamese musicians also experimented with new instrument construction. Combining the guitar and mandolin created the *ghita mando*; carving scoops in the fingerboard of the guitar created the *ghi ta phím lõm* so musicians could properly play and ornament pitches of Vietnamese scales (Nguyễn Vĩnh Bảo n.d.[a]).

Beyond generating new genres and instruments, colonization influenced conceptualizations of performance time and space. With the introduction of new recording technologies, records of French and Vietnamese music on the Victor, Columbia, Pathé, Beka, and Odéon labels, audiences consumed shortened songs that fit into the recording medium (Tô Vũ, Chí Vũ, and Thụy Loan 1977, 82). The French built new performance venues, including the Théâtre de Hanoi, Théâtre de Haiphong, and Théâtre Municipal de Saigon, where local French musicians performed instrumental works and traveling troupes staged operas (83; see also Pasler 2012, 204–5). Audiences who consumed music and theater in comfortable seats were protected from the elements outside (Pasler 2012, 205).

The French colonial project further cultivated opportunities in France for the consumption of Indochinese culture. Jann Pasler writes of donations of various instruments from French colonies, including Annam, to the Paris Conservatoire in the 1870s and of the hope that works would be written for these instruments "in strange and wonderful combinations" (2004, 34).[15] Audiences made comparisons between the instruments, understanding how "development" took place through the imitation of "superior" instruments, especially those in Europe. Early research on Vietnamese music presented data on melodies, genres, cultural uses of music, aesthetics, and even notation.[16] In terms of performances, a troupe performed as the "théâtre annamite" at the 1889 Universal Exposition (Exposition Universelle) in Paris.[17] Allegedly, this troupe and the Javanese music and dance contingent made famous by Claude Debussy's frequent visits became the principal attractions of the exposition (Devirès 1977, 25). Comprised of about forty "actors, musicians, and personnel attached to the troupe," the Vietnamese troupe performed a Buddhist ceremony and other "appropriate music . . . all dressed in appropriate ceremonial costumes" (27). In an eyewitness account, Julien Tiersot describes the instruments, including gongs, drums, flutes, kèn (oboelike instrument), and đàn cò (1889, 13). Tiersot also provides a narrative of the action and music improvised onstage alongside brief transcriptions of what he heard. He portrays certain melodies, for example, as "sad" or "warlike" (15). Members of this troupe were from Cochinchina, with a director from Saigon, but the "performances belonged to the traditional repertoire of Annam: long epics, of a heroic character, on themes borrowed from historical and religious legends, where military themes played a prominent role" (Devriès 1977, 27). The instrumentation aligns with music from central Vietnam, possibly from the court theater or Buddhist ritual tradition.

Vietnamese musicians also participated in the 1900 Universal Exposition (Exposition Universelle) in Paris. Writing in two issues of the weekly journal Le Ménestrel in 1901, Tiersot describes a different type of music performed in the Théâtre Indo-Chinois to that played in 1889.[18] Instruments again included the đàn cò, but also the tiêu (flute), đàn tranh, đàn kìm, đàn tam (three-stringed lute), đàn độc huyền (another name for the đàn bầu monochord), and various "delicate" percussion instruments, which he preferred over the "horrible drums" of the 1889 performances (1901a, 12). In the January 13 issue, Tiersot quotes the leader of the ensemble, a M. Viang—identified as Nguyen Viang by Judith Gautier (1900, 5)[19]—who describes the methods of improvising the music heard at the exposition. "All of my musicians," Nguyen Viang notes, "do not play identically the same thing: provided that, in each phrase, everyone begins on the same note and returns to the same note at the cadence, all is for the best; in the interim, everyone is free to vary the theme as they please" (Tiersot 1901a, 12). This suggests a number of Vietnamese musical traditions, including đờn ca tài tử.

Descriptions of the event do not provide a genre designation. Tiersot claims that the musicians were from Saigon and performed the music of Cochinchina (1901a, 12). In the January 20 issue, he publishes a transcription of a tune that "forms the essential based of the musical repertoire of the Théâtre Indo-Chinois" (1901b, 20). Nguyễn Lê Tuyên and Nguyễn Đức Hiệp use this transcription as published in a 1905 source to argue that the work appears to be the earliest notation version of đờn ca tài tử (2013, 85–89). The transcription lacks the nuance of traditional Vietnamese music and could be of one of any number of traditional Vietnamese tunes heard through the ears of Tiersot. In addition, a number of musicians moved from central Vietnam to southern Vietnam in the late nineteenth and early twentieth centuries, so it is conceivable that although they traveled from Saigon, they may have studied music elsewhere.

Gautier writes more descriptively than Tiersot of these performances and refers to the musicians as performing "la musique d'Annam." I hedge that these musicians, therefore, more likely hailed from central Vietnam. She indicates that to understand the music, one must refer to a volume of the Ministry of Rites in Huế, where the royal court was located (1900, 4). This text is probably the *Book of Rites* (*Liji* or *Kinh lễ* in Vietnamese) attributed to Confucius (Hoàng Yến 1919, 233) and could possibly be the *Yueji* chapter on music in *Liji*. More importantly, Gautier notes that the musicians used Chinese character notation "solely for aiding their memories since the rhythm and the duration of notes was not indicated" (233). Hoàng Yến (1919) provides extensive notation of this type in his description of *ca Huế* (sometimes *ca nhạc Huế*, or central Vietnamese folk music), and is something I have not seen used in southern Vietnam (see Nguyễn Phúc An 2019a for a transcription into staff notation). The musicians performed one work titled "l'Eau qui Coule" ("Flowing Water") or "Lưu thủy" (see Hoàng Yến 1919, 270–73, for notation). This is a well-known tune in the *nhã nhạc cung đình* (court music) and ca Huế repertory.[20] Gautier also suggested that local audiences praised this ensemble as more "authentic" than the other performers in the Indo-Chinese pavilion. "The Cambodian dances were of dubious authenticity, as were the dancers," she mentions (1900, 3). The dancer Cléo de Mérode, one upheld by Nguyễn Lê Tuyên and Nguyễn Đức Hiệp (2013) as dancing to an actual Vietnamese tune, "cannot fool anyone," according to Gautier (1900, 3). "Only the Annamite orchestra composed of men and women was authentic and faultless" (4).

Colonial Critique

Colonization ordered certain forms of cultural production in Vietnam for easy consumption in cosmopolitan space, which had significant impacts on traditional music. Musicians, officials, and others used music to introduce French and other European methods of expression, and Vietnamese traditions and methods of education ultimately "developed" toward certain French models. Vietnamese musicians then brought certain aesthetics concerning performance space back to Indochina following performances in Europe, which had a significant impact on music performance, including of đờn ca tài tử.

An effective summary of French influence appears in the bilingual Vietnamese and French memoir of Nguyễn Phụng Michel, the founding director of the National School of Music in Saigon. Although he adopted certain elements of French educational models for the school, he uses rather critical language to attack how colonization reorganized Vietnamese conceptualizations of appropriate spaces for music and the temporal aspects of music. French authorities used the newly constructed theaters in Hanoi and Saigon to demarcate spaces to hear high-art music.[21] "In Saigon as well as Hanoi, Western theaters were built with the goal of popularizing Western art but in practice they only were used to entertain the French population in the overseas colonies rather than focus the popularization of culture according to culture's true meaning" (Nguyễn Phụng Michel 1997, 2).

The ultimate impact of French colonization remains a topic of debate among cultural critics. Tô Vũ, Chí Vũ, and Thụy Loan (1977, 80) argue that musical practices imported by French colonial authorities served to "domesticate" and "assimilate" the Vietnamese people. They contend that such developments had the potential to erase traditional music (89–90), but ultimately they argue that "domesticization was not successful" (90). The reality is more nuanced. Vũ Tự Lân argues that although European music overran the predominantly oral traditions of Vietnam, the hybrid music that emerged from the interaction between Vietnam and France eventually helped the anticolonial cause and ushered modernity into Vietnam (1997, 32). Jason Gibbs echoes the analysis of others that the hybrid experiments "promoted the formation of a society to allow young people to escape rigid traditional mores" (2003/2004, 72). Western art even brought Vietnam out of the so-called "feudal era" and enabled the growth and development of Vietnam on its own terms (Vũ Tư Lân 1997, 149).

EMERGENCE OF ĐỜN CA TÀI TỬ

Đờn ca tài tử emerged in the colonial period of Vietnamese history. The music appeared following the migration of nhã nhạc cung đình and ca Huế musicians from Annam to Cochinchina in the late nineteenth century. According to some sources, musicians left central Vietnam during or immediately after the anticolonial Cần Vương (Loyalty to the King) movement from 1885 to 1889. The movement ultimately failed, but Nguyễn Quang Đại (alias Ba Đợi), one of the musicians who resettled, became known as one of the original musicians of đờn ca tài tử (Nguyễn and Đỗ 2007, 15–16; Nguyễn Tuấn Khanh 2014, 35–36; and Cannon 2016, 152). In informal music settings, they mixed central Vietnam musics, including court tunes and ca Huế, with those of hát bội (classical opera) and nhạc lễ (ceremonial music). (Listen to **Track 3** to hear an example of nhạc lễ.[22]) Nguyễn Thị Minh Ngọc and Đỗ Hương (2007, 14) argue that musicians improvised on these tunes in between or after hát bội and nhạc lễ performances. They sought some refuge from the more rigid performance settings and an opportunity for greater mixture with the other music present in southern Vietnam at the time (see also Vương Hồng Sển [1968] 2007, 25).

Đờn ca tài tử articulates an experience of the southern Vietnamese everyday, so all aspects of colonial governance potentially impacted the ways that musicians shaped đờn ca tài tử. Musicians did not confine themselves to one genre of music, and therefore brought in new tunes that they heard in theaters and on the radio. Some of these musicians had opportunities to perform in theaters and at colonial expositions abroad, thereby bringing đờn ca tài tử to new audiences and new spaces. When musicians encountered new instruments, they also brought them into private đờn ca tài tử performance spaces. One therefore should consider the history of đờn ca tài tử as emergent from, conversant with, and a reaction to the French colonial presence in southern Vietnam.

The positive reception of the work of Vietnamese musicians on the French stage, for example, had a powerful impact on the popularization of đờn ca tài tử in Vietnam. In his 1970 study of the early history of đờn ca tài tử, Trần Văn Khải describes a stage performance just south of Saigon of a *ban tài tử* troupe under the leadership of Nguyễn Tống Triều:

From 1910 in Mỹ Tho, there was a *tài tử* group comprised of Nguyễn Tống Triều, also called Tư Triều, who played the đàn kìm, Chín Quán, on the đàn bầu, Mười Lý on the tiêu, Bảy Vô on the đàn cò, Miss Hai Nhiễu on the đàn tranh, and Miss Ba Đắc, a singer. This tài tử group played and sang very well because the majority had been selected to perform traditional Vietnamese music at an exposition in Paris and just had returned. (1970, 81–83)

Vương Hồng Sển ([1968] 2007) and Nguyễn Tuấn Khanh (2014, 57–58) cite this story in their respective histories of music in early twentieth-century Cochinchina to indicate the importance of this event in đờn ca tài tử's history and development.

These musicians most likely returned from the 1906 Colonial Exposition (Exposition Coloniale) in Marseille, even though Trần Văn Khải states that they returned from an exposition in Paris. In a short description of theater productions at the exposition, the May 15, 1906, issue of *La Dépêche Coloniale Illustrée* makes reference to "a Cochinchinese orchestra that performed a suite of pieces," leading one to believe that a southern Vietnamese music troupe performed stand-alone works outside the context of a theater production (Trouillet 1906, 108). A photograph from the 1906 exposition published in Ferrière et al. (1906, 20) shows the *l'orchestre annamite de cochinchine* with sixteen participants, although not all of their instruments are visible: those that are visible include seven đàn tranh, one *đàn đoản* (short-necked lute), two đàn bầu, one đàn tam, one đàn kìm, one đàn cò, a small drum, and a small hanging gong.[23] Like the 1900 performance in Paris, M. Viang served as the director of the ensemble and appears to stand in the back of the ensemble (see Figure 3.1). Importantly, Nguyễn Tống Triều also stands in the picture, lending credence to the theory that the ensemble participants returned from the Marseilles exposition rather than the Paris one six years previous.[24]

When the ensemble returned to Cochinchina, Nguyễn Tống Triều drew on the experience to perform in public for large audiences. No longer did the music simply provide a diversion from everyday life for small ensembles, singers, and their connoisseur friends; it now served as entertainment in restaurants and casinos in the Mekong Delta. In these larger spaces, the singers eventually started to act out the scenes they described vocally, presumably to engage the visual and help audiences understand storylines. First called ca ra bộ, meaning "to sing while gesturing," this action developed into a genre of renovated opera called cải lương that became widely popular in southern Vietnam (Trần Văn Khải 1970, 81–84; Trần Văn Khê 2000, 59–60). Cải lương is viewed as one of the primary ways in which Vietnamese performing artists experimented and engaged with—or

FIGURE 3.1 Southern Vietnamese Music Ensemble at the 1906 Colonial
Exposition in Marseille *Ferrière et al. 1906, 20; source: Bibliothèque
nationale de France, used with permission*

perhaps assimilated—new theatrical forms, literature, fashion, and ideas circulating in the early twentieth century in cosmopolitan urban centers, including Saigon and Chợ Lớn. The stories presented were diverse, as producers adopted Vietnamese, Chinese, and French stories for the stage (Nguyễn T. Phong 1998, 493). The music, however, split from đờn ca tài tử given the restrictions placed on the musicians. They could no longer improvise to their hearts' content and had to play for specific durations. Đờn ca tài tử continued to prosper in private spaces in the Mekong Delta and Saigon, and drew from tunes on the cải lương stage just as it had done from theater and ritual spaces at its emergence.

CONSOLIDATING PRACTICE

In the section on the possible impacts of philosophy on a Vietnamese worldview, I asked how individuals maintain motion in life despite the trials and tribulations placed in front of them. I consider this again given the upheaval caused by the impact of French colonization on đờn ca tài tử musicians. Laozi and later commentators offer several methods of maintaining motion, the most important of which are nonaction (vô vi) and spontaneity (tự nhiên). Vietnamese musicians frequently mention these two concepts, as both help them "return to the source" (về nguồn) or cultivate the seed (hạt giống) of practice. This is not an exercise in nostalgia, but one of cycling back into the past and recapturing those elements discarded following colonization and modernization, which still have virtue (đức) and value (giá trị). Vietnamese musicians use this language to discuss how they are transformed in some way during a performance. Most importantly, they seek what inspires (cảm hứng) them. To be inspired implies feeling (tình cảm or cảm giác) and, specifically, drawing on how other musicians or objects in the performance space encourage others to play in a particular way.

Inspiration and Value

Inspiration is meant to occur naturally and with little or no forethought.[25] This is the tenet of vô vi, where one should not impose or intrude on others (Black 1989, 35).[26] Laozi's text makes multiple mentions of nonaction: Chapter 38 states that the "man of superior virtue takes no action, but has the ulterior motive to do so" (Chan 1963, 158); Chapter 57 argues that the "sage says: I take no action and the people of themselves are transformed" (167). Nonaction identifies a natural way of approaching a decision and enabling necessary change in the world (Thrasher 2008, 48). Alan Watts interprets Laozi's nonaction as understanding something through intuition rather than as "a result of some discipline" (Watts 1975, 88). Government officials or other leaders, for example, follow the model of nature to establish harmony (Liu 2016, 5). Musicians might use inspiration to generate musical material for a performance; indeed, this is foundational to đờn ca tài tử practice.

Knowing intuitively without calculated thought enables spontaneity (tự nhiên) or "self-so" (Chan 1963, 148); another translation of tự nhiên is "natural" or "naturally," understood as "intuitvely from the self" (Thrasher 2008, 49–50). Chapter 51 of Laozi's text suggests that the "Tao is esteemed and virtue is honored without anyone's order. They always come spontaneously" (Chan 1963, 163). Through spontaneity, one evaluates their surroundings and determines the best course. Alan Thrasher connects this directly to creation by arguing that Daoists advance intuition over blind observance of artificial rules (2008, 49–50).

The philosopher Zhuangzi (莊子) extends Laozi's evaluation of spontaneity and maintains that nature is never static but is constantly changing and trans-forming. Rather than viewing the *đạo* (way) as worldly, Zhuangzi understands it as "transcendental."[27] The individual should aim to transcend the earthly path in the valley and embrace "self-transformation" within a context constantly in flux. Transformation "is the final abode of life" (Chan 1963, 178). In his critique of Zhuangzi, Guo Xiang (郭象) offers that the sage must "profoundly and deeply respond . . . to things without any deliberate mind of his own and follows what-ever comes into contact with him. He is like an untied boat drifting, claiming neither the east nor the west to be its own" (Chan 1963, 327). The notion of being unmoored enables greater possibilities for creation through flowing; indeed, the metaphor of flowing in water appears not only in pieces like "Lưu thủy" ("Flowing Water"), as previously mentioned, but also elsewhere in southern Vietnamese music.

Musicians of đờn ca tài tử express similar sentiments. Nguyễn Vĩnh Bảo discusses how he engages his memory to produce "accidental" or spontaneous pitches in performance. The past, for him, constitutes a collection of memorized moments from which one generates something in the present.

> I memorize in my head my life in the past . . . Joy and sadness, everything is in my head. Sometimes I do not think I play with a memorized melody . . . A note I did not predict comes from my inspiration and my fingers go on the strings like that . . . accidentally. Sometimes it is very good; sometimes it is very bad. Everything comes from inspiration. And if you ask me to play it again, once more, it will not be exactly the same . . . because of my feelings [are different].[28]

Spontaneity also explains how musicians transition from one work to the next. In performance, they might perform works as discrete entities separated by breaks with chatter and liquor, or combine works into single units. They also might intersperse shorter and contrasting works—or portions of shorter works—into longer works. Nguyễn Vĩnh Bảo once described how he injects the slow and melancholy composition "Ngũ đối ai" ("Lament") into performances of the fast *Hạ* piece "Ngũ đối hạ" ("Lowering the Five Elements").[29] He might "not intend to play 'Ngũ đối ai' but accidentally, when [he] arrives to the sixth phrase of 'Ngũ đối hạ,'" he slowed down and made the transition. "I love to go to 'Ngũ đối ai,'" he added, suggesting that this spontaneity was built from his personal style. As a venerated musician, "everybody follows me."[30] Change therefore occurs when following a leading musician's inspiration.

Action and Motivation

Not all musicians idealize purely spontaneous musicmaking, and instead advocate a more guided approach; one might call this a guided spontaneity. Nguyễn Vĩnh Bảo presented his inclusion of "Ngũ đối ai" within "Ngũ đối hạ" as "accidental" and contingent on inspiration; however, this choice was far more strategic. He added the tune to generate variety and depict an expanded range of emotional sentiments. "Ngũ đối ai" is a melancholy work in contrast to the livelier "Ngũ đối hạ." Musicians therefore must effectively transition between modal areas by slowing down and introducing the new ornamentation and pitch center associated with sadness.[31] After a number of phrases, the musicians then speed up and transition back to "Ngũ đối hạ." They might return to the sad work again if they wish, but they always must end with the more upbeat "Ngũ đối hạ." Nguyễn Vĩnh Bảo followed his inspiration, but he steered his performance to uphold an aesthetic preference for contrast. Seeking an ideal, in order words, implies action rather than nonaction.

In a conversation I had with Huỳnh Khải, he offers some terminology for understanding this method of approaching performance. When discussing the music that he creates (*sáng tạo*), Huỳnh Khải uses the generic term *cách* (way), and more specifically *cách đàn* (way of playing), to describe a method of playing music.[32] Other musicians also adopt these terms when they speak generally about music creation. The terms designate an approach to producing sound and seem to encompass a technical facility with playing an instrument, a personal style, and an impetus for performing. Huỳnh Khải also adopts the terms *lối* (way, or passageway) and *lối chơi* (way of playing) as descriptors of a musician's approach to performance. Barley Norton suggests that the use of *lối* refers not to the style of the musician but to "the internalization of the fundamental melodic shape of a song" that operates as "a creative articulation of implicit musical knowledge" (2009, 136). Huỳnh Khải offers a similar suggestion but with a greater focus on the externalization of implicit musical knowledge and, perhaps more importantly, the shaping of understandings of this knowledge. *Lối* motivates—here, Huỳnh Khải uses the term *thúc đẩy*—the musician to perform in particular ways.[33] *Thúc đẩy* implies movement, pushing, or embarking (from the term *đẩy*). It opens the possibility for external forces, such as policy, to influence music creation—a concept described in further detail at the end of this chapter and in the next chapter. For Huỳnh Khải, this impetus generates music that is appropriate for twenty-first century audiences.

FIGURE 3.2 Sign for the "Kiều Kiều" Restaurant on Quang Trung Street in Cần Thơ featuring the đàn tranh and two-stringed đàn sến *photo by the author*

Inspiration and Impetus in Performance

In reality, spontaneity, nonaction, and motivation mix together in all the performance decisions. Memories of tunes combine with present conditions, and musicians follow their inspiration to craft a pleasing and moving experience for all involved. These approaches became apparent during my many trips to Cần Thơ in the Mekong Delta to listen to performances and speak with musicians who played traditional music nearly every day but rarely in a professional capacity.

Cần Thơ is a dynamic place for studying traditional music in the Mekong Delta. The city sits adjacent to the Hậu (Bassac) River, one of the two major rivers of the Delta, thereby making it a geographical, cultural, and economic intersection. Foodstuffs and people travel along these waterways, collecting and carrying sounds. Trucks, buses, cars, and motorbikes traverse the narrow and bumpy roads that crisscross the region, bringing clothing to worldwide markets, fresh produce to farm-to-table restaurants, and friends to gatherings at roadside and riverside cafés. From the early afternoon well into the evening, bankers, farmers, government officials, and tourists become musicians. They play instruments, sing songs, joke together, and share memories of departed friends. As they reflect together on everyday life in southern Vietnam, they reinforce old connections and forge new bonds of community.

One evening in 2009, three local musicians took me to a restaurant called Quán nhậu Kiều Kiều in Cần Thơ and taught me how music bridges idiosyncratic approaches to life and music practice (see Figure 3.2). When musicians inspire one another, they build comfort among friends and bring different approaches and musical materials to the space. In this setting, local university lecturer Lê Đình Bích conveyed an extensive knowledge of folk tunes and song texts, and his unbridled enthusiasm often encouraged us all to break out in song. Trần Minh Đức, my instrument teacher in Cần Thơ, brought his extensive knowledge of đờn ca tài tử and cải lương theater tunes. On the đàn sến, a two- or three-stringed lute in the shape of a plum blossom flower, he produced both intricate and fast virtuosic melodies that occasionally ended with rousing applause by his friends. He also was known for improvising amusing song texts to poke gentle fun at the exploits of his friends (and even me, on occasion). Their mutual close friend Phước, who had a day job working in a local office of the state (*nhà nước*), added tremendously to the jovial atmosphere as an adept player of the đàn tranh and the ghi ta phím lõm. He frequently engaged in tactical and nonverbal acts of instrumental commentary by repeating what seem to be passages of melody just performed by another in the ensemble and correcting their errors. These apparently emerged without warning and generated great amusement among other members of the group.[34]

On that evening, Thầy Phước made me feel especially welcome as a newcomer into the space of performance. He made sure that I knew the names of the tunes that we played and the meanings of the lyrical content. He also expressed excitement that I could bring him details about music played elsewhere in the world.[35] He asked if particular tunes sounded Indonesian or Chinese, as he considered the way that Vietnamese fit into larger networks of Asian musicmaking. He also pointed out the importance of alcohol in the space and the different ways that restaurants owners to try to get patrons intoxicated as a method of keeping their businesses solvent. (The sign for the restaurant in Figure 3.2 advertises the availability of "all types of alcohol.") At one point late in the evening, he rose from his chair with his beer glass in hand to address me. He said that he wanted to acknowledge the effort that I put into trying to understand Vietnamese music and to express sympathy for the difficulties I faced in getting there as an American. We clanged our glasses together, and he repeated again under his breath, "It's so hard, so hard," before drinking, putting down his glass, and smiling broadly at me. I think all present understood the significance of an American academic drinking and singing alongside an employee of the Vietnamese state. Beer motivates and builds bridges, and music solidifies them.

These musical practices join inspiration and motivation. Musicians in these spaces inspire one another through melodic snippets and styles, but performances also motivate participants to build closer bonds and include new individuals into community circles. This work continues in absence. Phước passed away not long after I completed my doctoral fieldwork. Whenever I return to Cần Thơ and meet Trần Minh Đức and Lê Đình Bích, we recall the performances we attended together and what we learned from one another. We still talk and laugh about Phước's style of providing musical commentary on the musicianship around him, and the wry smile with which he did it. Through intentionally replicating this style, we keep our memories of him alive.

CONCLUSION

Southern Vietnamese traditional music generates connections between people. Musicians sustain these connections not only through the tunes played but also through evoking sounds and advancing long-standing processes of creation drawn from Daoism, but also Buddhism and Confucianism. These are simple ideals, certainly, but teachers work hard to advance and explain them. To best understand how music works, musicians argue, southern Vietnamese persons must have a seed planted in them to later become an effective producer and consumer of culture. The seed represents an inner virtue everyone needs to cultivate. As they grow up and interact with the histories and narratives of a people and a nation, culture begins to germinate and blossom in that person, leading to the sharing of this culture.

Đờn ca tài tử is firmly rooted in southern Vietnam. This music has emerged from the interactions between long-standing residents and newly-arrived migrants into southern Vietnam and synthesized northern and central Vietnamese, Chinese, French, and other musics. As old practices change and give rise to new ones, đờn ca tài tử musicians continue to extend the stream of virtuous Vietnamese lived experience. They draw on tenets of nonaction, spontaneity, and motivation to maintain methods of expression when they meet new conditions. These practices fade in the background with new influences, but they do support musicianship in the present, a topic to which Chapter 4 turns.

FOUR
Portrait of Đờn ca tài tử

In November 2009, Nguyễn Vĩnh Bảo emailed a recording of the work "Lưu thủy trường" to his students in the Netherlands, New South Wales, and Texas. Meaning "Flowing Water" (long version), this is one of the most well-known, performed, and recorded works of the đờn ca tài tử repertoire. Before listening to the recording, I expected it to be similar to previous iterations of the work he and others have performed. Musicians typically begin with an improvised prelude called the *rao* to introduce the *điệu* (or *điệu thức*, meaning mode or model [Trương Bình Tòng 1996, 31]) of the work and the style of each performer. Following the sound of the *song lang* (a wooden clapper), musicians improvise (*đàn tùy hứng*) around the primary pitches of the backbone melody called the *lòng bản*. With a reference to water in the title, some musicians imitate the sounds of water flowing in nature. In a particularly memorable duet performed with Hồng Tấn Phát on the Ocora album *Viet Nam: Tradition du Sud* (1972), Thầy Vĩnh Bảo frequently uses glissandi on the *đàn tranh* to evoke the sound of cascading water. One glissando after another lands on a pitch of the lòng bản, and as the sounds of the water resonate in the instrument, listeners feel surrounded by nature.

The 2009 recording begins, however, neither with sounds of plectra strumming pitches on the đàn tranh nor with the sound of water. It begins instead with the sounds of a hammer striking metal. (Listen to **Track 4**.) At the time, a new café was being built adjacent to Thầy Vĩnh Bảo's home, and no room in the house could escape construction sounds. I initially cringed when I heard him try to compete with the hammer. When he allows the strings of the zither to resonate and disperse into silence during the most contemplative moments of the piece, the hammer comes in, sounding a metaphorical death knell of tradition. This interpretation is not accurate, however. Thầy Vĩnh Bảo elected to record the track during the day with the construction sounds in the background not to prove that traditional music is dying or dead, but to indicate how traditional music coexists and thrives alongside the rapid changes of the contemporary period. At one point in his *rao*, he matches the pitch the hammer produces as it hits metal and then bases his improvisation on this pitch. As the construction worker bangs away, he introduces the structure of the mode and lands on the pitch produced by the hammer: he hits the note once, twice, three times, and adds a bit of vibrato before continuing. He treats the hammer like a fellow musician in the performance space and crafts a time- and space-specific performance.

Đờn ca tài tử is not traditional music in an "antiquated" sense but instead resounds in the vibrant spaces of everyday interactions. In addition to drawing inspiration from a construction site, Thầy Vĩnh Bảo's performances have imitated the sound of a clock or a spoon accidentally falling to the ground.[1] He heard these sounds as he performed, and rather than ignore them, he recognized them as part of the same space that he inhabited. The sounds reflected on happenstance, and he encouraged listeners to hear these sounds and interpret their meanings alongside his music.

Inspiration (*sự cảm hứng*) in southern Vietnamese traditional music is not a free-for-all but a strategic blending of knowledge of past practice with sounds and people in the present performance space. The hammer duet may be the most memorable aspect of this Thầy Vĩnh Bảo performance, but it is supported by recollections of previous duets, the tunes played, and the individuals involved. Inspiration is emotional work, in which musicians reflect on the distance between past practice and the present—the individuals lost and tunes no longer played resonate in the musicians' minds as they perform. Thầy Vĩnh Bảo often sought inspiration in old commercial recordings in his collection. He used an old Sony Walkman to play recordings of musicians long passed, and then accompanied them on the đàn tranh or đàn kìm to give the recordings new life in the present.

This chapter explores how musicians bring memory and musicianship to life in đờn ca tài tử performances in Ho Chi Minh City and the Mekong Delta. Musicians have a wide array of practices at their disposal to follow their inspiration, from instruments to modes and tunes. These practices relay certain emotional sentiments and particular narratives to audiences. In these descriptions, I combine fieldwork interactions with musicians and summaries of theorizations of đờn ca tài tử practice published over the course of the past forty years. Given the number of musicians involved in this work, multiple histories and belief systems concerning authentic music practice emerge, but this richness helps elucidate the diversity of practice in existence.

INSTRUMENTAL FORCES OF ĐỜN CA TÀI TỬ

When southern Vietnamese musicians perform music with others—or others come to play with them—they *đi chơi* (literally, "to go play") or seek *vui chơi* (literally, "happy play," meaning "fun") with others.[2] Vocalists and five or six instrumentalists work together to produce sound appropriate for the performance environment. Vocalists extemporize texts based on the lives and actions of other participants in the performance space or sing fixed lyrics either memorized or read from a text. (Increasingly, today, singers read lyrics from their mobile telephones.) Instrumentalists *đờn (đàn)* or pluck string instruments and *thổi* or blow into wind instruments to produce sound.[3] The ensembles often entirely feature string instruments, and musicians have a wide range from which to select in order to make *vui chơi*, such as đàn tranh (zither); đàn kìm (two-stringed moon-shaped lute); đàn cò (two-stringed fiddle, also called the đàn nhị elsewhere in Vietnam); đàn gáo (two-stringed fiddle with a coconut as a resonating chamber); đàn bầu (monochord, also occasionally called the đàn độc huyền); đàn sến (lute in the shape of a plum blossom flower); đàn vĩ cầm (violin); đàn tỳ bà (four-stringed pear-shaped lute similar to the Chinese *pipa*); and several types of guitars, including the đàn ghi ta (guitar), ghi ta mando (similar to a mandolin), Hạ uy cầm (Hawaiian steel guitar), and ghi ta phím lõm (guitar with a scooped fingerboard). Aerophones include the sáo (transverse flute) and tiêu (vertical flute). My studies and performances of đờn ca tài tử focused on three instruments, which shaped my understanding of this tradition. I studied the đàn tranh and đàn kìm with Nguyễn Vĩnh Bảo in Ho Chi Minh City, and the three-stringed đàn sến with Trần Minh Đức in Cần Thơ.

Đàn tranh

The đàn tranh belongs to a family of zithers performed in Asia that also includes the Chinese *guzheng*, Korean *gayageum*, and Japanese *koto*. The semicircular shape of the instrument's body distinguishes it from some of the flatter zithers found in the region. Instrument makers often decorate the instrument with ornate mother-of-pearl inlay and a dark lacquer, further marking the instrument as Vietnamese. Musicians usually sit with the instrument in their laps and the end of the instrument resting on a chair or the floor. The bottom of the instrument must not lie flat against a solid surface, however, since sound needs to escape holes cut out from the bottom of the instrument.

The most typical Vietnamese đàn tranh have sixteen or seventeen strings, although others may have nineteen, twenty-one, or more strings. Lê Tuấn Hùng (1998) offers a great deal more detail on the construction of the zither and its history, but a few points are worth mentioning. When facing or sitting in front of the instrument, tuning pegs are inserted diagonally across the instrument on one's left, and the strings are attached to fixed points on one's right. The shortest and thinnest string is closest to one's body and the longest and thickest string is on the opposite side. A small moveable bridge (con nhạn), sometimes called a "moveable horse" (ngựa đàn), supports each string; musicians use these to retune the instrument as necessary. Musicians usually tune the strings to a pentatonic scale associated with the main pitches of the mode (điệu) in which they play. On the seventeen-stringed version with which I am the most familiar, musicians do not tune the first string to the first note in the Vietnamese scale, hò; instead, they tune it to the third or fourth notes of the scale, depending on the mode. The scale then begins on the second string.

The training of the musician's hands constitutes one of the most difficult parts of playing the instrument. The left hand moves across the instrument on the left side of the tuning bridges and produces the intricate ornamentation for which the instrument is well known. Unlike contemporary performance techniques of the Korean and Chinese zithers where musicians press the strings with some force to alter pitch, the technique of southern Vietnamese students is more delicate and subtle. While resonant, the instrument is not especially loud, so audience members often need to sit quite close to the instrument in order to hear the tapping, vibrato, and pressing needed to properly evoke the sentiments of đờn ca tài tử modality. The right hand moves up and down on the right side of the tuning bridges to pluck the strings. In the southern Vietnamese traditions, musicians use two plectra (phím gảy) on the thumb and pointer fingers (see Figure 4.1). Three plectra can be found as well, but this is more typical of the central and northern Vietnamese traditions. The đàn tranh plectra are designed as extensions of the curved fingernail; since they are curved inward, they only pluck the strings in one direction—toward the musician's body for the pointer finger, and away from the body for the thumb.

The sound of the zither is easily distinguished from other instruments played in a đờn ca tài tử ensemble. Improvisations often feature glissandi, especially at the beginning of a work. After the sound of the song lang that ends the rao and leads to the named work itself, đàn tranh musicians use a glissando to orient all players to the start of the work. (This glissando is indicated with á or Á in

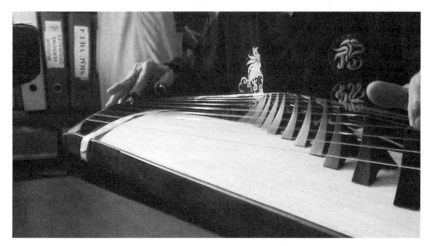

FIGURE 4.1 Close-up of a đàn tranh played by Nguyễn Vĩnh Bảo
still from video by the author, July 14, 2012, Ho Chi Minh City

FIGURE 4.2 Nguyễn Vĩnh Bảo playing the đàn kìm
photo by the author, July 26, 2019, Cao Lãnh

notation detailed in the next chapter.[4]) They listen for the descent to the first pitch of the tune and all play that pitch at the same time. Typical improvisations by đàn tranh players feature stepwise motion, extensive ornamentation, and occasional leaps. Musicians also use octave displacements in order to fill space in the improvisation and generate resonance in the instrument.

Đàn kìm

The đàn kìm (or đàn nguyệt, as it is known elsewhere in Vietnam) is a lute with a resonating chamber in the shape of a slightly pinched circle, hence why it is described as being in the shape of a moon. The instrument is made entirely from wood and has no sound holes on the face or back of its body, which means that it is relatively quiet and is not always easy to mic in performance settings. Two strings run from a fixed point on the face of the instrument to two tuning pegs (*trục đàn*) at the end of the long neck. The neck has eight bamboo frets (*phím đàn*), which produces a pentatonic scale on each string. Some methods of tuning the instrument maintain the same pentatonic scale on each string, while other methods generate different pentatonic scales. (Nguyen Th. Phong [1986] offers more detail on these tuning systems.) The frets are high, which enables extensive ornamentation of single pitches, including bending to several pitches above the fretted pitch. This yields melismatic and fluid melodies but impedes the production of fast improvisations, which are themselves not typical of đờn ca tài tử performances. Instead of plectra, musicians strike the stings with both sides of a guitar pick (see Figure 4.2).

Musicians playing the đàn kìm often serve as leaders of the ensemble. They typically play the *song lang* with the foot and determine when the *rao* ends and the named work begins. They also use the *song lang* to indicate when a piece ends. They control the tempo through the production of melody at a particular speed and the use of the *song lang* to articulate certain beats of each phrase played. In more contemplative works, đàn kìm players tap out slow rhythms on the face of the instrument to mark beats of rest not meant to be filled with melody.

Đàn sến

The đàn sến is a six-sided wooden lute in the shape of the plum blossom flower and has either two or three strings. No musician or scholar with whom I spoke in southern Vietnam presented a clear history of the instrument, although it does appear to have originated in China (Trần Văn Khê 1962, 150).[5] In China and among Chinese diasporic communities, it is known as the *qinqin* (秦琴) or *meihuaqin* (梅花琴, or plum blossom flower instrument).[6] J. Lawrence Witzleben points to the existence of a similar instrument in *Jiangnan sizhu* ensembles of southern China (1995, 49–50). A website maintained by the Guangzhou Bureau of Culture indicates that one also finds these instruments accompanying folk operas from southern China.[7] The website only features an image of the three-stringed instrument, although other sources point to the existence of the qinqin in both two- and three-stringed versions, particularly in Chaozhou (Teochew)—specifically in *xianshi* and *xiyue* ensembles, where the instrument serves a supporting role (Thrasher 2008, 8–10)—and greater Guangdong Province (Witzleben 1995, 49–50).[8] I surmise, therefore, that the instrument traveled to southern Vietnam with Chinese musicians emigrating from Fujian and Guangdong provinces primarily in the late seventeenth and eighteenth centuries. This supposition is bolstered by two additional details. First, many Chinese in southern Vietnam still speak the Teochew dialect—the language spoken in Chaozhou, where the qinqin was most popular; and second, one typically finds the đàn sến only in southern Vietnam and not in central and northern Vietnam—locations in which immigrants from Chaozhou did not settle.[9]

The wooden resonating body has a flat or rounded soundboard with no sound hole, and a rounded or flat back. The đàn sến has twelve or fourteen fixed frets made of bamboo or wood with a metal strip that serves as the contact point with the string. The twelve frets are attached to the neck, and if the instrument features two additional frets, they are placed on the face of the instrument. Unlike the đàn kìm, whose frets divide one octave into five notes, the frets of the đàn sến divide an octave into seven. This allows musicians greater flexibility, as they can easily switch between types of music involving different scalar structures. In addition, the musician can easily remove and replace the frets on the fingerboard. New or recently refurbished instruments oftentimes require frequent re-fretting as the wood of the resonating chamber settles, which causes the plucked pitch to fluctuate slightly. Musicians frequently reglue the frets onto the neck of the instrument in order to keep the instrument in tune.

Trần Minh Đức performs the three-stringed đàn sến rather than the more common two-stringed version (see Figure 4.3). The three-stringed instrument is a trademark for him, as there are few other musicians who play it in southern Vietnam. He first encountered the three-stringed đàn sến in the late 1990s and immediately started exploring what he views to be the increased versatility of the

FIGURE 4.3 Lê Đình Bích, the author, and Trần Minh Đức (from left to right)
playing the đàn sến in Cần Thơ *from the collection of the author*

instrument.[10] He assumes that the addition of the third string is an "advancement"
made in Vietnam and argues that the additional string enables the musician to
provide greater melodic elaboration, since more pitches are at the disposal of
the fingers of the left hand. He maintains that the improvements over the two-
stringed version help keep traditional vibrant and his music expressive.

ĐIỆU IN ĐỜN CA TÀI TỬ

Expression emerges partly in the performance of điệu, meaning mode or model.
Điệu codifies an expectation of a specific "ethos" or sentiment and collates practice of performing specific musical devices so it is retained in collective memory
(Trainor 1977, 65; see also Nguyễn T. Phong 1998, 462–64). Musicians debate điệu
precisely to craft, maintain, and control their own experiences playing.

Scholar-performers have taken part in these debates, both drawing from
and adding to the rich—and conflicting—archive of textual materials that have
circulated throughout Vietnam and abroad. Trần Văn Khê's foundational text on
traditional music describes two modal systems to organize southern Vietnamese
traditional music (1962, 216–46). Many contemporary musicians replicate this
theory in spoken descriptions of điệu today. *Bắc* mode works express happiness
and involve stable or largely fixed pitch ornamentation content, and *Nam* mode
works express more complicated emotional states—often involving sadness—and

feel musically unstable. Other musicians, including some interviewed by John Paul Trainor (1977, 64), describe four or five điệu; Nguyễn T. Phong (1998, 483) argues that there are eight. Since many artists divide the đờn ca tài tử repertoire into four categories, I argue that four điệu exist in southern Vietnam today. In addition to the Bắc mode, there also exists a related *Nhạc lễ* or *Hạ* (ritual music) mode; in addition to the Nam mode, there also exists a *Oán* (profoundly sad) mode. These modes have several important characteristics related to scale, interval, and ornamentation.

Scale

A điệu includes a particular set of pitches constituting a scale. In Vietnam, musicians use the following solfège syllables to distinguish these pitches:

Hò	Xự/Ú	Xừ/Xư	Xang	Xê	Cống	Phan/Oan	Liu
Sol	La	Si	Do	Re	Mi	Fa	Sol[11]

Vietnamese pitches are not found on the piano, but for ease of readability, I use the noteheads in Figure 4.4 to approximate pitch in all subsequent transcriptions.

Scholars disagree, however, on how many pitches make a scale "Vietnamese." Trần Văn Khê (1962) bases theories of modality on the pentatonic scale; he makes it clear that performances of particular modes feature pitches outside the five-note scale, but he does not suggest the presence of a hexatonic or heptatonic scale (206–12). Đắc Nhẫn and Ngọc Thới (1974) agree with the pentatonic-scale model; they further argue that the scale unifies and defines Vietnamese practice throughout the entirety of Vietnam (inclusive of the Republic of Vietnam and Democratic Republic of Vietnam that still existed when their text was published). Music "with origins in the south use the national scale [*thang âm dân tộc*], an inherited aspect of the national tunes that have existed for a long time and spread from the North to the South" (24). The structures of the scale are stable, from their perspective, and have moved from the so-called source of Vietnamese culture in northern Vietnam to central and southern Vietnam as part of the *Nam tiến*. It should nevertheless be noted that this is not universally believed.

Evidence from particular works and the construction of certain instruments suggests that Vietnamese music is actually not pentatonic. Certain instruments more easily produce a pentatonic scale, while others, including the đàn sến and ghi ta phím lõm, produce heptatonic scales. The đàn kìm produces many scales

| Hò | Xự | Xừ | Xang | Xê | Cống | Phan | Liu |

FIGURE 4.4 Vietnamese solfège syllables

	0	1	2	3	4	5	6	7	8
String 2 *Dây đại/dây to*	Xang	Xê	Cống	Liu	Xự	Xang	Xê	Cống	Liu
(Big string)	Do	Re	Mi	Sol	La	Do	Re	Mi	Sol
String 1 *Dây tiểu/dây nhỏ*	Liu	Xự	Xang	Xê	Cống	Liu	Ú	Xáng	Xê
(Small string)	Sol	La	Do	Re	Mi	Sol	La	Do	Re

FIGURE 4.5 Dây Bắc tuning on the đàn kìm

	0	1	2	3	4	5	6	7	8
String 2	Xê	Cống	Hò	Xự	**Xừ**	Xê	Cống	Liu	Xự
	Re	Mi	Sol	La	Si	Re	Mi	Sol	La
String 1	Liu	Xự	Xang	Xê	Cống	Liu	Ú	Xáng	Xê
	Sol	La	Do	Re	Mi	Sol	La	Do	Re

FIGURE 4.6 Dây Bắc Oán tuning on the đàn kìm

depending on how it is tuned. When tuned for the Bắc mode on both strings, the two strings are tuned a fifth apart, and the đàn kìm produces the pitches indicated in Figure 4.5. If musicians wish to play a work in a different mode, they easily change the tuning of one or both of the strings by turning the tuning pegs.[12] One might tune the strings in octaves, a tuning known as *dây tỳ*; separated by approximately minor sevenths, a tuning known as *dây tố lan* ("pure orchid" [Nguyễn Th. Phong 1986, 59]); or in approximate fourths, a tuning known as *dây bắc oán*, indicated in Figure 4.6. With the raising of the second string, the musician has access to *xừ* (bolded in Figure 4.6), a pitch often found in sad or melancholy works such as "Vọng cổ." This flexibility suggests that đờn ca tài tử should not be considered pentatonic.

Musicians may also adopt a fretted pitch as a new tonic rather than retuning the instrument. This method becomes especially important in performances where musicians quickly follow their inspiration and move to a new composition in a different mode. In other instances, this change might occur to accommodate two singers in performance with different ranges (Nguyen Th. Phong 1986, 62). If musicians elect a tonic pitch produced by pressing the string at the first fret (thereby producing the second pitch of that string), they use the *dây hò nhị* (making the tonic with the second pitch of the string) tuning.[13] If musicians press the string at the second fret (thereby producing the third pitch of the string), they use the *dây hò ba* (third pitch) tuning; the fourth pitch of the string yields the *dây hò tư* (fourth pitch) tuning.

The adept musician uses the instrument to perform a great diversity of pitch content in the service of multiple modes and diverse emotional associations. The tuning system therefore informs the understanding of southern Vietnamese music as not pentatonic. Musicians instead conceive of each modal scale as heptatonic, from which musicians use a subset of pitches to produce a composition (Vũ Nhật Thăng 1998, 107; see also Lê Tuấn Hùng 1998, 33).

Intervals and Pitch Pairs

No standard conceptualization of pitch exists in Vietnamese traditional music, so musicians must iterate and reiterate intervallic relationships to properly make the mode in performance. For some theorists, this is vitally important because the space between two pitches may differ depending on the mode or even the work performed. Vũ Nhật Thăng (1998)'s extensive study of intervallic content compares the number of cents separating pitches in each southern Vietnamese mode. He argues that the placement of every pitch besides *hò* and *xê* varies (Vũ Nhật Thăng 1998, 107). Some of these differences are small; others are more significant. Most musicians are not so pedantic about tuning and are willing to accept a certain degree of pitch imprecision as long as the imprecision did not prevent the production of a convivial atmosphere.

Students learn the importance of keeping certain pitches in tune with one another during lessons. After several inaccurate attempts at tuning the đàn tranh on my own, for example, Nguyễn Vĩnh Bảo suggested that I should think of these pitches not as discrete entities but as pitches that resonate together.[14] In studying his process of tuning up the instrument, therefore, I learned how to hear two pitches as being "in tune." When tuning the instrument, I made sure that *hò* and *xê* sounded an approximate fifth and *hò* and *xang* sounded an approximate fourth. The remaining two pitches, *xự* or *xừ* and *cống* or *phan/oan*, were more difficult to tune outside of the performance context, especially for performers, like me, who must retrain their ears to listen for Vietnamese "in tunedness." I therefore tuned the pitches approximately and then used the ngựa đàn to adjust the pitch as necessary when I played.

Pitches played in pairs appear frequently in performance and therefore enable the recognition of different modes in southern Vietnamese music. One pitch of the pair can be the tonic pitch (*hò*), but it does not have to be, and the other pitch is typically a fourth away. Following frequent repetition, certain pitches co-resonate or resonate as a single entity evocative of the mode. Rather than thinking of a mode as being comprised of a scale of pitches in stepwise order, musicians think of the modes as a series of co-resonances. This co-resonance is part of the aesthetic engagement with particular modes associated with đờn ca tài tử and, most likely, its central Vietnamese predecessor *ca Huế*. Connoisseurs and musicians therefore listen to modes as multiple intervals comprised of pitch pairs that resonate in their instruments. A listener builds an appreciation of an improvised melody based not simply on the artful generation of pitch content but on how pitches resonate together in the instrument.

Ornamentation

Along with co-resonating pitches, musicians consider ornamentation methods (*kỹ thuật*) fundamental to the production of the mode. In particular modes, musicians must perform the ornament to properly evoke the identity of the pitch. My lessons with Nguyễn Vĩnh Bảo and Trần Minh Đức required significant time developing the muscle memory for three ornaments in particular: *rung* (vibrato), *mổ* (tapping), and *nhấn* (pitch bending). Musicians produce vibrato by raising and lowering a pitch at a moderate speed for the duration of the sounding of the pitch. Importantly, not all *rung* in Vietnam are the same, since musicians use vibrato to identify their regional specialization and style. In central Vietnam, for instance, musicians of ca Huế produce a wider and more deliberate *rung* compared to the faster southern Vietnamese type.[15] The mổ ornament punctuates the note with a tap of the string (for the đàn tranh and various lutes), a tap of the *cần đàn vòi đàn*, the flexible bamboo (originally buffalo) horn of the đàn bầu (monochord), or a tap of a keyhole (for the flutes).

Ornaments often join disparate pitches together and explore the intervallic space between them. These include nhấn, where musicians bend one pitch up-

ward to another pitch (Nguyễn T. Phong 1998, 461–64). Vũ Nhật Thăng classi-
fies different types of nhấn: raising a pitch to another and then applying vibrato
(*nhấn rung*); raising a pitch and returning immediately (*nhấn láy* or *nhún*); and
augmenting (or borrowing) one string to produce the sound of another string
(*nhấn luyến*) (1998, 46–47).[16] Hoàng Đạm adds that one can also bend the string
to a pitch and then pluck (*gảy*) the new pitch a number of times before returning the string to its standard state (*vỗ* or *âm vỗ*) (2003, 121; 181). Combinations
of these ornaments called *luyến láy* also evoke the sense of the respective mode
(Nguyễn T. Phong 1998, 461–64).

Certain ornaments do not add to the modal sense of the tune. Trần Minh Đức
makes reference to two đàn sến ornaments in this category. Since the instrument
does not have a large resonating chamber, the sound of plucked pitches dies away
very quickly. Performers use *reo* (tremolo) with the pick in the right hand, and
chữ luyến (staccato tapping, or the onomatopoeic *búm dây*) with the left hand,
alongside repeated string plucks with the right hand, to elongate the iteration
of a particular pitch or pitches.[17]

Musicians exercise considerable flexiblity in how they ornament in actual
performance, often deploying ornaments differently to add nuance and emotional
weight to particular improvised passages. For instance, knowledgeable audiences
use differences in ornamentation to discern gradations of sadness imparted by
performers. Nguyễn Vĩnh Bảo often differentiated between profound sadness
and grievance in his improvisations. In lessons with me, he connected the ornamentation types to specific stories to make the distinction and the ways of
listening explicit.

> Vibrate the *do*, bend to *re*, and return to *do* . . . The expression—if you play
> like that, you want to express your sadness, but not a profound sadness. *Your
> sadness.* And if you play like this [instead]: you press down, bend the string to
> *mi*, and release to *do*, that expresses the grievance, a very profound sadness.
> You see, when I play like that, I see the image of a man who is dying. . . . They
> put him in the coffin and put him in the grave. [But] he wants . . . to stand up
> to say the last word . . . you know?[18]

When understood, specific musical devices, including pitch content and
ornamentation, connect sound to relatable ideas. One cannot understand the
meaning of these two types through notation or listening alone; one must also
make these connections outside of the concepts—that is, suffering and grievance—to listen for the performers' intent.

These connections rely on shared experiences in this everyday context. A non-Vietnamese national like me can only imagine the histories described rather than feeling them viscerally after having lived through them. As Thầy Vĩnh Bảo demonstrated both ornaments, he both pointed to the possibilities of individual expression through play and focused on the personal sadness often expressed through performance.

> You understand what I mean? The difference is this . . . for Vietnamese listeners, this is their reaction when they listen to this. They differentiate, they can see the image [of the man dying]. They feel very sad . . . This is the profound sadness, grievance, suffering!. . . . The ornamentation in Vietnamese music is of the utmost importance.[19]

The man depicted in this story could stand in for any of the men he has known over his long lifetime who left before their time: some died during the colonial period; some died during the Second Indochina War; some—including one of his closest friends—died in reeducation camps set up following the collapse of the Republic of Vietnam; and others died of natural causes. These men had more to say.

Frequent consumers of Vietnamese music often describe đờn ca tài tử as evoking some of the most nuanced and devastating sadness in Vietnamese traditional music.[20] They do not necessarily hear the same images that Nguyễn Vĩnh Bảo uses to craft the passage, but they draw on similarly melancholy images that are personal to their own lived experience.

Sound Aesthetics

Musicians spend considerable time making sure that their instruments sound and resonate appropriately, oftentimes adjusting the tuning of the instrument to ensure that the *âm sắc* (timbre) is appropriate when plucking or running the bow against a string. *Âm sắc* is related to *âm thanh* (sonority), which appears in discussions of aesthetics to indicate when a sound is pleasing and resonates effectively in the body of the instrument. Any instrument, including those with amplification, may be sonorous and produce a pleasing sound if played appropriately. Most đàn kìm players have replaced the lute's silk strings with nylon strings, and over the course of the twentieth century, musicians have adopted the electric guitar and violin as modernized versions of the đàn kìm and đàn cò respectively. These changes still produce a sonorous and pleasing sound, even if the timbre changes. Using a violin is acceptable in performance, since it also produces a sonorous sound, but it cannot replace the timbre of the đàn cò fiddle. To make such an argument "devalues" the đàn cò, as it suggests that the đàn cò timbre might so easily be replaced by an imported and colonial-era instrument.[21] Both *âm sắc* and *âm thanh* are part of the essence and *tâm hồn* (soul) of traditional Vietnamese music.[22]

Shaping the sonority of a work involves how pitches are produced and ornamented. For instance, Nguyễn Vĩnh Bảo frequently admonished me in lessons for stopping my vibrato before the pitch finished resonating on the đàn tranh. Even if I move to a new pitch on the instrument, I must continue to add *rung* if the left hand is not needed for the subsequent pitch or pitches. If the left hand becomes needed, I should add *rung* until the last possible moment and then move quickly and fluidly to the next ornament. For the mổ ornament, I must also ensure that the pitch resonates appropriately. In some instances, I might just tap once, but in cases where the note resonates for a longer length, I might tap two or more times to maintain the identity of the pitch.

Nguyễn Vĩnh Bảo insisted that I allow the sound to resonate and fully dissipate because of long-standing aesthetic practice. It aligns in particular with Laozi's assertion for making great music with barely perceptible sound. Vũ Thế Ngọc transliterates the original Chinese text (大音希聲) on this practice as "đại âm hy thanh" (literally, "great music, rare sound") and offers the explanation "âm lớn thì ít tiếng," or "significant music comes from only a little sound" (Lão Tử 2018, 128–29). In context, this forms part of four lines in Chapter 41 on appreciating existence through what cannot be perceived in nature: "The great square is boundless. The great vessel is slow to mature. Great music may be nearly inaudible. The perfect image has no form" (Laozi 2005, 61). The third line may be interpreted in any number of ways, but through conversations with musicians and practicing Daoists, it suggests that softer and emptier sounds, or the silence between sounds, make better music as they have greater inner depth and meaning.[23] This aligns with the teaching of Nguyễn Vĩnh Bảo, who spent considerable time making sure that I understood how to let sounds of the đàn tranh dissipate. When I stopped ornamenting a note prematurely, he stopped me and told me to continue ornamenting even after I thought that the sound had stopped—the imperceptible still needs to be ornamented.

The notion of inner depth and meaning suggests a connection to highly personal and very often emotion-filled music. Encounters with sound often include relating personal stories to students so they can understand how certain sonic qualities take on emotional meaning. Nguyễn Vĩnh Bảo spoke, for example, about how certain tunes reminded him of living in Cambodia in the 1930s, as well as of hopes and desires he had as a young man. When he played certain sad works, he recounted in late 2008, he remembered a woman whose advances he rebuffed in the early 1960s. She was young, and he was married. In his attempt to distance himself, he was callous toward her, and their last encounter made her quite upset. Seeking counsel on his actions, he went to visit a friend, who suggested that he play music to work through his emotional state. "Anyone who listened to this music feels suffering . . . In that situation, I was suffering for her. Not for me, but for her."[24] Knowing the work would be a moving one, the friend surreptitiously recorded the impromptu performance. The friend never disseminated the recording—"he kept it for himself," Nguyễn Vĩnh Bảo recalled—but they reflected on the recording later.[25] This recording captured the moment of encounter between the musician, his emotional state, and the space of his friend's home.

Musicians draw from personal reflections and experiences and direct them through commonly accepted performance practices to generate meaning. Musicians begin with a *rao*, or improvised prelude, to establish a mode and the musician's personal style. The named work in the mode of the *rao* then follows, and musicians use the skeletal melody called the *lòng bản* to guide their improvisation. To express the happy, sad, or melancholy nature of the tune, they draw on their structural understandings of pitch context of that mode. I offer descriptions of these structures as my teachers relayed them to me.

Rao

Performances of đờn ca tài tử open with preludes that shape listeners' expectations through length, style, and modality. Before the start of some types of vocal works, for example, singers begin with a nonmetrical recitative known as *nói lối* or "speaking the way" (Nguyễn T. Phong 1998, 454; see also Nguyễn Phúc An 2019b, 346). For instrument players, the *rao* establishes a musical language and style for performance. A less common way to do this is through the performance of a *dạo* precomposed prelude that also is used in central Vietnamese music (Hoàng Yến 1919). Both suggest visual images: *dạo* means to walk or stroll and *rao* means to announce or a "call to people to buy something" (Lê Tuấn Hùng 1998, 62).[26]

Musicians establish their way of playing through the rao and introduce the pitch content, ornamentation, and stock phrases attached to the mode of the tune (Cannon 2016, 143–44; Nguyễn Phúc An 2019b, 344–45). Musicians of đờn ca tài tử craft long and meandering rao when they meet at a friend's home or local café to complete a day's work with music, food, liquor, and camaraderie.[27] They use musical phrases typical of their styles and incorporate and extend musical material produced by the other musicians in the space. They therefore draw from past practice and a specific attempt to establish the performance as a meeting of musicians in that present. In this way, the rao has a role in playing with temporality. Nguyễn Vĩnh Bảo once mentioned that whether he plays a version of a work from the 1930s or the 1970s, he must properly evoke the character of everyday life from that period. Since these time periods typically featured more individuals walking from place to place rather than taking motorbikes, the rao should be slower and more deliberate.[28] Finally, on the most practical level, the rao gives the musicians time and space to retune their instruments, since the constant pressure applied to the strings in particular causes the instruments to go out of tune easily.

The length or absence of a rao helps listeners differentiate performances of đờn ca tài tử from works with the same titles that are associated with other genres. Rao of đờn ca tài tử may last for several minutes or possibly longer, depending on the whims of the performers. Short rao of ten to thirty seconds (or even less) begin works of cải lương. Since audience members typically want to focus on the visual action onstage, musicians provide enough musical material to the singers so they have their starting pitches in their ears. Precomposed works of *nhạc dân tộc* (national music) based on đờn ca tài tử and cải lương and performed by Phạm Thúy Hoan's Sounds of the Homeland Ensemble often do not feature a rao. The impetus of performance here is on the meaning crafted by composers of the precomposed work and not necessarily the musicians themselves; the individual expression enabled by the rao therefore has no place in the performance. In addition, not all of the performers are able to improvise, so they are not yet able to produce a rao.

Fundamental Works

A named work follows the rao. A diverse array of works comprises the đờn ca tài tử tradition, and many musicians, including my teachers, view the following twenty works as the most fundamental. (For recordings of the works, listen to the bolded tracks indicated.)

Điệu Bắc Pieces [29]

"Lưu thủy trường" ("Flowing Water" [long version]) **Tracks 4, 20, and 23**
"Phú lục chấn" ("Song of an Overland Journey" [long version]) (Lê 1998, 138)
   Track 6
"Bình bán chấn" ("Equal Measures" [long version]) (Pham and Whiteside
   1975, 108)
"Xuân tình chấn" ("Young Love" [long version])
"Tây thi" ("The Beautiful Tây Thi") (Pham and Whiteside 1975, 108) **Track 13**
"Cổ bản" ("Old Tune")

Nhạc lễ (Điệu Hạ) Pieces [30]

"Xàng xê" ("Alternating Do and Re") **Track 8**
"Ngũ đối thượng" ("Raising the Five Elements")
"Ngũ đối hạ" ("Lowering the Five Elements") **Track 7**
"Long đăng" ("The Dragon's Lantern") (Thái Văn Kiểm 1964, 82)
"Long ngâm" ("The Dragon's Voice") (Thái Văn Kiểm 1964, 82)
"Vạn giá" ("Ten Thousand Strands of Silk")
"Tiểu khúc" ("The Outer Coffin")

Điệu Nam Pieces

"Nam xuân" ("Southern Spring" or "Southern Youth") **Tracks 14, 15, and 17**
"Nam ai" ("Southern Lament") **Track 12**
"Đảo ngũ cung" ("The Inversion of the Five Fundamental Notes") **Track 10**

Điệu Oán Pieces

"Tứ đại oán" ("Four Generations" [*oán* version]) (Lê 1998, 138) **Track 11**
"Phụng cầu hoàng" ("The Phoenix Seeks a Mate") (Huỳnh Sanh Thông 1983)
"Phụng hoàng cầu" ("The Male and Female Phoenix")
"Giang Nam cửu khúc" ("Nine Tunes of the Southern River")

Musicians rarely perform these works in their entirety in performance due to their length; instead, they might play the first several—and most recognizable—phrases of the work. For Bắc mode works, musicians can play all six in order.[31] They may elect to skip works, but they should not play any in retrograde. For example, they could play "Lưu thủy trường" followed by "Xuân tình chấn" but not vice versa. If they want to play another piece that sits above the previous on the list, then they must pause for a number of minutes before playing the next piece.[32]

Many other works circulate throughout southern Vietnam, including tunes adapted from related genres of central and southern Vietnamese music and little ditties called *bản cà chía* (nonesense tunes). Musicians in the Cần Thơ performance spaces I frequent tend to prefer these shorter works since they quickly are played in their entirety. This sometimes occurs because the musicians want to get back to their beers and banter; more often, however, not everyone in the group knows the work selected, and they do not want to exclude that person from the musical fun. Popular works include folk songs from central Vietnam, including "Lưu thủy vắn" ("Flowing Water" [short version]); works from hát bội, such as the devastatingly sad "Xuân nữ" ("Young Woman") (Cannon 2016, 156; see also Pham and Whiteside 1975, 113–26); southern Vietnamese folk songs, including "Lý con sáo" ("Song of the Starling," **Track 9**), "Lý sương mù" ("Song of the Mist"), and "Lý cây bông" ("Song of the Cotton Flower").

A large corpus of short works associated with non-Vietnamese communities in southern Vietnam also make an appearance in performances. Chinese pieces include "Ú liu ú xáng" ("Alternating La Sol La Do") and a tune most likely named after a proper name titled "Cao phi" (Hoàng Đạm 2003, 17). Pieces with Khmer associations include "Ngũ điểm—Bài tạ" ("Five Grades—Song of Thanks," **Track 21**) and "Miên hậu hồi cung" ("Khmer Queen from the Time of the Court"), the latter of which Trần Minh Đức argues does not borrow a Khmer melody, but "Miên" in the title refers to the Khmer people.[33] Other works reflect French colonial influence, including "Nhạc Miên Nhạc Pháp" mentioned in Chapter 3, and even American tunes, including "Oh! Susanna."[34]

Musicians also incorporate new and longer works that have developed in cải lương performances. They transfer and develop these works separately in đờn ca tài tử performance spaces. Examples include works named after individuals, including "Trường Tương Tư" and "Văn Thiên Tường," and the most famous cải lương and đờn ca tài tử tune, "Vọng cổ." (Listen to **Track 5**.)

Stability in Bắc and Hạ Pieces

The Bắc works listed in the previous section imply an origin in the north—here, this means a real or imagined connection to Chinese territories (Trần Văn Khê 1962, 99). The mode is stable and rarely features pitch content outside of the pentatonic scale notated in Figure 4.7 (Nguyễn Th. Phong 1986, 62); listen to "Lưu thủy trường qua [to] Phú lục" performed by Trần Minh Đức, who plays the first two Bắc tunes in sequence (**Track 6**). Its stability also emerges from the frequent oscillation between *hò* and *xang*. Like the emphasis on the tonic and dominant in Western art music, or the use of *sa* and *ma* or *pa* in Indian *raga* theory, the work sounds grounded when musicians return to the most important pitches of the mode.[35]

Musicians adapted the Hạ works from the seven pieces of the southern Vietnamese nhạc lễ repertoire. (Listen to **Track 3**.) Given this connection, musicians argue that the works should not be grouped together with the "happy" works of the Bắc mode. These works feature the same scale and methods of ornamentation as the Bắc mode, but they sound slightly less stable and evoke more varied emotional content. Musicians frequently oscillate in performances of this mode between the pitch pair *xự* and *cống* (the second and fifth pitches of the scale as indicated in Figure 4.8), unlike the first and third pitches of the Bắc mode.

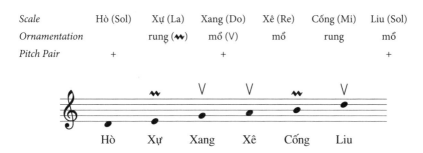

Scale	Hò (Sol)	Xự (La)	Xang (Do)	Xê (Re)	Cống (Mi)	Liu (Sol)
Ornamentation		rung (ᴧ)	mổ (V)	mổ	rung	mổ
Pitch Pair	+		+			+

FIGURE 4.7 Scale and ornamentation of the Bắc mode

Scale	Hò (Sol)	Xự (La)	Xang (Do)	Xê (Re)	Cống (Mi)	Liu (Sol)
Ornamentation	mổ	rung	mổ	mổ	rung	mổ
Pitch Pair		+			+	

FIGURE 4.8 Scale and ornamentation of the Hạ mode

(Listen to "Ngũ đối hạ," **Track 7**, and "Xàng xê," **Track 8**.) This difference allows the musician to "express . . . happiness with solemnity" associated with the ritual from which the Hạ works developed.[36]

Musicians sometimes call these Hạ works the *bảy bài cò*, or seven pieces of the đàn cò fiddle. Musicians and general audiences have associated the đàn cò not only with ritual music but also with funeral (*tang lễ*) music. During my first research trip to Ho Chi Minh City in 2007, I often heard the piercing sound of the fiddle early in the morning when Buddhist funerals took place next door to the building in which I stayed. Hearing these tunes in a funerary setting tinges the way they are understood in a convivial đờn ca tài tử setting.

Instability in Nam and Oán Pieces

The final two modes, *Nam* and *Oán*, feature additional degrees of instability and nuance to great emotional affect. Musicians generally accept that these works reflect varying degrees of sadness, and this emerges from a greater pitch flexibility and fluidity found in both modes. That said, musicians do not conceptualize pitch content of Nam and Oán in standardized ways, so there are debates concerning the number of pitches in a scale and which pitches are considered the most important. I surmise that this instability is a remnant of Bắc and Nam mode categorization by early music theorists: if the Bắc mode is conceived as stable and inflexible to generating generally happy and solemn music, the Nam mode becomes its opposite—as highly flexible to explore sadness, melancholy, and grief. Rather than focus on fixed pitches and pitch pairs, I examine pitch augmentation and ornamentation in this discussion of Nam and Oán modes.

In these pieces, musicians deviate in specific ways from standard intervallic relationships. They speak in particular of raising particular pitches to make them *già* (old) or lowering them to make them *non* (young).[37] The techniques are remnants of the influence exerted on the development of đờn ca tài tử from ca Huế of central Vietnam.[38] Dương Bích Hà explains that Huế musicians incorporated *già* and *non* pitches into Nam mode works of the ca Huế tradition in order to impart a certain "sad and mournful" quality of Nam works (1997, 124; see also Phạm Duy 1972, 140). These adjustments serve as a kind of "accent" or very slight deviation from the scale.[39] The Nam mode scale for the ca Huế tradition includes the pitches *hò* (sol), *xự non* (lowered la), *xang già* (raised do), *xê* (re), *cống non* (lowered mi), and *liu* (sol). This is not the same scale as one finds in the đờn ca tài tử version of the Nam mode; indeed, one finds *già* and *non* more often in ca Huế than in southern Vietnamese music.[40]

Musicians do not adjust the tunings of strings to craft these sounds but bend pitches in the course of performance only.[41] In the đờn ca tài tử tradition, *già* is the most prevalent technique. To create *già* on the đàn tranh or đàn kìm, musicians press a string slightly with the left hand and oftentimes add an ornament.[42] In well-known works like "Nam ai," "Lý con sáo," and "Vọng cổ," for example, musicians sharpen *xang* and add a *rung* ornament; hearing a widened fourth interval with the vibrato emphasis crafts a sense of biting sadness.[43] (Listen to **Track 9**.) *Non* also is found in đờn ca tài tử, but it is not common. In conversations I had with Nguyễn Vĩnh Bảo in 2013, Thầy Vĩnh Bảo explicitly indicated that *non* does not exist in đờn ca tài tử performance.[44] Later in one conversation, however, he argued that evocations of sadness do sometimes feature a flattened *cống* pitch; John Paul Trainor's lessons with Nguyễn Vĩnh Bảo in 1974 and 1975 corroborate the existence of a both raised and lowered pitches (1977, 170). Hoàng Đạm also identifies the same lowering of pitch in the "Vọng cổ" scale of the đờn ca tài tử and cải lương traditions, and labels it *cống non* (2003, 181).[45]

If one assumes that the Nam mode is the flexible antithesis to the stable Bắc mode, discussions of Nam modality involve many exceptions to the rules. Importantly, the Nam mode of the southern Vietnamese traditions appears differently than in the central Vietnamese traditions.[46] Exactly what pitches this involves depends on the performer and theorist. Trương Bỉnh Tòng (1996) argues that a fixed Nam mode scale exists, as indicated in Figure 4.9. This does not align with the practice of the three works in the Nam mode, however. "Đảo ngu cung" in the Nam mode features the pitch *cống* with the *rung* ornament, but includes *xự* as a primary pitch in the mode rather than *xử*. The work also emphasizes the pitch *xê* (as indicated in Figure 4.10), and often features a *nhấn* ornament from *xê* to *cống* (as indicated in Figure 4.12). Often this work is performed at a relatively

Hò   Xử/Y   Xang   Xê   Phan   Liu

FIGURE 4.9 Nam mode scale (adopted from Trương Bỉnh Tòng 1996, 46)

Scale	Hò (Sol)	Xự (La)	Xang (Do)	Xê (Re)	Cống (Mi)	Phan (Fa)	Liu (Sol)
Ornamentation	mổ	rung	mổ	rung	rung	mổ	rung
Emphasis				+			

FIGURE 4.10 Scale and ornamentation of "Đào ngũ cung," a Nam mode piece

Scale	Hò (Sol)	[Xự] [(La)]	Xử (Si)	Xang (Do)	Xê (Re)	[Cống] [(Mi)]	Phan (Fa)	Liu (Sol)
Ornamentation	mổ	rung	mổ	mổ	mổ	rung		mổ

FIGURE 4.11 Scale and ornamentation of "Nam xuân," a Nam mode piece

FIGURE 4.12 Types of *nhấn* in "Nam xuân"

quick tempo, and *già* and *non* do not feature prominently in this work. (Listen to Trần Minh Đức play "Đào ngũ cung" in **Track 10**.)

In contrast, "Nam xuân" and "Nam ai" feature a greater variety of pitch content. The main pitches of "Nam xuân" align with the theoretical scale indicated in Figure 4.9; however, the work features frequent *nhấn* to pitches *xự* and *cống*—pitches seemingly from the Bắc mode and outside the pentatonic scale in Figure 4.9. Figure 4.11 depicts the "Nam xuân" scale and associated ornamentation. (Listen to **Track 14** and **15**.) The pitches in square brackets (*xự* and *cống*) are not featured as prominently in performances of the work, but they are also not absent. Performers also bend frequently in this work from *hò* to *xự*, *xang* to *cống* and *xê* to *cống* (see Figure 4.12); the pitch to which the performer bends is given a *nhấn rung* (bending with vibrato). In addition, *phan* (Fa) is left unornamented.

As in "Đào ngũ cung," *già* and *non* do not appear in the versions I have examined; indeed, Nguyễn Vĩnh Bảo did not advise incorporating either adjustment into my performance of the work. There is some evidence to suggest, however, that some other musicians incorporate these augmentations into their practice. In Vũ Nhật Thăng's analysis of this work, he suggests that *xang* is performed over twenty-five cents higher than the *xang* found in a Bắc mode work, and *cống* is performed nearly twenty cents lower (1998, 97–101). These differences simply may be differences in style, or they may indicate the use of *già* and *non*.

"Nam ai" features additional complexity. John Paul Trainor identifies the following pitches: *hò xừ xang xê phan* (1977, 82). Unlike the other works in the Nam mode, performances of "Nam ai" often feature *xang già* with a *rung* ornament (see also Vũ Nhật Thăng 1998, 102). Vũ Nhật Thăng also identifies significant lowering of *cống*, lending additional credence to the existence of *cống non*. It also is worth mentioning the occasional use of *phan* with a *rung* ornament in "Nam ai."

The fourth mode is *Oán*, which receives less consideration in this book, so I do not examine it as thoroughly. Trân Văn Khê originally categorized *điệu Oán* as a variant of the Nam mode (1962, 244). Kiều Tấn (2002, 285–86) and Võ Trường Kỳ (2014, 95–97) do as well. Indeed, all classify the Oán pieces as sub-modes or nuances (*hơi* means literally, "air," or sometimes "scent") of the Nam mode.[47] *Hơi*, perhaps more than *điệu*, has a convoluted definition. As I have come to understand the concept, hơi involves an augmentation of điệu toward alternate evocations that do not overturn the overarching concept of the điệu associated with that piece. In other words, hơi adds and does not subtract from the production of the piece.[48] From this standpoint, Oán mode works depict a more severe sadness than that depicted in the Nam mode. (Listen to **Track 11**, an excerpt of "Tứ đại oán," a tune that Nguyễn Vĩnh Bảo prepared to help me learn on the đàn tranh.)

Many scholars and musicians today promote the Oán mode as a fully fledged mode not only because it contains some of the most emotionally powerful works in southern Vietnam but also because the Oán mode is not found in name outside of southern Vietnam. The works have their origin in southern Vietnamese folk songs of the eighteenth century and therefore have a different identity than the Bắc and Nam pieces (Cannon 2016, 162n11). Musicians and audiences consider these works as "tragic" due to the theorized influence of music of the Chăm people (Trương Bỉnh Tòng 1996, 29; 39; Lư Nhất Vũ and Lê Giang 1981, 110–11; 1983, 398–99). Contemporary interpretations add that this residual sadness emerged from the disintegration of the kingdom of Champa during the Nam tiến and the loss of the nation (Cannon 2016, 162n11).

Trương Bỉnh Tòng proposes, somewhat controversially, that Oán blends elements from the Bắc and Nam modes but remains more flexible and unstable. This description points to the play undertaken by the musicians with whom he has performed and studied.

The structure of the Oán modal system is a combination between certain rigid aspects of the Bắc mode and the flexible aspects of the Nam mode. And this combination is not only in every section and every phrase of music, but is ingrained in the pitches, always with different rigid and flexible elements. For example, with the pitch *cống*, when it is heard as *cống non* [at one point], when it returns, it is *cống già*. And all pitches generally, sometimes they are ornamented, sometimes not. (1996, 47)

The hybrid construct yields seven pitches: it uses the "variable pitches" of *xự* and *cống* of the Bắc mode, and the variable pitches of *xừ* and *phan* of the Nam mode (51). He advocates that the Oán scale truly is heptatonic, rather than pentatonic with some additional notes that occasionally make an appearance. The mode also includes two additional "sounds" (*thanh*) over the seven sounds produced by the heptatonic scale, as certain pitches have slightly sharpened and flattened gradations (48). Many musicians would contest the point that *cống non* and *cống già* exist in a single work—indeed, I have heard no such performance— so this claim may be an exaggeration in an attempt to conclusively depict the Oán mode as unique.[49] Trương Bình Tòng's theory therefore may not be accepted by all musicians, but as a theory, it indicates the importance of playing with pitch content in southern Vietnamese traditional music performance.

CONCLUSION

Đờn ca tài tử is not a genre of music of the ethnomusicological canon, therefore requiring an extended description and synthesis of basic music theory. Although admittedly dense at times, the descriptions in this chapter offer insight into the performance practices and musical materials deployed by musicians. Musicians have a great deal of musical tools at their disposal to follow their inspiration. Whether embodying nonaction and spontaneity or seeking to motivate audiences, they use particular modes and tunes to create effective performance settings. Performance practice, and therefore the tradition as a whole, is not fixed, and significant disagreements exist concerning "authentic" practice. This flexibility enables musicians to gauge the performance environment, select from the practice they have studied, and create meaningful sound.

I have drawn on a number of voices in this chapter, but the voice of the musician who started this chapter looms large. Nguyễn Vĩnh Bảo donated a great deal of his time and energy to me, starting in 2007, and fundamentally shaped my understanding of southern Vietnamese music practice. He did the same for musicians in the Mekong Delta, Ho Chi Minh City, and among Vietnamese diaspora communities around the world. As suggested with the opening anecdote, he advocated that past practice remains viable because it is malleable. Until his passing, he continually worked to expand the space of performance to encompass not simply the room, neighborhood, or concert hall but also the globe. The concomitant music that intertwines inadvertent and inspired sounds embraces not only the hammer and the Walkman but also the internet, including email, online forums, Facebook, and YouTube. In making a larger space of performance and meaning-making, he taught a group of disparate individuals to listen in similar ways and reflect on developments in Vietnam to which they also belonged.

The next chapter evaluates how musicians move from inspiration to performance. I investigate the metaphors they use to externalize and auralize sounds based on internal sentiments. These metaphors have long lives in southern Vietnam and related antecedent genres of music, and they provide greater insight into the processes of creation practiced by musicians of đờn ca tài tử.

FIVE

Playing with Metaphor

Bông xanh bông trắng rồi lại vàng bông ơ rường ơ.
Bông lê cho bằng bông lựu ơ rường ơ.
Là đố í a đố nàng.
Bông rồi lại mấy bông,
Là đố í a đố nàng.

The green leaf and white cotton ball have yellowed by the house, oh yes!
The same as the pears and pomegranates by the house, oh yes!
La la la, make a guess, mademoiselle.
How many flowers are there?
Make a guess, mademoiselle.

Visual images abound in the spoken Vietnamese language and in Vietnamese song lyrics. The descriptions of objects in nature, for example, articulate understandings of beauty, virtue, and morals. They are metaphors, and their appearance offers powerful insight into the production of meaning. The opening stanza of the southern Vietnamese folk song "Lý cây bông" ("Song of the Cotton Flower") reproduced here, for example, offers two metaphors: the flower and the house (or the frame). The cotton flower is the clearest and most immediate metaphor. The green leaf and white fluff of cotton depicted in the lyrics capture beauty and the passage of time. That cotton plants turn yellow as they age indicates a readiness for harvest; indeed, the Vietnamese word for yellow, *vàng*, also means "gold," or "golden," suggesting that the plant has its greatest value at this stage. The lyrics further invite listeners to compare the cotton plant to other plants that produce fruit. In particular, the text connects the yellow leaf and ripe fruit, when the fruit is at its most delicious. The third and fifth lines then introduce a woman (*nàng*) into the scene and ask her to estimate the number of beautiful flowers around the house.[1] The term *nàng* brings to mind any number of fictionalized young women in Vietnamese literature, perhaps most especially Kiều, the protagonist of the Vietnamese epic poem *Truyện Kiều* (*The Tale of Kiều*), by Nguyễn Du. In the metaphorical connection between nàng and the flower, beauty takes on a living and sustaining quality. The lyrics suggest, then, that the beauty of cotton enables a vibrant future in southern Vietnam, since the region produces much of the world's cotton clothing and therefore requires the cotton plant to support the economy.

The second metaphor present here is the support structure, which provides a kind of backdrop for the beauty of the scene. The term *rường* means "frame"; a *nhà rường* is a kind of one-story traditional home found in central and southern Vietnam. Some versions of this house are open-aired, providing a frame for shelter, but also open spaces to fill with decorative objects. Even though it sits in the background, the frame plays an important role in steering the production of meaning: it provides space for expression; without it, the flowers may not be noticed. Beautiful flowers in an open field are undifferentiated; flowers surrounding a living space for humans provide a pretty view for inhabitants. The rường in the lyrics therefore structures the listener's engagement with the beauty of the cotton flowers and ripe fruit.

The performance of these lyrics carries their potency and makes them applicable to everyday circumstances. As one of southern Vietnam's most treasured folk songs, children learn it at a relatively young age in school, and musicians perform it on national television, in provincial festivals, and in classrooms. I first learned the song in Tiếng Hát Quê Hương rehearsals in 2008 when Phạm Thúy Hoan worked to cultivate the seed of tradition in participants. We sat in close quarters, sharing notation and lyrics, and singing. Cô Thúy Hoan occasionally stopped us, encouraging us to shape the lyrical content a bit more elegantly around the contours of the melody. Elegant performances, she advocated, are more entertaining and spur the development of the seed of tradition. Our jobs were to sow the seed among audiences and cultivate the flower of tradition in ourselves. I also performed it on Vietnamese national television (Đài truyền hình Việt Nam) in January 2009 for the opening segment of an episode of the English-language talk show program *Talk Vietnam*. I produced a fairly basic version of the tune on the đàn tranh alongside Nguyễn Thuyết Phong on the đàn kìm and Khương Cường on the tiêu. As a production of the VTV4 station, it appeared both on domestic Vietnamese and on satellite television around the world over the Tết Lunar New Year holiday at the end of that month. The program presented the power of a Vietnamese folk song to bring together a foreigner, an overseas Vietnamese, and a Vietnamese national through music.

The metaphor builds camaraderie and new meaning. My third performance of "Lý cây bông" occurred in Cần Thơ during the same evening with Lê Đình Bích, Trần Minh Đức, and Phước described in Chapter 3. Toward the end of the evening of music, camaraderie, and laughter, Lê Đình Bích slapped me on the back and gave me the honor of selecting the final song of the evening. We had consumed nearly a case of *Sài Gòn đỏ* (Saigon red) beer and were happily inebriated by this point. I therefore wanted to select a tune that we could all recall in that state and that had meaning for everyone in attendance. When we happily sang "Lý cây bông," we aimed to create what Trần Minh Đức calls *xuất thần* (ecstatic state), where music emerges spontaneously from the conditions of performance, akin to the flowers emergent around the house described at the beginning of this chapter. Active collaboration through structures of mode and improvisation of melody suggest that we all have adequate knowledge to generate these beautiful melodies together given the right conditions.

Metaphors connect different realms of experience, thought, and inquiry, which steer musicians toward particular performance practices over others. "Multiple musical metaphors," Timothy Rice argues, "guide action and thought in individual lives, in society and through time" (2001, 22). As musicians play and sing, they draw connections between sound and language or nature. These metaphors "make claims about the nature of music and . . . bring music closer to other domains of human experience" (2003, 159). This enables musicians to attach sound to particular ideological frameworks so listeners better interpret the sound produced (159).

I describe a number of metaphors separately in this chapter; when they interact together, they generate a dynamic environment of performance. In đờn ca tài tử, a metaphor of a frame works alongside metaphors of a flower, leaves, and branches to guide four creative (and related) processes: thinking about the inner experiences of the musician to make them explicit in performance; connecting musical experience in performance to everyday life in some way; engaging with and structuring musical knowledge for later use; and shaping appropriate inspiration in the performance context from the sounds and individuals around them. The philosophical worldview presented in Chapter 3 permeates these processes: musicians follow the guiding principles of nonaction and spontaneity as they make particular performance choices.

This chapter begins with a brief synopsis of how ethnomusicologists have engaged with the metaphor. I focus in particular on metaphors found in other Southeast Asian musical traditions, as there are some areas of overlap with southern Vietnamese music (if only by coincidence). I examine the "frame" and "flower" metaphors as đờn ca tài tử musicians described them to me, and analyze how the metaphors interact in performance contexts. I then examine how their interaction leads to certain performance goals, especially the creation of xuất thần (ecstasy), which musicians describe as a feeling of being both overpowered and empowered by knowledge and the experience of camaraderie among performers.

I advise some caution before I start this discussion. Metaphors are valuable and imaginative, but they are not rules of performance and should not be rigidly applied. As Nguyễn Vĩnh Bảo once remarked to me, "When I play for me, I do not observe the rules strictly. Because if you apply the rules strictly, you are not you."[2] Effective metaphors guide and should not prescribe. They work across disparate realms of human existence, so the rules of one realm never completely align with another. They do not fully embody the rules of particular philosophies or ideologies, and one should not attempt to pigeonhole them. Metaphors also carry risks: they leak, generate misunderstanding, and distract. They may ultimately help musicians and ethnomusicologists "understand our world" (Rice 2001, 24; see also Perlman 2004, 30), but we must try not to invoke them flippantly.

METAPHOR IN ETHNOMUSICOLOGY

Metaphors allow musicians and the ethnomusicologists who interact with them to ascribe linguistic meaning to sonic performance. Metaphors can be powerful in this regard. Ebuka Elias Igwebuike (2017) pinpoints ways that musicians of a kind of Igbo folk music called *Egwu Ekpili* use metaphor to join together different realms of everyday life and "creat[e] new conceptual realities" (68) in southeastern Nigeria. A study of these metaphors in performance ultimately reveals identity and ideological frameworks within which a community operates (63). Often the metaphors serve as poignant social commentary and critique well-known social figures in humorous ways, as Raphael Chijioke Njoku (2020, 188) also indicates in another Igbo performance context. This kind of humor is "encoded" and subject to interpretation, thereby giving users a degree of protection (133). Metaphor rewrites power—who has it; who can use it—and protects methods of expression for social contexts.[3]

The metaphor offers a way of understanding the agency of creativity deployed across different domains and performance events. Samuel A. Floyd Jr. (1995) proposes what he calls an "orational metaphor" for understanding Black music-making in the United States. That is, he identifies "rhetorical turn" or a kind of Signifyin(g) that enables expression through musical form in Black music (1995, 236–37); indeed, as mentioned in Chapter 2, Signifyin(g) enables experimentation with power (Gates 1988). Floyd offers ways of hearing the voices suggested through Signifyin(g), enabling musicians to compare across musical works and understand the power of Black musical expression as emergent from a corpus of music, rather than single examples (1995, 247).

In various works on traditional music genres of Asia, ethnomusicologists have written about methods of expression enabled through "flower" and "frame" metaphors similar to those found in đờn ca tài tử. In *Jiangnan sizhu* of southern China, musicians "add . . . flowers" or *hua* (花) to "ornament" melody (Witzleben 1995, 61; see also Thrasher 2008, 131). Balinese *gamelan gong kebyar* performers also invoke a flower metaphor to describe embellishment of the basic structural melody, called the *pokok* (trunk). Colin McPhee, in his characteristic language in *A House in Bali*, writes:

> Music, I learned, had its "stem," its primary tones (which it was possible to preserve in writing) from which the melody expanded and developed as a plant grows out of a seed. The glittering ornamental parts which gave the music its shimmer, its sensuous charm, its movement—these were the "flower parts," the "blossoms," the *kantilan* . . . It was in these flower parts . . . that a teacher showed his inventiveness, a gamelan its ability. The style was always changing, although the stem-tones remained the same. (1946, 41)[4]

The visual metaphor of expanding from the "trunk" as a seed sprouts serves as a lesson in aesthetics, depicts appropriate "flower parts" as natural, and serves as a useful heuristic device for musicians.

The metaphor generates knowledge about sound by offering insight into internalized performance processes. Marc Perlman's well-known example of the "unplayed melody" in central Javanese *karawitan* highlights the ways that musicians use terminology to describe how they perform. Javanese musicians might learn the *balungan* or skeletal melody played by the *saron* instrument as a structural guide of a specific work, but they do not necessarily follow that melody when improvising pitch content on one of the embellishing instruments. They instead follow the "unplayed melody," a melody learned over the course of the musician's lifetime engagement with the work (2004, 1). To make this implicit knowledge of melody explicit and heuristic, then, musicians draw on "creative thinking" to devise effective language to describe their knowledge (27). They simultaneously reach a new understanding of their own practice and articulate knowledge of the tradition with this metaphor when creative thinking spurs the "engines of creativity" in performance (28). Practice therefore leads to questioning and creative thinking; thinking makes a metaphor to structure knowledge; structured knowledge through metaphor then starts the engines of continued practice. Creativity in the central Javanese context therefore constitutes not only the "creative thinking" undertaken to apply language to process but also the process of applying this thinking in performance to generate melody.

Other performance traditions in Southeast Asia offer other metaphors to describe separate parts of the creative process. In Deborah Wong's work on Lao *maulam* (singer) Khamvong Insixiengmai, two different metaphors, *lam* (passageway) and *taeng* (beautify, adorn), "represent two abilities, two skills, two kinds of training and two ways to create performances" (2004, 26). Musicians view *lam* as a kind of "course or passageway" from the *maulam* to an audience; it involves the performance of poetry while accompanied by a *khaen* (mouth organ) player (26–27).[5] *Taeng* designates practice or composition when a *maulam* considers how to craft *lam* for a performance; the term also designates a kind of embellishment to "fix up" or "beautify" something that already exists (29).

> Seen as composition, *taeng* takes on a special shade of meaning found in many Southeast Asian notions of creativity. Rather than make something utterly new and original (the kind of creativity romanticized and valorized in the West), to *taeng* a song or poem implies adding material on to preexisting material in such a way that the configuration is new but built on something old. (29)

Musicians therefore view their work as extensions of what previously emerged, and as moving in directions amicable and acceptable to contemporary audiences. Working together, both Lao metaphors acknowledge the experience of the individual *maulam* and recognize the role of the audience in accepting (or rejecting) the beauty produced in live performance.

In both of the Javanese and Lao examples, musicians conceive of their practice as part of a wider field of social and linguistic understanding. Musicians use metaphors to connect what is felt or experienced in music with larger societal discourse of thinking or beauty (Perlman 2004, 24; Wong 2001, 77–78). Other ethnomusicologists have invoked metaphor in similar ways. The "cross-domain mapping" of carpet making and Azeri *mugham* described by Inna Naroditskaya (2005) shows how metaphor connects different realms of everyday life. Musicians and carpet makers do not simply inspire each other with their output: they can view a carpet as akin to "reading" music, and hear music as akin to "listening" to a carpet (46–47). Thinking about music performance as akin to making a carpet strengthens understandings of both domains.

The metaphors present in these examples constitute feedback loops between musical knowledge, social engagement, and music performance. These feedback loops build, akin to the "engines of creativity" metaphor suggested by Perlman. For improvised music, this building happens both within a performance and between performances. Ingrid Monson offers that thinking about musical improvisation in jazz serves as a metaphor of conversation. Studying these musical conversations elucidates the "structural affinities" that emerge in that performance—or the sense of camaraderie I also describe in performances of "Lý cây bông"—and the "accumulation and communication of cultural feeling" over time (Monson 1996, 77).

Musicians of southern Vietnamese traditional music engage with similar metaphors to express and describe various elements of musical creativity. Huỳnh Khải uses the metaphor of the "way" to guide his performances; Nguyễn Vĩnh Bảo and Trần Minh Đức use the metaphor of the announcement (*rao*) to designate how musicians start a musical exchange by establishing a mode in an improvised prelude. They think creatively about inner experience and make this experience explicit to audiences, other musicians, and students; connect experience in performance spaces with those in everyday life; structure the musician's engagement with knowledge; and generate inspiration in performance toward producing particular sounds over others. Most importantly, these metaphors extend local understandings of creation from the Daoist belief systems described in the previous chapters to generate sustainable đờn ca tài tử.

METAPHORS OF CREATIVITY
IN SOUTHERN VIETNAMESE MUSIC

When musicians of đờn ca tài tử describe creation, they use the verb *sáng tạo* or use the nouns *sức sáng tạo*, which designates the power or strength of creation, or *sự sáng tạo*, which means "creation" or "creativity," depending on its context. In an article that describes widely held understandings of creativity by đờn ca tài tử musicians, the late ethnomusicologist Trần Văn Khê (2013) argues that he "best internalizes *sự sáng tạo* in *đờn ca tài tử*" with the phrase "học chân phương mà đờn hoa lá" (literally, "study the simple and plain but play the flowers and leaves").[6] The reference to internalization suggests a metaphorical conceptualization of performance process. Creativity requires understanding the simple and plain (*chân phương*) of music in order to improvise just as flowers and leaves (*hoa lá*) grow on a tree. Trần Văn Khê continues, connecting this concept to a generalized Vietnamese philosophy of life, whereby one follows a particular moral truth but allows for change.

Musicians use particular language to describe an internalized and learned process of both thinking about and creating music in performance. Musicians express creativity, then, through the interaction of metaphors chân phương and hoa lá or, more often, a related term *hoa lá cành* (literally, "flowers, leaves, and branches"). Chân phương provides the structure or frame of the performance—the plain or rustic essence replicated in one performance to another—and hoa lá cành provides the embellishment required for beautiful performances. These terms are not specific to đờn ca tài tử; indeed, Thầy Phước Cường of the Bửu Sơn Temple in District 5 of Ho Chi Minh City described the importance of a musician in southern Vietnamese music first understanding chân phương and then generating hoa lá cành once one has developed an appropriate familiarity with chân phương.[7] The similarity to the lyrical content of "Lý cây bông" described at the start of this chapter is not a coincidence; much of traditional music involves generating beauty within a frame. Like the cotton flowers, however, this beauty is not necessarily everlasting, as described in more detail in the following section.

Chân phương Frame

Chân phương implies foundation and structure. Dictionaries define the concept as "clear," "neat," and "plain"; more broadly, the word can mean "rustic" (Ban biên soạn chuyên từ điển 2003).[8] Some works of literature suggest meanings of "basic" or even "simple"; taken with "rustic," the concept might suggest rurality where the foundation of the Vietnamese identity can be found. A remembrance of the late singer Bạch Huệ suggests the concept of "rules" to indicate the structure upon which she built effective performances (Thanh Hiệp 2014).[9] Nguyễn T. Phong translates the concept as "square" (1998, 465), evoking an image of a closed entity with a clearly defined structure. Võ Trường Kỳ suggests a definition of model or exemplar (*mực thước*) (2014, 42). Lastly, Lê Tuấn Hùng offers "standard" but also makes a connection to "frame" (1998, 56; see also Norton

2009, 135). Although not a literal translation, I favor the description of a rustic frame for chân phương, as it captures the foundational nature of the term and its connection to past practice in music.

Musicians use the frame to teach audiences about certain musical routines that make the performance effective, and they prepare audiences for how to understand what is to follow.[10] For Gregory Bateson, the "frame is involved in the evaluation of the messages it contains, or the frame merely assists the mind in understanding the contained messages by reminding the thinker that these messages are mutually relevant and the messages outside the frame may be ignored" ([1972] 2000, 188). The wooden house in "Lý cây bông," for instance, focuses the listener's attention on the flowers in view and encourages a particular kind of engagement with them. Certain structures of music play similar roles. Thomas Turino's introductory text to ethnomusicology encourages undergraduate students to view the frame as a structure into which one steps to "interpret . . . a particular slice of experience" (2008, 14). The "slice" metaphor is effective for undergraduate teaching, but really is too limiting. Steven Feld (1984, 12) instead points to the simultaneous open and closed nature of the frame, where musicians let meaning in and out. He suggests movement between the open and closed parameters as the musician or audience member focuses on the meaning of very specific components of the frame and imagines new possibilities through engaging with the frame. This negotiation between open and closed elements generates and maintains connections with musicians inside and experiences outside the performance space. In other words, the frame exerts some control on what musicians allow into performance and what is kept out of improvisation. This is ultimately vital for supporting creativity.

Musicians forward a rich discourse of the fundamentals as part of chân phương. Thầy Phước Cường used *chân phương* to describe the basic rhythmic material supporting nhạc lễ (ceremonial music), which serves to connect older and new performance practices.[11] As my lessons with Trần Minh Đức started, he argued that musicians must play what he termed "đờn bản," meaning to "play the basics"; another friend suggested it meant playing the "whole original steps." The term therefore refers to both *căn bản* (the basics) and *bản nhạc*, meaning the song being performed.[12] The musicians who properly play the basics therefore understand how to effectively generate a piece of music. He contrasted đờn bản with "đờn ngón," meaning to "play by the fingers," which designates a simple imitation of a teacher's work without any thought to the work's structure.[13]

A fundamental frame in đờn ca tài tử is the basic structural melody, or *lòng bản*, associated with each đờn ca tài tử tune (Trần Văn Khê 2013). Barley Norton (2009, 135) and Võ Trường Kỳ (2014, 40) define *lòng bản* as the "guts of the piece" (*ruột bài*). Võ Trường Kỳ offers that "lổng bản" (with the use of *ô* rather than *o* as the first vowel) is a more accurate term to describe the musical frame of the work. Meaning "cage," "the word *lổng* has the meaning of a container with which one frames the fixed limits of the melodic and rhythmic elements of the musical phrase" (2014, 40). Both *lòng bản* and *lổng bản* pinpoint the core identity of the work as located in this basic structural melody; I adopt *lòng bản* given its more prevalent usage in Vietnam today. Vietnamese musicians use *lòng bản* to carry the identity of the tune; this includes not only a recognizable melodic contour and beat structure but also evocations of implied lyrical content.

The lòng bản refers to the fundamentals necessary to craft coherent melody in performance; it also helps musicians identify works. Like Feld's description of the Kaluli "lift up over sounding" metaphor, the lòng bản also encourages fellow musicians and listeners to "sense" sound in cohesive ways (1988, 78). The lòng bản consists of various pitches within a metrical structure that should be sounded to identify the tune played. These melodic points oftentimes align with *nhịp* (beats) or locations of metrical importance within a phrase. Musicians improvise between these points, often by listening to what others play and extending the motives crafted. Heterophony emerges from this performance context.

Students learn a lòng bản through performance with their teacher, and not every version is the same. "In Sài Gòn, we have a different lòng bản than the lòng bản in Mỹ Tho, Bạc Liêu, or Bình Dương," Huỳnh Khải argued. "Each one has its own personality, its own personal character."[14] Musicians from these different regions still may play together, as the basic modal characteristics remain the same. In Huỳnh Khải's performances, he "preserves the richness . . . and the character of the" work; however, he still maintains certain modal and scalar connections between different versions of the works. "I unify the nuance [*hơi*] and the mode [*điệu*] so the lòng bản has those things" even if he adopts a slightly different lòng bản played with another musician.[15] Musicians prize their lòng bản's locality, but not at the expense of potential camaraderie.

Musicians use the implicit guiding framework of the lòng bản to produce melody. Like the Javanese "unplayed melody," however, the lòng bản is not easy to extract from the melody produced.[16] Practicing musicians rarely abstract the lòng bản; notable exceptions are the game shows described in Chapter 8 that require contestants to perform lòng bản as proof of their competence. When I interviewed Huỳnh Khải about this concept, he demonstrated the lòng bản of "Nam ai" on the đàn kìm as a melody of twelve beats. (Listen to **Track 12.**) He then demonstrated his *kiểu*, meaning "pattern" or "example," in which he added embellishment, but it had fourteen beats, which aligns with the first phrase of other versions of "Nam ai" of which I am aware. In crafting something abstract for my benefit, he skipped two beats (indicated by the absence of beats three and four in the fourth notated measure of Figure 5.1). The lòng bản still serves a pedagogical purpose for his students and me, as it provides the general trajectory of melody and appropriate beat structure, including the main beats heard articulated with the *song lang*, as indicated with a + symbol). His *kiểu* gives the work a clearer and more interesting sense of direction, and even included *song thinh* (literally, "same sound," to be described later in this chapter) embellishment, as indicated by the parenthesis around particular pitches. He still maintains the structure of the hơi and điệu, a point he made repeatedly in my interview with him.

Musicians debate the fundamentals, suggesting that the rules of metaphor are not fixed. Lòng bản are not standardized, so musicians debate those pitches that should be included in the lòng bản to make it "more interesting." In December 2014, I attended several tapings of a đờn ca tài tử weekly competition at the Voice of the People Radio Station in Ho Chi Minh City (Đài Tiếng nói Nhân dân Thành phố Hồ Chí Minh, or VOH) that was simultaneously broadcast on a local television station and the radio. During the two-hour competition, a series of đờn ca tài tử groups performed for an audience and three judges; at the end, the three judges gave their feedback (*nhận xét*) on the musicality of the performances. One judge approvingly noted that the lòng bản crafted by one player was very appropriate for đờn ca tài tử. The judge then turned to another player in the group and noted that one pitch used in the melody should be replaced by its neighboring pitch; such a choice would make the piece "more interesting."[17]

Although abstracting the lòng bản is a theoretical exercise and open to interpretation, hearing the strategic points of the lòng bản enables the novice student in particular to understand the core identity of the work around which embellishment ultimately is crafted. This is one reason, perhaps, why the judge offered the commentary concerning an interesting versus a less interesting pitch selection. The identity of the tune was at stake, which ultimately impacted the way that the embellishment emerged in performance.

The structural logic that helps musicians play and audience members recognize the tune emerges from an evaluation of the theoretical lòng bản. Figure

FIGURE 5.1 First phrase of "Nam ai" as played by Huỳnh Khải (August 14, 2013)

FIGURE 5.2 Outline of the first two phrases of "Lưu thủy trường"

5.2 presents a lòng bản of the first two phrases of the Bắc mode tune "Lưu thủy trường."[18] The lòng bản clearly indicates the Bắc mode and beat structure. The initial preponderance of hò (D) with the inclusion of its paired note *xang* (G) in measure four helps establish the Bắc mode; the gradual introduction of other pitches in later measures solidifies the mode. The beat structure emerges from patterns of silence and sound. The first *nhip* of the work falls in the third notated measure. Musicians articulate this beat with the *song lang* wooden clapper and then follow this with embellishment on the notated *xang* and a return to the tonic hò articulated with another beat of the *song lang*. Taken together, the musician perceives the general trajectory of the tune: this work features a sense of gradual addition of pitch content and diminution. If a musician were to sing the pitches from the notation, listeners would recognize it.

Hoa lá cành Embellishment

Musicians embellish the lòng bản to craft pleasing and memorable melodies. For Trần Văn Khê, "instrumentalists do not need to copy the lòng bản but should attach hoa lá [flowers and leaves] to produce a sound that is lilting and romantic, in any way that does not detract from the tune . . . [I]t is not correct to simply play the lòng bản" (2013). Nguyễn Vĩnh Bảo and other musicians use hoa lá cành (flowers, leaves, and branches) to describe this embellishment. I hereafter refer to hoa lá cành, since it has a wider presence in Vietnamese public life to designate flower arranging, visual beauty, and even romantic feelings.

Invoking flowers in metaphors of music practice connects the production of sound with the visual realm, philosophy, and religious traditions. Hoa lá cành implies spontaneous musical creation and natural (*tự nhiên*) production. One nonmusician friend even suggested to me that the metaphor was fitting for southern Vietnam since "southern people are closer to nature."[19] This poignant characterization connects the land and musical practice to an awareness of the philosophical worldview described in Chapter 3.

Hoa lá cành denotes a specific kind of creativity that respects and extends specific melodic rubrics considered central to the rendering of the tune. Musicians draw on their understanding of the lòng bản and knowledge of appropriate performance practice to create a beautiful, embellished melody.[20] These extensions occur through spontaneous improvisation, or *đàn tùy hứng*. Musicians express what they feel in the moment, drawing, for example, from the instrument played; the individuals in the room; understandings of the "characters" of one's fellow musicians heard through their technique and musical embellishments; and even inadvertent sounds that occur in the performance space.

Appropriate hoa lá cành, according to Nguyễn Vĩnh Bảo, may be tasted, smelled, and full of color.[21] The musician might play with rhythm and anticipate the placement of beats and certain notes to generate interest between the notes of the structural melody. During a lesson in 2009, Thầy Vĩnh Bảo recorded a version of "Tây thi" on the đàn kìm and then played over the recording to demonstrate embellishment techniques—he included neighbor notes, passing tones, anticipated beats, and subdivided the beat, playing two or four times as fast as the first recording. (Listen to **Track 13**.) "This is an elaborate version," he indicated. "It depends on the situation, depends on the audience, depends on the partner."[22] In the 1972 recording of "Lưu thủy trương" performed with Hồng Tấn Phát for the label Ocora, he maintains certain structural melodic moments of lòng bản, but fills the space between these notes with glissandi. This use of the đàn tranh technique of running one's fingers up and down the strings of the instruments mimics the sounds of water flowing and serves as a direct aural reference to nature. He also draws on the clear and lasting resonance of the đàn tranh as a source of inspiration for his playing.

Other musicians might use specifically named techniques, such as *chuyền*. Chuyền is a technique where southern Vietnamese musicians subdivide the beat in an effort to provide directionality toward a particular strategic pitch.[23] Musicians only use it in Bắc and Hạ mode pieces, since the embellishment of the lòng bản expresses happiness.[24] This technique is found in ensemble performances

FIGURE 5.3 Example of *chuyển* in "Lưu thủy trường"

FIGURE 5.4 Nguyễn Vĩnh Bảo's đàn tranh template of "Lưu thủy trường"

as well, but musicians also use it strategically to create momentum or generate anticipation for the final note of a phrase or section. Nguyễn Vĩnh Bảo taught me the name of the technique, but Trần Minh Đức often used it more frequently. Figure 5.3 indicates the way that a musician might expand a version of a melody by adding neighbor notes and passing notes, as well as adding glissandi on the đàn tranh, that lead to a main structural pitch of the piece—here designated by the penultimate G.

The type of embellishment produced depends on the instrument played.[25] In addition to the use of glissandi described here, musicians of the đàn tranh often produce more stepwise melodies with frequent leaps up or down the octave, as indicated in a version of "Lưu thủy trường" produced by Nguyễn Vĩnh Bảo on the đàn tranh in Figure 5.4. After the glissando, he plucks the *hò* (D) string with the index finger, then the *liu* (D) string and *cống* (B) string next to it with the thumb, the *hò* with the index finger, and the final *liu* of the first full measure with the thumb. As the embellishment continues, Nguyễn Vĩnh Bảo continues the frequent octave displacements and begins to build a sense of an arc: in measure five, for example, *cống* emerges from the texture as a destination pitch rather than a passing tone as in measure three; measures five and six introduce *xê* (A);

and measure seven features *xự* (E). When the lòng bản indicates a greater sense of motion during the last two beats of the *song lang* (see Figure 5.2), he uses the chuyển technique to generate melodic content and emphasize the sense of motion to the end of the phrase.

Other instruments also build the lòng bản like this, adding idiosyncratic embellishment as the work progresses, either as a solo or in an ensemble. Players of the electric guitar, for instance, contrast stepwise motion with melismatic passages to demonstrate the range of sounds possible on the instrument. These musicians therefore embellish through timbre alongside melody and rhythm. In a recording of "Xàng xê" by ghi ta phím lõm virtuoso *Nghệ sĩ ưu tú* (Artist of Merit) Nguyễn Thiện Vũ (n.d.), he descends part of the way through the work into the lower register of the instrument. As he subdivides the beat, he adopts the style of a rock guitarist strumming multiple strings of the guitar with his pick to create distortion while presenting the last few notes of the phrase. (A perusal through the copious number of ghi ta phím lõm videos on YouTube indicates that the timbral distinction and reference to an external genre is common.) Although perhaps simply an interesting and offhand effect at the end of the phrase, it serves as a poignant nod to other methods of playing the guitar and even a suggestion of methods of incorporating new techniques into generating hoa lá cành in performance.

Another method used to embellish a melody is called *song thinh* (also called *song thanh*, or "same sound"). Performers of both the đàn kìm and đàn sến use song thinh, and it is one of the more recognized playing techniques of the đàn sến in particular. Players place the index finger of the left hand between two frets and press down—a movement indicated by the vertical dashed line in Figure 5.5. They begin the song thinh technique by plucking the lowest note of the motif with the right hand—the note created with the index finger on the lowest string (string 3) and indicated as *hò* in Figure 5.5—and then use the third, fourth, and fifth fingers of the left hand to produce other pitches.

One of the most common song thinh involves producing pitches one octave above the tuned pitches of the strings, as indicated in Figure 5.5. The *xang* created using strings two and three are in unison, but the timbre of the two pitches is different, as performers, stretching their fingers, do not place as much pressure on the third string with the fifth finger. The xang on string three appears thinner or airier, so its sonority is not as resonant, but the difference enables the performer to reiterate the pitch in a more interesting way than simply applying tremolo.

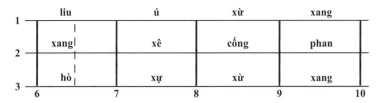

FIGURE 5.5 Pitches at the sixth to tenth fret of the three-stringed đàn sến for strings 1, 2, and 3

Performers of the two-stringed đàn sến and the two-stringed đàn kìm incorporate song thinh for some limited melodic elaboration. On the three-stringed đàn sến, however, the musician produces one set of pitch equivalents — *xang* on strings two and three — and five octave displacements without needing to move the position of the hand since strings one and three are separated by an octave and *xang* is sounded on strings one and two. Players therefore use song thinh frequently as pitches over one and a half octaves are available in a single hand position; in addition, it allows performers to easily perform rapid sequences of notes. At its most basic, however, musicians use the technique to produce the same pitch in the same tessitura with different timbral qualities. (Uses of song thinh appear in my transcriptions as notes with parentheses placed around them.)

The Danger of Flowers

Spontaneity should not be unbridled, however, as it is indeed possible to improvise hoa lá cành in inappropriate ways. (To extend the metaphor, one should not improvise an orchid flower for a cherry tree.) In my zither lessons with Nguyễn Vĩnh Bảo, we spent considerable time perfecting the *nhấn* (bending) ornaments as these endow performances with *tâm hồn* (soul). He noted in one lesson that one can go too far when bending a pitch on the zither to the point that the song loses its identity. He turned to his computer to find a well-known recording of an improvised prelude preceding a performance of "Nam xuân." The performance featured so many glides in succession that the work "gave the listener the impression that he plays Indian music!"[26]

Flowers, too, may inspire through their beauty, but they also are dangerous. (The rose has thorns; the oleander is toxic if ingested.) According to Chapter 38 of Laozi's text, flowers have ulterior motives and therefore must be approached carefully.

Those who are the first to know have the flowers (appearance) of Tao but are the beginning of ignorance. For this reason the great man dwells in the thick (substantial), and does not rest with the thin (superficial). He dwells in the fruit (reality), and does not rest with the flower (appearance). (Chan 1963, 158)

Flowers are superficial; focusing on the superficial prevents the attainment of knowledge and wisdom. Those who grow flowers seek to distract from truth. Those who do have ulterior motives operate with "foreknowledge" or attempt to steer the consequences of their actions. "Foreknowledge reveals the flowering of the Tao and yet delusions begin" (Laozi 2005, 55). The sage, on the other hand, pursues wisdom and has no ulterior motives (Chan 1963, 158).

In everyday usage, hoa lá cành carries a similar warning. While a source of beauty and inspiration, hoa lá cành also refers to a kind of literary, verbal, or visual expression that is not always prized—think here of the negative connotations of flowery or over-the-top language or actions. It also indicates a kind of extravagance. In an article oriented toward young people, the *kenh14.vn* website contrasted a male celebrity's simple, elegant, and "manly" attire—consisting of a black turtleneck and black trousers—with extravagant hoa lá cành fashion.[27] As the article states, "One does not need to be hoa lá cành" to be beautiful.

For musicians, flowers are pretty but they distract listeners from the foundations or essence of practice. Musicians must temper their production of melody so they do not become overly flowery. To do so would move practice too far away from its source. As a Vietnamese translation of Laozi's text suggests, "Knowledge as the symbol of a flower is outside of the Tao and the source of complete stupidity."[28] The flower may emerge from knowledge, but it is not knowledge itself.

METAPHOR AS MEDIATOR OF CREATIVITY

Flowers constitute an ideal engaged in performance but not embraced. This is one of the most important parts of creativity in southern Vietnamese music: a frame structures or grounds spontaneity to keep improvisation appropriate and beautiful. Chân phương upholds some sense of the past, largely in the form of value judgments: musicians maintain mode, melodic content of the lòng bản, associations with past musicians, and other elements. Hoa lá cành indicates departure from the chân phương in the form of appropriate methods of đàn tùy hứng. They reconstruct the tune for the present; indeed, musicians reiterate over and over again that improvisation is body-bound in the context-specific performance space.

Đờn ca tài tử musicians draw from past performances and memories and filter them through a metaphor of appropriate performance practice. They think about particular approaches to the aesthetic production of sound and use particular techniques to generate this sound. In this sense, musicians use the chân phương and hoa lá cành metaphors together to gather, collect, and organize their resources. Since metaphors are the primary means of creative expression in đờn ca tài tử, creativity also should be understood in the same way. Musical creativity manages and orients musical knowledge and competence to be more efficient and effective in the performance setting. Creativity primarily involves the best use of resources to sustain practice, just as nature sustains itself.

Metaphors work together in performance to bring together musical resources and produce engaging performance. By way of example, I evaluate the convergence of chân phương and hoa lá cành in several performances of "Nam xuân." I evaluate the first two phrases of the tune to highlight how musicians draw from the frame to approach embellishment through flowering. This is a Nam mode work: it is not cheerful like other works attached to the happy or Bắc mode, but it is not indicative of someone grieving loss. For Nguyễn Thuyết Phong, "to Vietnamese, this is not sad"; instead, it is "relax[ing], calm[ing], tranquil . . . [and] solemn . . . but it's not really sad."[29]

Southern Spring, Southern Youth

Trần Văn Khê (1962, 99) points to the origins of "Nam xuân" (along with "Nam ai") in Quảng Nam Province, and the tunes later migrated to southern Vietnam (see also Phạm Duy 1972, 142–44). They entered đờn ca tài tử from nhạc lễ and hát bội, carrying vestiges of these earlier southern Vietnamese traditions. When I asked Nguyễn Vĩnh Bảo to explain the meaning of the tune, he said that many misunderstand the title of the work—most translate it as "Southern Spring" (Nam for "south," a term that also designates the mode, and xuân for "spring"). With a laugh, he argued that southern Vietnam does not have a spring season— the weather is either hot and dry or hot and wet—so "southern spring" does not make sense; instead, the work depicts youth and coming of age. The work "expresses the sentiment of the young man, or 'thanh xuân' . . . [at] the age of . . . seventeen or even sixteen."[30] The arrival of the lunar new year uses the same term (*mùa xuân đến rồi*). Although celebratory, the new year brings a period of reflection, reverence to one's ancestors, and hope—indeed, one greets guests and family members with wishes for good health and success.

I evaluate "Nam xuân" through a comparison of five versions of the tune. I depict the commonalities of these five versions as representative of the chân phương, or foundations of the tune. I propose a lòng bản reflective of contemporary performance practice; as Huỳnh Khải has noted, musicians from different locations in southern Vietnam produce different lòng bản, so the lòng bản proposed in Figure 5.6 should not be considered authoritative. The differences between the versions constitute hoa lá cành and the ways that musicians extend certain structures of the foundation to generate practice; that said, several common ways of embellishing the lòng bản emerge, thereby suggesting the way that the metaphor guides improvisation in specific ways. To undertake this analysis, I draw from commentary made by musicians, but also infer meaning based on my own study of đờn ca tài tử. The analysis is descriptive and not prescriptive; indeed, others may propose other viable alternatives.

I begin with two text-based versions of "Nam xuân" taken from printed and archival sources. The first source is from notation published in 1909 by Phụng Hoàng Sang. This is the earliest known notation of đờn ca tài tử published in southern Vietnam. As an aide-mémoire, the pitch content is relatively spartan, but provides good clues about the nature of the lòng bản.

Phụng Hoàng Sang 1909
1 á XANG xang hò xê hò xang XANG
2 xê xê xảng xê xang hò xang xang—

The next source is from unpublished notation prepared by Sáu Hóa and given to me by Lê Đình Bích. Sáu Hóa performed frequently for Emperor Bảo Đại in Saigon and later moved to the Mekong Delta, where he taught Trần Minh Đức. At the start of the notation, he pairs *hò/liu* with *xê* and *xang* (notated as *xan*) to establish the scale, and later adds neighbor notes and octave displacements to generate variety.

Sáu Hóa n.d.
1 Á xan xan xế xãn xản—xế san lìu lìu—xế xan lìu xế lìu xan xàn
2 xan xế cổng xế—lìu xế xế xãn xán xan xế xể xế xan lìu xế lìu xan xàn—

Both Phụng Hoàng Sang and Sáu Hóa crafted written notation that indicates melody and not rhythm. For this reason, in Figure 5.6, I have aligned the pitch content in measures as stipulated by the original notation, but their placement within the measure should be seen as approximate. That said, in a number of places, it is clear where pitches should fall because all other versions maintain this placement. The notation does provide, however, some approximate sense of meter: Phụng Hoàng Sang's notation capitalizes solfège in the first phrase to indicate important beats in the phrase. Sáu Hóa's notation, as is typical in most solfège notation I have seen, indicates the placement of each of the four beats in the phrase with an underlined syllable. Note that both sets include a dash at the end of the second phrase to indicate *nhịp ngoại*, or "outside beat," where silence is heard on the beat indicated.

The third example is a standard version taught by Nguyễn Vĩnh Bảo to his students through lessons and notation. His work is highly ornamented, pays attention to sound resonating in the instrument, and plays with the sense of beat as if to anticipate material to appear next. (Listen to **Track 14**.) I transcribed the fourth version from a version released in 2014 on the French INEDIT label that features Quang Dũng on the đàn bầu and Hoàng Cơ Thụy on the đàn tỳ bà. These players manage to mediate the sounds of two very different instruments into a coherent performance; indeed, it is clear that they listen to one another closely. I transcribed the final version from a performance I attended at the Lá Thơm (Fragrant Leaf) Restaurant in November 2008. (Listen to **Track 15**.) The musicians had played together extensively and therefore played similar melodic material.

An analysis of chân phương begins with the mediation of the mode. In Figure 5.7, I have replicated the mode as it is presented in these two phrases. Although musicians play with an expanded palate, they still ground the mode through the repetition of primary notes *hò* and *xang*. Hoàng Cơ Thụy's improvisation on the đàn tỳ bà for instance features the rhythmic repetition of *xang* (G) in measure two to establish the placement of the pitch; he follows this at the end of measure two and into measure three—and later in measure seven—with *hò* (D). The use of both *xự* and *xứ* (E and F) appears common in "Nam xuân," generating a sense of ambiguity. In addition, only Nguyễn Vĩnh Bảo's version and the Lá Thơm performance include a *cống* with the rung ornament; others only pass over *cống* and view it as relatively unimportant.

The lòng bản in Figure 5.6 suggests points of convergence across the five versions of the work. The lòng bản emerges from past versions, indicated by the text

FIGURE 5.6 Five versions of the first two phrases of "Nam xuân" and a lòng bản

FIGURE 5.7 Pitch and ornamentation in "Nam xuân"

versions from the early twentieth century, and today helps a listener understand the sense of direction crafted. This lòng bản begins with important pitches and intervals so as to suggest the identity of the work. It not only includes pitch content and the placement of the *nhịp ngoại*, but also places where the musical texture becomes denser both meldocially and rhythmically. Measures four and six for example feature greater subdivision of the beat and, particularly in the latter case, a greater sense of movement. Both of these in turn lead to the generation of faster embellishments — this occurs to some degree in measures four and five and to a greater degree in measures six and seven.

Notating a lòng bản helps examine how musicians craft flowers. As previously suggested, one understands the creativity of hoa lá cành through the conditions and results of spontaneity and motivation toward a particular goal. Nguyễn Vĩnh Bảo aimed to craft sounds that resonate well in the instrument. For example, he uses octave displacements in measures two, four, five, and seven, and also generates a melody that saunters rather than races toward the main beats of the lòng bản. He also uses *song thinh* to highlight timbral variety: he bends from *xang* to *xê* (G to A) and then through the repetition of *xê* soon after, and indicates the distinction between a pitch produced through bending the *xang* string and a pitch produced on the *xê* string. Importantly, the resonance still remains clear.

The two ensemble performances indicate ways that musicians create a sense of camaraderie and community through spontaneous pitch production. The melody produced by the Lá Thơm musicians seems more motivic than the others; indeed, all the musicians played the same turn motive together in measures two, four, and eight. Although they do improvise, the musicians have produced through repeated practice a standard way of performing the work, upon which they then deviate in individual ways. The INEDIT recording presents two individuals with very different styles that require some mediation in context. On the đàn bầu, Quang Dũng crafts a melody in the first few measures that appears similar to the Lá Thơm performance. He bends from one pitch to the next and only adds a hint of rhythmic variety. Hoàng Cơ Thuỷ's performance on the đàn tỳ bà focuses on establishing a modal center. He then quickly jumps from one octave to another and presents a melody that has an offbeat quality. Once they establish their respective styles, they begin to respond to one another — this, too, is a form of framing the improvisation so a unified improvisation can emerge from two styles. When Hoàng Cơ Thuỷ offers a sixteenth-note passage in the first beat of measure six that obscures the placement of beat one and involves *song thinh* on *xê*, Quang Dũng replicates the rhythm of the motive in the second and third beats of the measure. In measure seven, Hoàng Cơ Thụy introduces another octave leap, and Quang Dũng does so for the first time later in the measure. The musicians clearly listen to each another and react to what the other plays. This is central to crafting the sense of naturalness attached to đờn ca tài tử creativity.

MAKING ECSTASY FROM METAPHOR

The creativity described here connects different realms of experience into a temporary unified whole of some kind. This occurs when "everything around you belongs to the art."[31] For some musicians, the use of knowledge and the intersection of metaphors does not simply generate effective and moving performances; it also creates ecstasy. Trần Minh Đức foregrounds this ecstatic state, or what he calls *xuất thần* (literally, "exporting the spirit"), in his descriptions of the goals of performance.[32] Xuất thần linguistically denotes an altered state of mind of the musician who appears so engrossed in the creation of music and the conviviality of the social performance setting that other events just beyond the performance space go unnoticed. This is a kind of practice that envelops one's being and is something to which he strives when he performs.

My understanding of xuất thần first emerged in Cần Thơ during lessons with Trần Minh Đức and in social settings with his friends. When Hai Đức performs in the xuất thần state, he develops phrases, builds on preceding motives, lingers upon particular ornamented notes, or plays rapid passages at the top of the đàn sến fingerboard. He does not pause to explain a particular technique or take a drink, but smiles broadly and finishes phrases with a flourish of the right arm. He continues, often becoming more and more engrossed in his playing. At particular moments, those around him also become engrossed, leaning forward in their chairs and ignoring the ringing of their mobile phones—a rare occurrence in Vietnam today. When he stops playing, those around him clap and yell, "Hay quá!" (Really good!). Through this performance, he presents his expansive experience with the tradition but also his ability to shape sound for the context. Those methods of organizing and guiding knowledge through metaphor therefore work to generate the xuất thần state.

Ecstatic Practice in Ethnomusicology

When ethnomusicologists engage with altered states, they often call them *flow* or *flowlike*. Turino (2008, 4–5) draws on Csikszentmihalyi (1990) to define *flow* as the state of intense focus that enables one to tackle a music task with precision, which ultimately "is fundamental for psychic growth and integration" (Turino 2008, 4). This is a tidy explanation, and one might be tempted to connect various forms of musical ecstasy found throughout the world, including in Sufi temples, Santería rituals, and Arab classical music to the feeling of timelessness and unity seen in flow; however, this state is not universal, needs to be learned, and is often only learned by certain individuals over others (Sutton-Smith 1997, 186).

Other ethnomusicologists prefer *ecstasy*, the term I adopt here. Ecstasy is a messy but powerful condition that draws on biological processes of the brain to serve context-specific practices.[33] One of the most important evaluations of music and ecstasy in ethnomusicology comes from Ali Jihad Racy, who breaks down the creation of the ecstatic state in Arab classical music into two components: *tarab* and *sulṭanah*. Tarab is an ecstatic environment comprised of the participation of and connections between audience and music (1998, 101). Improvised music emanates from this environment and sustains it. For Sabah Fakhri, a musician whom Racy quotes at length, "we become reflections of one another. I consider the audience to be me and myself to be the audience" (Fakhri as cited in Racy 1998, 130). Creativity emerges through the "interactive cycle of communication" between the stage musician and audience (Racy 1998, 101).

Sulṭanah serves as the most complementary concept to Vietnamese xuất thần. Racy defines it as "modal ecstasy," which emerges from the performance of modes, or *maqāmāt*, by Arab musicians (100). This is a learned reaction to sonic "preconditions and procedures" to which musicians listen and respond in performance (2003, 126). During a performance, musicians feel both empowered through and overpowered by music. Although seemingly paradoxical, this state proves that a musician has achieved "artistic authority by succumbing to the ec-static hegemony of the melodic mode" (122). Musicians further describe a feeling of "temporal transcendence," as they no longer perceive the passage of time in the ecstatic state (124–26). Like sulṭanah, xuất thần is the apogee performance experience for musicians in a social setting. The production and experience of sound empowers and overpowers the musicians, and if successful, they perform good music effortlessly.[34]

My interviews with musicians throughout southern Vietnam did not pinpoint the origins of xuất thần, but their descriptions are reminiscent of Daoist and Buddhist concepts. These connections indicate the ways that xuất thần diverges from other understandings of ecstatic and spontaneous music practice in eth-nomusicology. Spontaneity, Zhuangzi advocates, "is the universal process that binds all things into one, equalizing all things and all opinions" (Chan 1963, 177). Spontaneity emerges, of course, from nonaction. Rather than becoming fully conscious of the self, however, nonaction enables the individual to forget the self, a Daoist ideal known as *wangwo* (忘我). For musicians of some Chinese music, this designates a state where one "forgets everything but music."[35] Forgetting the self enables the individual to "reach the true perspective of individual freedom," according to Liu Jianmei (2016, 5). Liu continues, noting that "Zhuangzi's philosophy lifts individuality to a universal and spiritual ideal, which has a much deeper impact on literature and the other arts" (5). Invoking the Liezi (fourth century BCE), considered the third most important work in Daoist philosophy after that by Laozi and Zhuangzi, Alan Watts further argues that that nonaction is a "dreamlike state of consciousness" or a "floating . . . so that the physical world lacks the hard reality normally present to common sense" (1975, 93). There is overlap here with the Zen Buddhist concept of "breaking through the obsession of self" or *powozhi* (破我執) (Liu 2016, 5).

To be creative and reach a sense of "individual freedom" in Daoist philosophy, one must dismiss the self rather than develop it. This is a very important distinction, as it identifies one of many distinctions between local understandings of creativity over imported Western understandings of creativity. Musicians like Hai Đức attempt to achieve this "floating" quality by enacting certain processes of gathering, collecting, and organizing knowledge in the performance context. This is a learned state, hence why he raised the importance of cultivating it through practice during a number of my lessons with him.

Xuất thần occurs when the musician performs alone or with a group of friends in small settings where all take part in musicmaking. No individual is elevated above the others. In this sense, the listeners are also the performers, and no clear demarcation between performer and listener exists. The ecstatic state emerges from the musician's engagement with the logic and structure of the music itself and the collective knowledge of the musicians themselves, much like the description of sulṭanah. When musicians like Huỳnh Khải aim to commodify and "develop" this music, as described at the end of this chapter, they create a new category of a listening audience that is clearly separated from the musicians, who then become foregrounded. They then reject xuất thần as "superstitious" because it gets in the way of the "development" of this listening and consuming audience.[36] Xuất thần remains, however, an important concept for understanding creativity in the Mekong Delta.

Social Ecstatic Practice

When musicians generate xuất thần together, they seek ways to build a specific kind of ecstatic atmosphere through sound. I attended a performance like this in June 2010 with a documentary film crew and wrote the following reflection in my field notes:

The taxi stopped abruptly in front of the restaurant, Quán Nhớ, and we jogged through the rain and hopped over a puddle to get to the entrance. To actually get to the dining room/performance space, we had to walk through the owner's home. We passed his daughter hanging laundry and an elderly woman with blackened teeth [from chewing betel nut] preparing vegetables in the kitchen. When we reached the space, I could smell the pungent scent of the river and realized that the room was on stilts. I walked to the end of the room, pulled back the tarp that kept out the heavy rain, and considered what would happen if the room collapsed into the river . . . There were a few tables scattered in the space, although only two were occupied. Besides Thầy Bích, his friend Thầy Hải, Lộc (the cameraman), Quân (the producer), and myself at one table, a group of individuals in their early twenties sat drinking beer and smoking cigarettes at the other table. Not long after our arrival, a blind gentleman was led to the front of the room and began playing the guitar. A woman at the other table took a cordless microphone and began to sing. Like the other restaurants that I have visited, it seems that groups come to these restaurants to both eat dinner and perform. They aim to perform not only within their group but also with the other individuals in the restaurant. This became clear when the owner took the guitar and Thầy Bích sang, and later, when Thầy Hải sang an improvised version of the piece "Vân thiên tường," and he made reference to the foreigner (me) who had traveled a great distance to Vietnam to listen to this music. The environment was casual, and as more individuals entered the restaurant, we introduced ourselves, and in between jokes and laughter, performed for and with each other.

Over the course of this performance, I observed several musical and social moves that built and maintained xuất thần over the course of the evening. The sound was continual and filled the space; this particular performance featured an electric guitar with ample reverb and a number of singing voices. Musicians incorporated a diverse range of works and often made seamless transitions between these works. Musicians encouraged participation, so they selected recognizable works so that everyone could take part; if anyone was left out, they moved to a new work. Collaboration involved frequent musical interactions through the use of each other's improvised music and the invention of new lyrical content involving the everyday lives of those participating.

During another performance on a rooftop café overlooking Cần Thơ in January 2015, I observed other ways that musicians incorporated themselves into their sonic environment. As voices of other patrons continued constantly in the background, musicians tuned their instruments and played snippets of various melodies, only pausing to take a drag on their cigarettes or to open another bottle of beer. Upon hearing a particular melody, another musician stopped his conversation and yelled, "Okay, let's sing that. One, two, three!" As the beer flowed, musicians moved fluidly from one song to another and from one exchange to another. In the recording of this evening, I made specific note of the opening of beer bottles and the sound of pouring the beer over ice that filled the short gaps between songs and conversations. It is not just the consumption of liquor that encourages conviviality and abandoning the self (as liquor does); it is also the sound of it as an index of past, present, and future enjoyment.

These elements work also work together to craft a narrative for or structure around the performance—that is, a closing off from the pressures of the outside to craft this sense of conviviality—that builds from one song to the next. In the January 2015 performance, Hai Đức at one point gave his đàn sến to a friend and started singing a text that elicited laughter from those around him; he sang a melody recognized by others who occasionally joined in, and when he paused, the sound of đàn sến and đàn tranh players moved to the foreground with a very lively melody often found in cải lương theater and sometimes in đờn ca tài tử. As Hai Đức took on the personas of multiple characters, these musicians provided constant accompaniment, which served to maintain the emergent xuất thần atmosphere. With a rousing ending, Hai Đức exclaimed that his generation of Cần Thơ musicians was just as good as the musicians in Ho Chi Minh City. With shouts of approval, we all drank.

Hai Đức expanded the xuất thần atmosphere that led directly into the next performance. The musicians began with calls of "thanks," and we clanged our beer glasses together. A new singer entered with an announcement to his compatriots (bà con) that he would tell a story. (Listen to **Track 16**.) Hai Đức returned to playing the đàn sến, and the đàn tranh followed. The text sung here had some fixed elements, as evidenced by the occasional interjection by other men in the group who sang along, and improvised elements crafted by the singer. The singer adopted a young man's persona and described his youth—he liked to go out and play and sing (đờn ca) with his friends—but relayed his mother's concern that he really should spend his time finding someone to marry. He made a note of the disadvantages of marrying a woman in the countryside and a woman in the city—this mention stands in for larger debates about both the applicability of urban styles of đờn ca tài tử performance in rural settings and the development of traditional music in line with global creativity models discussed in the next chapter (see also Cannon 2016, 156–60). The narrator then made a gesture to Lê Đình Bích, one of the singers in this coterie, saying that the young man could follow Thầy Bích and study at the university. The group erupted into laughter and Hai Đức chimed in, "And what else?" suggesting that the young man might follow Thầy Bích into other less scholarly pursuits like drinking beer and flirting. The story then continued.

In addition to the amusing lyrical content, the narrator/singer also spliced different and recognizable melodies into the texture to my great surprise and to other listeners' great enjoyment. At one moment, for example, he singer launched into the tune "Miên hậu hồi cung" ("Khmer Queen from the Time of the Court"; see Figure 5.8) with lyrics that the other musicians recognized.[37] After the first phrase of the tune, the musicians laughed and joined him. I knew the tune—but not the lyrical content—because it was one that Hai Đức had taught me in his lessons; it evidently was a favorite of the group of musicians with whom he sang.

The musicians performed this cải lương favorite not to feature the influence of Khmer music on Vietnamese music, but to inject a Khmer voice or Khmer history into narratives of Vietnamese traditional music.[38] In my conversations with Hai Đức, he indicated that he knows little about Khmer music but has encountered many Khmer Krom in southern Vietnam. By incorporating this piece into the performance, the musicians allowed a voice to speak that resonates

FIGURE 5.8 Excerpt of "Miên hậu hồi cung"

Playing with Metaphor **133**

not necessarily with Khmer or Khmer Krom but with other Vietnamese who understand this composition as representing the diversity of locality. As they did at the end of the previous tune, the musicians reveled in the unique cultural space of Cần Thơ and the Mekong Delta.

The performances of this particular evening sustained xuất thần throughout the night, but this is not always the case. Xuất thần breaks down when there are too many interruptions by other patrons or waitstaff in the restaurant and when certain individuals become too intoxicated to participate appropriately (either through nonparticipation or obtrusive behavior). Instances also occur where performers seem to be visibly uncomfortable because they are either made to feel unwelcome or do not have the requisite musical experience to participate when asked. In the June 2010 performance with the film crew, for example, one of the singers, Thầy Hải, wished to perform a particular work that the accompanying guitarist did not know well. When the guitarist stumbled and played incorrect pitches, Hải stopped singing and gave the guitarist instructions. This did not destroy xuất thần in the scene, but rebuilding the feeling required some effort.

Solo Ecstatic Practice

In our lessons, Trần Minh Đức attempted to replicate the musical aspects of building an ecstatic state without the required social components of ecstasy. He drew on his own recollections of the ecstatic experience to reproduce the appropriate sonic material so that I understood the sonic construction of xuất thần. Being a novice, I could not participate easily in generating xuất thần with him during the lessons because I did not have the musical skills required. I therefore observed his entry into and exit out of xuất thần and tried to ask him questions after he finished. He often still appeared to be engrossed, so I had to wait until the ecstatic state dissipated for him to respond.

Trần Minh Đức's xuất thần emerges through sonic engagement with the characteristic of điệu and musical material. He builds a sense of unity in his improvisations, drawing on his practice of spontaneity. To describe this, I draw on a field recording of "Nam xuân" that he made for me in June 2009. (Listen to **Track 17**.) As indicated in the discussion of this tune earlier in the chapter, the meaning of the mode is somewhat ambiguous, so a number of characteristics of the rao, transcribed in Figure 5.9, point to the uncertain nature of the mode. He begins with an octave displacement followed leap from *hò* (D) to *xê* (A), introducing the *mổ* (tapping) ornament on *xê*. He introduces *xang* (G), which together with

FIGURE 5.9 *Rao* preceding "Nam xuân" performed
by Trần Minh Đức (recorded June 24, 2009)

hò grounds the mode; however, he passes over *xang* relatively quickly, indicating a predilection to avoid grounding. He continues by introducing other pitches of the mode and a common cadential motive, *xang—liu—cống—xê* (indicated with stems in Figure 5.9 as it was played in steady rhythm), but he does not end the phrase with *xang*—he ends it with *xê*. He quickly passes over *xang* again in favor of *xự*, playing with the *rung* (vibrato) ornament. When he reaches the end of the *rao*, notated as halfway through the second stave of Figure 5.9, the notes become quite indistinct. The sound is muddied and uncertain before ending with a clear sounding of *liu* and *xang* (the last of which he plays using the *reo* ornament).

After the click of the *song lang*, Hai Đức begins "Nam xuân" with an entry phrase resembling that played by the đàn bầu in the INEDIT recording and the Lá Thơm performance, as transcribed in Figure 5.6. An ecstatic performance must align with the expected parameters of the work—one comprised of four-measure phrases, featuring the *song lang* at the end of the third and fourth measures of each phrase, and evoking the Nam mode throughout (see Figure 5.10). Hai Đức uses recognized motives associated with the work (especially the opening motive) and evokes the lòng bản, but these alone do not make xuất thần. Xuất thần emerges as Hai Đức generates a sense of sonic unity through self-imitation, incorporating rhythmic and melodic variety, and building a sense of momentum. When Hai Đức performs alone, he cannot rely on sounds produced by others in the performance space, so he returns to motives previously played occasionally in different guises. The common cadential motive I referenced in the *rao* analysis appears in measure 4 and again in measures 7–8 and 15–16, although they do not fall in the same place in the phrase. The second and third iterations start in the last beat of the penultimate measure of their respective phrases to accommodate the appearance of *nhịp ngoại*, or an articulation of silence at the end of these two phrases. Another longer self-referential motive appears in measure 7

Playing with Metaphor **135**

and again in measure 10 but is displaced by a half beat. In context, the measure 7 iteration seems out-of-sync with the beat structure: when he reaches the *liu* (D) in the second half of the second beat of measure 7, he seems to change the position of the beat or reach the main beat too early. The listener loses the sense of beat momentarily and only regains it with the start of the cadential motive at beat four of that measure. When he returns to this motive in measure 10, it does not feel out of place, and he ends the motive on beat three of measure 10; listeners feel that they have arrived in the correct place this time around.

This last example shows the kinds of rhythmic interplay that Hai Đức incorporated into an increasingly rich and dense improvisation. He frequently obscured the placement of the beat, even introducing a motive in the second and third beats of measure 3, which repeats throughout. In this motive, he anticipates the placement of the next beat and also incorporates timbral variety by playing the second iteration of *liu* (D) using *song thinh*. This is repeated in measure 12 and a version obscures the placement of beat one in measure 15. Additional rhythmic obscuring of beat occurs in measures 12–13. With sixteenth-note leaps from *xê* to *phan* (A to C), one might expect him to complete the motive with a return to *liu* (D), the de facto tonic. Instead, he repeats the motive twice, and then leaps from *xê* to *cống* in measure 13. He plays with expectation here before finally playing a *xê—phan—liu* motive that the listener expects.

The motivic development, play with rhythm, and return to repeated material all contribute to the sense of building an effective improvisation. He evokes similar chân phương structures of mode and lòng bản, but quickly incorporates increasingly complicated patterns of embellishment. He introduces fast passages, such as those in measures 6–7 that drive the work forward; incorporates dynamic contrast, indicated by the crescendo in measure 5; plays with timbral contrast, indicated by the staccato markings in measure 9. He is not out of control here; indeed, he knows how to generate material that sustains a sense of internal logic and order. He brings himself into that logic and, in so doing, builds xuất thần.

Questioning Ecstasy

The ecstatic nature of xuất thần is not accepted by every musician; indeed, I did not learn of xuất thần during my musical experiences in Ho Chi Minh City. When I asked Huỳnh Khải, a notoriously reserved individual, about xuất thần, he surprised me by laughing loudly. He recognized its existence but did not practice it and suggested what might be called a more rational or empirical understanding

FIGURE 5.10 First four phrases of "Nam xuân" performed by Trần Minh Đức

of the concept. He therefore used xuất thần to explain the difference between a performance of improvised versus composed music.

> I think that this word *xuất thần* means that when [embellishing] . . . a fixed melody, we vary the notes but we do so without thinking about it. When we play, things outside of us inspire us. . . . We play the notes without ever thinking about them beforehand. . . . Sitting and thinking about what to write out or when I compose music—this is not xuất thần.[39]

He used similar language to describe xuất thần as Nguyễn Vĩnh Bảo used to describe hoa lá cành with an emphasis on producing a melody "without thinking" and being inspired by something "outside" the self. Huỳnh Khải may reject xuất thần, as it suggests ignoring impetus or motivation for change, which is very important to his practice. As with the "flower" metaphor, musicians do not wish to escape from the frame and produce something ugly, misleading, or directionless.

The concept remains important, however, for musicians in the Mekong Delta. Xuất thần involves more than social camaraderie—it also involves the achievement of a momentary balance between knowledge held and present experience had. As musicians draw on what they know and how they perceive their environment, xuất thần emerges to make temporary wholes. In performances where xuất thần is present, I hear combinations of discrete musical elements, expansions of preexisting elements, and the redefinition of genre through the inclusion of Vietnamese and other tunes. These performances also congeal wisdom imparted in lessons and transmit knowledge about practice. This inspired state involves the release of some self-control, but as long as musicians have the musical knowledge and ability—and also do not become too drunk—the release yields a powerful sense of freedom of expression. It generates effective musical content in performance and upholds a model of creativity that has been in practice in Vietnam for a long time. I therefore understand why some musicians view xuất thần as irrational and yet inspired practice.

CONCLUSION

In this chapter, I have pointed to the importance of metaphor in structuring the ways musicians think about đờn ca tài tử. These metaphors close the loop of practice, allowing musicians to define the content to be mediated in performance. They connect to external constructs that are themselves closed loops and sustainable: chân phương (frame) constitutes knowledge that has been codified in some way, including điệu and lòng bản, and hoa lá cành (flowers, leaves, and branches) proposes a way of thinking about improvisation and embellishment as spontaneous and natural. Xuất thần (ecstasy) music practice emerges from the use of these metaphors and proposes a way of thinking about the unified whole crafted by listening intently to one another. These performances draw on elements of past practice, augmenting them for present conditions and anticipating future uses based on those that have come before. They use knowledge and practice learned from teachers and members of the community to suggest more beautiful flowers, leaves, and branches for future use. The next chapter examines how musicians have developed these methods of thinking about practice throughout the political and economic changes of the twentieth and twenty-first centuries.

SIX

Developing Creativity

Established in 2000 as a collaborative effort between Thừa Thiên—Huế Province and the Embassy of France in Vietnam, the Huế Festival takes place every two years and features domestic and international music groups. I attended in June 2010 on a summer research trip to observe how musicians presented đờn ca tài tử in a large concert setting. The organizers of the 2010 festival touted the event as an opportunity for musical and cultural exchange between the participants, who hailed from many provinces in Vietnam, as well as China, Japan, India, Senegal, Cuba, and elsewhere. Indeed, it served as "the meeting place of the ancient capitals [and] the assembly point of world cultural heritage" ("nơi gặp gỡ các thành phố Cố đô—Điểm hẹn các di sản văn hóa thế giới").

The most important goal, however, was to advance "integrating" and "developing" cultural heritage. The main byline of the festival repeated frequently for the duration of the festival was "2010 Hue Festival: 'Integration and Development within Cultural Heritage'" ("Festival Huế 2010: 'Di sản văn hóa với hội nhập và phát triển'"). Integration took the form of assembling music and dance performances from within Vietnam and presenting these diverse musics as representative of a flourishing and integrated population alongside other musics reflective of national integration from elsewhere in the world. Development took the form of using old musical forms to deliver new content, as well as the occasional use of synthesized sounds to revitalize traditional forms. The performances organized by specific provincial governments in Vietnam, in particular, took up integration and development in earnest.

On the second day of the festival, a performance of the An Giang Artistic Group (Đoàn nghệ thuật An Giang) of An Giang Province next to the Cambodian border in southern Vietnam featured "culture of the four sibling ethnic

FIGURE 6.1 Chăm dance of the Đoàn nghệ thuật An Giang
still from video by the author, June 6, 2010

groups: Vietnamese, Chăm, Chinese, and Khmer" living in the province.[1] Like other performances by provincial-level groups, this performance highlighted the music of minority groups living in those provinces through a Vietnamese nationalist lens: they used the Vietnamese language and only a few words of those represented ethnic groups, and prominently featured Vietnamese (Việt) performers accompanied by prerecorded popular music. In the opening act, women dressed as Chăm danced in red headscarves to what appeared to be approximated *maqāmāt* (see Figure 6.1). This performance was followed by a duet between a woman dressed in the same red attire and a man who made frequent movements with his shoulders—akin to a shimmy—whenever he did not sing. The performers appeared to replicate a well-worn European exotified version of Arab popular music.

The third act was a đờn ca tài tử ensemble. The emcee described đờn ca tài tử here as a "type of national art [*nghệ thuật dân tộc*] that has been passed down through the generations for a long time,"[2] found in the shared border regions, and evoking both the mentality (*tinh thần*) of the people of An Giang Province and the soul (*tâm hồn*) of national artistic expression. The second work performed, titled "Người là Hồ Chí Minh" ("He is Hồ Chí Minh"), with lyrics composed by Phường Hồ Tấm, espoused the virtues of Vietnam's revered chairperson and uncle (Bác Hồ) of the nation. These kinds of performances are common: the propagandistic lyrical content is safe in the public sphere and the music is traditional and considered innocuous. The festival audience heard the amplified voices clearly, but the instrumental music was not well amplified (see Figure 6.2). The performers of the *"ghi ta Việt Nam"* or ghi ta phím lõm, đàn kìm, and đàn cò played live even through the rainstorm that developed in the middle of the performance. At times, I was not sure that the musicians could hear one another appropriately; when the musicians landed on important structural beats—especially those of the *song lang*—the sound seemed disjointed.

The performance of the An Giang Artistic Group presented a clear ideological message through the artistic resources of one of Vietnam's southern provinces. It displayed how musicians and cultural cadres use overt nationalist iconography to connect selected sources of Vietnam's past with a visually engaging present and idyllic future. It invoked Hồ Chí Minh as national hero and An Giang Province as a microcosm for the nation, where individuals from different ethnicities live harmoniously and work together to produce national culture. (Listen to **Track 18**.) The lyrics in particular "disseminate culture" and teach audience members about the Vietnamese mentality and soul, as my friend Phạm Ngọc Lanh was fond of saying.[3] Presenting the performances on television further presented Vietnam as a technologically-savvy nation with the ability to commercialize and deploy its own cultural resources for consumption. These choices were strategic and carefully planned, even if they were not all well executed.

The nationalization, popularization, preservation, and deployment of technology all serve the paradigm of *phát triển* (literally, "development") in contempo-

FIGURE 6.2 Performance of "Người là Hồ Chí Minh" by Thanh Kim on ghi ta phím lõm, Thiện Vũ on đàn kìm, Quốc Tuấn on đàn cò, and singers Thúy Phương and Thái Ngọc Lợi *still from video by the author, June 6, 2010*

rary Vietnam. Strategically shaped since the beginning of the postcolonial era, development has become a handy paradigm frequently evoked in economic, political, and cultural spheres to index policies of modernization and glorification of the future.[4] In the words of anthropologist Erik Harms, development is "a means of transcending the imperfections of the present and to elide the failure of space to fit into ideal categories of cultural order" (2011, 91). Focused on the future, cultural practices uphold certain ideologies of the present directed toward the future; even when these ideologies change, development still drives and motivates.

Invoking development is an overt strategy to disassociate from methods of the past, especially those methods of music practice discussed in the previous chapter. Political economist Pietro Masina describes development as a "process whereby socioeconomic change, rather than evolving through some 'spontaneous' dynamic, can be organized and promoted consciously by some organizing and directing agent; and that agent par excellence is the state" (2006, 27; original emphasis removed). In cultural development programs, the state exerts significant control over cultural production by organizing festivals and conferences, and directing state funds toward these events. In so doing, they remove the "spontaneous" component to cultural production that so fundamentally supports traditional music. Will đờn ca tài tử perish, or will musicians find new ways to craft traditional music within frameworks ordered by the state?

For musicians of đờn ca tài tử and other genres of traditional music, the concept of phát triển denotes a new way of thinking about creation emergent over the twentieth century. Adopted from economic policy, development became a metaphor to describe experiments and changes to traditional music. The metaphor links music creation to the economic development strategies of late socialist and post-socialist Vietnam, where musicians craft music like economists and policy makers to cultivate economic growth. Development therefore guides the ways practitioners, civil servants, and audiences think about, talk about, and conceive of practice. No longer entirely spontaneous, natural, and involving nonaction, "developed" music is rehearsed, debated, and motivational; indeed, Huỳnh Khải's use of "thúc đẩy" (motivate) upholds development ideals.

Development discourse plays a significant and specific role in shaping music creation in southern Vietnam. In this chapter, I identify how phát triển emerged as a potent postcolonial metaphor and became a blunt discursive strategy following the end of the Second Indochina War, and later embodied new promises and dreams of international collaboration and cooperation following the reforms of the 1980s and 1990s. What I witnessed in southern Vietnam aligns in considerable degrees with work by Barley Norton, who focuses on the development of new folklorized versions of *lên đồng* in the late 1990s (2009, 201–16), and Lauren Meeker, who investigates the transformation and popularization of *quan họ* for the television screen (2013, 104–14) and the revival of the village festival (117–37). Musicians of đờn ca tài tử undertake similar uneasy negotiations between past practice and state discourse of development, but their approaches methods differ.

Since development is oriented toward the future, politicians first debate policy and theory concerning cultural development. This occurred in both the Republic of Vietnam and later in the Socialist Republic of Vietnam. Given the attention paid to future prosperity and motivation, these political leaders designated mastery in the service of development. Indeed, as Julietta Singh (2018) describes, mastery intrudes in similar ways in Vietnam as other postcolonial contexts. The state-appointed titles of Nhà giáo ưu tú (Teacher of Merit) and Nghệ sĩ ưu tú (Artist of Merit), for instance, label certain individuals with state-sanctioned abilities to direct the development of culture. Two artists in this text hold these titles: Phạm Thúy Hoan holds the first, and Huỳnh Khải holds the second.[5]

Musicians and teachers with mastery then apply theories of development to practice. To perform developed music requires an attention to appropriate pedagogical methods. Phạm Thúy Hoan's work with the Tiếng Hát Quê Hương Ensemble serves as a case study in this work. Musicians who participate rehearse in groups under her leadership and that of other professional musicians. Their work often focuses on young people, who do not yet have mastery and therefore can be shaped appropriately to later convene the better and brighter future represented in development policy.

POSTCOLONIAL DEVELOPMENT DISCOURSE

Postcolonial discussions often begin in colonial-era debates, and Vietnam is no different. In the early twentieth century, a new Vietnamese intelligentsia (*giới trí trúc*) rose in Hanoi and Saigon, as well as among Vietnamese populations abroad (Tai 1992; Marr 1981, 8–12; 31).[6] In the 1910s and 1920s, they searched for an alternate model of Vietnamese life that could be situated as a third space between the neo-Confucian or "traditional" and the French models (Marr 1981, 9). In other words, they sought to establish a coherent Vietnamese national identity founded on shared characteristics and aspirations. At this time, for instance, Phan Kế Bính (1915) codified a list of shared customs in the book *Việt Nam phong tục* (*Vietnamese Customs*), which outlines the ways that Vietnamese parents, children, wives, and husbands have interacted with one another throughout time, as well as the foods, professions, and beliefs that unite Vietnamese people together through culture.

Hồ Chí Minh declared Vietnam an independent nation following the August Revolution in 1945. Transmitted from Hanoi radio, this statement allegedly did not reach Saigon, although Hanoi representatives did organize a rally to hear the independence address (Marr 1995, 525). The French did not give up their rule, however, and the ensuing First Indochina War (1945–1954) pitted the Việt Minh (Việt Nam Độc Lập Đồng Minh Hội, or Vietnam Independence League) against the French military and colonial structures. The war ended with the defeat of French troops at Điện Biên Phủ (in northern Vietnam) in 1954, and the subsequent signing of the Geneva Accord, which divided Vietnam into two at the seventeenth parallel. Hồ Chí Minh led the Democratic Republic of Vietnam (North), and Emperor Bảo Đại and Ngô Đình Diệm led the State of Vietnam (South). Unification of the North and the South should have occurred in 1956 as the Geneva Accord stipulated, but the two countries remained separate with the Democratic Republic of Vietnam (DRVN) led by the Vietnam Communist Party and the renamed Republic of Vietnam (RVN), supposedly led by democratic electoral processes but actually led by a series of self-serving dictatorial and military figures. The ensuing Second Indochina War sought to forcibly reunify the country under the ideological frameworks of the victor and their international allies—the United States and a handful of other allies bolstered the South, and China and the Soviet Union supported the North.

In spite of clear ideological differences between the DRVN and RVN, both strategically pursued policies to counteract French influence, repair damage to Vietnamese cultural production, and expand traditional music to new audiences. Authors on both sides of the seventeenth parallel described French authorities as using strategies to keep French culture at the pinnacle of artistic endeavors and depict the Vietnamese as static, meek, and in need of guidance. French policy largely ignored the continuously evolving nature of culture in Vietnam, and this needed to be repaired under the guise of developing traditional music. Nguyễn Phụng Michel (introduced in Chapter 3) wrote in his memoir:

> The French government's mistake, the most unsuccessful and clumsy of all
> during the colonial period, was to view ethnic culture of all of the colonies
> as it was in the past; they did not appreciate the issues related to developing

[phát triển] and building general cultural knowledge of the Vietnamese people. They only focused on deliberately obscuring to easily engineer the most opportune way of colonizing. They intentionally forgot that every race, however uncivilized they may be, still has a traditional culture always preserved in the activities of its people. Without knowledge of this, how can they understand thoroughly the mentality of the people and to emphathize with them with any intention whatsoever? To summarize, my underlying motive here is that when returning to one's country after studying in France or in any Western country, deliberately try to prove my ideas [regarding making a music school] to the French so they see the ill-advised, absurd ways of treating the cultural sphere undertaken by the past colonial regime. (1997, 2)

This metaphorical call-to-arms recognized the "absurd" beliefs injected into Vietnamese cultural production during colonization and encouraged current students to repair them through development.

The RVN and DRVN both advanced cultural policy to "develop" the arts in the making of the modern (and competing) Vietnamese nations. In southern Vietnam, RVN policy directed cultural production until 1975 and encouraged certain forms of musical experimentation regarding ensemble performances and international collaboration. After 1975, northern cadres implemented DRVN policy in the South, and they viewed some southern Vietnamese music with suspicion. After several years, however, signs of previous experiments reemerged, as these former practices found in the RVN were not entirely incompatible with socialist cultural policy of the DRVN. In particular, Phạm Thúy Hoan drew from previous RVN models when she started her Sounds of the Homeland Ensemble in the early 1980s and encouraged collaborations with musicians of East and Southeast Asia. The following descriptions explore specific approaches to cultural development in the RVN and in the Socialist Republic of Vietnam after 1976 with a particular focus on how musicians deployed metaphors of development to preserve traditional music generally and đờn ca tài tử specifically.

The Republic of Vietnam Period

Policy documents in the Republic of Vietnam period offer insight into nation-building ideals advanced through cultural development. For RVN commentators, culture served to unify the RVN population and advance easier reunification with the North. Some of the clearest policy positions appeared in the pages of *Văn hóa nguyệt san* (*Culture Monthly*), a journal published under the auspices of the Directorate of Cultural Affairs in the Ministry of National Education.[7] The first issue appeared in 1955 and published a speech made in the preceding year by Nguyễn Đăng Thục, an academic and occasional civil servant in the Ministry of Culture. Politics, he argued, has a role in the advancement (*tiến hóa*) of society and the encouragement of civilization (*văn minh*). Culture, according to him, "indicates the function of morality" and ultimately enables societal change and innovation; without culture or change, humans simply are "brutish or have no sense" (2). This advancement or development occurs through unity of culture and population. "Our realistic aspiration today is unification," he wrote, "unification of the country, unification of the heart" (8).

Articles published in the journal include descriptions of development and unity that mirror those offered by Vietnamese musicians today. In a series of articles published on "developing culture" (*phát triển văn hóa*) in 1963 and 1964, Nguyễn Đình Thi, a Sorbonne-trained philosopher then based in Paris, argues that cultural production should address imbalance within society.[8] Within the borders of the RVN, the "mission of democracy is to create the necessary conditions to realize possibilities. For this reason, the work to develop a nation-state primarily involves finding a way to close the distance between real imbalance and balance of which we are aware" (1963, 1683). This pronouncement resonates with one made by Huỳnh Khải, where music performance "produces compatibility" between different segments of the population (Cannon 2016, 157). Nguyễn Đình Thi then advances unity through nationalist sentiment. "When we speak of culture here, we understand this as meaning 'all the activity levels of a people [*dân tộc*].' Developing culture primarily is the enhancement of the levels of this activity" (Nguyễn Đình Thi 1964, 7). Producing culture enables connections between people, which Huỳnh Khải, Phạm Thúy Hoan, and others in contemporary Vietnam also advocate. Lastly, Nguyễn Đình Thi argues that developed culture must "promote humanity" (7); develop the consciousness of the people (13); and "expand the economy" (20). The commercialization of culture for economic gain is something that disappears in southern Vietnam after 1975 but does reappear in earnest in the late 1990s and early 2000s.

Institutions and professional performance troupes directed this advancement and unity work in Saigon. In 1956, the first year of the existence of the RVN, the Ministry of National Education established the National School of Music (Trường Quốc gia Âm nhạc), which was renamed the National School of Music and Drama (Trường Quốc gia Âm nhạc và Kịch nghệ) in 1960 (Nguyễn Phụng

Michel 1997, 8).[9] The school had a Vietnamese traditional music branch, which taught a variety of traditional instruments and music from northern, central, and southern Vietnam; it also had a Western art music branch that taught performance, composition, and music theory. Nguyễn Vĩnh Bảo noted that in the traditional music branch, in which he taught until the mid-1960s, students specialized in certain regional types of music but took lessons in all. Students studied both traditional and Western art music using European solemnization, a pedagogical decision with which he did not agree; rather than being indicative of a lack of scientific rationality, Vietnamese pitch names enabled students to better understand and produce the unique qualities of Vietnamese traditional music (Nguyễn Vĩnh Bảo n.d.[b], 5).

Nguyễn Phụng Michel, the first director of the school, described the original impact on the music of Vietnam in his memoir and provided further insight on RVN cultural policy as it pertained to institutional practice. His descriptions use the terms "develop" and "popularize" to indicate the goals of the National School of Music in building a "national character" and unify the fledgling nation. The school aimed to:

(1) Train artists-as-connoisseurs to serve and develop [*phát triển*] the singing, dancing, and music of Vietnam;[10]

(2) Popularize [*phổ biến*] music in school and among the public [*đại chúng*];[11]

(3) Collect, research, preserve, and develop [*phát triển*] folk songs, singing, dancing and traditional music of Vietnam, as well as promote high-quality compositions with the rich nuance of the national character [*dân tộc tính*]

(4) Train professors for a career of singing, dancing and playing music in the education industry in Vietnam. (1997, 4)

These guidelines further indicate an emergent professionalization to keep traditional music alive, keep it vibrant, and keep it entertaining for the public.

Popularization, development, and building a national characer for the public involved performing traditional music, including đờn ca tài tử, in professional ensembles. What ultimately emerged in the RVN has its origins in the 1940s and 1950s, when a number of new ensembles in Saigon created a vibrant music and theater scene in the immediate postwar period. These ensembles performed traditional music as well as excerpts from hát bội and cải lương featuring music with similarity to đờn ca tài tử (Nguyễn Phương 2011). In some sources, these groups are called *gánh* or *gánh hát* (troupe), or *đoàn* or *đoàn hát* (ensemble).[12]

Some members of these troupes later worked in the new National School of Music and helped organize ensembles there.[13] These experiments suggested methods of maintaining elements of traditional aesthetics while transforming traditional music for modern audiences. In 1960, Nguyễn Vĩnh Bảo recalled, he orchestrated "Lý con sáo" and other works for a large ensemble comprised of nine different instruments. This kind of ensemble is larger than any typical ensemble of traditional music.[14] These did not always involve musicians playing simultaneously: he divided the works into different parts involving solos, duets, trios, and the full ensemble. During the former three, the musicians were free to improvise, but this was not possible during the full ensemble portions. The works also included an improvised prelude. In "Lý con sáo," the sáo and the đàn bầu played the prelude. The three bowed instruments opened the precomposed portion of the piece, then the flute and the monochord finished the first phrase; the second phrase involved the whole ensemble. The performance, he argued, was "very appreciated by connoisseurs."[15] The performance still would not be considered "traditional" per se, but it drew on traditional music aesthetics.

Alongside education and public performances of traditional music, international collaboration fostered new consuming audiences. Nguyễn Đình Hòa, a well-known figure in RVN cultural affairs and in Vietnamese lingusitics, points to the active participation of the RVN in the United Nations Educational, Scientific and Cultural Organization (UNESCO) in his 1999 memoir and in *Văn hóa nguyệt san* (1964).[16] The State of Vietnam (later the RVN) joined UNESCO on July 6, 1951, as an entity overseen by the Ministry of National Education, and collaborated closely with UNESCO members in Asia (Nguyễn Đình Hoà 1964). The RVN worked with "Saigon embassies of friendly nations," for example, to organize research assistance and cultural events (354–55). In Saigon, Nguyễn Vĩnh Bảo gave performance demonstrations at the Vietnamese American Association in 1965 and the French Cultural Center in 1974 (Cannon 2012, 129–30). He recalled performing at the South East Asian Cultural Festival in Singapore in August 1963, where he met Singaporean politician and then Parliamentary Secretary in the Ministry of Education Lee Khoon Choy, whom Nguyễn Vĩnh Bảo gave a đàn tranh.[17] He also performed in Tokyo in 1969 and in Paris with Trần Văn Khê in 1972. In 1971 and 1972, he held a visiting position at Southern Illinois University in Carbondale where Nguyễn Đình Hòa served as Director of the Center for Vietnamese Studies. International cultural engagement with UNESCO, Japan, Singapore, and other non-Communist states ceased after 1975, but collaboration started again in the 1990s.

Reunification of People and Policy

With the collapse of the Republic of Vietnam government on April 30, 1975—a day known in Vietnam as the Day of Reunification and the Liberation of Saigon but known elsewhere as the Fall of Saigon—the Communist Party in Hanoi set policy for a country officially reunified in 1976 as the Socialist Republic of Vietnam (SRVN). Everyday life changed as Party members started the process of reorganizing the political, economic, cultural, and social lives of citizens of the overthrown RVN (Jamieson 1993, 360). The new regime established reeducation camps for politicians, soldiers, writers, poets, journalists, and others perceived as formerly loyal to the RVN regime to "educate" these individuals about Marxist-Leninist ideology through indoctrination classes, communal singing of *nhạc đỏ* (revolutionary songs; literally, "red music"), and forced labor. Many families considered leaving the country on rickety and overcrowded boats, hoping to elude the Vietnamese coast guard and find a ship or cargo vessel that would eventually arrange passage to refugee camps throughout Southeast Asia.[18]

The immediate post-1975 period in Vietnamese history was quite bleak. The state extended the DRVN system, which was "based on the creation of joint state-private enterprises in modern industry, the collectivization of agriculture and handicraft industries, and the attempts to bring domestic circulation of goods under state control through the creation of a state trading network and administrative pricing system" (Masina 2006, 54; see also Beresford 1988). During the 1970s and 1980s, Vietnam had little contact with other countries besides the Soviet Union and members of the Eastern Bloc. The United States also placed Vietnam under embargo, hampering trade and international relations. Furthermore, the state diverted what little resources they had to military fronts: the Vietnamese government invaded Democratic Kampuchea in December 1978, eventually toppling the Khmer Rouge regime; as a result, China invaded Vietnam in early 1979, resulting in a six-month border war. Although the Sino-Vietnamese War (also known as the Third Indochina War) was short, fighting on two fronts depleted resources.

During this period, cadres implemented certain tenets of cultural policy to unify cultural production in the country. Many genres of music—especially popular music of the RVN period—disappeared from stages, airwaves, and television screens. Some southern Vietnamese musicians refer to the period as the "era of non-Vietnamese music" since one of the only permissible genres seemed to be nhạc đỏ (P. Taylor 2001, 150). Cải lương was performed, but in diminished form.

Directors eliminated visual and musical elements of Chinese origin, as well as so-called western tunes, to make the works didactic, celebrate of the revolution, and serve other political purposes (151–53; see also Khai Thu Nguyen 2012). Some music, including đờn ca tài tử, was performed in private spaces—as evidenced by Nguyễn Vĩnh Bảo's archive of recordings from the late 1970s and 1980s—but it was not completely untouched by policy given its place in the Conservatory and elsewhere in the public sphere.

Cultural policy in the SRVN had its origins in intellectual and revolutionary debates of the 1930s and 1940s that were designed to craft culture in a new society free from oppressive foreign influence.[19] The earliest document of DRVN cultural policy emerged with *Đề cương về văn hóa Việt Nam* (*Draft of the Fundamentals of Vietnamese Culture*) in 1943. Although unattributed to specific authors, Trường Chinh (1907–1988), later a general secretary of the Communist Party, allegedly played a pivotal role in producing this document (Ninh 2002, 28). He also later penned documents on cultural policy and helped establish the guidelines by which artists produced culture and art advocated by the Party (28; Đức Huy 2003). Initially circulated to a small number of Party members who dealt with cultural politics and policy, they disseminated the document more widely after 1945 (Ninh 2002, 27).

Cultural policy generated national culture in line with historical, political, and economic narratives present elsewhere in the everyday sphere, including published in print media and discussed in television and on the radio. Sustaining this national culture and the associated national identity imagined by the state involved the replication of similar language in these multiple spheres. The *Đề cương về văn hóa Việt Nam* document outlines three basic tenets or principles to guide cultural production: (1) "nationalization" (*dân tộc hóa*); (2) "popularization" or progress through the masses (*đại chúng hóa*); and (3) progress through science (*khoa học hóa*).[20] (Nationalization and popularization also are central tenets of RVN policy.) In a document prepared in 1944, Trường Chinh ([1944] 1985, 24) argues that each constitutes a part of an unbreakable chain and works in tandem to generate sustainable narratives, including a so-called "mass consciousness," that remain applicable in the present (Marr 1981, 364).[21]

The first of three principles, nationalization, emphasizes *dân tộc*, which is a potent concept meaning both nation and ethnicity. Since every *dân tộc* has specific qualities particular to a nation and its people, Vietnamese artists must search for those qualities or characteristics that are fitting for the entire Vietnamese nation and stress them in art and music. Vietnamese folk songs (*dân ca*) and folk opera (*chèo*) songs from northern Vietnam are, for example, Vietnamese because they exist in Vietnam and have become associated with the Vietnamese identity or consciousness. Replicating the sonic characteristics of these songs therefore teaches others what the Vietnamese nation sounds like.

The second principle, popularization, involves drawing inspiration from the masses, who are at the center of the revolutionary project, to produce a cultural product applicable to their lives and experiences. As Trường Chinh argues, "the masses are the ultimate art connoisseurs since they have many ears, eyes, intelligent brains, and a responsive collective sentiment" (Trường Chinh [1948] 1985, 121, translation by Ninh 2002, 44). Art serves the audience and the revolution; the concerns of the artist are secondary. "Art for art's sake" (*nghệ thuật vị nghệ thuật*), a category defined in the 1944 statement, should not exist, as this type of artistic endeavor distracts from revolutionary causes (Trường Chinh [1944] 1985, 23). This is an important difference from RVN policy and practice, although both policy systems invoke the public as ultimate arbiter of culture.

The third principle, making progress through science, deploys "rational thought" rather than "pure morals, feelings, and supernatural influences" in the production of art (Ninh 2002, 33). Barley Norton shows that concerns about superstition (*mê tín*), for example, prevented the public performance of northern Vietnamese lên đồng spirit possession practices from the 1950s to the 1980s (2009, 28–32). Huỳnh Khải's rejection of *xuất thần*, noted in Chapter 5, is most likely a result of this policy as well.

Deploying musical propaganda involved complex organization directed from high-level officials down through various structures of the government and Party. The *Đề cương về văn hóa Việt Nam* advocated that "cultural revolution must come after political revolution" ([1944] 1985, 17). Once officials solidified the political message, it was transformed properly into a cultural message and delivered through state apparatuses. The "government sought to coordinate and control all cultural expression," Norton argues, "through nationalizing and professionalizing the material bases of artistic creativity and cultural production, from publication presses and newspapers to music and theater troupes" (2009, 33). Creativity, in essence, became part of state bureaucracy. One of its main arms in the 1950s and 1960s was the performance troupe (đoàn); again, one sees similar ensembles (gánh) in southern Vietnam from the same time period. Aligned with political organizations, including the Army, these đoàn produced and disseminated national and revolutionary music (Lê Tuấn Hùng 1998, 110–11; Nguyễn T. Phong 2003, 172–74). The RVN ensembles did not serve the same purposes, although professionalization did occur in educational institutions.

Making music through various state authorities did not mean that the message and music remained fixed. This was a strategic departure from French colonial practice, for which Nguyễn Phụng Michel (1997) advocated. Early DRVN cultural policy advocated that as conditions changed, culture and music must also change. This is fundamental to the discourse of phát triển, where music develops to best suit contemporary conditions. In a description of the national character (*tính dân tộc*) that should be present in all Vietnamese music, former Vice Minister of Culture and poet Cù Huy Cận argued:

> If we do not start from national capital and from the nation's foundational traits that have been gathered, then we are rootless and view ourselves negatively. Furthermore, if we understand the national character as a fixed and formulaic item, then we deny ourselves a future, which is very dangerous because we thwart our growth and progress. If our ancestors also "closed the door," then we could not have developed *chèo*, for example, to the level of today. ([1974] 1976, 126)

Musicians followed certain ideological constraints, but flexibility remained to allow the national identity to evolve and change. As noted, RVN policy makers presented a similar perspective and even used a similar concept, dân tộc tính, to describe this national character. To have a sustainable and viable future, therefore, culture and music should grow and develop in new directions.[22]

Policy presented few specific musical details, making the creative process open to interpretation. In Cù Huy Cận's statement, for example, he highlighted the development of chèo, but provided no description of proper development in musical terms and little guidance toward developing performance practice. Hà Huy Giáp, an important figure in the early days of the Vietnamese revolution, described how old forms (*hình thức*) may reflect new ideology (*nội dung*) for forming a socialist society as long as musicians or other performers either use suitable forms or change existing forms to suit that ideology ([1974] 1976, 9–10). How one should transform traditional music for new ideological contexts, however, is not apparent in these documents.

The policy and practice divide actually left room for experimentation in the production of traditional music in the late 1980s and into the 1990s. Miranda Arana (1999) and Lê Tuấn Hùng (1998), for instance, examine this experimentation in a genre of music called *nhạc dân tộc hiện đại* (neotraditional music) inclusive of newly composed works and those that evoke traditional music.[23] In my experience in southern Vietnam, musicians no longer attach the "hiện đại" (neo) designation, but use the term *nhạc dân tộc* to designate both traditional music and neotraditional music that draws on traditional music aesthetics. National music emerged because many believed older "forms" of traditional music, drawing on Hà Huy Giáp's language, no longer represented the ideals of a new Vietnam; musicians therefore used new forms to make ideology understood by the population. These forms included optimistic lyrics and more upbeat and faster tempos than those found in traditional music (Lê Tuấn Hùng 1998, 98–99). European musical influence abounded as well, including the use of the equal tempered scale, tonal harmony, and European-influenced musical forms. In terms of instrumentation, large ensembles, such as those with many đàn tranh, played works in unison (98–99).

Southern Vietnamese music today draws together elements of RVN and DRVN (later SRVN) cultural policy. This means that the musical experiments started in Saigon before 1975 continue to live today. These experiments develop national music culture and advance nationalistic narratives of unity. Musicians advance the roots of traditional practice and popularize traditional music for contemporary tastes and audiences. At the same time, ensembles are professionalized and large and therefore perform rehearsed music in visually engaging settings to solidify the message of unity through national music. This work rationalizes the ideological framework for commercialization and consumption. Although nhạc dân tộc takes many different forms today, southern Vietnamese music often draws on đờn ca tài tử to espouse a clear southern regionalism within the national fabric. One of the major proponents and developers of nhạc dân tộc in Ho Chi Minh City is Phạm Thúy Hoan, who disseminates knowledge of practice through her Tiếng Hát Quê Hương (Sounds of the Homeland) Ensemble.

SOUNDS OF THE HOMELAND ENSEMBLE

Phạm Thúy Hoan started Tiếng Hát Quê Hương in 1981 at the request of her daughters, Hải Phượng, who is perhaps the most famous musician of traditional music in southern Vietnam today, and Hải Yến, who lives and continues to perform in the United States. Evidently, friends of Hải Phượng enjoyed listening to her perform and expressed an interest in learning to play the đàn tranh. Cô Thúy Hoan therefore agreed to teach both of her daughters in addition to their friends. She began her lessons in the Triệu Thị Trinh School of District 10 in Ho Chi Minh City, using the name *Bản Tiếng Hát Quê Hương* (Sounds of the Home-land Group). At various points in the early 1980s, she moved the lessons to the Ho Chi Minh City Children's House (Nhà Thiếu nhi Thành phố) and the Đuốc Sống School. It became a resident ensemble at the Palace of Culture and Labor (Cung văn hóa lao động) in Ho Chi Minh City in 1984. The secure rehearsal and performance location enabled, in her words, the development of a movement of national music performance in Ho Chi Minh City.[24] Momentum soon developed whereby students had a rehearsal space to which they could always return and invite friends to participate without worrying that the ensemble would be forced to move to a new location. As of this writing, Tiếng Hát Quê Hương still meets at the Palace of Culture and Labor every Sunday morning. Students study the đàn tranh and several other traditional instruments, and learn to sing folk songs.

Phạm Thúy Hoan's goals for the ensemble synthesize cultural policy pro-nouncements of both the RVN and the SRVN. She aims to (1) preserve (*bảo tồn*) and maintain (*giữ gìn*) traditional music; (2) popularize (*phổ biến hóa*) national music; and (3) develop (*phát triển*) national music.[25] In an interview for a televi-sion program about the ensemble, she also indicates an interest in broadening (*rộng rãi*) national music (HTV 2007; see also Cannon 2013, 99–100). She argues that Vietnamese youth do not understand the national character and the music that protects and develops the specific qualities of this character. Instead of being directed by the masses, however, she addresses a perceived knowledge gap and cultivates societal wisdom. She implores her students not to disregard the past in the present, and encourages them to learn to draw on this past as a source of strength. These hopes for inclusivity and unity in the national music genre very possibly have their roots in RVN policy or at least at the National School of Music in Saigon before 1975, but they remain firmly in line with DRVN policy imported after 1975.

The ensemble preserves, maintains, popularizes, and broadens as part of a larger discursive strategy of development. Phạm Thúy Hoan develops national music to build communities, make better sense of external forces in Vietnam, and both address and redress a knowledge gap about traditional music. In so doing, as I have described in Cannon (2013), she seeks to inject a southern Viet-namese voice into national traditional music production that has largely been based on northern Vietnamese cultural production. Cô Thúy Hoan disseminates this regional "culture" under the rubric of national music to generate a powerful sense of national unity and community among her students.

FIGURE 6.3 A Tiếng Hát Quê Hương rehearsal *photo by the author, August 24, 2008*

When Phạm Thúy Hoan started the ensemble, she enjoyed teaching the children, but faced difficulties typical of the period: they were very poor and did not have enough instruments for every student. She could not give individual instruction and therefore taught students in groups. She asked one student to play a composition or an excerpt of a composition while another wrote out the pitches on the blackboard using *Sol La Do Re Mi* syllables. Born out of difficulty, this group-learning technique later became a foundational pedagogical tool of her Sunday morning lessons at the Palace of Culture and Labor.

These teaching principles continue today. When teaching a song, Phạm Thúy Hoan sings the melody and indicates rhythm using solfège pitches to help the beginning instrumentalists play properly and hear the relationship between one pitch and other. Student-to-student instruction also occurs spontaneously, where one student with advanced knowledge and experience helps other students learn (see Figure 6.3). At one rehearsal in May 2009, I observed four đàn tranh students practicing a new composition titled "Quê Mãi" ("Forever Homeland").

One student had more experience with the piece and began leading the small rehearsal without a specific request from Cô Thúy Hoan or one of her other teachers. She sang out solfège pitches in rhythm and indicated the meter of the composition with slight movements of her arm and head so others could learn the melodic and rhythmic content of the composition.

Building communities assures strong bonds between individuals to operate in an urban setting where many genres of local and global music pervade. Cô Thúy Hoan therefore views herself as a type of social activist, where she ensures knowledge about traditional music in particular and national music in general continues to flow freely among individuals in contemporary Vietnam. She adopts the development initiative of unifying and broadening practice by asking students, who often are of very different ages, to gather to sing folk songs typically thirty minutes after the officially designated start time of the Sunday morning rehearsal. Folk songs, as both she and ethnomusicologist Nguyễn T. Phong (2003, 178) argue, developed from farmers singing in fields and did not initially require instrumental accompaniment. Instrumental arrangements only emerged after musicians collected folk songs for concert performances. One needs to learn the vocal versions of these songs to get closer to their source and understand from where they emerged. Singing them therefore brings the students closer to the notion of the nation, a sentiment echoed by Gustave Dumoutier when he wrote that the folk song is "the heart of a nation all exposed" (Dumoutier 1890 as cited and translated by Nguyễn T. Phong 2018, 100).

In all of the rehearsals that I observed over several years, Phạm Thúy Hoan drew songs from throughout Vietnam to generate a sense of national unity through group singing. She had several favorites that she asked students to perform, including "Trống cơm" ("Rice Drum") from northern Vietnam. (Listen to **Track 19**.) She frequently asked students to sing several folk songs in succession from various parts of the country. During one rehearsal, students first performed "Lý bông sen" ("Song of the Lotus Flower") from the Mekong Delta (Cannon 2013, 89–90). They continued with "Bèo giạt mây trôi" (also "Bèo dạt mây trôi," or "The Water Fern Drifts Like a Cloud"), a folk song from the *quan họ* genre of repartee singing from northern Vietnam. The third was another southern Vietnamese folk song titled "Lý đất giồng" ("Song of the Fertile Soil"). The final folk song was the upbeat "Hò đi thẻ mực" ("Going Fishing") from Kiên Giang Province in southern Vietnam.[26] Unlike the other folk songs from southern Vietnam, the singers mimicked the stereotyped and thick southern accent or *miền Tây* dialect from Kiên Giang: they pronounced /s/ like /sh/, /v/ like /j/, and

FIGURE 6.4 Phạm Thúy Hoan teaching in her home *photo by the author, August 17, 2013*

/anh/ like /an/. This use of a stereotyped dialect was not accidental but served as central to the nationalization of regional identity under the rubric of nhạc dân tộc.[27] These four songs taken as a group therefore reveal Phạm Thúy Hoan's strategy of aurally producing the entire nation.

Phạm Thúy Hoan incorporates multiple genres of instrumental traditional music, including đờn ca tài tử, into her teaching, albeit in arranged and standardized forms. She builds knowledge about national music by drawing on what the "ancestors" taught, composing both old (*cổ*) and new (*cải tiến*) works, and performing these together for audiences.[28] Since students learn five-lined staff notation in school, she arranges (*soạn*) the works to teach them quickly and to enable large ensemble performances with many instruments playing one version in unison. She teaches some of the ornamentation required of đờn ca tài tử but does not include all. Excessive ornamentation and improvisation produce a cacophony of uncoordinated sound, which might countermand her professed goal of creating unity through beauty in performance.

In addition to the Sunday morning rehearsals, Phạm Thúy Hoan also holds group lessons in her home on Saturday afternoons. She mostly teaches beginning students but also holds rehearsals for advanced students late in the afternoon when they prepare for upcoming concerts. The students have a range of ages and careers—some are full-time university students and others are professionals.

During the lessons I visited in August 2013, Phạm Thúy Hoan worked particularly hard to train the ears of students, as this was possible in the relatively quiet space of her home compared to the noisy Palace of Culture and Labor. In one instance, she used the *song thinh* technique to test their knowledge of what constitutes being in tune. Some students plucked one string and then generated the same pitch in tune on the next string; other students tried but could not hear that the notes were out of tune. Phạm Thúy Hoan therefore had to indicate to specific students whether the bent pitch was "too high" (*cao quá*) or whether the student should raise (*lên*) or lower (*xuống*) the pitch for it to match that of the unaugmented string. She also trained students to move their hands with some degree of uniformity to play glissandi on the đàn tranh by starting close to the moveable bridge (*con nhạn*) of the highest string and then moving their fingers downward in a diagonal motion away from the moveable bridges (see Figure 6.4). Although this instruction aimed to craft a certain visual aesthetic of unity, students still had to listen to the strings to make sure that each one was in tune.

In one particular lesson, she did this work with the đờn ca tài tử tune "Lưu thủy trường" using notation in her teaching guide *Phương pháp đàn tranh (Đàn Tranh Method)*. As is typical in a method book, études preceded the work so the students could build muscle memory to perform works in the correct mode. (Listen to **Track 20**.) They practiced the *rung* (vibrato) and *nhấn* (bending) ornamentation and some lively and syncopated rhythmic characteristics of the version she notated. As she taught, she focused not only on playing the pitches correctly but also on uniformity. To produce an enjoyable performance, the students plucked the strings at the same time, produced vibrato at the same rate, and bent between pitches the same way. She encouraged an exactitude that is usually absent from đờn ca tài tử performances. The đờn ca tài tử musicians described in the previous chapters certainly needed to play the appropriate pitches of a mode, but they did not need to produce vibrato at the same rate. As such, improvisation and spontaneity were absent from Cô Thúy Hoan's approach.

While some development involves paring down a work, other forms of development are additions. Phạm Thúy Hoan takes inspiration (*lấy hứng*) from older compositions, such as folk songs (*dân ca*) and traditional compositions (*nhạc cổ*, literally, "old music") and adds new techniques.[29] In comments she made at a performance in May 2009, for example, she described two new techniques

FIGURE 6.5 Performance by Nguyễn Thái Hoà, Hải Phương on đàn bầu,
and Uyện Trâm on đàn tranh *photo by the author on May 9, 2009*

included to "make the pieces richer." The first involved a new form of ornamentation using the right hand: using the two plectra, the musician very quickly alter-
nated between two pitches to create a climactic moment. The second involved
strumming up and down the full length of the right side of the instrument with
the right and left hands to generate a constant sound of running water.[30] This is
similar to the technique used by Nguyễn Vĩnh Bảo in his 1972 recording of "Lưu
thủy trường," although he only uses his right hand.

Tiếng Hát Quê Hương also performs publicly to spread her versions of development to a broad audience of students and admirers. In Cannon (2013,
104–5), I describe formal performances called "Hoa Quê Hương" ("Flower of
the Homeland"), which take place throughout the year and were once the most
frequent performances of nhạc dân tộc in Hồ Chí Minh City (Minh Tân 2002;
Cannon 2013, 111n7). Other categories of performance offer more relaxed settings, including informal evening performances called *buổi sinh hoạt* that I
attended in 2009 and 2012, titled "Giới thiệu câu lạc bộ Tiếng Hát Quê Hương"
("Introducing the Sounds of the Homeland Ensemble"). Phạm Thúy Hoan advertises the events outside the Palace of Culture and Labor, as well as via the
Ensemble's websites and Facebook page. Word of the concerts also passes from

current students to their friends. Phạm Thúy Hoan serves as emcee and guides the audience through an understanding of the sounds produced. She asks Tiếng Hát Quê Hương instructors to perform solo and ensemble performances of the most popular instruments, including the đàn tranh and đàn bầu, to indicate the high quality of professional musicmaking (see Figure 6.5).

Students actively participate in this informal setting as well. She asks them to perform on a small stage in a courtyard of the Palace to introduce the type of music performed by the ensemble and highlight the role of students in disseminating knowledge about nhạc dân tộc. Students also sit in the audience and participate in group performances of folk songs. This not only produces a more relaxed environment in which to experience national music but also allows the current students to encourage visitors to socialize and ultimately join the Tiếng Hát Quê Hương program. They share sheet music provided by Phạm Thúy Hoan and sing folk songs that she has arranged. In so doing, the "seed" of knowledge of folk songs held by prospective members begins to germinate into a nhạc dân tộc flower in a field of shared knowledge under her guidance.

I cannot underestimate the success of the Tiếng Hát Quê Hương project. In addition to the performances she crafts, Phạm Thúy Hoan is frequently featured on television and always foregrounds the work of her students. I met a number of musicians through Tiếng Hát Quê Hương, and they lauded her creative energy and hard work even after they departed the school. One friend, Lê Hồng Sơn, once noted that Phạm Thúy Hoan crafted songs that were more accessible to children and has been able to encourage young people to listen to, perform, and appreciate traditional music creation.[31] Another friend described her as extraordinarily kind since she did not speak ill of others, in contrast to many other musicians of traditional music.[32]

Phạm Thúy Hoan's work is also strategic and savvy. Although she had been a professor at the National School of Music and Theater in Saigon, many of her pedagogical methods, compositional practices, and music presentations in performances intersect with policy structures of the DRVN. Her methods also align with development and national music policies of the RVN. In this way, her work cogently synthesizes DRVN and RVN policy in the immediate postwar period, when artistic expression no longer needed to be consolidated and rallied to defeat a common enemy or to form a unified Vietnam under the Communist Party, as this goal had already been achieved. Through Tiếng Hát Quê Hương, she engages in nationalizing music through strategic musical adoption, popularizing music through multiple types of performances and developing both traditional and new music. She does not appear to advocate that one might draw from the revolution or the Party but instead advocates alternate locations of inspiration in music and community. She promotes a lived everyday nationalism, where musicians and citizens interact with one another in performance spaces to develop national music together.

ADVANCING VIETNAMESE CULTURE
THROUGH INTERNATIONAL COLLABORATION

Phạm Thúy Hoan's work occurred in conversation with and alongside the many economic and political changes of the 1980s and later. The mid-1980s in particular saw pivotal changes in Vietnamese policy to combat food shortages and limited economic development in the country. The Communist Party's Sixth Party Congress in 1986 instituted a series of reforms known as Đổi Mới (Renovation) to reorganize state bureaucracy and allow development of the private sector (Masina 2006, 59–64). This has been described as a "socialist market-oriented economy under state guidance" (Beresford and Tran 2004, 3). Following the collapse of the Soviet Union, which had provided ideological and monetary support to Vietnam, the Communist Party sought what historian David Elliott terms "deep integration" into the global market economy (2012, 329). Integration also ushered changes in the cultural sphere. For instance, these reforms opened "a space for revisiting the past," which "allowed discrepant interpretations of the past to come to the fore," and led new "actors besides the state to occupy the space of memory" (Tai 2001, 3). Musicians of traditional music, including Phạm Thúy Hoan, soon found many more spaces in which to operate and negotiate history and memory among audiences in Vietnam and in the diaspora. After Đổi Mới, for instance, she took part in international collaboration, which became a foundational part of her educational model.

Continuing the logic of the *Đề cương về văn hóa Việt Nam*, cultural change on the surface occurred after the economic changes in the late 1980s. In reality, musicians like Phạm Thúy Hoan either preempted Đổi Mới or worked concurrently with these changes, and only later did official cultural policy catch up. After the Eighth Party Congress in 1996, the Communist Party drafted and, in 1998, signed the document "Resolution of the Fifth Conference of the Central Executive Committee (of the Eighth Congress) on Building and Developing an Advanced Vietnamese Culture Imbued with the National Identity" or "Nghị quyết Hội nghị lần thứ năm Ban Chấp hành Trung ương Đảng (khóa VIII) về

FIGURE 6.6 Street poster in Ho Chi Minh City reading: "Building
and Developing an Advanced Vietnamese Culture Imbued with the
National Identity is the Responsibility of the Entire Party and Every
Citizen" *photo by the author, August 13, 2013*

xây dựng và phát triển nền văn khóa Việt Nam tiên tiến, đậm đà bản sắc dân
tộc" (Ban Chấp hành Trung ương Đảng [1998] 2003). The street poster in Figure
6.6 popularizes the policy for Ho Chi Minh City citizens.

The document outlines the methods and challenges of strengthening socialist
practice and developing Vietnamese culture. To a limited but important degree, it
reconciles certain parts of RVN and DRVN policy statements. As a work of socialist cultural policy, it depicts culture as a "front" of the August 1945 Revolution;
however, it also provides insights into the perceived challenges facing cultural
production and the changing nature of cultural synthesis in the last decade of
the twentieth century. Importantly, the Resolution indicates an official pivot
concerning international collaboration. By the 1990s, Vietnam had few Communist allies remaining. The "collapse of the Soviet Union and socialist European
countries," according to the document, "was a great disturbance in the ideology
and sentiments of officials, Party members and workers" ([1998] 2003). Vietnam's
relationship with China also remained strained following a decline in relations
since the 1960s and the border war in the late 1970s. Old allies could no longer
provide ideological support, so new ideological parameters were sought to support and guide the development of national Vietnamese culture. The Resolution

therefore suggests new forms of international cooperation and exchange to help develop and increase exposure to Vietnamese culture. "We have the opportunity to continue to expand on the cultural achievement of humanity [and] at the same time, introduce to people from other countries the beautiful and unique value of Vietnamese culture." This culture must "facilitate the good implementation of the task to preserve and promote the national cultural identity compatible with the quintessence of world culture" ([1998] 2003). Vietnamese culture adopts certain elements from the outside and in return introduces the outside world to the beauty and development of Vietnamese culture. The document even encourages the introduction of national art and culture to Vietnamese living abroad. These initiatives work to build Vietnam's "cultural capital" (vốn văn hóa) (Xuân Hạ and Đất Mũi 2013).

Asian Zither Festival

International collaborations with these new potential partners began slowly. One of the first initiatives involved reviving the Nguyễn dynasty-era court music in the 1990s, where French, US, and Japanese institutions provided support (Norton 2018). In southern Vietnam, collaboration was more ad hoc, relying on personal contacts and considerably less funding. Phạm Thúy Hoan was at the vanguard. She frequently collaborated with the late ethnomusicologist Trần Văn Khê while he was based in France and after he relocated to Ho Chi Minh City. She also pursued grassroots collaborations with musicians in Japan and, later, South Korea, Taiwan, China, and Singapore. With her daughter Hải Phượng, they participated in a series of concerts in Japan in August 1998 alongside Japanese and other musicians from Asia; they also performed in Singapore in 1999. In September 2000, Phạm Thúy Hoan hosted a festival in Ho Chi Minh City showcasing zitherists from Vietnam, Japan, South Korea, and Singapore. She later participated in similar festivals in Singapore, Korea, and Taiwan, and organized the Second Asian Zither Festival in 2008 (Nhạc hội đàn tranh châu Á lần II).[33] She followed this with three zither festivals (Hội ngộ đàn tranh) in 2010, 2012, and 2014 that also involved performers from elsewhere in Asia. I attended only the 2008 festival, which featured performances from Japanese, South Korean, Taiwanese, and Chinese musicians.

Phạm Thúy Hoan invited these musicians to Ho Chi Minh City specifically to solidify the place of the đàn tranh as sonically evocative of the Vietnamese nation and national character for audiences in Vietnam and elsewhere in Asia

(Cannon 2013, 102–8). She professed four ways of building toward this goal. First, she raised awareness among members of the Vietnamese public of the existence of other forms of the zither in East Asia. She hoped that by having the Japanese *koto*, Korean *gayageum*, Chinese and Taiwanese *guzheng*, and Vietnamese đàn tranh side by side onstage, members of the Vietnamese public would make comparisons and learn why each instrument is unique. Second, she wanted audiences to learn more about the sound of the đàn tranh, and specifically understand how one sonically differentiates between the đàn tranh and the other zithers. She hoped that Vietnamese listeners would learn to hear how musicians from different countries emotionally evoke certain sentiments in performance, and in particular, the sentiments that Vietnamese musicians evoke using the đàn tranh. Third, she hoped that members of the Vietnamese public would, after attending the festival, develop a sense of pride in the richness of the Vietnamese zither tradition and, specifically, the traditional and national music produced by the zither.[34] Finally, she sought exchange between zither performers and encouraged đàn tranh performers to borrow from techniques used by other zithers. New techniques "build and develop an advanced Vietnamese culture [still] imbued with the national identity," invoking the vision of the 1998 Resolution. Vietnam then becomes an equal partner in the exchange of musical ideas via the regional flows of culture in twenty-first-century Asia.

During the four days of the 2008 festival, Phạm Thúy Hoan organized workshops and performances to achieve her goals. On the opening day, she hosted an open workshop where performers of each of the four Asian zithers allowed members of the Vietnamese public to touch and play each of the instruments. Simultaneously, they spoke with the performers through translators to learn more about the construction of the instruments, the materials used, and proper playing techniques. On the evening of the first day, the opening concert took place at the Palace of Culture and Labor, which featured instruments and the ensembles from each country to the primarily Vietnamese audience. The concert began with lengthy remarks by invited political officials, including the Vice Chancellor of the Labor Confederation in Ho Chi Minh City. She characterized the performance as a "coming together" of the musicians from different East Asian countries to celebrate the "centuries of common history" between the nations.[35] In the English translation provided, one of the two Masters of Ceremony used the term "transcultural" to indicate the emergence of a pan-Asian identity in the process of exploring the commonalities between zither performance traditions of five Asian nations. With the increasing influence and growing number of

FIGURE 6.7 Vietnamese music performance at the Second Asian Zither Festival 2008 held at the Ho Chi Minh City Conservatory of Music *photo by the author, September 2, 2008*

performances of Western music, the officials continued, performances such as those produced during the festival could "save traditional music" in Asia. The risks of cross-cultural interaction (or fertilization) do not outweigh the reward of a unified attempt to save the musical traditions represented at the festival. The goal therefore appeared to be strength through alliance and camaraderie.[36] The concerts on the two following days featured opportunities for each delegation to perform longer compositions of both ensemble and solo music. On September 2, the Vietnamese, Japanese, and Chinese delegations performed, and on September 3, the Korean and Taiwanese delegations performed. The final day featured performances by all musicians, including a collective performance of the Vietnamese folk song "Lý ngựa ô" ("Song of the Black Horse") (Cannon 2013, 108–9).

The second performance, which featured the Vietnamese delegation (see Figure 6.7), took place on Vietnamese National Day (*Ngày Quốc khánh*) or Independence Day—the day commemorating Hồ Chí Minh's declaration of independence from France on September 2, 1945. This symbolism was not lost on the organizers and members of the audience, as the emcees reiterated the significance of September 2 as one of the most important days for the Vietnamese people. During the one-and-a-half-hour set, which lasted longer than the performances from both Japan and China, Vietnamese musicians performed ensemble and solo compositions. The evening began with the performance of a new composition by the Tiếng Hát Quê Hương Ensemble, followed by traditional music, including "Long ngâm" ("The Dragon's Voice") from central Vietnam, and

Developing Creativity **165**

new compositions, including Phạm Thúy Hoan's "Tình ca miền Nam" ("Love Song of the South").

The performance of "Tình ca miền Nam" for solo đàn tranh appears to particularly uphold the goal of exchange of musical material or the encouragement of strategic hybridity. The composition uses the đàn tranh as gatherer of regional sounds and crafts a narrative using the rondo form (Lê Tuấn Hùng 1998, 98–99, 103). The work references melodic excerpts from southern Vietnamese folk songs and adopts methods of playing the đàn bầu on the bottom string of the zither. The composition also incorporates brief performance techniques played by non-Vietnamese zitherists during performances on preceding evenings, especially during the Taiwanese guzheng solo and ensemble performances. These techniques include glissandi followed by a tremolo produced with either the thumb or index finger using both sides of the finger plectrum. This technique, called *yaozhi* (搖指) on the guzheng, is more difficult to produce on the đàn tranh, as the đàn tranh plectra are designed as extensions of the curved fingernail and are therefore curved inward as opposed to the flat guzheng plectra. Musicians of the đàn sến and other Vietnamese lutes use a similar tremolo technique called *reo*, but the technique is not found in historical đàn tranh performance. The composition also calls for glissandi using the fingernail of the left hand—as, unlike a guzheng player who tapes plectra to four fingers of each hand, the đàn tranh player only uses plectra on two or three fingers of the right hand—while the performer continues to produce a tremolo using the thumb or index finger of the right hand. Lastly, the composition includes a imitation of *fanyin* (泛音), a *guqin* (seven-stringed Chinese zither) and guzheng technique of producing harmonics by shortening the length of the resonating string with the left hand and tapping the string with the fingers—or in the case of the guzheng, the artificial nails—of the right hand (Mitani 1981, 135). In this work, the performer taps a string with the plectrum of the right hand while continuing to ornament the pitch with the left hand.

With these techniques, and particularly the inclusion of this piece in the context of the Asian Zither Festival, Phạm Thúy Hoan has developed Vietnamese traditional music through strategic borrowing from Chinese traditional music and elsewhere. The effective blending of Vietnamese melodies and non-Vietnamese techniques has made "Tình ca miền Nam" one of her most successful compositions. The work piques the curiosity of listeners in its divergence from traditional music and suggests ways for Vietnamese music to be considered both traditional and modern. Placing the composition within the Asian Zither Festival only heightened these associations, as the work came to be seen as traditional, modern, developed, and international.

The Asian Zither Festival fit very well with the pronouncements of the 1998 Resolution on "building and developing" culture. Under Vietnamese leadership, participants heard the intersections and differences between different zither styles with a particular focus on the place of the đàn tranh in the fabric of Vietnamese music. Since Vietnam was considered the weakest regional and global player among the group of nations that participated, audience members and Tiếng Hát Quê Hương could further take pride in the ways that Phạm Thúy Hoan headlined the đàn tranh over the others. Over the course of the festival, participants heard how Vietnamese musicians might draw from external models to strengthen Vietnamese national music. Through manipulation of the processes of the festival, the message to the Vietnamese audience was that Vietnamese music and the related national identity are dynamic, traditional but modern, and advanced like other Asian nations.

CONCLUSION

Traditional music changes. In the past and present, musicians of đờn ca tài tử follow various Daoist ideals to craft their spontaneous performances. Over the course of the twentieth century, musicians replaced this approach with a discourse of development. This development (phát triển) was a response to the French colonial attempts to undermine and fix traditional practice and existed as a postcolonial endeavor to preserve the traditional arts for a free and independent Vietnam. Several iterations of development emerged over the course of the second half of the twentieth century. In southern Vietnam, the cultural policy of the Democratic Republic of Vietnam replaced that of the Republic of Vietnam in 1975, but there were several clear connections between the two policies. Following the reforms of the 1980s, international collaboration and integration became an important part of development. As these changes occurred, traditional music in Ho Chi Minh City as performed by Tiếng Hát Quê Hương and directed by Phạm Thúy Hoan engaged the theories of policy and made them understandable to young audiences in particular.

This chapter started with a story concerning an international festival in Huế that featured propagandistic versions of traditional music. Not all experiments in development are successful, but these still have a role to play in the experimentation related to development. I learned this on more than one occasion.

In April 2009, my friend Lê Đình Bích and I took a music river cruise along the Bassac River in Cần Thơ. The large boat had three stories of simultaneous performances, and as he and I walked from story to story, we heard instrumental đờn ca tài tử and loud pop tunes interspersed by drunken karaoke. At the end of the evening, he told me, "You have to experience everything to understand those things that are truly good."[37] The good and the paltry work together to help audiences understand what is truly effective; at the same time, one should recognize the important role of the musically questionable in creating a living space of musical development. The next chapter takes up an example of how musicians identify and deal with the questionable.

SEVEN
Tradition, Still Remains

Holding a Sony Walkman, Nguyễn Vĩnh Bảo played the crackling sounds of a television program he recorded earlier in the day. He paused the tape and looked directly at me—"That is wrong," he said sternly—and pressed the play button again. We sat in his small studio in Bình Thạnh District of Ho Chi Minh City, and I shuffled closer to hear the recording over the sound of the motorbike traffic flowing through an open window. Written for the đàn tranh, the work evokes modal structures associated with southern Vietnamese traditional music and references local folk songs. The work also features performance techniques not associated with traditional Vietnamese music, such as tempo changes (including a climatic *accelerando* at the end of the work) and methods of plucking the strings associated with the Chinese *guzheng* and Korean *gayageum*. The work is virtuosic, and only professional players are able to read it from staff notation and produce it accurately. He stopped the tape again and admonished the blending of multiple techniques by likening the performance to a hodgepodge meal of "steak, hamburger, spaghetti" and anything else one wished to include. The performance had no direction and no "soul" (*tâm hồn*), in his opinion. Before embarking on a long discussion of how one should preserve traditional music authentically, he pointed to the Walkman and rearticulated his critique in English to ensure I understood: "Wrong," he said; the zitherist "makes the noise of a train."[1]

In this interaction, Nguyễn Vĩnh Bảo critiques "Tình ca miền Nam" by Phạm Thúy Hoan, the work analyzed at the end of Chapter 6. That chapter describes the new ways that musicians experiment with preservation through development and international collaboration. These experiments increasingly divide commentators—some find the performances aesthetically pleasing, while others find them putrid. For musicians who embrace the development metaphor, the new connection of music to economic policy and political directive ignores

FIGURE 7.1 Nguyễn Vĩnh Bảo tuning the đàn tranh
photo by the author, December 27, 2014

present circumstances in favor of a more prosperous and harmonious future. For Nguyễn Vĩnh Bảo and others, music must necessarily engage with conditions of the present, and they use hoa lá cành and other techniques of improvisation handed down from teacher to student for centuries to do so. These two groups argue over how to best preserve traditional music, ultimately depicting their specific approach as more sustainable.

This chapter investigates how Vietnamese musicians sustain traditional music through a reliance on the metaphor of "the ruin." The ruin emerges under specific conditions. Initiatives that encourage economic and cultural development spawn new interpretations of traditional practice, new histories, new compositions, new instruments, and new performance spaces. Musicians like Nguyễn Vĩnh Bảo depict these initiatives as ruining traditional music, and undertake extensive work to propagate their own understandings of traditional music based on past practices. The existence of the ruin therefore suggests a clash of creativity models, but is also generative of creativity itself. Importantly, the musical ruin is not specific to the Vietnamese case but emerges as a creative impetus at particular historical moments where musicians generate new opportunities for personal expression after periods of war or strife, often navigating government-sanctioned or community-generated policy. Following some period of experimentation, too many opportunities crowd the market, necessitating the building of boundaries to protect the creative outlet from being forgotten. This attention to preservation by limiting the growth and development of music helps musicians to maintain their practices and ultimately be heard in an increasingly dense sphere of cultural production.

THE RUIN AS PRODUCTIVE DECAY

I define the musical ruin as a metaphor for a sound object that has undergone devastating and alienating alteration against which a musician reacts in order to perform innovative music and educate others. In Vietnam, musicians refer to the process of ruining traditional music as *làm hư* (to damage or decay) or *làm loạn* (to make disorderly). Nguyễn Vĩnh Bảo and others cannot change the music in ruined form—it already exists in print, in recordings, or on television—and instead of ignoring these forms, they engage with them to produce knowledge of proper practice, instill this knowledge in others, and spur future creativity.

The ruin drives creativity by culling inappropriate contemporary practice through disassembly. Decomposition or decay constitutes an important part of the communal negotiation between disparate discursive musical practices. In Laikwan Pang's evaluation,

> we need a more profound understanding of creativity—one that both builds and destroys, one that connects individuals and also points toward one's own alterity, and one that belongs not only to a few gifted individuals but to all of us. It is our willingness to grant, or simply acknowledge, the full potentiality of creativity that might help us to counter the late capitalist desire for total control. (2012, 45)

One becomes productive through destruction, especially of debilitating structures like development; indeed, the ruin "allow[s] us to step out of history and question the neat linear temporality of historical progress" to recouperative effect (Arnold-de Simine 2015, 95). Furthermore, destruction or ruin serves as activism: one engages alterity, exposes implicit power dynamics of society, and fosters collective identity through practices involving more than the privileged few.

Musicians like Nguyễn Vĩnh Bảo pursue a form of reparative creativity through their invocation of the ruin. They consider the possibilities afforded by limiting development and returning to the seed of tradition. For Diana Taylor, the experience of the ruin "root[s]" the perceiver or receptor of the ruin, "to place reactivated as practice" (2009, 18). The ruin activates, which is fundamentally different than cycles of decline and revival (c.f. Bithell and Hill 2014) described in ethnomusicology, including those revivals taking place elsewhere in Vietnam where musicians seek some kind of sanctioned authenticity (Meeker 2013, 117–37). The ruin enables the activiation of grassroots agency and provides a space within which musicians "can perform the unimaginable, keep the past intact as *past* even as we bring it up close and move through it" (D. Taylor 2009, 14; emphasis in original). I therefore use the ruin to continue the move "away from a deficit discourse of cultural loss" (Bendrups, Barney, and Grant 2013, 154), and propose a different course toward sustainability through repair enabled by rejecting progress and development discourse.

Sustainability, in Jeff Todd Titon's formulation, consists of diversity, limits to growth, interconnectivity, and stewardship (2009, 123). Stewardship often appears the most visible when investigating spheres of traditional music creation in southern Vietnam. Memoirs of, newspaper interviews with, and television programs featuring well-known scholars, musicians, and teachers flood the public sphere with methods of preservation and suggestions for the best ways to teach tradition (Cannon 2013). Nguyễn Vĩnh Bảo, for instance, drew on his extensive experience to present himself as a steward with legitimate knowledge of traditional music performance (Cannon 2012, 128–33). Although not difficult given his age and reputation, he continued to the end of his life to gather musical objects in his studio and add his own commentary. He then curated these intertextual snapshots for his students in Vietnam, France, Canada, the United States, and elsewhere with whom he communicated by telephone, email, and Skype. Conversations with visitors, newspaper articles, and documentary films about him built and maintained his prowess outside of the studio (see Hà Đình Nguyên 2014 as an example).

Limits to growth—or cutting back the old to enable the new—in emic sustainability models are less evident but just as imperative to keeping traditional music active. In other words, processes undertaken by practitioners themselves enable the "viability" and "vitality" of music but, like language, are sometimes naturalized and require some digging to make visible (Grant 2012, 34; 2014). Cycles of sustainable practice involve "production and consumption, increase and decrease, birth, growth, death, decay, and recycling back to life" (Titon 2009, 123). The decay that inevitably follows growth cannot be ignored, nor can the regeneration that occurs following reflection on decay. Nguyễn Vĩnh Bảo undertook this process, for example, by categorizing certain performance techniques as "ruined" and then rehabilitating these ruined musical forms to structure lessons on authentic practice. While many revere Nguyễn Vĩnh Bảo for his work, others continue the cycle, arguing that his practice diverges from other understandings of tradition. In private conversation and over forms of social media, they, too, invoke the rhetoric of the ruin, claiming that certain musicians misrepresent the meaning of tradition and even restrict practice to the point of alienating young people. In essence, all who invoke the ruin draw from their understandings of the past to restore what has been lost, and refurbish a Vietnamese traditional music that will, in their opinion, serve future generations better.

Ruins occur at specific historical moments when individuals react with disgust to the destruction around them. Katherine Bergeron (1998, 5–8) offers an example from nineteenth-century France, but historical Vietnamese music practice also offers a rich example.[2] In his discussion of the influence of Chăm music on central and southern Vietnamese music, historian Thái Văn Kiểm indicates the impact of ruin or decay not only on sound but also on the soundscape or scene of performance in a specific location.

> Above all, the "southern airs," such as *Nam Ai* or *Ai giang Nam, Nam Bình,* [*Nam xuân,*] *Nam thương,* [and] *Vọng phu* or *Quả Phụ,* always transmit the nuance of profound sadness and disappointment that aligns at the same time to the soul of a people in decay [*điêu tàn*], such as the Chăm people, or at least it creates an ambiance of melancholy close to the peaceful sites of Huế, bathed by the unhurried Perfume River. (1950, 22–23; 42)[3]

The influence of this sadness made its way to southern Vietnam and, in particular, into "Vọng cổ," which was extremely popular by 1950 in southern Vietnam and remains so today. In other words, the decay of the Chăm Empire generated of some of the most powerful and sad music of southern Vietnam.

Theorists of the ruin in Euro-American sociology and philosophy offer further insight into the breakdown of structures of knowledge and protection—or perhaps simply "form"—and how individuals reconstitute these structures or forms in new guises following interaction with the ruin. In a description of ruined buildings, Georg Simmel pinpoints its emergence when "nature" overtakes the "spirit"—the human spirit or, perhaps, human creativity—either by destructive forces or by abandonment ([1911] 1959, 262). When one views (or hears) the ruin, one's understanding of nature and spirit changes, thereby stirring the "unfinished and formless" soul (264). Philosopher Felix Ó Murchadha pairs this work with that of Martin Heidegger on the ontology of the dwelling—or what precedes the ruin and provides "protection from damage and threat" (2002, 13). The dwelling therefore provides a space for the negotiation and protection of identity. In the home, for example, threats exist outside in the form of bad weather or political change, and inside in the form of conflicting personalities of inhabitants. The existence of a ruin indicates that due to some sociohistorical circumstance, the boundaries safeguarding identity have broken down, allowing internal contents to spill out and be used by those on the outside, and external forces—often those forces that put cracks in the walls—to infiltrate and inhabit the dwelling.

The ruin does not emerge accidentally but as a result of something sinister (Baudrillard 1989), often where human actors are culpable. "We cannot consider" the ruin, according to Ó Murchadha, "without remembering human action and suffering" (2002, 11). Philosopher Dylan Trigg describes the ruin as an index of trauma and a site imbued with memory both where trauma occurred and that remains tied to traumatic events (2009, 88). In discussing the return of Holocaust survivors to concentration and extermination camps that now only exist in ruined form, Trigg analyzes the rupture that occurs when the body as retainer of memory, place, and actuation of the past in the present encounters a broken or ruined physical location. The ruin serves as "an appearance without spatio-temporal ground to support it," thereby producing "a disbelief [that] intervenes in [the] scene of return" (91). This spectral presence or "haunted undercurrent" in the bodily perception of place brings "voices in the past" into contact with those in the present and produces a "standoff" that confers an "afterlife upon the temporality of trauma, one that outlives the immediacy of the event" (91–93). The "standoff" serves as powerful impetus to generate new methods of protection. "Ruins in this sense are not merely the contingent failure of human action, but rather embody human action beyond the sphere of its possibilities" (Ó Murchadha 2002, 15). In other words, if left unchecked, the decay of the ruin feeds off borderless possibility and grows to topple other boundaries.

This concern necessitates a return to past practice, inclusive of nonaction and spontaneity. In Chapter 29 of the *Tao Te Ching*, Laozi writes: "Everything under heaven is a sacred vessel and cannot be controlled. Trying to control leads to ruin. Trying to grasp, we lose" (2005, 42). Human action through control generates the ruined form, which stands in opposition to memories of previous practice. At

FIGURE 7.2 Graffiti in Ho Chi Minh City *photo by the author, June 10, 2007*

the same time, however, any attempts to recuperate may be interpreted as direct actions and diversions from the natural streams of practice; indeed, one may interpret the ruin or uncontrolled as a kind of natural Daoist state. This disconnect generates a similar kind of "standoff" mentioned by Trigg, and cultivates creation, even if not in completely Daoist ways.

DEVELOPMENT'S FAILURES

The reaction to the ruin serves as a kind of reparative creativity, and contemporary Vietnam is replete with examples undertaken to stifle further decay and erosion of identity. Consider Figure 7.2, an image of the remnants of a bridge anchorage in Ho Chi Minh City. The area of Bình Thạnh District where I took this picture is a cloistered periphery within and surrounded by the rapid and uneven expansion of the urban center. Today, if I were to stand in the same spot and pivot 90 degrees to the right, I would see Landmark81, an 81-story mixed-use tower and the tallest building in Vietnam; if I turned an additional 90 degrees, I would see Bitexco Financial Tower, a 68-story skyscraper. Both remind Ho Chi Minh City residents of the profound disparity between the wealthy and poor in contemporary neoliberal Vietnam. As residents ponder the ruined bridge as a discard of development, they also consider their place within a rapidly changing Vietnamese civil society. Erik Harms's (2016) poignant ethnography of Thủ Thiêm Ward in Ho Chi Minh City points to the ways enforced destruction of and compensation for residential homes and land creates new perceptions of values and individual rights. The ruined anchorage, too, serves as a location for the creation of new meaning—the graffito's message that "hip hop is bullshit! rock is the best!" indicates that the expression of opinions for specific kinds of foreign popular music take place through proficiency in a foreign language.

Contemporary observations of Vietnamese urban planning point to the existence of the ruin and its emergence from development policy. In her evaluation of crumbling buildings originally built in Vinh City with the assistance of East Germany in the 1980s, Christina Schwenkel notes that "late and postsocialist urbanization has targeted devalued 'ruins' for demolition and advocated the construction of architecturally sound and sustainable structures that use and organize space in ways that are more profitable" (2012, 452). Wiping away the vestiges of failed socialist dreams makes way for new capitalist realities of the immediate Đổi Mới period in which Vietnam has very quickly tried to catch up.

Phát triển should not be understood as a unified discursive strategy in Vietnam. Development brings failure with external shocks to the fledgling global participation of domestic Vietnamese markets. With external events, such as the 1997 Southeast Asian and 2008 global financial crises, and with organizations such as the World Bank and the World Trade Organization placing restrictions on economic policy, Communist Party leaders have been unable to sustain a "well-defined national development strategy" (Masina 2006, 3; see also Beresford and Tran 2004, 6–9). Inconsistencies and "contradiction[s] in governance" emerge as the state absorbs external conditions into the paradigm of development (Nguyễn-võ 2008, xix; original emphasis removed). Social media has presented particular difficulties; many Vietnamese now connect with each other and with friends abroad through various media, but occasional restrictions to access remain. State entities unevenly work out methods of subsuming new technologies under the ideology of "development." Perpetually catching up, it seems, takes time (Harms 2011, 23).

The existence of the ruin therefore reminds that development leads to certain types of failure. It is impossible to control a global economy and contain the spontaneity so fundamental to effective cultural practice. Those graffiti artists who marked the anchorage and musicians like Nguyễn Vĩnh Bảo preserve the ruin, rather than demolishing it. They preserve it for heuristic purposes to comment on specific conditions of Vietnamese everyday life and sustain memories pushed aside in development. The disorderliness of the ruin generates and sustains evidence of past practice.

For contemporary musicians, the ruin interrupts development discourse and produces new trajectories of music creation. "What [the ruin] offers aesthetically is the unknown, the innovative that requires participatory receptivity," philosopher Robert Ginsberg argues. "We discover newness and it invites explanation" (2004, 155). The ruin itself is not new, but the reactions to it, as well as the "springing forth" and "activation" of the imagination that takes place, are new (157). In the opening anecdote to this chapter, for example, Nguyễn Vĩnh Bảo hears in the ruined composition references to Chinese and Korean traditional music juxtaposed with folk music from Vietnam. This is "against the rule" of traditional music performance, and he spends significant time interacting with his students, highlighting particular sounds heard in the ruined music and how to recreate these sounds properly.[4]

"DO NOT SELL SOUND TO THOSE WHO BUY HAPPINESS"

The identification of the ruin is not simply an academic exercise. Musicians and consumers of traditional music observe the conditions of practice and begin to discuss—in metaphor—the crumbling of the dwelling or frame of the music. When musicians point to the existence of the ruin, they describe the decrepit structures of practice. The metaphors fundamental to traditional music performance, including đờn ca tài tử, break down, leading to dissolution of meaning. The task then becomes rebuilding the frame to restructure engagement with the outside. They do not seek control of the outside environment, only their engagement with it, so meaningful sound can emerge again from metaphor. Flowers, too, can grow from decay.

Musicians of đờn ca tài tử craft a highly adaptable practice, which continues to generate debates about authenticity. In the past, musicians incorporated Vietnamese, Chinese, Khmer, and French songs into the đờn ca tài tử repertoire, and today, as indicated in previous chapters, musicians continue to compose new tunes and adopt techniques and sounds from East Asian music. With the proliferation of these adoptions in the contemporary context, however, musicians and cultural brokers frequently express concern that unmediated borrowing dilutes traditional practice.[5] Musicians and government officials propose initiatives to secure the essence (*tinh hoa*) of the national identity to đờn ca tài tử, limit borrowing, and establish more secure places of performance.[6] Inaccurate performance practices and improper borrowing therefore become seen as attacks not simply against tradition but also on the essence of a Vietnamese identity itself. A 2011 article in the English-language *Thanh Nien Daily* advocates further measures in an article titled "Save a folk music genre from crassness" (Thanh Nien 2011).

National newspapers indeed raise awareness of these discussions. A 2008 article titled "The music of talented amateurs, therefore . . . amateurish?" in the national newspaper *Người lao động* (*Laborer*), for instance, laments the lack of quality instruction on đờn ca tài tử performance practices in the Mekong Delta in particular.

> Youth who like đờn ca tài tử in the Mekong Delta today still do not have teachers who have achieved a skill level comparable to the level of the previous generation; a number of [these] artists are approximately sixty years old or older. Therefore, in order to develop đờn ca tài tử into a sure means of livelihood . . . [we] cannot simply wait for [even] part of the young generation to become fond of the traditional arts. For a long time, the work [done] to spread đờn ca tài tử in the Mekong Delta [was] mostly done by the previous generation of . . . artists [teaching] the next generation through artistic activities, but [we] do not yet have classes to teach compositions of professional quality. (Lê Như Giang 2008)

The author continues with descriptions of temporary measures taken in Tiền Giang and Bạc Liêu provinces south of Ho Chi Minh City to teach đờn ca tài tử to young people, but notes that more must be done. Six years later, *Người lao động* published a series of articles titled "Return to the space of đờn ca tài tử," which both advocate for appropriate practice and warn connoisseurs and artists to be on the lookout for ill-conceived preservation practices. One article in the series notes that certain inauthentic music featuring poor melodic construction and beat patterns is available in some restaurants on the outskirts of Ho Chi Minh City. The article also quotes one musician's warning on augmenting practice too much to suit the desires of others: "Do not sell sound to those who buy happiness" ("không bán tiếng đờn cho kẻ mua vui") (Minh Nga 2014). This kind of critique of commercialization, and even capitalism, encourages discussion among musicians about not just the possible drawbacks of foregrounding the economic benefits of đờn ca tài tử.

The ruin metaphor emerges in part because of a lack of clarity concerning what constitutes appropriately "developed" practice. Newspaper articles and television reports interview conservatory officials and academics who rarely provide specifics. One article titled "Don't alter đờn ca tài tử" quotes Trần Văn Khê as saying that performers should not augment đờn ca tài tử to be more suitable for the stage and for garnering a profit; instead the genre should "develop naturally" through the sound of the instruments and the voices of the people (Tấn Đức and Chí Quốc 2014). In the same article, Võ Trường Kỳ suggests that the

Institute for Musicology [in Hanoi] immediately needs to organize recordings of the twenty primary pieces [of the đờn ca tài tử repertoire] with the assistance of veteran artists to achieve the highest precision, and to disseminate these for people to consume. (Tấn Đức and Chí Quốc 2014)

The article provides some basic guidelines of development; however, the lack of clarity as to what practitioners should undertake in their everyday practice yields consternation among musicians. One cynical Vietnamese musician refers to this verbiage as "speaking like a parrot" (*nói như con vẹt*).[7] Simply repeating the term *development* indicates the existence of a theory whose practical applications persistently remain unclear (Cannon 2013, 91–94).

This kind of critique often takes place in private spaces where musicians speak with one another over social media, on online forums, and in person to debate newspaper articles, television programs, and festival performances. Some of these discussions are based on gossip, although, as Joseph Roach has noted wryly, "often the best hedge against amnesia is gossip" (1996, 31). In other words, those with a vested interest in traditional music steer debate into the realm of gossip to retain practice and the strengths or errors contained therein. Following "developed" performances, I notice a considerable increase in these debates. Some musicians belabor the over-the-top nature of these large-scale performances, while others retort that they were inspired by what they heard.

During the 2010 Huế Festival performance of the An Giang Artistic Group described at the start of Chapter 6, the musicians fought hard against the weather and technical glitches to perform a work titled "Người là Hồ Chí Minh" to the tune of "Vọng cổ." Like the immediate postwar performances of "Vọng cổ" described by Philip Taylor (2001, 151–54), the ensemble performed a melancholy tune while two singers sang happy lyrics describing the vision and moral values of Bác Hồ. The performance appeared jarring, and members of the audience did not appear to enjoy it. They did not cease their conversations and the applause was short and lackluster; indeed, one performer sitting on the stage looked at the audience and clapped in an exaggerated fashion as if to encourage an audience response, but nothing changed. This seems to corroborate Taylor's claims that even today, attempts to mold "Vọng cổ" still prove unappealing to audiences. When I mentioned the experience to Nguyễn Vĩnh Bảo on my return to Ho Chi Minh City, his reaction was disbelief and laughter. We spoke of it for a few minutes, but he appeared to become forlorn, and eventually asked if we might find a new topic of conversation.

RESTORING AND SUSTAINING MUSICAL TRADITION IN SOUTHERN VIETNAM

Development was not always an ugly term for Nguyễn Vĩnh Bảo. In a series of recordings that he made in the 1980s, he defined *phát triển* as the addition of "hoa lá" to music, or what he called in French the "version élaborée."[8] Since that time period, however, new cultural experimentation brought new understandings of development, and Nguyễn Vĩnh Bảo started to reject the overly political and propagandistic sentiments in "developed" works. "Tình ca miền Nam" and others ceased to accurately southern Vietnamese modes and their associated emotional sentiments. When sustainability came into question, he responded in earnest.

While traveling to a conference in 2016, I received a flurry of emails from Nguyễn Vĩnh Bảo with several of these types of responses. Although not able to move physically as much as he used to, he moved virtually with nimbleness and adeptness as he had done since the early 2000s. The emails, sent to a list of students, admirers, and fellow master musicians, ranged in content from recordings of "Dạ cổ hoài lang" and interviews students had conducted with him, to emails forwarded from students returning to Vietnam to visit their families and take lessons with him. He also sent three emails in quick succession musing on the ills of everyday life in different languages.[9] He sent the first in English and titled it "Suggestions on Simple Faith." It begins ominously with reference to struggles that afflict everyone universally. "We [are] often angry, nervous, excitable, and our disease [grows] worse. That is one of the worst moments of our life," he wrote, and advocated the use of music to overcome these difficult periods.

> Based on my own experience, music can be considered as a philosophy, a kind of meditation helping us to release from tension . . . purify our mind, to develop our love, our compassion and [be] friendly to all beings, remember what is right and forget what is wrong.

The next email, titled "En marge d'une désagrégation" ("On the margins of disintegration"), suggests, with some urgency, the reasons why the fabric of contemporary society seems to be unravelling right before his eyes.

L'individu vise une fin, une seulle: vivre hâtivement dans une frénésie irrationnelle, en cherchant à assouvir ses désirs, et pour y arriver, tous les moyens sont bons. . . . Le danger est réel, il faut le parer. Ayons le courage de reconnaître les ravages causés à notre patrimoine de notre civilisation et faisons des efforts pour les réduire. Mon vœu le plus ardent est que tout Vietnamien médite sérieusement sur ce problème capital de la désagrégation du pays que déchire depuis plus d'un quart de siècle la bêtise des hommes.

Translation:

The individual has one purpose, alone: live hastily in an irrational frenzy, seeking to satisfy desires, and succeed by any means. . . . The danger is real, one must avoid it. Let us have the courage to recognize the damage caused to our heritage by our civilization and make efforts to address it. My most ardent wish is for all Vietnamese to consider seriously the main problem of the disintegration of the country that over a quarter of a century has been caused by the folly of men.

Rampant individualism undermines the music that he crafts, and when the "folly of men" caused the catastrophic events of the twentieth century, heritage generally and traditional music, too, were ravaged. The last message, titled "Cách xử sự của tôi trong cuộc sống" ("My ways of behaving through life"), responds to—among other things—individuals who recently had lambasted him on Facebook and elsewhere for being false and a fraud.

Khi ai đó có dã tâm bịa ra đủ thứ chuyện trên trời dưới biển, nhằm nói xấu tôi, hạ uy tín tôi. Thay vì buồn, giận, tôi chọn cách im lặng để họ thoái mái tiếp tục bắt nạt. Nếu cần trả lời, thì tôi bình tĩnh suy nghĩ trước những lời nói của họ và xử lý sự việc một cách nhẹ nhàng với những lời lẽ êm tai để đánh vào tiềm thức của họ. . . . Nếu họ là người có giáo dục, có học, khi ngẫm ra ẩn ý đằng sau từng câu nói của tôi, thì có thể sẽ phải im lặng ngay.

Translation:

When someone has wicked ambitions, and fabricates all manner of things [literally, "things on land and under the sea"], they stoop to speak ill of me and discredit me. Because of my sadness and anger, I choose the way of silence for them to comfortably continue to bully. If I must respond, I calmly consider first their words and settle on a gentle way to [craft] sweet words to hit them in the subconscious. . . . If they are educated and erudite, when they consider the implications of the phrase I have just said, they will immediately be quiet.

A developed society is a selfish society—one supported by fabrications of "all things on land and under the sea." He and musicians like him have worked hard to acquire knowledge of past practice and sustain in for contemporary use; indeed, musicians of đờn ca tài tử innovate and make the vagaries of everyday life more manageable. Despite preserving the chân phương and hoa lá cành necessary to maintain heritage, he was attacked for his efforts. When threats became personal, he was silenced, but he did not recede into the background. He hoped to generate sound that would convince them of their envy and callousness.

Music Still Remains

Nguyễn Vĩnh Bảo's prose was powerful, but in his French-language poetry he offered some of the most poignant ways to speak about the failure of development. Melancholy but defiant, his poetry reflected on the conditions he faced and plotted effective solutions to work around these conditions. The first lines of one poem composed in 2008, "Mes hivers, mon vrai trésor . . ." ("My Winters, My Real Treasure"), position his practice in opposition to the development paradigm advocated by Vietnamese socialism:

> Le reste de mes ans ne sont que des hivers,
> Dans la nuit, je compose la musique et les vers,
> L'Art pour l'Art j'y consacre mes énergies.

Translation:

> My remaining years are nothing but winters,
> During the night, I compose music and verse,
> I devote my energy to art for art's sake.

He produced "art for art's sake," an ideology explicitly rejected by cultural policy makers and those advocating socialist realism in music (Ninh 2002, 44; Trường Chinh [1944] 1985, 23; [1948] 1985, 121). Another poem composed in 2010 titled "Le déserteur" ("The Dissenter") starts with more despondent language:

Ma vie est un naufrage,
Je crains les eaux et demeure au rivage,
Mais ma musique est comme la mer,
Qui jamais, ne se tait tout à fait . . .

Translation:

My life is a shipwreck,
I fear water and dwell on the shore.
But my music is like the ocean,
That never completely keeps me silent.

The first two lines imply that others deserted him, so he dwells (*demeure*) in a solitary place; the next two lines, however, indicate a respite found in music. Although abandoned, he continued to resound by drawing on an expansive source of inspiration, and students across the world heard him.

The word *demeure* in the second line stands out given its complicated meaning in the French language. The word does not simply mean "to dwell" or indicate abandonment but also suggests that something precipitated the ensuing emotional state of feeling shipwrecked. In the text *Demeure, Athènes*, Jacques Derrida uses *demeure* frequently to reference a simultaneous sense of boundedness and motion that torments. Derrida writes how the term enters his mind and takes hold as he examines a series of photographs of ancient ruins and everyday life in Athens. "Everything having to do with debt and delay can . . . already be found in the word *demeure* . . . everything, eternally, having to do with obligation and time, everything and the rest—remains, destiny, deferral, delay" ([1996] 2010, 9). *Demeure*, therefore, references a particular ontological state in which one is stalled or stationary not necessarily by choice but to repay a debt of some kind.

In Nguyễn Vĩnh Bảo's poem, *demeure* designates the memories with which he contended in the fracture produced by the ruin. These memories "return . . . in [their] absolute fullness, as [were] never experienced in the instance of [their] occurrence or in the rational recollection that took place afterwards" (Trigg 2009, 92). Nguyễn Vĩnh Bảo did not speak specifically of trauma in his century-long lifespan; however, in addition to labeling the "follow of men," he often described his life as "stormy."[10] Recall, for example, that many of his friends were placed into reeducation camps or left Vietnam after 1975.[11] History—or destiny—silenced him, leaving him to *demeure* on the margins of cultural production in Ho Chi Minh City and watch new forms of traditional music proliferate without his participation. In the encounter with the ruin, therefore, a standoff occurred in the present between the past retained in his memory and the development brought by post-1975 policies. He heard the ruin and reacted through music to generate new obligations and histories—the equivalents of the photographs that Derrida views—and restored the ruin to its former glory. No matter how tired he felt, he drew upon his ocean-sized knowledge and undertook this task as his "duty" to disseminate practice to new communities of musicians.[12] In a context where language might make trouble, music relays the complicated positionality and emotions of the performer. Not everyone aspires to rebel or revolutionize; many simply wish to have points made to those who understand them correctly and to wash over those who do not understand them without fear of retribution.

Nguyễn Vĩnh Bảo's reactions to the musical ruin took two general forms: he had a direct reaction to it and also attempted to reproduce indirect reactions in others. In the first case, the ruin spurred the production of music immediately after encountering it. As he listened to the ruined music described in the opening anecdote to this chapter, he strummed the đàn tranh and started to recognize quoted songs, techniques, and other musical elements within the ruin. These brought to mind additional performance practices and compositions of traditional music that were not directly quoted in the performance. Larger components such as form, function, and technique did not align with his memory, however, creating the standoff between his memory and what he heard in the present.

His reactions were strongest when he listened to performances and compositions of "developed" works. He faulted "readymade" compositions instead of improvised ones, the mixing of different folk songs together to produce a new work, limiting the use of ornamentation, and adopting non-Vietnamese techniques without the preservation of Vietnamese aesthetics.[13] In lessons, he distinguished specifically between melodies produced as a result of hoa lá cành and those produced as a result of phát triển. Importantly, this was a relatively new distinction for him that resulted from the emergence of ruined music. Unrestrained development, in his view, "kills the beauty of traditional music";[14] for example, it might involve replacing certain structural notes of a composition with whenever a musician wishes. Nguyễn Vĩnh Bảo used the entry phrase of "Lưu thủy vắn" ("Flowing Water" [short version]) to illustrate this type of development on the đàn tranh.[15] In a typical entry phrase, performances start with a glissando from the highest string of the zither to the tonic pitch *hò* (notated in Figure 7.3 as D). From here, the melody should follow the implied lyrical content

FIGURE 7.3 Different versions of the beginning of "Lưu thủy vắn" for the đàn tranh

of the phrase "Ngày từ ngày đợi chồng" ("Day after day, I wait for my husband"). Although not always performed with a vocalist, the contour of the melody helps audiences recall the lyrical content, connecting the contemporary performance to past performances—a central tenet of tradition, according to Edward Shils (1981, 12–14). As indicated in the bottom line of Figure 7.3, the zitherist brings out the lyrical content with the melody *hò* (D)—*xự* (E)—*hò* (D)—*xự* (E)—*xang* (G), with octave displacements embellishing the initial iteration of these pitches as per the typical zither style of southern Vietnamese music. This melodic line without the octave displacements may be seen as the lòng bản upon which musicians build their improvisations.

Development occurs when the musician replaces certain pitches with new pitches. The musician of the zither might replace the second pitch of the phrase (associated with the word *từ*) while adding another octave displacement to depict an extended part of the range of the instrument, yielding line C of Figure 7.3. This example does not fit with the implied lyrical content, as the octave jump is too far a reach for the imagined vocalist. The beat also does not follow the implied lòng bản of the work, opting for *hò* (D) instead of the necessary *xự* (E). Nguyễn Vĩnh Bảo argued that this type of development, while potentially interesting and deriving from a musician's inspiration, is inappropriate as it does not fit with the character of the composition derived from the memory of lyrical content and past performances. Deviating from the melodic contour especially at the beginning of the performance blurs or disrupts the memory and rewrites the remembered associations with the work. Development, it seems, encourages revisionism and disruptions with the past, which is antithetical to the propagation of traditional music.

The accurate method of rendering a melody is hoa lá cành. In this instance, musicians should draw on the implied lyrical content directly. Furthermore, as long as they maintain the structure of the lòng bản, they may anticipate beats or pitch content, add passing notes, use glissandi, and incorporate other methods used to beautify a work based on their inspiration in the present. In line A of Figure 7.3, Nguyễn Vĩnh Bảo demonstrated the way that the musician adds rhythmic variety by displacing the *xang* octave leap by one-half of a beat; the required move to *xê* is condensed into one-half of a beat before the leap to *xang* (G). In line B, he demonstrated brief syncopation and additional rhythmic variation.

In the discussion of the musical ruin, Nguyễn Vĩnh Bảo proposed a middle ground between so-called "authentic" or "quintessential" sounds and so-called "developed" techniques borrowed from elsewhere. Indeed, embellishment also involves tactical borrowing from outside the đờn ca tài tử tradition; however, as he invoked imaginary European and Chinese interlocutors, he observed in this interview excerpt that over-adoption obscures meaning.

NVB: In Vietnamese music, we prefer the deepest of the musical traditions. Listening to music [is like] looking at the cathedral. You look at the form, architecture and the equilibrium of the general form. When you enter the home of a European . . . [the] furniture is in very good harmony, but the wood is ordinary wood. . . . In the home of a Vietnamese, everything is . . . in very bad order. . . . [But] if you look at the furniture, you see the decoration; you admire the beauty of it. . . . Vietnamese music expresses the sentiment . . . the feeling of the musician . . . I play classical music . . . but I try to embellish old pieces of music, you know? I embellish them.

AMC: Would you call it updating an old piece of music . . . but using your own self as opposed to some other model?

NVB: Yes, but I always keep the basics of the piece, and the listener can recognize the name of the piece when I play. Some musicians . . . renew the piece. . . . You listen to it, but you don't [know] the name of the piece. You must [spend] at least ten or five minutes to recognize the . . . piece.

AMC: I see what you mean. . . . Do you think it makes it more exciting for a listener when they have to discover . . .

NVB: (interjecting) Yes . . . the music offers listeners [in] each performance a special reaction, a special feeling.

AMC: Do you think there are Vietnamese performers . . . who try to perform . . .

in a more Western way? So, for example, using your furniture metaphor, trying to rearrange the furniture in the Vietnamese house to be more harmonious, like in the Western house, and maybe bring in some new pieces with wood that [is] not very good. Do you think there are some musicians who try to westernize Vietnamese traditional music?

NVB: I think such a thing does not enrich Vietnamese music, does not express correctly the real Vietnamese traditional music, because if you speak Vietnamese, you must respect the grammar. . . . If you speak Vietnamese with Chinese grammar, it is wrong. For example, the word "simple": Vietnamese say "đơn giản" . . . and Chinese [say] "jiandan" [簡單]. . . . In Vietnamese, "I beat you to death" [is] "Tao đánh mày chết"; in Chinese, "Wo da si ni" [我打死你] is "I beat to death you." You can take a few elements from others' music in the world [on] the condition these combinations do not destroy your own music.[16]

When one borrows from another tradition, one must augment the adopted technique to fit the rules of the home tradition—in other words, "respect the grammar" and methods of expression in traditional Vietnamese music. For example, in a 2009 recording of "Lưu thủy trường," he experimented with timbral phenomena in the improvised introduction and adopted the *fanyin* technique of producing harmonics from *guqin* and *guzheng* performers. This is one way to "shape" the note in Chinese *guqin* music, a technique that "does not generally change the perception of pitch or the overall form of the piece but subtly helps mold phrase structure, enrich the sound texture, and even project modal characteristics" (Yung 2009, 84). Although Nguyễn Vĩnh Bảo's technique sounded similar, he moved a rubber band onto the strings to produce the harmonics so he still had use of his left hand to ornament the pitches. He did this because his conception of pitch and ornament were not separable; in order to borrow the technique appropriately, he still needed to be able to ornament the pitch to express the emotion associated with the work. In his opinion, this differed from other Vietnamese musicians, like those described in the previous chapter, who also incorporate the technique but use both hands to produce harmonics, thereby leaving no hand to produce ornamentation. Without ornamentation, the Vietnamese content is missing from the performance, and one cannot identify the home tradition or dwelling as Vietnamese.

Nguyễn Vĩnh Bảo as restorer then became educator, invoking the ruin indirectly as a strategy of resemblance or, in the words of Lawrence Kramer, "a closed system within which to construct a critical narrative of imitation, innovation, maturation, development, transformation, evolution [and] decline" (2011, 165). The decayed music needed to be made iconic — so the music heard on television was recognized as neotraditional music, for example — to build "heuristic, not aesthetic" value (166). In Nguyễn Vĩnh Bảo's case, it was doubly heuristic — labeling others' succumbing to neotraditional practice and his triumph in persevering to preserve tradition. Ultimately, the ruin must crumble, yielding an authenticity that, for Kramer, "begins where resemblance ends" (166).

In the indirect case, Nguyễn Vĩnh Bảo drew from his initial reaction to the ruined form to forge a pedagogical tool. To produce knowledge about traditional music for his students, he first constructed a logical case that certain music exists as ruined since few, especially young students, may understand it as such. In the case of the physical ruin, for instance, they do not realize the power of the remains of a bridge or building until they hear stories and understand individual memories about the place, and then, with the help of those who told the stories, adopt them as collective memories. The same holds true for the students' interaction with the musical ruin: they did not understand it until he presented a case for the music as ruined and then shaped their understanding of it. Students can only internalize so much, however, if they have not experienced dispossession and loss. The reproduction of spectrality therefore depends upon how well Nguyễn Vĩnh Bảo both linguistically and musically rhetoricized the musical ruin for those who could only experience it indirectly.

In lessons, he crafted a strategic methodology to impart his understanding of the ruin. He first played a recording of the musical ruin that he encountered, and remarked that something was "wrong" and "against the rule." The recording exemplified what Robert Ginsberg calls "pure duration" (2004, 161). The ruin is, in effect, uninhibited by time, similar to a museum object hanging in a gallery outside of time and outside of ordinary existence (Barndt 2010, 276). The recording enabled him to replay the ruin and, during each playing, choose different parts of the performance to critique. By bringing out various "inauthentic" techniques and establishing their "authentic" counterparts, he created new meaning, element by element. As he played a recording, he tuned his đàn tranh to match the tuning of the zither in the recording. He occasionally stopped and pointed to his cassette player to visually emphasize certain moments to which he later returned in the lesson.

As he replayed the recording, Nguyễn Vĩnh Bảo attempted to produce disbelief. "This is pure invention," he declared when playing the hodgepodge work.[17]

The composition was precomposed and therefore not subject to the inspiration of the individual musician who improvises traditional music. The work also incorporated disparate musical styles and pieces with little or no transition between them. One must learn, therefore, how to make the transition not just between parts of a composition but also between different compositions; he then showed the student how to do this. The conversation continued to how one should approach improvisation. This process continued, oftentimes, for one or two hours.

Nguyễn Vĩnh Bảo used the musical ruin to inspire creativity and imagination as a vital part of tradition. He described ensemble performances of traditional music as "conversations," and after interacting with the ruin, he seemed particularly eager to perform with others. On one occasion, for example, he drew from his reaction to the ruin to teach and then play "Vọng cổ" with me.[18] Strumming the moon-shaped lute, he began with the improvised prelude. He first explored the proper ornamentation of xàng già. As indicated in Chapter 4, combined with the vibrato ornamentation, the pitch properly evoked the tension associated with the mode of the work, oftentimes described as a sadness that aches or torments and does not dissipate. (Listen to **Track 4**.) He then introduced the other pitches of the scale and other characteristics of the mode. After he completed the prelude, I began to improvise on the zither a metered section based upon the lòng bản of the work. Being aware of the microphone turned toward me, I appeared nervous and initially played too quickly. After he entered, he slowed me down and took the lead, as the moon-shaped lute player is often expected to do. Our melodies intertwined and diverged, and we landed on the same pitch at specific structural moments of the work. We improvised, ornamented, and embellished out of his engagement with the ruin.

THE RUIN IN SOCIAL MEDIA

Invoking music in ruin has spread recently through new media to generate additional trajectories. Online forums, such as Cổ Nhạc Quê Hương (con-hacquehuong.com) and Đam San.net (damsan.net), have played a significant role in disseminating information to those who have subscribed. Since 2014, Facebook also has become a forum for disseminating opinion more publicly. The social media website offers new means to establish contact between and develop communities of musicians and their followers in southern Vietnam and in the diaspora. By posting photos of recent concerts and announcements about upcoming programs, users disseminate information more quickly than newspapers articles, television programs, and word of mouth.

Facebook also has become a forum for commentary on personality and practice; due to the permanence of the posts, like the ruin, they remain outside of time and are publicly viewable for many months or years. Individuals post their opinions about particular musicians under real or assumed names; they tag friends and master musicians with whom they are friends and perhaps with whom they hope to curry favor. Such tactical tagging provides legitimacy—which is sometimes temporary before those tagged remove their names from the post—to oftentimes vitriolic comments. Two examples of this kind of commentary that took place in 2014 reverberated throughout traditional music communities based in Vietnam and abroad. In July 2014, a poster to whom I refer here as "Phi" criticized on her publicly accessible Facebook page two leading đàn tranh performers.[19] She took issue primarily with the English translation of the đàn tranh as the "sixteen-stringed zither" in the title of a music festival and various associated concert programs that took place in Ho Chi Minh City and featured the two musicians. The translation devalued the original term. Posting in Vietnamese, she wrote: "When presenting [music] to the international community, the koto is the koto, the guzheng is the guzheng, the đàn tranh is the đàn tranh, the violin is the violin to preserve the original language of the instrument's name. Who recognizes the '16-string zither' as the Vietnamese đàn tranh? Respond clearly to this issue." This language indicated a concern for international recognition. By translating the term, the organizers of the festival blocked the potential prestige afforded by foreigners referring to the instrument in its original Vietnamese.

The post also advocated a brand of nationalism based on a perception of authentic traditional music besieged by foreign influence (see also Harris 2012, 463). Although both đàn tranh musicians she attacked were trained in Vietnam, one already moved abroad. The poster directed highly insulting language—described by one commenter as "nặng lời" (heavy words)—at the musician based abroad. She insinuated that moving abroad and using the English translation blinded the musician to the đàn tranh and, by extension, the Vietnamese nation. She continued by devaluing the contemporary musical experiments undertaken by the musician while living outside of Vietnam.

A few months later, another poster I will call "Hoà" began writing messages criticizing Nguyễn Vĩnh Bảo's character and simultaneously started to request the friendship of many musicians and scholars of Vietnamese music.[20] He wrote very little about Nguyễn Vĩnh Bảo's musical output. In one post, he called recent claims made at a ceremony honoring Nguyễn Vĩnh Bảo's contributions to traditional music preservation in Vietnam and abroad "boasts" or "lies." In these statements, he used the pronoun *mi*—a term with origins in central Vietnam—to refer to Nguyễn Vĩnh Bảo. This usage is considered extraordinarily disrespectful and, unless speaking with a close friend, it imparts significant condescension or disgust toward another in conversation. Although many originally tagged untagged themselves and unfriended this individual, some—including Phi— expressed encouragement and support for bringing these details to light.

Both comments caused many private discussions between musicians in Vietnam and in the diaspora and indicated the increasing propensity of individuals—shielded in some cases by anonymity—to express their opinions publicly. Like other online forums for musical exchange, the discussions become vitriolic and insulting (see Harris 2012, 461–62). Posts on Facebook and other forums pointed to perceived detrimental practices and linked to previous conversations on preservation. This made coherent the increasing amount of information available online about musicians and generated more effective social commentary. Tagging other musicians lent legitimacy to the comments, and new communities of likeminded individuals emerged. The communities drew on interpretations of the sound produced and generalizations of the character of musicians to identify ruined music that required reconstruction.

TACTICS OF THE HIDDEN RUINS

Nguyễn Vĩnh Bảo features prominently in this chapter because he advanced a particular discursive strategy in his lessons and written work. Other musicians also invoke the ruin in more subtle ways; they take a more tactical approach, working without spoken language to support their reparative work. This work occurred throughout my research in southern Vietnam, but I try to capture the vibrancy of đờn ca tài tử reparative experimentation over a month of research I conducted over December 2014 and January 2015. These examples offer ways that musicians try to popularize traditional music, bring in new audience members, and work within the rules of đờn ca tài tử to sustain it. These examples attempt to reestablish the rules or chân phương, perhaps, of traditional music for twenty-first century audiences, and there is a clear attempt to demonstrate to audiences that traditional music is worth saving.

On Sunday, December 28, my friend Việt and I attended a concert advertised primarily on Facebook at the Palace of Culture and Labor in Ho Chi Minh City. Touted as a concert featuring "âm nhạc cổ truyền" (traditional music), it featured collaborations between two local music clubs (câu lạc bộ). The audience was relatively small, and most of the audience members with whom we spoke appeared to be friends of the performers. The music ensemble initially consisted of đàn cò, đàn kìm, đàn tranh, and ghi ta phím lõm; a đàn bầu player arrived late. The đàn cò player also played a keyboard for certain songs and sections of pieces, introducing triad-based harmony. The musicians sat to the side of the stage, and it quickly became clear that singers were the primary focus of this concert (as I also found in the 2010 Huế Festival concert). When the performance began, the sound was deafening; we clearly heard the singers through the sound system, but save for the ghi ta phím lõm player, the instruments were barely audible. The performance featured an array of different genres and styles: the first tune performed was most like đờn ca tài tử, and each subsequent one seemed to take on more and more characteristics of cải lương: the singers used a greater range of gestures as they sang, which is more indicative of the theatrical tradition, and the musicians produced relatively fast melodies with little improvisation, which I really could only discern by following their movements on the fingerboards of their instruments. At one point in the fourth piece, the musicians stopped playing and an electronic dance track took over; this continued for a few minutes before the musicians started up again. At this point, the đàn bầu player had arrived, and I also could hear his melody more clearly since the đàn bầu is also typically connected to the sound system. As I tried to gauge audience reaction to these tunes, I saw one of the singers walk toward the stage wearing a sailor's outfit. Given the volume and the probability that the sailor singer would next sing about the defense of the Vietnamese islands in the Eastern Sea from Chinese aggression, I suggested to Việt that we depart; he quickly agreed. In our postmortem discussion, he encouraged me to think about the concert in positive terms and how the music experimented with new sounds and subjects and attempted to encourage the participation of young people on terms that may be better understood by them. As Lê Đình Bích had also advised during the 2009 boat performance described in Chapter 6, one needs to experience everything to appreciate what is the most interesting.

For traditional music to compete with a fast-paced everyday life that includes a good deal of popular music, it needs to complete on popular music's own terms. In other words, tradition needs to become a new icon of modernity. My friend Việt made these points clear to me early on this trip. To accomplish this, he suggested that foreigners might encourage young people to think of tradition as popular and invited me to attend one of his university classes to speak with his students about my interest in Vietnamese traditional music and culture. When I suggested that I would benefit from some visuals in a PowerPoint presentation, he politely told me that he was not looking for that. He wanted the presentation to be engaging for the students: I would generate excitement in the students and then field questions about the possibilities of expression enabled through music. Traditional music, even in popularized form, needs to live and breathe in vibrant ways—young people need to be able to talk to it and through it; it also needs to talk back. I could not simply present pretty pictures on a PowerPoint and expect that students would find them attractive.

On Saturday, January 3, I returned to the Palace of Culture and Labor to attend an evening performance titled "Hoa Quê Hương 57" ("Flower of the Homeland, Concert 57") at the invitation of Phạm Thúy Hoan. She worked hard to organize this and other small and intimate performances, and often worried that the young people invited would not attend, instead opting to spend time with friends on a Saturday evening. On this particular Saturday, she had a further concern that potential attendees would be out of town for the New Year holiday weekend.[21] She competed, here, with an increasingly modernized Ho Chi Minh City, with its many cafés, movie theaters, and low-cost flights to destinations in Vietnam and elsewhere in Asia. Although this was not an unfounded worry, participants filled the space that evening, indicating the popularity of her efforts.

Phạm Thúy Hoan recognized the need to complete for the time of students since she has difficulty retaining students in her lessons.[22] Students study for a short period of time and then leave after only learning a few short tunes. With the Hoa Quê Hương performance in particular, she generated a sense of musical camaraderie between younger and older performers with disparate abilities. She hoped that the younger students would take inspiration from the older and more advanced students. They would then be encouraged to stay in the ensemble.

Phạm Thúy Hoan did not invoke the ruin specifically, but did imply that she needs to recuperate the young person's experience with the sounds of tradition. In the ninety-minute performance, she guided participants through a musical journey through the Vietnamese homeland. She started with the sounds of beginners: the first ensemble featured three rows of đàn tranh, a *đàn tứ* (four-stringed lute in the shape of a rectangle) providing a bassline, two drummers, and a *sáo trúc* (transverse flute). Although they played relatively simple songs with limited ornamentation, the group captured the multigeneration and supportive ethos of the Tiếng Hát Quê Hương project. The đàn tranh players featured older women in the back row and progressively younger students in the front two rows; two men played the drums and a little boy played the sáo trúc. Phạm Thúy Hoan used the *song lang* as a metronome to keep the beat since the students had a tendency to rush. The second set featured eight đàn tranh musicians; three men and five women of various ages participated. During her remarks, Phạm Thúy Hoan noted that the musicians "studied older pieces as well as newer ones," which presents "old" and "new" as complementary. The first piece was the đờn ca tài tử standard "Bình bàn vắn," and the second performance was a new work titled "Việt Nam Quê Hương Chúng Tôi" ("Vietnam, Our Homeland"). Phạm Thúy Hoan passed around lyrics and invited everyone to sing. Performances of increasing degrees of difficulty followed, and the evening ended with two folk songs and a rousing performance of ABBA's "Happy New Year" to celebrate the start of 2015 in a further effort to bring the old and new together in performance.

Three days later, I traveled to Cần Thơ for a day at the invitation of Lê Đình Bích, who was giving a lecture to a group of American university students during which Trần Minh Đức was on hand with a group of musicians to provide a live demonstration of đờn ca tài tử. I have previously seen Lê Đình Bích give this lecture: He centered his lecture on the multicultural nature of the Mekong Delta, and how Chinese, Vietnamese, and Khmer populations work together to create a unique space of cultural production different than that found elsewhere in Vietnam. On the surface, he advanced the Nam tiến narrative described in Chapter 3, where Vietnamese expanded into the south and absorbed cultural elements along the way. Unlike the common Vietnamese-language histories of the Nam tiến, however, he did not make any remarks about "civilizing" the largely unused land of the Mekong Delta. He instead advanced a tricultural mixing to produce art and music, including đờn ca tài tử. He then had the musicians play "Ngũ điểm — Bài tạ" ("Five Grades — Song of Thanks"), a piece he argued is claimed by Vietnamese, Chinese, and Khmer musicians in the Mekong Delta. (Listen to **Track 21**.) This is not an unfounded assertion. In a 1980 recording given to me by Nguyễn Vĩnh Bảo, he asserted that this tune expresses a "Guangdong style" or mode (*điệu Quảng*).[23] Khmer Krom and Vietnamese musicians occasionally play the piece together in live and televised performances in the Mekong Delta.

"Ngũ điểm — Bài tạ" is an introductory work designed to help beginning instrumentalists perform đờn ca tài tử. Nguyễn Vĩnh Bảo starts all of his beginning đàn tranh students with the work; Trần Minh Đức taught it to me in the first month of our đàn sến lessons. (Listen to **Track 22**.) Neither musician emphasized the multicultural nature of the work in their lessons with me, but given their use of the tune as foundational to the đờn ca tài tử tradition, as well as their frequent reference in their conversations to Chinese, Khmer, and Chăm influence, the work does fit nicely into a narrative about the cocreated nature of traditional music in the Mekong Delta as involving participation of all groups living there.

Vietnamese musicians and listeners may be too wedded to the idea that đờn ca tài tử belongs only to Vietnamese audiences. By teaching đờn ca tài tử to foreign students as multicultural and selecting a piece belonging equally to Vietnamese, Chinese, and Khmer communities living in the Mekong Delta, these musicians attempt to rectify some of the damage caused by the Nam tiến narrative. Rectifying the ruins left by the southern advancement, they build bonds between communities.

Nguyễn Vĩnh Bảo most likely would consider all three of these examples "wrong," given the popularization and fast melodies produced. Like him, however, the Palace of Culture and Labor musicians, Phạm Thúy Hoan, Lê Đình Bích, and Trần Minh Đức respond to the exponential growth of traditional music by trimming back Vietnamese cultural practice. They work together in groups, engage with foreigners, and advance new (and more inclusive) histories of tradition. Instead of going to the cinema, young people build a sense of belonging through multigenerational and multicultural traditional music. They, too, reclaim tradition from the clutches of development.

CONCLUSION

Therefore the one who lacks no goodness
is fit to lead those who lack,
and those who lack
are themselves a resource. (Laozi 2005, 39)

Traditional music in Vietnam, for some, is placid and unmoving; it represents a bygone era with which one flirts nostalgically. For others, it remains a viable method of engaging with contemporary conditions. I evoke this dualism in the title of this chapter adopted from *Athens, Still Remains*, a translation of the title of Derrida's *Demeure, Athènes*. The Vietnamese musicians described here seek to sustain traditional music and establish themselves as part of history, part of the present, and strategists of future cultural function. This is not a new process; in the epigraph that starts this section, Laozi could have been writing of sustainability, where the steward draws on the ruin—something lacking "goodness"—to solidify the position of teachers and their lessons.

In this chapter, I have defined the concept of the musical ruin, or a decayed musical form, sound, or composition that conflicts with memory of practice. The ruin emerges in particular historical moments and, when deployed, serves to facilitate enunciation for those who feel increasingly unheard. Musicians use the rhetoric of the ruin to limit development and to repair perceived damage to traditional music. The ruin establishes a dialectical interlocutor to break open the logic of musical praxis and specify more appropriate trajectories of performance. It brings into stark relief the passage of time and the discomfort of simultaneous separation and immediate standoff; when engaged, it reveals complete experiences that do not dissipate easily and therefore spur creativity.

I draw specifically on the case of music practice in southern Vietnam where the recent reliance on development paradigms advanced after Đổi Mới without clear guidance concerning music practice produces too many possible trajectories of đờn ca tài tử practice. Nguyễn Vĩnh Bảo responded to these conditions by deploying his knowledge of traditional music effectively and crafting viable alternatives to neotraditional and newly composed music that permeate everyday spaces of contemporary Vietnam. In performance, he dismissed "development" in favor of "embellishment"—one might also see this as exploiting the inconsistencies of development policy toward new ends. Other musicians also take part, although in less vocal forms, to maintain their understandings of the viability of tradition in an increasingly crowded sphere of traditional practice. Nguyễn Vĩnh Bảo exploits *demeure*, and others use tactics of commentary to recuperate traditional music from perceived decay or ruin. They cannot ignore the metaphorical "noise of the train," so they reshape and sustain đờn ca tài tử for vibrant uses in the twenty-first century. Chapter 8 offers a further evaluation of the roles that technology and media play in this process.

EIGHT

Creativity in New Directions

In July 2012, a Vietnamese Canadian friend invited me to attend a rehearsal of đờn ca tài tử in downtown Ho Chi Minh City. Huỳnh Khải organized the rehearsal, which took place in the multistoried City Cultural Center in District 3 of the city, in preparation for a performance to be held in Cà Mau City at the end of the week. The building was created for a metropolis—narrow, nondescript, and unobtrusive—much like perceptions of live traditional music in urban centers in southern Vietnam. Indeed, while I waited for my friend, the construction workers smoking cigarettes with whom I loitered outside of the building appeared oblivious to the goings-on of the cultural center. After my friend arrived, we climbed a steep concrete ramp leading to a narrow entryway and ascended in a dingy elevator to the rehearsal room. The doors opened right into the space, and a reporter and cameraperson from a local newspaper greeted us. Their presence surprised me initially, but I understood later that they represented growing interest in traditional music performance among Vietnamese media outlets. The labor of the musicians and the documentation by these media outlets generated interest in this music among the general population; working together, they hoped to find new ways to compete with the rapid development of the city and maintain enthusiasm for traditional arts alongside other contemporary artistic forms.

I initially occupied myself with arranging my camcorder and considered the complicated nature of the rehearsal space—one very different than those I encountered during my research in the Mekong Delta. This rehearsal and the performance to happen a few days after were presentational in nature and required capturing the relatively quiet sound produced by each instrument and amplifying it.[1] As icons of modernity and development, the microphones and the amplification system clashed with the ways that đờn ca tài tử has been performed and consumed in the Mekong Delta for more than a century. Small groups of friends assembled in courtyards and in outdoor drinking establishments to smoke cigarettes, drink beer, reminisce, joke, and perform the music that most studied from childhood. The musicians improvised around loose structural melodies on various kinds of string and woodwind instruments, as well as sang prewritten or improvised lyrics. Musicians imbued these performances with a sense of local identity; even musicians who traveled often from Cần Thơ to Long Xuyên to Rạch Giá performed with local musicians to exchange musical ideas and build new pieces. Taking a form of music that emerged out of local engagement in the Mekong Delta, preparing it in a rehearsal in Ho Chi Minh City, and then representing it to an audience in Cà Mau without engaging local performers struck me as urban arrogance that was perhaps akin to colonial projects that concertized đờn ca tài tử for French audiences in the early twentieth century. Silenced into presentation, musicians did not engage with local audiences and enable embodied understandings of music practice.

A reporter interrupted my train of thought with a request to interview me. Since the musicians had started to tune their instruments and improvise onstage already, I assumed that she wanted to interview me quietly with the music playing in the background. I reluctantly agreed, as she was on assignment and needed material for her piece, and I hoped we would finish before the rehearsal started. I sat where she directed me, and right before she started to ask me a question, she paused, turned to the musicians, and asked them to stop playing. Horrified, I protested and suggested we speak later; she dismissed my concerns with a wave of her hand, and since the musicians had started to wait already, I resolved to get through the interview as quickly as possible. I proceeded to give a forgettable interview filled with silence and pleading glances to my friend to stop this and allow the rehearsal to start. When the reporter realized, finally, that little could be salvaged from the recording of my halting prose, she allowed the rehearsal to begin.

The rehearsal began like many đờn ca tài tử performances found throughout southern Vietnam. (Listen to **Track 23**.) The đàn kìm started the *rao*; the players of the đàn tranh and ghi ta phím lõm then joined in turn, providing the feathered introduction typical of ensemble *rao*. The last musician to enter was Huỳnh Khải on the violin.[2] With a sudden slowdown, however, the đàn kìm player gave him only a few seconds to add to the overlapping melodies and timbres produced by the other musicians. After the tap of the *song lang*, the musicians played "Lưu thủy trường," but it was shorter than what I observed in the Mekong Delta and elsewhere in Ho Chi Minh City. Since this was a rehearsal for a performance with a fixed program, the musicians were under time constraints.

FIGURE 8.1 Hải Luận on ghi ta phím lõm, Huỳnh Khải on đàn viôlông (or đàn vĩ cầm), Duy Kim on đàn tranh, and Trường Giang on đàn kìm, while a bust of Hồ Chí Minh looks on from behind *still from video by the author*

After they finished, an emcee walked out onstage and welcomed the invisible audience. She introduced the musicians, the piece played, and she started to describe the next piece when Huỳnh Khải interrupted her and corrected the title and the writer of the lyrics. Huỳnh Khải wanted the information to be accurate to teach listeners about authorship and how musicians and writers continue to write lyrics that deal with contemporary life and everyday conditions. This enthusiasm for shaping the staged performance contrasted with the facial expressions of other musicians, who simply looked like they wanted to get on with it. The emcee laughed, looked at her cue card, and started again. The rehearsal soon continued with a range of other đờn ca tài tử pieces for voice and ensemble.

This is the đờn ca tài tử tradition in the early twenty-first century (see Figure 8.1). As an example of developed (phát triển) music, one also saw the manipulation and controlled dissemination of aesthetics and meaning with mechanisms designed to generate legitimate understandings of traditional culture: a group based in a major urban center crafted a performance in a rehearsal space established by a local government authority. An emcee holding a microphone practiced how to narrate the meaning to the audience. Media outlets recorded the music and interviewed participants so others could also witness the active preservation of tradition.

Despite the use of technology and the presence of state media, one still found many indications that Huỳnh Khải and the other musicians continued local models of creativity in the practice of đờn ca tài tử. One found visual and aural icons of historical performance practice with the use of the zither and moon-shaped lute. The form was rooted also in history: a feathered, improvised prelude introduced the mode of the piece and lead to collective elaboration on an elusive structural melody. Other instruments possibly associated with colonial or Western music traditions, namely the guitar and violin, were incorporated almost a century earlier to perform traditional music. These musicians on the stage still practiced spontaneity and followed metaphor even when confronted with microphones in rehearsal.

Mediation with new technology does not automatically lead to more development or even an acceleration of development. One instead sees experiments in synthesis between a Western creativity and development model with a local Vietnamese one based on nonaction and spontaneity. In this chapter, I examine the many ways that musicians mediate between these models. I pay particular attention to the time period between 2011 and 2019, when southern Vietnam witnessed significant economic growth and đờn ca tài tử also become more widely recognized in public discourse on cultural sustainable development. By 2011, more individuals in Ho Chi Minh City knew of the genre with the Vietnamese government's application to request recognition of đờn ca tài tử by the United Nations Educational, Scientific and Cultural Organization (UNESCO) as intangible cultural heritage representative of humanity (Hà Đình Nguyên 2011). During a trip to Vietnam in 2013, many more individuals I encountered recognized the term đờn ca tài tử, knew something about traditional practice, and expressed a hope for UNESCO recognition. Journalists even suggested ways for local and national officials to encourage interest in the art form. In October 2013, an editorial that appeared in the national newspaper *Tuổi Trẻ* described a frequent worry that đờn ca tài tử was not "strong enough to cope with the process of global cultural integration," so the government should implement "investment and training policies" to advance knowledge of đờn ca tài tử practice (L. T. Ngã 2013). This has occurred; in that same year, a newspaper reported that Kiên Giang opened a number of new performance grounds "to create opportunities for cultural exchange between Kiên Giang and other music clubs" (Thế Hạnh 2013).

As everyday life changes, a young generation of musicians and consumers have emerged in southern Vietnam who consume Daoist aesthetics and older Vietnamese literature alongside American television and K-pop. Instead of adopting cosmopolitan understandings of creativity verbatim, musicians work to craft a fertile middle ground between historical and local notions of creativity—and more contemporary ones. These audiences are savvy, and musicians of traditional music experiment with many ways of catering to them and shaping their tastes. I begin this discussion with a review of cultural policy currently in play in southern Vietnam and how musicians have tactically adopted from these policy pronouncements to undertake their experimentation.

RENEWING RESOLUTIONS

Cultural policy needs circulation for the purposes of implementation. Early in my research, few seemed aware of the 1998 Resolution discussed in Chapter 6, so policy makers used the fifteenth anniversary of its passing to popularize understandings of its central tenets. The adoption of the Resolution had been very slow, evidently, as an article from the national *Thanh Niên* newspaper indicated with the title: "Cultural policy: decide quickly, implement slowly" (Trinh Nguyễn 2013). Cadres organized conferences to celebrate the perceived successes of the policy and advocate its continued relevance. According to one conference, the policy had a "pervasive, deep and wide impact in life; it creates strong changes in social life; makes appear many cultural movements in every region; attracts widespread public participation; contributes to the work to maintain political stability [and] social order; preserves the national cultural identity; [and] promotes economic development" (Duy Việt 2013). These events also served as fora to discuss viable methods of implementation. These exchanges were restricted and imbued with Party rhetoric, but they offered insight into the new spaces in which individuals took part in debate about the development or advancement of Vietnamese culture. In the case of đờn ca tài tử, conferences in Ho Chi Minh City and throughout the Mekong Delta included performances, short speeches, and opportunities for open discussion. On August 9, 2013, for instance, I attended a conference titled "Traditional Music and Today's Lives" ("Âm nhạc dân tộc với cuộc sống hôm nay") at the newly refurbished Rex Hotel—the same hotel mentioned in the Introduction. The organizers welcomed musician and educator "comrades" to the now glamorous hotel to discuss the challenges in promoting and developing a genre of southern Vietnamese traditional music.[3]

Media outlets reported on this conference (and others) to encourage broader social dialogue. Newspaper articles, television reports, YouTube videos, and Facebook posts summarized who attended, what they said, and gently encouraged audiences to enhance Vietnam's "cultural capital" (Xuân Hạ and Đất Mũi 2013). The Rex Hotel meeting generated greater buzz than others because of the attendance of actress and model Lý Nhã Kỳ (Anh Thư 2013). Her brief remarks at the start of the conference quickly spread in the "hot news" (*tin nóng*) blogs attached to newspapers and provided greater spotlight to the other issues covered in the conference.

Despite increased interest in traditional music among the general public, many musicians have grown tired of the rhetoric of these conferences, which entails perpetual diagnoses of preservation problems and encouragements to do more to teach young people. The end of the Rex Hotel meeting clearly indicated this fatigue. The organizers concluded with a call for reactions to the presentations made, but no one volunteered. They resorted to asking individual musicians and academics to offer remarks, but all politely declined. I had a sense that everything already discussed had been covered before and would be again in the future. A quick conferral with a friend in attendance confirmed this. A well-known musician with whom I spoke later made a similar observation, noting that attendees only spoke about their ideas at these conferences and then never made any attempt to implement them.[4] Speaking publicly on policy posed risks; it is safer to stay quiet and then return to one's pedagogical practice without scrutiny from government officials. These events showed a considerable distance between policy pronouncements advocated by officials who have little knowledge of music practice and the labor of musicians and teachers who have dedicated their careers and personal energy to traditional music preservation.

This conference, therefore, was a mixed blessing. On the one hand, it was long, often quite repetitive, and, for some participants, one in the line of countless similar meetings. Researchers and officials had to endure the discussions of "hurried ideas" decided by policy makers that were not necessarily grounded in the reality of everyday practice (Trinh Nguyễn 2013). On the other hand, some discussion occurred; media outlets reported on the event for major newspapers and television programs, and a media personality with everyday name recognition took an interest and participated. These meetings encouraged exchange and maintained the flow of tradition.

UNESCO *Preservation*

A central aspect to the perceived success of the 1998 Resolution involved collaboration between the Vietnamese state and international partners, including UNESCO, to recognize the value of traditional culture. For its part, UNESCO became (and remains) a major contributor to cultural policy and preservation throughout Vietnam.[5] UNESCO's inscription of the Complex of Huế Monuments as a World Heritage site in 1993 served as a pivotal moment in the Vietnamese government's increasing willingness to preserve tangible and intangible heritage, as well as its attunement to international cultural policy. UNESCO also organized a symposium on royal court music in Huế in 1994 (Norton 2018, 310). Vietnam later applied in earnest for UNESCO recognition of music genres as intangible cultural heritage.

Recognition introduces new forms of hegemonic power into practice, leading to occasions where those in power usurp agency from local musicians. David Harnish has written of the attempt by governments to "detraditionalize" music "from its context and inherent meanings and reposition ... these for other ends" (2007, 7).[6] In a discussion of *ca trù* (northern Vietnamese sung poetry), Barley Norton cautions that "the weight of cultural heritage threatens to limit *ca trù*'s musical and ritual meanings, to define its contemporary social relevance in primarily nationalistic terms, and to make it more difficult for a vital, innovative musical culture to emerge" (2014, 177). *Innovation* is an imperative term here, although a potentially misleading one. Musicians already have processes in place to make traditional music viable and conversant with everyday conditions; đờn ca tài tử musicians already are innovative, although many do not strive for such a description given the practice of nonaction and spontaneity.

UNESCO inscribed đờn ca tài tử as intangible cultural heritage of humanity on December 5, 2013, in Baku, Azerbaijan. Vietnamese newspapers and television programs celebrated the inscription and posted pictures online of the Vietnamese delegation waving Vietnamese flags and celebrating the announcement. On February 11, 2014, Ho Chi Minh City hosted a ceremony to celebrate the conferral of intangible cultural heritage status on đờn ca tài tử. The then prime minister, Nguyễn Tấn Dũng, marked the importance of the occasion by attending and making public remarks, as did many revered teachers from all over southern Vietnam. Katherine Müller-Marin, UNESCO's representative in Vietnam, also spoke on behalf of UNESCO. The performance took place in front of the Reunification Palace (Dinh Độc Lập), formerly the home and seat of the Republic of Vietnam, with an impressive stage that included a body of water and individuals rowing themselves around and collecting lotus flowers during the concert. The ceremony featured the participation of Huỳnh Khải on the đàn tỳ bà and Phạm Thúy Hoan's daughter, Hải Phượng, on the đàn bầu.

The performance offered a history of đờn ca tài tử and several works by small and large ensembles. One of the participants relayed through a friend of mine that the performance was quite stressful: the musicians performed on a large stage in front of the prime minister, many well-known musicians, and foreign dignitaries; the large ensemble comprised of ten musicians played in a row of chairs in an open-air environment, making it very difficult to hear one another.[7] Indeed, when the large ensemble performed the second work, "Lưu thủy trường," they did so without a *rao* most likely because the acoustic conditions were not suitable to responding to what the other musicians performed in a typical prelude. Few of these musicians had experience performing at such an important event simultaneously broadcast on national and Ho Chi Minh City television. Despite these worries and the control exerted over the narratives presented, the long performance offered significant exposure to elements of đờn ca tài tử's history, the diverse ways that performances take place, and the musicians themselves. The performances placed đờn ca tài tử alongside other related genres of music, including nhạc lễ and cải lương, allowing audiences to consider the commonalities between them. The musicians performed a nhạc lễ work first before a series of instrumental and vocal tunes; indeed, the number of instrumental works performed surprised me, as previous public concerts focused on vocal music. The concert also featured small ensembles, including two women playing đàn kìm and đàn tranh on a small boat with a picture of Hồ Chí Minh next to them. Although well executed, it became apparent that the organizers relied on a prerecorded track for the performance, as it included the distinct sounds of the đàn bầu even though the instrument was not present onstage. As musicians played more tunes, dancers and singers appeared on the stage, many wearing the *khăn rằn*, a black and white checkered scarf often used to distinguish southern Vietnam from elsewhere in Vietnam. These actors depicted a bustling scene of life in the Mekong Delta; although not to everyone's liking, the performance presented the diverse ways đờn ca tài tử exists in southern Vietnam and as an art form carefully preserved though collaboration between Vietnamese musicians and international experts.

FESTIVALS

Who gets to participate in performances and to whom these performances are directed remain important considerations in the analysis of musical creativity. The February 2014 performance commemorating UNESCO recognition involved the participation of a foreign UNESCO official, who helped lend legitimacy to recognition beyond the borders of Vietnam. The Huế Festival described in Chapter 6 did not specifically involve the participation of foreigners, but was oriented toward foreigners in the audience. Other multiday festivals have been organized to focus on local methods of preservation without the participation of foreigners, and occasionally take place in locations not frequented by foreign tourists. Like the February concert and the Huế Festival, these local festivals were tightly choreographed and featured emcees relaying scripted information to local audiences. Under bright lights, choreographed dances, and, occasionally, lip syncing and the instrumental equivalent, these festivals advanced new uses for music traditions to new audiences. With the exception of opening and closing ceremonies, tickets were priced quite cheaply to encourage attendance, and local or national television networks sometimes broadcasted the performances—particularly those of the opening and closing ceremonies—within Vietnam. These festivals therefore provided significant insights into the experiments directed toward Vietnamese musicians and consumers themselves. They were more overtly propagandistic, but were in many ways more experimental in terms of shaping contemporary Vietnamese taste.

One of the more lavish—and derided—examples is the First International Đờn ca tài tử Festival (*Festival Đờn ca tài tử Quốc gia lần thứ nhất*) that was held in Bạc Liêu from April 24 to 29, 2014.[8] Bạc Liêu serves as the mythical origin of đờn ca tài tử in state-directed narrative. The town is the birthplace of Cao Văn Lầu, who wrote "Dạ cổ hoài lang," a tune that later developed into "Vọng cổ." Televised on national and regional television stations, the opening concert on April 25 began with a troupe of dancers in matching *áo dài* (national dress) holding either two lotus flowers or a conical hat—both of which served as visual representations of the Mekong Delta. Two well dressed singers sang a newly composed work welcoming audience members, introducing the quintessentially "southern" nature of Bạc Liêu Province and describing the instruments associated with đờn ca tài tử. In this performance, a dissonance emerged between oral histories of the genre and the attempt to present a "developed," modern, and hip version of it in performance. The singers, for instance, did not use a đờn ca tài tử vocal style with appropriate modal ornamentation, but something closer to a pop or *nhạc trẻ* (youth music) style. In addition, aside from a brief instrumental prelude on the đàn tranh zither, the ensemble featured no musical instrument associated with the genre. It instead started with a string orchestra following tonal harmony, and a choir that later sang vocables. The most striking component of the performance, however, was the extraordinary number of dancers. As the performance continued, women appeared in blue áo dài mimicking the movements of birds; men waved palm leaves; men and women danced in circles with lotus flowers in their hands; and boats floated across the stage. Later in the performance, sounds of đờn ca tài tử finally emerged with a work arranged by Huỳnh Khải titled "Nhớ ơn tổ nghiệp" ("Gratitude for the Founding Musicians"). The musicians accompanied dancers moving across the stage holding the major instruments associated with the ensemble. When one instrument was heard more prominently than others, those dancers held the instruments high in the air for the audience to see them. The work borrowed the melodic structure of "Ngũ đối hạ" with precomposed lyrical content but was not performed live. Unfortunately, some sounds, including the đàn cò, were synthesized, which added to the fantastical nature of the large presentation.

The festival featured a number of well-known performers who have dedicated their lives to performing đờn ca tài tử, but it was not well received.[9] Many dismissed the incessant dancing and popification as divergent from all appropriate understandings of the tradition. There also were concerns about the crowding out of local resources, as well as rumors of corruption. Newspapers even questioned certain decisions made by organizers, including the amount of money spent on the festival. Bạc Liêu lacks significant infrastructure, so many argued that the money was used to pave roads and build new performance facilities to encourage tourism to the area (H. T. Dũng and C. Quốc 2014); organizers also built a đàn kìm moon-shaped lute sculpture and water feature in downtown Bạc Liêu. Prime Minister Nguyễn Tấn Dũng even chimed into the debate, advocating that "improving the lives of the poor is more important than building theaters" (Quý Lâm 2014).

Despite these problems, the festival organizers did attempt to revitalize Vietnam's national engagement with đờn ca tài tử. The lyrical content, choreography, and sound presented the genre as appealing, entertaining, and evocative of southern Vietnam. Those who took part attempted to provide an educational experience for the entire country. Lyrical context described instruments; dancers took replicas of instruments out onstage for audience members and viewers at home to see; and musicians provided sound so audiences could connect the visual icon to the sound produced by a professional musician. This work gave southern Vietnamese musicians an opportunity to establish a space for đờn ca tài tử performance in the rich and crowded tapestry of Vietnamese cultural traditions; this was a space they never had before. The sound emerged from the people and location of southern Vietnam, and for those who wished to visit, Bạc Liêu was open and welcoming.

TELEVISION PROGRAMS

Drawing on existing infrastructure and relatively inexpensive models of knowledge dissemination, radio and television stations throughout southern Vietnam also have created programming for đờn ca tài tử performance to generate interest in the genre. Some in the Mekong Delta already broadcasted đờn ca tài tử performances before the genre's renaissance in 2011 and 2012; since then, they have also added popular competitions. These performances have initial lives on television and radio stations, but are later posted to the websites of these stations, YouTube, Facebook, and elsewhere. As of this writing, YouTube in particular contains an extraordinary archive of short-lived and successful experiments. Two different game shows with similar titles, for example, featured young singers accompanied by professional đờn ca tài tử instrumentalists. *Gameshow Hò Xự Xang Xê Cống* (*Sol La Do Re Mi Gameshow*) aired in 2013 on Vĩnh Long television (Đài Phát Thanh—Truyền Hình Vĩnh Long) and *Giọng Ca Nhí Hò Xự Xang Xê Cống* (*The Voice of Young People Singing Sol La Do Re Mi*) aired in 2015 on Bạc Liêu television (Đài Phát Thanh—Truyền Hình Bạc Liêu). Participating contestants, who mostly were young women aged under fifteen, competed for points. In both programs, they sang tunes in two different ways: first, they sang the lòng bản on solfège syllables of the tune selected (or assigned), and then they sang an embellished version of the tune. The game shows sometimes featured one performer at a time; at other times, they featured singers who sang the lòng bản in unison and then each offered snippets of embellishment in turn.

The judges and producers endeavored to make strategic educational points with these contests. The narrative of the third episode of *Gameshow Hò Xự Xang Xê Cống* in particular sought to reward a contestant's appropriate singing ability, her abilities as a stage performer—all the contestants were women in this episode—and general knowledge of đờn ca tài tử. Following the singing of the lòng bản in unison, one singer sang part of a phrase, which then was continued by the next singers. It provided no opportunity for individual expression, however, and when the singers sang the embellished melody in unison, it became clear that they had memorized a tune for the performance. Following this exercise, the emcee appeared on the stage with the three contestants, accompanied by dramatic music akin to that found on *Who Wants to Be a Millionaire?* Each contestant selected a question out of a fishbowl, and they were given an opportunity to study the question. Each question related to some element of đờn ca tài tử performance practice: one question provided the contestant with a series of solfège pitches and asked her to identify the melody; to assist in this identification, Thiện Vũ, who has featured in my earlier descriptions of improvisation and participated in the 2010 Huế Festival, played the tune on the đàn kìm. The second question related to the impact of Trần Văn Khê's research on traditional music, and the last question asked the contestant to identify the musicians who first popularized the vocal version of "Vọng cổ." Like *Who Wants to Be a Millionaire?*, the emcee gave each contestant four possible responses to the question. The contest ended when the judges provided commentary on each performance and indicated whether the contestant's response was correct. The three judges included an instrumentalist, a singer, and a scholar, and they were paired with the question associated with their specialty: Huỳnh Khải provided commentary to the contestant who answered the lòng bản question; Dr. Mai Mỹ Duyên, a scholar of đờn ca tài tử, responded to the second question; and cải lương singer Phượng Loan responded to the third question. Each judge then provided a score to the three participants, and the emcee declared a winner.

Contests for music clubs that have long experience playing with one another also take place in Ho Chi Minh City and the Mekong Delta. The Voice of the People Radio Station in Ho Chi Minh City (VOH) has organized radio programs, such as the 2013 *Liên hoan đờn ca tài tử: Hoa sen vàng* (*Gathering of Đờn ca tài tử: Golden Lotus*), and weekly televised competitions, such as the 2014 *Hội ngộ tài tử Phương Nam* (*Southern Vietnam Tài tử Competition*). In December 2014, I visited two of the latter programs at the radio station and the final competition at the Ho Chi Minh City opera house. In each two-hour program, two sets of two đờn ca tài tử clubs from the outer districts of Ho Chi Minh City and bordering provinces of the Mekong Delta performed a series of similar works organized around a particular theme. The performance depicted in Figure 8.2, for example, featured works meant to evoke *ca ra bộ*, the precursor to cải lương in which singers sing while making gestures. The singer from an army ensemble from Bình Tân District in Ho Chi Minh City made a gesture while the đàn bầu and đàn kìm accompanied him. A panel of judges comprised of Cao Thị Thắng, Huỳnh Khải, and Ngô Hồng Khánh evaluated the singing, instrumental, and presentational abilities of the groups with point values and commentary on the effectiveness of the musicians' practice at the end of the one-hour segments.

The performance space is not typical for đờn ca tài tử, especially given the raised stage and equipment needed to create the live radio and television feed. That said, the atmosphere of the space was convivial and relaxed. Each perfor-

FIGURE 8.2 A performance from the 2014 Southern Vietnam Tài Tử
Competition at the VOH Studios *photo by the author, December 21, 2014*

mance featured friends and family of those performing as well as a number of
the public who attended almost every week. During the performances at the
radio station, I saw families with small children who occasionally made noise,
but this was tolerated by the sound technicians. Audience members frequently
turned to speak with those around them; even if they did not know one another,
they all shared an interest in this genre of music. During a December 2014
performance, I made friends quickly and was joking with two elderly women
who came to this performance every week. They mentioned that they had other
friends who joined the performance by listening the radio, indicating that they
paid attention to the larger audience taking part through other means, which
also included watching the live feed or the full performance after it was posted
on YouTube and the VOH website.

In both the game show and VOH competition, Huỳnh Khải appeared as a
judge and commentator, indicating his wide influence in developing and disseminating đờn ca tài tử to new audiences. As of this writing, he continues this
work in earnest on YouTube and Facebook. His use of social media appears to be

an outgrowth of development initiatives in which he disseminates information about the national identity in Vietnamese music. He uploads evidence of this practice and a wealth of information regarding traditional music to YouTube. His most popular video from 2011, for example, has over 194,000 views as of this writing, which is an extraordinary number for a genre of traditional music.[10] On his Facebook page, he also frequently posts clips from competitions so his followers may be introduced to new talent. Members of the public comment on these posts and occasionally ask questions. He responds in thorough detail, often posting lyrical content or solfège notation so musicians can study the works he has written. This work reaches a wide audience in Vietnam and abroad.

POPULAR CONTESTS

Very recently, there appears a shift in public discourse away from international collaboration and recognition through UNESCO and toward the reality television show model promoted by American, European, and Thai television networks. New television contests in Vietnam have sought to recycle the *America's Got Talent* (or *Vietnam's Got Talent*) model to popularize the đờn ca tài tử contest for wider audiences. Rather than featuring participation from Huỳnh Khải and others close to the đờn ca tài tử music scenes in southern Vietnam, they involve well-known cải lương stars. In 2018, Đồng Tháp television (Đài Truyền Hình Đồng Tháp) produced a program titled *Tài Tử Miệt Vườn* (*Countryside Tài tử*).[11] The three judges, *Nghệ sĩ nhân dân* (People's Artist) Việt Anh, *Nghệ sĩ ưu tú* Thanh Hằng, and Nghệ sĩ ưu tú Ngọc Huyền, as well as the emcee, Nghệ sĩ ưu tú Quế Trân, are well-known actors and singers in Vietnam and have greater name recognition than the đờn ca tài tử judges of the earlier television competitions. Contestants are young and old with seemingly ordinary lives, and the producers work to craft a particular narrative and rapport between the judges and the contestants. One of the more celebrated performances as of this writing is of Nguyễn Thị Chiệp, who walked out on the stage selling lottery tickets (*vé số*). She indicated that she needed to sell all of the tickets before she could perform, suggesting that livelihood comes before art. The judges gladly agreed to purchase the rest of the tickets, which elicited a great deal of laughter from *chị* (older sister) Chiệp and the audience. Quế Trân invited her to approach the judges, which significantly reduced the distinction between judge and contestant. Ngọc Huyền purchased ten tickets and then told Việt Anh that he must take nine; he seems startled, but readily agreed. To encourage the lighthearted nature of their interaction, he then asked chị Chiệp if he is handsome. She responded with "ừ," which is a colloquial way of indicating agreement. This yielded additional laughter from the audience, as she continued to emphasize the "countryside" vocabulary. She returned to stage, and Quế Trân realized that she had not yet introduced the contestant. Chị Chiệp introduced herself, but her thick *miền Tây* accent from the Mekong Delta caused confusion over her name. When the judges appeared unable to repeat her name properly, she resorted to spelling it for them; again, they all laughed at the situation and at her performance of the "country bumpkin" archetype.

Chị Chiệp performed a very moving rendition of the sad work "Phụng hoàng." She adeptly altered the timbre of her voice, occasionally thin and airy in some parts, and deep and husky in other parts. During the *rao*, her voice shook with gravitas. Thanh Hằng immediately found it moving and jumped up to express her encouragement, exclaiming, "Wow! That's impressive! Impressive!" ("Trời ơi! Hay quá vậy! Hay!"). (See Figure 8.3.) As chị Chiệp continued, Thanh Hằng responded with snippets of lyrical content, asking chị Chiệp to elaborate on a sung point she just made with a quick "Why is that, sister?" ("sao chị?"). Thanh Hằng then left her seat at the judging table and walked onto the stage to sing additional lines of encouragement. (See Figure 8.4.) The *pièce de résistance* occurred at the end when chị Chiệp worked her line to a dramatic and climatic moment and substituted the final lyric with Thanh Hằng's name. As the audience erupted into applause, they laughed and embraced each other. The emcee summarized the feelings of the panel and audience that performance was "really very creative" ("sáng tạo nhiều quá").

The performance by the contestant, judges, and emcee promoted đờn ca tài tử as a developed genre of music in line with a popular context. The producers crafted a storyline and drew on different emotions through effective comedy in parts and sad music in others. The comment that the work was "creative" particularly solidified the work as being engaging for this medium. After two weeks on YouTube, the clip had over two million views and was even "trending" for a period of time in Vietnam on the platform (Hồng Nhung 2018). At the time of this writing, the video has been viewed over ten million times (Truyền Hình Đồng Tháp 2018). The number of views—as well as use of the English-language term "trending" in announcements about the popularity of the video—indicate the turn toward new forms of development and popularization of đờn ca tài tử.

Rather than simply replicating a previous development model, however, Nguyễn Thị Chiệp's performance effectively blended the Western and local un-

FIGURE 8.3 Nguyễn Thị Chiệp (right) performs for three judges (left) on *Tài tử miệt vườn* screenshot from the Truyền Hình Đồng Tháp YouTube channel, used with permission

FIGURE 8.4 Thanh Hằng (left) and Nguyễn Thị Chiệp (right) perform a duet on *Tài tử miệt vườn* screenshot from the Truyền Hình Đồng Tháp YouTube channel, used with permission

derstandings of creativity into a very appealing performance. At the start of the performance, it appeared to be a typical Csikszentmihalyi-identified evaluation with a panel judging the performance. The judges used their expertise to determine whether chị Chiệp was worthy of praise and possible fame. A *rao* started the performance, however, indicating that the audience would hear improvisation and spontaneity. Her rich evocation of the Oán mode immediately pulled at the hearts of the panel, and after an especially moving passage with emphasis on the *rung* ornament, Thanh Hằng leapt to her feet to provide praise. The distance between judge and performer disappeared when the judge walked to the stage to sing with her. The judge referred to herself as "em" (younger sister) and embraced the contestant as "chị," generating a familial and close relationship.

In many ways, this performance would easily have been found in a private home or singing café like those I described in Cần Thơ. Chị Chiệp crafted a performance based on personal experience, bringing her everyday life into the performance space—initially selling lottery tickets and only pursuing a leisure activity after she completed her work. Her chân phương frame properly constructed the mode with its requisite pitch content and ornamentation, and also effectively relayed the rhythmic structure of the tune. Using hoa lá cành, she used timbral richness and melody to improvise around the lòng bản evoked by the instrumental ensemble that accompanied her. The lyrical content was similarly moving, and she concluded with a spontaneous reference back to the performance space with the mention of Thanh Hằng by name. Although the performance certainly evoked a flashy and developed contemporary Vietnam, chị Chiệp maintained older notions of creativity through spontaneity and effective embellishment.

TO WHERE DO YOUTH TURN?

Traditional music and đờn ca tài tử remain vibrant today, and young people take part in their maintenance, despite criticism to the contrary. As traditional music changes—as it always has—and certain performance practices become less prevalent, commentators try to pinpoint what has disrupted the fragile ecosystem of traditional performance. They sometimes resort to scapegoating an amorphous and not-easy-to-define group. Returning to remarks the August 2013 Rex Hotel conference, Ho Chi Minh City Conservatory instructor Đỗ Tấn Việt suggested that students need to be trained in traditional music at a younger age. Đỗ emphasized that investment in human capital, in particular, would yield better results in promoting traditional music. Later, Deputy Minister of Culture, Sport and Tourism Vương Duy Biên argued that this type of work music must raise young people's perception of the value of traditional music to "build the Vietnamese soul." Reiterating a common dismissal of youth taste, Vương Duy Biên suggested that young people drive around in large cars and do not speak with one another; they seem to only be interested in business; and when looking for inspiration, they look outside to places like South Korea and its music industry. He expressed particular dismay when he hears K-pop used as Vietnamese telephones' ringtones. "Tradition is number one," so the participants must endeavor to "create a space for preservation."[12]

Not only do Vietnamese musicians and music scholars make this accusation, but ethnomusicologists and foreign commentators do as well. Dale A. Olsen (2008, 3) has argued that Vietnamese popular musicians publicly aim to dispense with the past and entirely focus on the present. He even suggests that Vietnamese youth have a "somewhat collective lack of concern about the past" (21). Such a description does a tremendous injustice not only to popular musicians and young people who are well versed in the music of the past but also to music creation as a whole. Vietnam, furthermore, does not forget.

Based on my conversations with young people, they have far more nuanced understandings of traditional music than their parents or scholars give them credit. In July 2018, over a cup of coffee, a friend of mine in his final year of university expressed his irritation with being blamed for destroying the traditional arts. "Both đờn ca tài tử and cải lương live on in youth culture," he argued, but in a very different sense than in the past.[13] Young people mix đờn ca tài tử and cải lương tunes into works of the internet-based microgenres of vaporwave, trap remixes on YouTube, and hip-hop remixes featured on television programs such as *The Remix*.[14] These artists spend time listening to and drawing on an extensive online archive of traditional music in order to use it creatively and strategically. My friend pointed out that even films use traditional music to tell stories of great interest to young people. One such film titled *Song Lang* features a love story between two men—one a musician and member of an organized crime syndicate; the other a cải lương actor—in the 1980s. Named after the wooden clapper used in đờn ca tài tử and cải lương, the film seeks to tell a powerful story but also feature the traditional arts; indeed, Studio68, the film's production company, filled their Facebook page with videos and stills of cải lương in an effort to teach followers about the sonic and visual materials used to craft it. At the time of this conversation with my friend, only a teaser trailer for the film had been made available, but it generated quite a great deal of interest among not just the LGBTQIA+ community and young people but also members of an older generation. Phạm Thúy Hoan, for example, went with a group of musicians to a screening of the film on the first day of its release, indicating in a Facebook post that she wanted to "support" the film and the musicians in it. In telling new stories about cải lương and đờn ca tài tử, young people preserve these arts using new technologies and new forms of spontaneity.

CONCLUSION

Traditional music in southern Vietnam today has many vibrant lives that bridge the approaches to creativity present in the country. As Vietnam has changed considerably in the twenty-first century, musicians have adopted new forms of technology to disseminate their message and understanding of sound. Rather than simply accelerate development practices, however, they effectively mediate past creative practice and current modern conditions. "Rather than impeding the development of new ideas," Susan Felch writes, tradition "is actually the vital force that propels them into existence. Tradition, in other words, is generative, not deadening" (2005, 55). Whether in private homes, at conferences, on television, or in live festivals, musicians—young and old—foster dynamic approaches to performance that keep traditional music spontaneous and meaningful.

CONCLUSION

Creativity appears regularly in Euro-American discussions of education, artistic freedom, and artistic greatness; however, given the roots of creativity discourse in the myth of the white male genius, those deploying the term can unwillingly perpetuate inequity and discrimination. Creativity is not a universal truth, but a kind of evaluative discourse deployed by those seeking to maintain their power. Outside of the West, however, creativity is practiced in far more nuanced, playful, and socially conscious ways. Artists are knowledgeable about and may strategically adopt from Western understandings of creativity, but they continue to draw extensively from local understandings toward socially engaged goals. Any future of creativity studies, therefore, lives in the Global South; if these studies are not written by globally marginalized peoples and inhabitants of the Global South, then they must engage primarily with these voices to tell their stories.

In my view, ethnomusicologists remain particularly well-disposed to study creativity, whether musical or otherwise, but this remains an ideal rather than the reality. Ethnomusicologists sit at the intersection of musicology and anthropology, and work alongside ethnic, queer, and cultural studies. Many ethnomusicologists can therefore deploy a greater number of tools with which to analyze the richness of expression through both social interaction and individual artistic expression. I have undertaken this kind of affinity-building to describe musical creativity practiced by musicians of southern Vietnamese traditional music. I have written neither *the* book on creativity in ethnomusicology nor *the* book on southern Vietnamese music, but I have tried to advance conversations on both topics with the hope that future ethnomusicologists will engage with creativity in different ways.

In the descriptions of creativity included in this ethnography, I have critiqued the globalized and neoliberal understandings of creativity understood simply as the individual prowess of the genius. Many ethnomusicologists fundamentally need to find new lenses through which they observe and practice musicmaking. I propose three lenses here, although more certainly exist. First, rather than viewing music performance as an endeavor to make something novel or new, creativity should instead be understood as something that cannot be mastered. Music is never static. How can one master the constantly moving, shifting, evolving, and disappearing? Second, creativity is historical, by which I mean that it exists in history and memory, and draws from these concepts to generate contemporary practice. Third, creativity is reparative and recuperative; it seeks to repair fractures between individuals and make advancements toward a more equitable society.

These three fundamental assumptions about creativity are not mine, I should note, but have emerged from my reading of scholarship outside of ethnomusicology and marginalized scholarship within ethnomusicology. As noted more fully in Chapter 2, Julietta Singh critiques mastery and embraces a dehumanist approach to bring powerful (and vulnerable) readings of texts and performance into scholarship; the works of Samuel A. Floyd Jr. and Kyra D. Gaunt advance an engagement with history and memory to uncover and name that which drives contemporary musical practice; finally, the work of Dorinne Kondo in particular encourages scholars to consider the reparative potential of the arts, and the moves of specific individuals in making these repairs. I mention these scholars in particular because their work guided me as I wrote and revised this monograph.

For artists, creativity plays an important role in understanding, confronting, and negotiating the crises of our time. I understood the increasing importance of sáng tạo (creativity) as I studied southern Vietnamese traditional music from 2007 to 2019, but the wide significance of the concept was only made known to me in a speech made by Municipal Party Secretary Nguyễn Thiện Nhân. As described in Chapter 1, he saw creativity as the solution to crisis: if people had creativity, it would enable the city to develop and prosper; people would no longer see the need for any kind of protest. This is a simplistic understanding of creativity deployed to quell freedom of expression, but it indicates the power and promise of the concept. His comments further indicate a commonly held view in Vietnam today: that sáng tạo as practiced in Vietnam blends global and local understandings of creativity, creation, and expression.

Creativity in southern Vietnam is a product of the region's place at a crossroads of migration and cultural influence from East Asia, South Asia, and Europe. Musical creativity brings together ancient philosophical traditions in Asia, especially Daoism, which advances nonaction (vô vi) and spontaneity (tự nhiên) in one's life and music practice; East and South Asian musical practice, including Chăm musical modality; and French literary traditions and performance practices. Đờn ca tài tử musicians gathered these elements in the late nineteenth and twentieth centuries to ultimately form a named genre that bore witness to and was influenced by anticolonial sentiment, war, regime changes, and other shifts in southern Vietnamese everyday life. Vietnamese musicians continue to synthesize them for appropriate use in the present.

My understandings of creativity in đờn ca tài tử of southern Vietnam draw on interactions with several musicians who kindly provided me with extensive guidance. These musicians draw on long-held understandings of creativity in southern Vietnam and increasingly engage with Western models of creativity to augment their practice. Phạm Thúy Hoan advocated that young people need to cultivate an inner virtue or seed (hạt giống) to create appropriate and effective traditional music. This is not static engagement by simply drawing on the past. As Nguyễn Vĩnh Bảo has argued, musicians change and carry over (đổi qua) to make sure people, locations, and events have an imprint on music.

These musicians oftentimes spoke of creativity through metaphor. Unlike historical musicologists who sometimes describe metaphor as ephemeral (see Cook 2006), ethnomusicologists forward the use of metaphor as an important and vibrant structuring mechanism for practice. Metaphors suggest routes of music production so that meaning remains significant and sustainable. Drawing from work by ethnomusicologists and others, I offer that metaphors help musicians think about life experiences and make these experiences aurally manifest in performance; further bridge these sounds with everyday life; structure knowledge used and generated in performance; and steer interactions in the performance context to generate inspired sound.

The metaphors described in this text have been powerful enough to sustain the production of đờn ca tài tử through the violence and upheaval of the twentieth century. The chân phương (frame) provides structure and logic to the mediation of practice, as noted by Trần Văn Khê, Nguyễn Thuyết Phong, Lê Tuấn Hùng, and Thầy Phước Cường. Hoa lá cành (flowers, leaves, and branches), as described by Nguyễn Vĩnh Bảo, suggests various ways of spontaneously improvising beautiful melodies akin to what is found in nature. Musicians, including Trần Minh Đức and others in the Mekong Delta, explore the intersections of these metaphors and strive for ecstatic practice called xuất thần, a state of performance achieved through a proper evocation of mode accompanied by the encouragement of one's peers that serves to mediate the self within a community of practitioners. The twentieth century also saw the emergence of phát triển (development) as a metaphor for music that advances or improves what came in the past. Policy adopted from the importation of French and Marxist-Leninist discourse encouraged the creation of so-called "developed" music to serve various needs of unifying the nation, whether it be the Republic of Vietnam or the Socialist Republic of Vietnam after 1976. This metaphor spawned numerous experiments in the last quarter of the twentieth century, which were led in the public sphere by Phạm Thúy Hoan. She and others collaborated with international partners to produce a modernized and inclusive traditional music for young people. For some musicians, the developed performances get too far away from authentic performance practice; they therefore invoke the musical ruin to forcefully advocate for a return to certain practices of improvisation. This return to hoa lá cành has cleared away overgrowth in the đờn ca tài tử music scene and has made musicianship more sustainable for the twenty-first century.

As southern Vietnam continues its rapid development, musicians find new ways to engage with traditional music and mediate between local understandings of sáng tạo and global understandings of creativity. These mediations sit at the core of đờn ca tài tử practice, and this ethos has continued into the twenty-first century. Even with new technologies at the disposal of musicians, and both UNESCO and the Vietnamese state playing roles in the stewardship of đờn ca tài tử, performers continue to maintain connections to the old "seeds" of practice; indeed, some even return to them in earnest to enrich contemporary performance with ancient ideas.

In the Introduction, I relayed how Nguyễn Vĩnh Bảo described đờn ca tài tử as a "music without a name" in order to reclaim the genre from appropriation by others who ascribe inaccurate meanings to tradition—in other words, he attempted to reseed the tradition. In this short statement, Nguyễn Vĩnh Bảo reminded me that the language we use mediates powerful meanings but also generates considerable slippage. The genre has a number of different names, but the harder that musicians, policy makers, and audiences work to establish these names, the harder others respond to redo this work to creative effect.

The practice of ethnomusicology, then, is never fully complete and mastered: as much as we try to name, those names can easily slip away. As ethnomusicologists consider the nature of our methods and research practices, we might spend more time listening to those with which we engage to understand music. After all, those in a position of marginality see the world more completely than we do.

GLOSSARY

Bà: term of address for a woman about the age of one's grandmother
bài bản: composition (implies both instrumental and lyrical content)
bản: composition (implies instrumental content)
bản tổ gồm: fundamental compositions of *đờn ca tài tử*
Bắc: see *điệu Bắc*
buổi sinh hoạt: activity (Tiếng Hát Quê Hương event)

ca Huế (also *ca nhạc Huế* or *nhạc Huế*): music from Huế, central Vietnam
ca trù: sung poetry from northern Vietnam
cải lương: renovated opera of southern Vietnam
cảm hứng: inspiration
chân phương: metaphor for "frame" (also "basic," "rustic," "ordinary")
châu văn: music used to accompany the *lên đồng* mediumship ritual
chèo: folk theatre from northern Vietnam
chiến tranh chống Mỹ cứu nước: War Against America to Save the Country
chuyển: melodic expansion toward a cadential point
Cô: female teacher, also a term of address for a woman about the age of one's mother
cống: Vietnamese solfège representing Mi

"Dạ cổ hoài lang": southern Vietnamese song translated as "Listening to the Sound of the Drum at Night, I Think of You" (*đờn ca tài tử* tune)
dân ca: folk songs
dạo: pre-composed prelude (literally, "stroll")

đàn: to play (a string instrument)
đàn bầu (or *đàn độc huyền*): monochord
đàn cò: two-stringed fiddle (southern Vietnamese term)
đàn gáo: two-stringed fiddle with coconut as a resonating chamber

đàn ghi ta phím lõm: guitar with a scooped fingerboard

đàn kim: moon-shaped lute (southern Vietnamese term)

đàn nguyệt: moon-shaped lute (northern Vietnamese term)

đàn nhị: two-stringed fiddle (northern Vietnamese term)

đàn sến: plum blossom flower lute (Chinese *qinqin* or *meihuaqin*)

đàn sến hai dây: two-stringed *đàn sến*

đàn sến ba dây: three-stringed *đàn sến*

đàn tam: three-stringed lute

đàn tam thập lục: hammered dulcimer of thirty-six strings

đàn tranh: zither of sixteen, seventeen, nineteen, or twenty-one strings

đàn tùy hứng: improvisation

đàn tỳ bà: four-stringed pear-shaped lute

Đảng Cộng Sản Việt Nam (or *Đảng*): Vietnamese Communist Party

đao: way (i.e., a spiritual direction)

Để cương về văn hóa Việt Nam: Draft of the Fundamentals of Vietnamese Culture

điệu thức (or *điệu*): or model

điệu Bắc: "happy" mode (northern mode)

điệu Hạ: ritual music pieces

điệu Nam: "sad" mode (southern mode)

điệu Oán: "melancholy" mode

đoàn: ensemble, also *đoàn hát* (RVN and pre-RVN southern Vietnam); government-sponsored performance troupe (DRVN and SRVN)

Đổi Mới: Renovation (reform period begun after the Sixth Party Congress)

đồng chí: comrade

đờn: southern Vietnamese dialect term for *đàn*

đờn ca tài tử: music of talented amateurs or music for diversion

đức: virtue

gánh (or *gánh hát*): troupe

gảy: strum or pluck the strings

già: sharpening a pitch slightly (literally, "old")

ghi ta Hạ uy: Hawaiian lap-steel guitar

ghi ta phím lõm: see *đàn ghi ta phím lõm*

Hạ: see *điệu Hạ*

Hạ uy cầm: Hawaiian lap-steel guitar

hát bội: classical theatre

hạt giống: seed

hình thức: form

hò: Vietnamese solfège representing Sol

hoa lá cành (also *hoa lá*): flowers, leaves, and branches, or creative embellishment

Hoa Quê Hương: Flower of the Homeland (performances organized by Phạm Thúy Hoan)

hơi: nuance

kèn: oboe-like instrument

Kinh (also *Việt*): Vietnamese majority ethnic group

kỹ thuật: ornamentation

lên đồng: spirit medium ritual found in northern Vietnam

liu (and *líu*): Vietnamese solfège representing Sol

lòng bản (or *lồng bản*): structural or basic melody

lối (or *lối chơi*): a way of playing that involves motivation or *thúc đẩy*

"*Lưu thủy trường*": "Flowing Water" [long version] (*đờn ca tài tử* tune)

"*Lưu thủy vắn*": "Flowing Water" [short version], also "*Lưu thủy* đoản" (*đờn ca tài tử* tune)

luyến lên: upward inflection ornament

luyến xuống: downward inflection ornament

mổ: staccato ornament

Nam: see *điệu Nam*

Nam tiến: southern expansion/advancement

"*Nam xuân*": "Southern Spring or Southern Youth" (*đờn ca tài tử* tune)

nghệ nhân: revered musician

nghệ sĩ: artist

nghệ sĩ nhân dân: People's Artist

nghệ sĩ ưu tú: Artist of Merit

nghệ thuật vị nghệ thuật: art for art's sake (*l'art pour l'art*)

nghị quyết: Party resolution

Người lao động: daily national newspaper meaning "laborer"

nhà giáo ưu tú: Teacher of Merit

nhạc dân tộc: national music

nhạc dân tộc hiện đại: neotraditional music

nhạc đỏ: revolutionary songs (literally, "red music")

Nhạc hội đàn tranh châu Á: Asian Zither Festival

nhạc lễ: ceremonial (or ritual) music performed in temples

nhạc sĩ: musician, composer

nhạc sư: master musician

nhạc tài tử miền Trung: another term for *ca nhạc Huế* (rarely used)

nhạc tài tử Nam bộ (or *nhạc tài tử*): another term for *đờn ca tài tử nhạc trẻ*: youth music

nhấn: pitch bending ornament

nhận xét: feedback, often after a competition performance

nhịp: beat

nhịp ngoại: outside beat

nhịp nội: inside beat

non: flattening a pitch slightly (literally, "young")

nội dung: ideology

Oán: see *điệu Oán*

phan (also *oan*): Vietnamese solfège representing Fa

phát triển: develop, development

phím đàn: frets

phím gảy: finger plectrum

quan họ: genre of repartee singing from northern Vietnam

rao: improvised and unmetered prelude (literally, "announce")

reo dây: tremolo

rung: vibrato ornament

Sài Gòn Giải phóng: Liberation of Saigon (also a daily newspaper of the Communist Party in Ho Chi Minh City

sáng tạo (also *sự sáng tạo* and *sức sáng tạo*): creativity

sáo (or *sáo trúc*): flute

song lang: wooden clapper (timekeeper for the *đờn ca tài tử* ensemble)

song thinh (also *song thanh*): performance technique literally meaning "parallel sound"

Tam giáo: three belief systems (Daoism, Confucianism, and Buddhism)

tâm hồn: soul

thanh niên: youth (also a national daily newspaper)

Thầy: male teacher (and a term of address for monks)

thổi: to play (a wind instrument)

Tiếng Hát Quê Hương (or *câu lạc bộ Tiếng Hát Quê Hương*): Sounds of the Homeland Ensemble

tiêu: flute

tính dân tộc (also *dân tộc tính*): national character

tinh hoa: essence

tự nhiên: natural or spontaneous

trục đàn: tuning pegs

Trường Quốc gia Âm nhạc: National School of Music (Republic of Vietnam)

Trường Quốc gia Âm nhạc và Kịch nghệ: National School of Music and Drama (Republic of Vietnam)

tuổi trẻ: young people (also a national daily newspaper)

Văn hóa nguyệt san: Culture Monthly journal published by the Republic of Vietnam's Directorate of Cultural Affairs in the Ministry of National Education

"*Vọng cổ*": "Nostalgia for the Past" (*đờn ca tài tử* tune)

vô vi: nonaction

xang: Vietnamese solfège representing Do

xây dựng và phát triển nền văn khóa Việt Nam tiên tiến, đậm đà bản sắc dân tộc: primary slogan from the 1998 Resolution of the Fifth Conference of the Central Executive Committee (of the Eighth Congress) on Building and Developing an Advanced Vietnamese Culture Imbued with the National Identity

xê: Vietnamese solfège representing Re

xừ or *xư*: Vietnamese solfège representing Si

xự or *ú*: Vietnamese solfège representing La

xuất thần: state of ecstatic performance (literally, "exporting the spirit")

NOTES

Introduction

1. For Vietnamese city names well known in English, I adopt more recognizable spellings like "Ho Chi Minh City" and "Hanoi" without diacritics. For other place names, I adopt Vietnamese spellings.

2. The addition of the term *Nam bộ* (south) indicates the music's origins in the southern region of Vietnam and to differentiate the music from a similar kind of music from central Vietnam called *nhạc tài tử miền Trung*. (This is more often described as *ca Huế* or *ca nhạc Huế*, or "music from the city of Huế.")

3. Nguyễn Vĩnh Bảo, interview with the author, December 18, 2014. Many interviews cited in this book took place in Ho Chi Minh City. I therefore only indicate interview locations outside of Ho Chi Minh City in these citations. All "personal communications" occurred over email or an instant-messaging platform.

4. Nguyễn Vĩnh Bảo, interview with the author, July 18, 2013; see also Cannon (2016, 160).

5. Nguyễn Vĩnh Bảo, interview with the author, December 18, 2014.

6. Nguyễn Vĩnh Bảo, interview with the author, December 18, 2008.

7. Nguyễn Vĩnh Bảo, interview with the author, July 26, 2019, Cao Lãnh.

8. Nguyễn Vĩnh Bảo, interview with the author, July 26, 2019, Cao Lãnh; emphasis verbalized.

9. I have provided more extensive detail about this life and work in Cannon (2013) and (2018).

10. The members of the *Hoa Sim* National Folk Music Ensemble also included Ngọc Dung (who now lives in San Jose), Quỳnh Hạnh, and Phương Oanh (Trần Quang Hải 2010).

11. Many locations in rural areas in southern Vietnam are not described as being on specific streets. Many southern Vietnamese instead use established physical landscape markers to describe where they live. Hai Đức describes the location of his birth as Cái

Chanh Cái Muỗng, where *Cái Chanh* indicates a place where a lemon grove meets a river, and *Cái Muỗng* indicates a place where senna plants meet a river.

12. Trần Minh Đức, interviews with the author, June 28 and 29, 2010, Cần Thơ.

13. He also mentioned that he has students who moved abroad after 1975, but he does not currently instruct them.

ONE *Framing Contested Creativities*

1. The original is published in Vietnamese. All translations from Vietnamese and French are my own unless otherwise indicated.

2. This discourse mirrors some elements of both Charles Landry's (1994) work on the creative city and the United Nations Educational, Scientific and Cultural Organization (UNESCO) Creative Cities Network.

3. The return of Vietnamese popular music stars from the diaspora is evaluated in more detail by Caroline Kieu-Linh Valverde (2012).

4. The popularization of the board game Monopoly is another example of this practice. Lizzie Magie initially created the game, but Charles Darrow then augmented it very slightly and sold it to Parker Brothers. Presenting himself as creator and master of the game, he earned millions from its sale while Magie earned nearly nothing (Mould 2018, 55–57).

5. In so doing, Csikszentmihalyi takes part in the large-scale stabilization of creativity. These ideas circulated and ultimately underpinned New Labour's attempt in the United Kingdom to support creative industries and usher in the next chapter of Britain's economic development (Mould 2018, 8; see also Cook 2018, 182; and Williamson and Cloonan 2007, 318). The results of this policy were mixed, with Robert Hewison (2014) arguing that the investment in societal creativity benefited only the few.

6. Ethnomusicologists advance a similar notion. Juniper Hill advocates that "an environment in which diverse solutions are allowed and accepted" best enables the encouragement of creativity (2009, 89). Gil-Sung Park (2013) points to the similarities between Csikszentmihalyi's creativity model and the way that creativity has been "managed" and "manufactured" in the South Korean popular music industry.

7. Artists and musicians may accept this and deploy their efforts as part of a structured collective to drive development. If they have stable or salaried work, however, the work they do belongs to corporate elites in the neoliberal and capitalist context. Jason Toynbee, for instance, evaluates the impact of superstructure on individual creative practice and understands the underlying mechanisms of musicmaking in capitalist spheres (2017, 37). In these settings, the labor undertaken by musicians does not belong to them; any creativity generated therefore does not belong to them either (48). The structures of copyright law uphold this alienation from labor and creativity. Matt Stahl, for instance, examines the ways that the copyright law in the United States gives ownership of the recorded work

to major artists rather than their hired collaborators (2013, 210; see McLeod and DiCola 2011 for an examination of the sampling system).

8. For Maureen Mahon, music practice involves "processes of social construction" that attaches labels of "natural" and "unchangeable" to musical forms and techniques (2014, 329).

9. Theories of practice emerge largely out of the social sciences and have been referenced by ethnomusicologists for decades (Danielson 1997, 16–17; Sugarman 1997, 27–30; see also Rice 2017). Nooshin (2015, 27) examines creativity as practice in some detail.

TWO *Creativity in Ethnomusicology*

1. This did not follow concurrent trends in psychology and related fields. Cook notes, for instance, that creativity studies began in 1950 in the field of psychology (2018, 4).

2. Nooshin (2015, 4) also identifies this humanistic/social scientific division.

3. Nooshin notes that Constantin Brăiloiu and A. L. Lloyd make similar arguments in the 1958 and 1967 respectively (2015, 14).

4. Brăiloiu further views individual creativity in various processes of variation (Ramnarine 2003, 20).

5. One important exception for Nooshin is Percy Grainger, who evaluated of the creative abilities of individual singers and musicians (2015, 14).

6. Ed Sarath makes similar arguments for consciousness. He argues that "self-awareness, transcendence, realization of wholeness and interconnectedness, noetic experience, and the wide range of feeling and emotion that are thought to distinguish human beings from other species" emerge from creative action and expression (2013, 2).

7. The concept of work here invites Marxist critique. I invoke some of this here, particularly through my reference to the work of José E. Limón (1992) summarized in Chapter 1; however, a more sustained synthesis of play, work, and creativity must be put aside for now.

THREE *The "Seed" of Creativity in Southern Vietnam*

1. As I prepared Cannon (2013) for publication, I sent the draft to Phạm Thúy Hoan for her review. She was startled that I quoted her student using the term *Việt Cộng*. It is a disparaging term allegedly coined by Ngô Đình Diệm, the first president of the Republic of Vietnam, to mean *Việt gian cộng sản* ("Communist traitor to Vietnam"); it later referred more generally—but still in a pejorative way—to *Việt Nam cộng sản* (Communist Vietnamese) and was used by non-Communists in South Vietnam, among Vietnamese in diaspora, and among non-Vietnamese speakers during and after the war (Turley 2009, xiv). Cô Thúy Hoan wondered why one of her students had said this and why I had repeated it in a work about her ensemble. She gave the article to another student who had studied in the United States and asked him to provide a summary of the context to her. When

the three of us met, I explained that her student had probably used the term because as an American, I would understand both the connotative and denotative meanings of the term. The two members of the ensemble had been on opposite sides of a violent conflict, but the student wanted to impart that Cô Thúy Hoan's music had brought them together and helped them heal the deep wounds of the war. She seemed relieved; she still had some concerns about how someone might misinterpret the term in context, but she agreed to allow me to use it. Unfortunately, her worry ultimately proved correct: an undergraduate thesis I found online uses my article to argue that some cultural production in Vietnam advocates a non-Communist southern Vietnamese nationalism; the thesis writer does not replicate the use of the term *Việt Cộng*, but misunderstands the point of the article.

2. Nguyễn Vĩnh Bảo, interview with the author, June 28, 2007.

3. Importantly, O. W. Wolters makes the argument that Funan should not be considered the first Southeast Asian state (Wolters [1982] 1999, 23–24). The prevalence of the Chinese term for the region, *Funan*, carries forward a Sinitic historiographic understanding of Funan (109–10).

4. The architecture of cities with large Khmer Krom populations, such as Sóc Trăng, indicates the influence of Theravada Buddhism of many Khmer Krom communities over the Mahayana Buddhism of the Vietnamese populations.

5. Some advance a longer history, as evidenced by a series of poems by Vũ Huy Chân (1955) titled "The Five-thousand-year History of Vietnam" that ran in the Republic of Vietnam (South Vietnam) journal *Văn hóa nguyệt san* in the mid-1950s.

6. This continued long-standing cultural exchange between the lands given the relatively open borders in the region (Whitmore 2011). According to Trần Văn Khê (1962, 22), the rulers of Đại Việt had a particular interest in the music of Champa. After Lê Đại Hành invaded Champa in 982 AD, he brought one hundred royal dancers and singers to Đại Việt. In 1060, Lý Thánh Tông transcribed a Chăm song for inclusion into Vietnamese music practice, and in 1212, Lý Cao Tông commissioned work with the title "Chiêm Thành âm" ("A Song of Champa"). Vietnamese sources commonly point to this connection and describe how Chăm music influenced the creation of sad tunes in southern Vietnamese music. Meanwhile, Khmer music appears less frequently in Vietnamese literature, although musicians frequently debate in private conversations the presence of Khmer tunes and song titles in southern Vietnamese music.

7. Nguyễn Vĩnh Bảo, interview with the author, December 18, 2008.

8. Most of the Vietnamese scholars cited to support these conclusions, including Lê Tuấn Hùng, Nguyễn Thuyết Phong, and Võ Trường Kỳ, are accomplished performers. Their words align with the beliefs professed by the other musicians discussed here.

9. Thầy Phước Cường, interview with the author, October 23, 2008. In Cannon (2012, 132), I referred to this temple as "Chùa Bửu Lâm," which I later realized is an error. The temple is called Chùa Bửu Sơn.

10. Nguyễn Vĩnh Bảo, interview with the author, October 23, 2008.

11. McHale translates the lyrics of a 1935 version of the tune that was printed in Romanized script for ease of understanding by the general population (168–69). Lyrics included "enter[ing] the land of Nirvana," "spreading the Way," and "escap[ing] from sinking into suffering."

12. There is some debate as to whether Laozi actually lived or serves as a stand-in for the collective knowledge of early Daoist practice.

13. In Cannon (2016), I offer the "thematic loop" as a similar concept.

14. The cities of Hanoi, Hải Phòng, and Đà Nẵng (Tourane) also came under direct control. See Firpo (2016, 4) for a discussion of the application of French law in Hanoi and Hải Phòng during this period.

15. Although Annam served as the French name for an administrative unit comprised of the central Vietnamese provinces, "Annam" or "les annamites" often differentiated Vietnamese culture and language speakers from the Khmer and Lao areas of French Indochina.

16. Gustave Dumoutier (1890) describes mostly lyrical content from central and northern Vietnam; see Nguyễn T. Phong (2018) for a more extensive evaluation. Hoàng Yến (1919) describes methods of performing the đàn tranh and đàn kìm and also provides the Chinese character notation of a number of pieces from Huế in central Vietnam; this notation provides the best glimpse of performance practices in the early twentieth century in Huế. E. Le Bris (1922) provides notation and French translations of lyrics of music that constituted *ca Huế*, or a genre of music from Huế that existed outside of the royal court. Gaston Knosp ([1907] 1922) has published a detailed encyclopedia article on the music of Indochina that discusses Vietnamese music history, music aesthetics, and genres, in addition to providing illustrations of many types of Vietnamese instruments; indeed, Pasler (2012) describes the work of Gaston Knosp as that of "comparative musicology." A genre-specific study on *quan họ* from northern Vietnam by Nguyen Van Huyen appeared in 1934. Georges de Gironcourt (1943) provides some detail of Vietnamese music, but more detail—including intricate illustrations—of the music of minority groups.

17. Sasagawa Hideo notes that monuments at Angkor often served as models for the Indochinese pavilions, including those at the 1889 and 1900 Universal Expositions in Paris and the 1906 Colonial Exposition in Marseille. Vietnamese music and theater were the only ones featured at the first two events (2005, 426). It was not until the 1906 event that organizers featured Cambodian dance (421; see also Diamond 2003, 148).

18. The January 13 and 20, 1901, issues featured descriptions of music from the Indochinese pavilion. These are from an eighteen-part series by Julien Tiersot on the music of the 1900 Universal Exposition that ran from October 7, 1900, to January 27, 1901.

19. I am not aware of the use of the Vietnamese first name "Viang." Most likely, this is a misspelling of "Giang."

20. Musicians perform a version of this tune in southern Vietnam today called "Lưu

thủy vắn" ("Flowing Water" [short version]). This is a different tune than "Lưu thủy trường" ("Flowing Water" [long version].

21. Jann Pasler's (2012) descriptions of Gaston Knosp's music criticism of opera and other European art music in northern Vietnam at the turn of the twentieth century point to the prevalence of music for French and other European audiences.

22. In this example recorded in the Bửu Sơn Temple in District 5 of Ho Chi Minh City, the musicians play a section of "Ngũ đối hạ" on the *mõ* (drum), *đẩu* (small hanging gong), and đàn cò (fiddle). The drum and gong then play a transition involving rolling (*đổ*) on the drum to a *bóp* section featuring the *kèn thau* (oboe). The *bóp* is nonmetered and serves as an upbeat introduction to the next section (not heard in clip). My thanks go to Nguyễn Thuyết Phong for helping me understand this clip (personal communication with the author, February 22, 2021).

23. Postcards created from this image label the ensemble as "Orchestre de la Maison du Repos des Notables Cochinchinois."

24. The image of Nguyễn Tống Triều published in Trần Văn Khải (1970, 82) appears to be the same gentleman on the left-hand side of the Marseille picture. Nguyễn Lê Tuyên and Nguyễn Đức Hiệp (2013, 92–93) agree with this assessment.

25. In Chapter 63, Laozi writes, "Act without action. Do without ado" (Chan 1963, 169).

26. In Vietnamese, *vô vi* often is taught through the phrases "bất hành nhi hành" and "không làm nhưng làm," meaning that one does not act in order to act.

27. According to Thrasher (2008, 49–50), Zhuangzi connects music performance specifically to spontaneity.

28. Nguyễn Vĩnh Bảo, interview with the author, August 21, 2008.

29. Nguyễn Vĩnh Bảo, interview and email exchange with the author, April 30, 2009.

30. Nguyễn Vĩnh Bảo, interview with the author, March 17, 2009.

31. Nguyễn Vĩnh Bảo, interviews with the author, April 2 and May 6, 2009.

32. Huỳnh Khải, interview with the author, August 14, 2013; see also Huỳnh Khải (2011); Meeker (2013, 52).

33. Huỳnh Khải, interview with the author, August 14, 2013.

34. Lê Đình Bích, interview with the author, May 26, 2009, Cần Thơ.

35. Thầy Phước, interview with the author, April 8, 2009, Cần Thơ.

FOUR *Portrait of đờn ca tài tử*

1. Nguyễn Vĩnh Bảo, interview with the author, December 18, 2008.

2. Thầy Phước Cường, interview with the author, October 23, 2008; see also Nguyễn Tuấn Khanh (2014, 38).

3. The terms *đàn* and *thổi* have antecedents in the Chinese language in the terms *tan* (彈) and *chui* (吹), respectively. My thanks to Jonathan Stock for alerting me to these terms.

4. Other kinds of glissandi also exist in Vietnamese music but will not be covered in this text. Players of the *đàn tỳ bà* use a kind of glissando called *rải*, for instance.

5. Although Trần Văn Khê provides a spelling for the instrument that I have not seen elsewhere (*dan xên*), he argues that the term also originates in China (1967, 89). Thrasher argues that the instrument is related to the *yueqin* (four-stringed moon-shaped lute with a short neck), while Yuan-Yuan Lee and Sin-yan Shen argue that the instrument is a "cousin" of the *ruan*, an "ancient" four-stringed moon-shaped lute with a long neck and typically two decorative sound holes on the face of the instrument (1999, 119–20; see also Thrasher 2008, 58n9).

6. For the *qinqin* name, the prefix *qin* (秦) refers to the Qin region in northwest China (present-day Shaanxi Province), after which the instrument was perhaps named (Thrasher 2008, 99n37). The second character *qin* (琴) refers to the instrument, and is equivalent to the Vietnamese word *cầm*. The Vietnamese translation of meihuaqin is *mai hoa cầm*.

7. Guangzhou Municipal Bureau of Culture, accessed May 23, 2009 (and no longer available online), http://2007jzj.gzwh.gov.cn/yyzs/2005zgyq/zgyq.asp?id=83.

8. See also Thrasher (2001). François Picard (1991, 162) also notes the existence of the three-stringed *qinqin*.

9. In Hanoi, I once saw a shop on the road to the airport with a sign that depicted the đàn sến. In addition, Vũ Nhật Thăng analyzes the pitch content of a đàn sến owned by Xuân Khải, a well-known composer of *nhạc dân tộc* in northern Vietnam (Vũ Nhật Thăng 1998, 32). I have never, however, heard of performances of the đàn sến in any other location besides southern Vietnam.

10. The three-stringed version of the instrument does have a long history in southern Vietnam. The cover of a book of sheet music from 1930, for instance, includes a picture of a musician playing the three-stringed version (Trần Sanh Lại 1930).

11. Others suggest that *hò* should be classified as *Do*, but I do not adopt this method here. Nguyễn Phúc An (2019a) and Kiều Tấn (1993, 323–24) provide an extensive summary of pitches proposed in theoretical treatises on đờn ca tài tử.

12. The đàn tranh, on the other hand, requires the retuning of each individual string, whereas the retuning of the đàn kìm might take five seconds.

13. *Nhị* here is the Sino-Vietnamese term for "two."

14. Nguyễn Vĩnh Bảo, interview with the author, August 11, 2013.

15. Nguyễn Vĩnh Bảo, interview with the author, March 26, 2009.

16. Vũ Nhật Thăng (1998, 47) also describes this as *mượn cung phím*, or borrowing the pitch from another fret place on the fingerboard. For the đàn cò and đàn gáo, he also specifies that one can slide to a new pitch (*vuốt*). *Vuốt* is also used to describe slides on various guitars.

17. Trần Minh Đức, interview with the author, June 4, 2009, Cần Thơ.

18. Nguyễn Vĩnh Bảo, interview with the author, May 6, 2009.

19. Nguyễn Vĩnh Bảo, interview with the author, May 6, 2009.

20. For Vietnamese musicians aware of the Delta blues in the United States, they suggest that the Mekong Delta has its own form of blues in đờn ca tài tử.

21. Nguyễn Vĩnh Bảo, interview with the author, July 18, 2013.

22. Changes to an instrument sometimes provoke nationalist ire as well. Nguyễn Vĩnh Bảo told me of an attempt to fashion a đàn gáo in northern Vietnam, where the instrument is not often found. The instrument maker used a piece of wood and surrounded it with cowhide. The resulting sound might be considered sonorous, but it had the timbre (and "soul") of a Chinese instrument rather than a Vietnamese one (Nguyễn Vĩnh Bảo, interview with the author, July 18, 2013).

23. Ko On Chan, personal communication with the author, April 16, 2020.

24. Nguyễn Vĩnh Bảo, interview with the author, December 2, 2008.

25. Nguyễn Vĩnh Bảo, interview with the author, December 2, 2008.

26. The term *rao* also appears in "rao hàng bán vặt," the phrase for classified ads. My thanks to PQ Phan for alerting me to this phrase.

27. In some instances, *rao* grow into long stand-alone ruminations on particular emotional states. This is especially true of commercial recordings and recordings shared between friends. Nguyễn Vĩnh Bảo features *rao buồn* (sad preludes) on the Ocora recording *Vietnam: Tradition du Sud* ([1972] 1992). He also records these works in his studio for distribution among his online community.

28. Nguyễn Vĩnh Bảo, interview with the author, December 27, 2014.

29. I place translations of titles published elsewhere in parentheses. Other translations are my own. I adopt the ordering of the Bắc pieces proposed by Nguyễn Vĩnh Bảo, Trương Bình Tòng (1996, 64), and others. "Tây thi" and "Cổ bản" sometimes—but not always—have an indication of length after the title. There is a discrepancy as to whether these pieces are "vắn" (short), as indicated by Nguyễn Vĩnh Bảo, or "trường" (long) (Kiều Tấn 2002; Nguyễn Văn Ngưu 1995). To prevent confusion here, I omit the length designation.

30. The titles of these seven works are difficult to translate, and the possible meanings of the titles are not often debated by the musicians with whom I interacted. For some of the titles, I looked through several dictionaries, including a Latin-Vietnamese dictionary originally published as A.J. L. Taberd (1838), to gather a composite understanding of these terms. Lê (1998, 138) provides several alternatives.

31. Playing all Bắc pieces in order without any transition phrases between them is possible, musicians argue, because each piece starts with a subsequent pitch of the scale of the Bắc mode. "Lưu thủy trường" begins with the note *hò* (sol); "Phú lục chấn" begins with *xự* or *u* (la); "Bình bán chấn" begins with *xang* (do); "Xuân tình chấn" begins with *cống* (mi); "Tây thi" begins with *líu* (sol); and "Cổ bản" begins with *xê* (re). Playing the work in order does not outline the scale in its exact sequence, but Nguyễn Vĩnh Bảo argues that the general progression has a clear upward scalar trajectory (interview with the author,

July 18, 2013). Kiều Tấn (2002, 278) and Nguyễn Văn Ngưu (1995) list "Cổ bản" after "Bình bán chấn" so the pitches are introduced in their scalar order; Nguyễn Văn Ngưu's notation does not construct the scale using the first pitch performed but with the pitch iterated on the first beat of eight in the first phrase. In other words, the six pieces begin in the following ways, respectively: xê xáng **liu** (notated as **hò** with one set of lyrics provided); xê liu **u**; líu cóng xê **xang**; xừ cóng líu **xê**; xề u liu **cọng**; xáng xề xàng **liu**. (All solfège syllables have been replicated exactly as they are found in the notation.) There are other variants as well. Writing about cải lương in Hanoi, Đắc Nhẫn and Ngọc Thới (1974) place "Cổ bản" at the end of the six works but list "Tây thi" after "Phú lục chấn" (44–53); this is an outlier. (Đắc Nhẫn and Ngọc Thới also argue that some of these works developed from similarly titled works in of the Huế tradition; the exception is "Tây thi" [49]. This may have been a replicated argument made by Trần Văn Khê [1962, 98–99]. Most musicians today do not agree with such a direct melodic connection to the central Vietnamese musical tradition.)

32. Nguyễn Vĩnh Bảo, interview with the author, May 6, 2009.

33. Trần Minh Đức, interview with the author, May 26, 2009, Cần Thơ.

34. Lê Đình Bích, interview with the author, June 26, 2010, Cần Thơ.

35. One also does not hear the use of *già* or *non* pitch augmentation (to be described in note 37) in this mode.

36. Nguyễn Vĩnh Bảo, interview with the author, October 15, 2008.

37. The term *non* often is made in reference to young plants in nature. The word for "young bamboo" is *cây tre non*, and fresh bamboo juice from a young plant is called *nước ép tre trúc non*. For additional descriptions of *già* and *non*, see Kiều Tấn (1993, 323).

38. Nguyễn Vĩnh Bảo, interview with the author, July 29, 2013; see also Vũ Nhật Thăng (1998, 88).

39. Adjustments to *xự* and *xang* maintain an important intervallic "fourth" equivalence between *hò* and *xang*, and *xự* and *xê*: here, *hò* and *xê* are fixed pitches and serve to stabilize the performance of the mode. When *xang* is raised slightly, it increases the intervallic space between *hò* and *xang*; to maintain intervallic equivalence, one lowers *xự* slightly to increase the space between *xự* and *xê*. Dương Bích Hà further argues that these adjustments may be due to the construction of particular instruments found in Huế; in particular, the *kèn bóp*, a kind of small double-reed instrument, crafts a seven-note scale that replicates the *già/non* "accent" (1997, 125–26). Going further back into history, she connects this scale to one described by Trần Văn Khê (1962, 231) as the Javanese *pélog* scale that he believes influenced the early development of music on now-Vietnamese lands. All of these claims are titillating but unproven at this point.

40. Nguyễn Vĩnh Bảo, interview with the author, July 18, 2013.

41. Nguyễn Vĩnh Bảo was emphatic about this point. "When you tune the string, you must use the accurate pitch." If not, "no one will want to play together with you!" (interview with the author, July 18, 2013).

42. Nguyễn Vĩnh Bảo, interview with the author, July 23, 2012; see also Trainor (1977, 110).

43. Although he does not mention *già* and *non* by name, Trần Văn Khê does mention the use of raised and lowered pitches in "sad pieces" of southern Vietnamese music (1962, 230). He further suggests that this usage indicates influence from Chăm music (1962, 231; see also Addiss 1971, 36). Although little is known about the music of the ancient kingdom of Champa, scholars invoke the music as some of the melancholiest in Vietnam.

44. Nguyễn Vĩnh Bảo, interviews with the author, July 18 and 29, 2013.

45. Both John Paul Trainor (1977, 110) and Lê Tuấn Hùng (1998, 83) identify "Vọng cổ" as related to the set of pitches used to create "Nam ai," a Nam mode work. Hoàng Đạm identifies "Vọng cổ" as a Oán mode work.

46. Trần Văn Khê (1962, 99) argues that "Nam xuân" and "Nam ai" are closely related to Quảng Nam pieces and are different than similarly titled works in the ca Huế tradition.

47. They also categorize the nhạc lễ or Ha works as hơi of the Bắc mode.

48. I most often heard performances of a composition played in the *hơi Quảng* (Guang-dong nuance) style, which aimed to temporarily transform a piece into a "Chinese" composition by using different ornamentation.

49. Trương Bình Tòng continues by detailing the specific ways that the rigid and flexible components emerge in performance context. He argues, for example, that Oán features certain rigid intervals that do not involve any neighbor tone or passing tone movement and land definitively on a pitch; flexible intervals involve a bit more motion and do not seem as conclusive (1996, 52).

FIVE *Playing with Metaphor*

1. I thank my friend Phan Huy for suggesting the interpretation of the lyrics in this way. In several versions of the lyrics that I collected, the nonsense syllables in the third and fifth lines are "Là đô í a đô nàng," which I translated simply as "la la la la lady." He proposed that the lyrics actually are "Là đố í a đố nàng," where the first *đố* in the line indicates a solfège name, as it sits next to *là*, and the second *đố* means "guess," suggest-ing that the lady (*nàng*) referenced in the line is invited to count the flowers. Although the melodic content of the tune does not suggest a "La Do" relationship, I still find this argument plausible. Phan also suggested I used the French term *mademoiselle* as it bet-ter captures the imagery of the elegant woman standing in nature as the lyrics intend.

2. Nguyễn Vĩnh Bảo, interview with the author, December 2, 2008.

3. Kyra D. Gaunt desribes how "being 'in the game'" serves as a metaphor for not simply "working in the music industry" but also having access to the power and prestige that comes with this work (2006, 115).

4. McPhee mentions as well that musicians demonstrate the flower embellishment

through dance (1946, 41). For other uses of a flower metaphor in Javanese gamelan, see descriptions of the *sekaran* or "flower pattern" (Brinner 1995, 225–26) and *kembangan* (Alves 2001, 30; Sutton 1991, 157).

5. Wong mentions that Maria Roseman makes a similar observation in her discussion of the Temiar in Malaysia (1991, 8–9).

6. Nguyễn T. Phong (1998, 465) also makes reference to chân phương and hoa lá as structural components to performance, but without the reference to creativity.

7. Thầy Phước Cường, interview with the author, October 23, 2008.

8. The lyrics of the contemporary rap song "Đơn giản" ("Simple") by Hoàng Rapper place chân phương alongside "rustic" (*mộc mạc*) and "ordinary" (*bình dân*): "Nhiều lần nhận ra trong tôi chợt yêu thương sao cuộc sống giản đơn thôi / Mộc mạc bình dân chân phương từ trong từng điều nhỏ nhoi nhất trên đời / Giấu giếm làm chi quan tâm làm chi bao nhiêu cảm xúc kia / Cứ sống thật đi nên tôi cười khi tôi vui, tôi khóc khi tôi buồn." ("Many times I have realized that inside me, I suddenly love why life is so simple / Rustic, ordinary, and chân phương from even the smallest thing in the world / Why do I conceal my concerns and emotions? / To live a truthful life, I need to smile when I am happy and cry when I am sad") (cuoimim n.d.).

9. She "developed 'hoa lá cành' but still preserved the correct rules of playing. [She] primarily followed these rules but trained herself to know how to sing in the *tài tử* style . . ." (Lê Duy Hạnh as cited by Thanh Hiệp 2014).

10. Ethnomusicologists draw on Erving Goffman's (1974) and Gregory Bateson's ([1972] 2000) definitions of the frame to pose how musicians and audiences structure meaning in performance in different ways (see Shannon 2003, 17; Stone 2008, 118–20). Ingrid Monson (1996, 17) uses the Goffman's frame concept to better understand how musicians viewed her. She posits, for example, that it is better to think of the ethnomusicologist in the field as a journalist rather than as a scholar studying a more abstract project. Here, I follow Thomas Turino (2008, 14) in his application of Bateson's description of the frame as an interpretive lens.

11. Thầy Phước Cường, interview with the author, October 23, 2008.

12. The reference to *căn bản* as "basic" recalls another term, *cái căn*, or "root," to describe chân phương (Lê Tuấn Hùng 1998, 56). The root refers not only to the fundaments of performance practice but also to the source of knowledge about the tradition. This, too, is found in Daoist practice, where Daoists advocate staying close or returning to the source as an important element of creative practice. The source also constitutes a kind of root in nature: in Chapter 59, Laozi writes, "the roots are deep and the stalks are firm, which is the way of long life and everlasting existence" (Chan 1963, 168).

13. Trần Minh Đức, interview with the author, April 16, 2009, Cần Thơ.

14. Huỳnh Khải, interview with the author, August 14, 2013.

15. Huỳnh Khải, interview with the author, August 14, 2013.

16. Hoàng Đạm (2003) has done extensive work on this topic, identifying key lòng bản associated with particular đờn ca tài tử tunes.

17. Cao Thị Thẳng, public commentary, December 21, 2014.

18. There is disagreement among musicians concerning the length and beat structure of this work. It is most often described as a work of thirty-two phrases where each phrase has four beats (*nhịp tư*), but it is sometimes performed as a work of sixteen phrases where each phrase has eight beats (*nhịp tám*). In this example, I follow the most common thirty-two phrase version.

19. Anonymous research collaborator, personal communication with the author, July 19, 2018.

20. Nguyễn Vĩnh Bảo, interview with the author, July 22, 2009; see also Lê Tuấn Hùng (1998, 56).

21. Nguyễn Vĩnh Bảo, interview with the author, October 22, 2008.

22. Nguyễn Vĩnh Bảo, interview with the author, June 12, 2009.

23. Translated as "pass" and "decant," the term designates the addition of tones to fill out the melody, so as to improve its flavor as a decanter does for wine.

24. Nguyễn Vĩnh Bảo, interview with the author, March 26, 2009.

25. Nguyễn Vĩnh Bảo, interview with the author, May 18, 2009.

26. Nguyễn Vĩnh Bảo, interview with the author, March 13, 2009.

27. The 2016 article about David Beckham was titled "Chẳng cần hoa lá cành, David Beckham vẫn khiến khối cô chết mê tại show Louis Vuitton," or "One Does Not Need to Be *hoa lá cành*, David Beckham still is a lady killer in the Louis Vuitton show" (Cô Kim 2016).

28. "Còn trí thức là biểu hiệu cái hào hoa bên ngoài của Đạo và là nguồn gốc của ngu muội." (Lão Tử 2018, 122)

29. Nguyễn Thuyết Phong, interview with the author, November 5, 2008.

30. Nguyễn Vĩnh Bảo, interview with the author, March 13, 2009.

31. Nguyễn Vĩnh Bảo, interview with the author, December 25, 2008.

32. Trần Minh Đức, interview with the author, June 29, 2010, Cần Thơ.

33. Judith Becker (2004) writes extensively on the ways that music serves and enables trance states; importantly, like Gilbert Rouget (1985), Becker understands "trance" and "ecstasy" as separate categories. As Rouget notes, for example, "ecstasy is a keenly memorable experience which one can recall and ponder over at leisure and which does not give rise to the dissociation so characteristic of trance" (9).

34. Importantly, they do not enter a trance. For Gilbert Rouget (1985, 11), trances involve the kind of disconnection to one's immediate environment, while ecstatic states involve connections to that environment (see also Becker 2004, 27). The social environment works alongside the sound produced to generate the xuất thần environment; there is no theoretical separation between the social and the musical here. Trance traditions exist elsewhere in Vietnam. Barley Norton (2009) describes spirit possession in lên đồng that

emerges from the performance environment inclusive of the live *chầu văn* music played; a similar ritual occurs in central Vietnam (PQ Phan, personal communication with the author, Bloomington, Indiana, May 11, 2014).

35. Chen Rong, interview with the author, January 16, 2016, Kalamazoo, Michigan.

36. Huỳnh Khải, interview with the author, August 14, 2013.

37. In Track 16, one hears this fragment of melody between 3:36 and 3:52.

38. Trần Minh Đức, interview with the author, May 26, 2009, Cần Thơ.

39. Huỳnh Khải, interview with the author, August 14, 2013.

SIX *Developing Creativity*

1. Transcribed from recorded emcee public comments, June 6, 2010.

2. Transcribed from recorded emcee public comments, June 6, 2010.

3. Phạm Ngọc Lanh, interview with the author, March 22, 2009.

4. A similar concept, *fazhan* (發展), exists in the contemporary Chinese context (Chumley 2016, 197; Wilcox 2018, 87).

5. The titles of *Nhà giáo nhân dân* (People's Teacher) and *Nghệ sĩ nhân dân* (People's Artist) designate a higher status that teachers and artists can attain.

6. Before this time period, the Nguyễn court in Huế oversaw the production and maintenance of knowledge and governance through the literati system, which was dissolved in 1918.

7. The evaluation of the journal in this setting is only cursory. Besides an evaluation of *Văn hóa nguyệt san* by Claudine Ang (2013) in her larger historiographic study of intellectual debates in RVN scholarly literature and a citation of one article on central Vietnamese music in Lê Tuấn Hùng (1991), this journal has received little attention. There is no mistake, however, that this journal is important in the ways that it highlights how politics and culture were combined in the RVN. In the April 1956 issue, an adage attributed to then-president Ngô Đình Diệm appears in a blank space at the end of one article. Reminiscent of the contemporary practice of posting the guiding morals of Hồ Chí Minh in public spaces in contemporary Vietnam, it reads: "Học đến tận nơi, hỏi đến tận chốn, hiểu thật thông suốt, hành thật chu-đáo" (Study until the very end; ask until there is nothing left to ask; understand clearly and thoroughly; practice makes perfect). Following the November 1963 coup that deposed Ngô Đình Diệm, the journal published military decrees and resolutions describing the president's government as "ineffective" and "betraying the most sacred rights of the populace" (Dương Văn Minh 1963, n.p.).

8. This Nguyễn Đình Thi was an academic in exile about which I have found little, except for a newspaper article in the Vietnamese press (Đỗ Ngọc Quang 2003). He should not be confused with the well-known northern Vietnamese writer of the same name who lived at the same time.

9. In 1961, Nguyễn Phụng Michel opened the National School of Music in Huế (Trường Quốc gia Âm nhạc địa phương Huế) to focus on teaching the folk and court music of the region.

10. I translate the term *phụng sự* here as "serve," but it also indicates a kind of devotion, often of a patriotic nature.

11. Instead of translating the term *đại chúng* as "the masses," as one would do for an ideological text based on Marxist-Leninist ideology, I borrow the term *le public* from the French translation that Nguyễn Phụng Michel provides.

12. Hoàng Chương et al. (2011) list a number of troupes: *gánh "Con tằm"* in 1946; *gánh Nam Tinh* and *gánh Thanh Minh* in 1949; *gánh Hoa Sen*, *gánh Kim Thanh*, *gánh Hương Hoa*, and *gánh Kim Thoa* in 1950 (2011, 187–89); finally, after the dissolution of the *gánh "Con tằm"* in 1952, Năm Châu and Tư Trang established Ban Việt kịch Năm Châu, "the first troupe organized in the model of a managed group" (2011, 188). In 1954, the Saigon scene also included the *đoàn hát Kim Chung*, which moved to Saigon from northern Vietnam, although one source indicates that Saigonese audiences did not receive this ensemble well since their singers sang southern Vietnamese songs with a northern Vietnamese accent (Nguyễn Phương 2011). These troupes included singers and well-known musicians of both đờn ca tài tử and cải lương: Năm Cơ—a performer of the đàn kìm, đàn sến, and đàn ghi ta—was associated with Hoa Sen and Kim Chung; Năm Nghĩa—a performer of the đàn tranh and đàn ghi-ta, and one of Nguyễn Vĩnh Bảo's teachers—was associated with Thanh Minh (Nguyễn Vĩnh Bảo n.d.[c]).

13. The troupe *gánh "Con tằm"* was comprised of "lifelong friends" Năm Châu, Ba Vân, Duy Lân, Năm Bở, Phùng Há, Ngọc Sương, Kim Cúc, and Kim Lan (Hoàng Chương et al. 2011, 187). Nguyễn Phụng Michel lists Nguyễn Thành Châu (Năm Châu), Duy Lân, and Trương Phụng Hảo (Phùng Há) as cải lương voice and movement faculty at the National School (1997, 7). Nguyễn Vĩnh Bảo also recalls that the faculty included Kim Cúc and Kim Lan as well (n.d.[b]).

14. The instruments included the đàn sến, đàn kìm, đàn tỳ bà, đàn tam, đàn bầu, two đàn cò, đàn gáo, three đàn tranh, and the six-holed sáo. (Nguyễn Vĩnh Bảo recalled that he played the third đàn tranh part.) He said that the ensemble consisted of fifteen members, but I only count twelve in his list. Other performers may have included singers and percussionists, both of which perform in similar ensembles today.

15. Nguyễn Vĩnh Bảo, interview with the author, March 5, 2009.

16. Nguyễn Đình Hòa (1924–2000) simultaneously served as head of the Directorate of Cultural Affairs in the Ministry of National Education and as Secretary General of the National Commission for UNESCO Affairs from 1962 to 1966 and later as a counselor for education and culture in the RVN Embassy in Washington, DC, from 1966 to 1969 (Nguyễn Đình Hoà 1999, x; 157). He held various teaching posts in the Republic of Vietnam over his career, and ultimately served as director of the Center for Vietnamese

Studies and later as a professor in the Department of Linguistics at Southern Illinois University–Carbondale. He was a friend of Nguyễn Vĩnh Bảo and facilitated his visiting professorship at SIU in 1971 to 1972.

17. Nguyễn Vĩnh Bảo, personal communication with the author, April 9, 2016; see also Chew 2008, 2009.

18. Arranging passage on one of these boats required considerable funds. Phạm Ngọc Lanh told me that many sold their cars and bicycles to collect enough money, leading to an increase in the number of people who began walking to their destinations in Ho Chi Minh City after 1975 (interview with the author, January 26, 2009).

19. With the origins of the Indochinese Communist Party (later the Communist Party of Vietnam) in southern China, these policies adopted certain ideas from Mao Zedong's well-known Yan'an speech of 1942, "Talks on Literature and Art" (Ninh 2002, 28).

20. I have adopted Ninh's translation of *dân tộc hóa* as "nationalization" (2002, 29). Marr translates these three tenants as "patriotism, mass consciousness [and] scientific objectivity" (1981, 364).

21. The three principles enacted strategic policy "formulated to weed out contending ideas and insist on a particular view of Vietnamese culture past, present and future" (Ninh 2002, 34).

22. Many other socialist contexts have advanced the production of particular forms of "national music," occasionally through the use of state ensembles and newly composed work (see Buchanan 1995; Rice 1994; and Stock 1996).

23. The research of both authors is largely complementary, although they have slightly different foci. Arana discusses general attributes of the genre based upon her research in Hanoi and, in particular, research conducted with musicians associated with the Hanoi Conservatory. (She also suggests the translation of "neotraditional music.") Lê concentrates on the role of the đàn tranh in producing national music and attempts to describe the place of nhạc dân tộc in both southern and northern Vietnam. He briefly mentions, for instance, Phạm Thúy Hoan's role in propagating national music in southern Vietnam through composing new works and the Tiếng Hát Quê Hương Ensemble (1998, 114–16).

24. Phạm Thúy Hoan, interview with the author, July 7, 2009.

25. Phạm Thúy Hoan, interview with the author, July 7, 2009.

26. Thẻ "mực" is a term used specifically in Kiên Giang to describe fishing by the sea; this is also known as "câu mực." The fishing technique involves a flexible rod, a large hook, and fishing line wound around a large plastic reel.

27. For some nonparticipants, the practice of stereotyping dialect negates particularities and appears ostracizing. A friend of mine seemed puzzled when I described the practice. He grew up in central Vietnam but does not speak the stereotyped "central" accent, which he characterized as more representative of Huế rather than all of central Vietnam (personal communication with the author, March 7, 2009).

28. Phạm Thúy Hoan, interview with the author, July 7, 2009.

29. Huỳnh Khải undertakes similar compositional work (interview with the author, August 14, 2013).

30. Phạm Thúy Hoan, interview with the author, May 9, 2009.

31. Lê Hồng Sơn, interview with the author, August 7, 2013.

32. Việt, interview with the author, August 13, 2013.

33. Given the success of the first and second festivals, the Third Asian Zither Festival was scheduled for 2014 in Ho Chi Minh City. It would have enabled interactions not only between Vietnam-based musicians with zitherists from China, Japan, and Korea, but also between diasporic Vietnamese based in Seattle, Portland, Houston, and San Francisco who had planned to travel to Ho Chi Minh City to take part. It was rumored that a few months before the planned start of the festival, concerns were raised about inviting Chinese artists due to the frosty relationship between Vietnam and China. Although Vietnamese artists with whom I spoke thought these concerns were unwarranted, the festival ultimately was canceled out of an abundance of caution. The 2014 Zither Festival seems to have replaced it.

34. Phạm Thúy Hoan, interview with the author, July 7, 2009.

35. Transcribed public remarks, September 1, 2008.

36. The concert on the opening night featured performances by all of the delegations, including a performance of the southern Vietnamese tune "Xàng xê" described in further detail in Cannon (2013, 106–7).

37. Lê Đình Bích, interview with the author, April 16, 2009, Cần Thơ.

SEVEN *Tradition, Still Remains*

1. Nguyễn Vĩnh Bảo, interview with the author, March 17, 2009.

2. In addition to the works described here, other texts that investigate the notion of the ruin in music include Anderton (2019) and Stamatis (2011).

3. Thái Văn Kiểm (1950) includes both a French and a Vietnamese version of the text. I surmise that the Vietnamese version (42) is the original since it includes "Nam xuân" in the list of "southern airs," while the French translation (22–23) does not; the Vietnamese version also makes a citation to Đào Duy Anh's 1938 text *Việt-nam Văn-hóa Sử-cương* (*An Outline of Vietnamese Culture*) whereas the French version does not.

4. Nguyễn Vĩnh Bảo, interview with the author, March 17, 2009.

5. For recent scholarship on the impact of international recognition and tourism on traditional music in Vietnam, see Anisensel (2012); Jähnichen (2011); Meeker (2013); and Ó Briain (2014).

6. The term *quintessence* (*tinh hoa*) appears often in descriptions of the preservation of culture (Hà Huy Giáp [1974] 1976; Meeker 2013, 25). A 2012 government decree

concerning what is allowable onstage and what can and cannot be recorded—and by whom—stipulated that it would encourage "investment for the work to collect, research, preserve, promote the value of the traditional artistic performing arts and acquire for selection the quintessence of world art" (Chính phủ Việt Nam 2012).

7. Anonymous research consultant, personal communication with the author, May 8, 2014.

8. Private archival recording, n.d.

9. Nguyễn Vĩnh Bảo, personal communication with the author, October 5, 2016.

10. Nguyễn Vĩnh Bảo, interview with the author, December 2, 2008.

11. Nguyễn Vĩnh Bảo, interview with the author, October 22, 2008.

12. Nguyễn Vĩnh Bảo, interview with the author, July 17, 2009.

13. Nguyễn Vĩnh Bảo, interview with the author, December 18, 2008.

14. Nguyễn Vĩnh Bảo, interview with the author, December 18, 2008.

15. "Lưu thủy vắn," which was mentioned briefly in Chapter 4, is also known as "Lưu thủy đoản" and is found as the first piece in the suite "Lưu thủy Bình bán Kim tiền" ("Flowing Water, Equal Measures, Golden Coin"). For a recording, see the first track of Nguyên Vinh Bao and Trân Van Khê ([1972] 1992).

16. Nguyễn Vĩnh Bảo, interview with the author, December 25, 2008.

17. Nguyễn Vĩnh Bảo, interview with the author, March 17, 2009.

18. This occurred on January 15, 2009. As Svetlana Boym has indicated, the ruin and nostalgia are tightly bound (Boym 2001). I therefore do not find it surprising that Nguyễn Vĩnh Bảo was frequently drawn to "Vọng cổ," a composition evocative of nostalgia, after he engaged with music in ruin.

19. I refer to this individual with the pronoun "she" since she uses the pronoun *chị* (older sister) to discuss her opinions, some musicians with whom I spoke believe that she wrote under a pseudonym. Although all posts described here are publicly available as of this writing, I use a common first name to refer to the writers and do not provide links to the individual posts. I do not agree with the rude and occasionally vulgar language used by Phi and Hoà; however, all who participated in these discussions used Facebook as a stand-in for a closed discussion forum. By linking to a conversation in which I only observed, I open the forum to international observation—and possibly additional "trolls"—and run the risk of ultimately eliminating the very "limits to growth" I study here.

20. I refer to this individual with the pronoun "he" since the profile photo posted is of a young man. Like Phi, mentioned above, it is believed he wrote under a pseudonym.

21. Phạm Thúy Hoan, interview with the author, January 3, 2015.

22. Phạm Thúy Hoan, interview with the author, January 3, 2015.

23. Nguyễn Vĩnh Bảo, transcription from a private archival recording made on July 9, 1980.

1. I adopt language here from Thomas Turino (2008) to describe the differences between presentational and participatory performance.

2. The violin is not a strange sight in đờn ca tài tử. According to Trần Văn Khê (2004, 214), Jean Tịnh introduced the violin into đờn ca tài tử performance in the early twentieth century. Musicians used the instrument to glide up and down the fingerboard and replicate the highly ornamented and melismatic tunes typical of vocal practice.

3. The conference opened with the greeting *kính thưa các đồng chí* (welcome, comrades), which typically marks the space as aligned with the government and Communist Party.

4. Anonymous research consultant, personal communication with the author, August 9 and 17, 2013.

5. The Ministry of Foreign Affairs established the Vietnam National Commission for UNESCO (Uỷ ban Quốc gia UNESCO của Việt Nam) on June 15, 1977. The SRVN officially joined the United Nations several months later on September 20, 1977. Both UNESCO and the SRVN maintain the official entry of the Republic of Vietnam in 1951 as the entry date of the Vietnam.

6. Describing an object or a site without the relationships that constructed it therefore misrepresents the object or site and also produces inaccurate knowledge. Anthropologist James Leach (2003, 137) has noted that groups living on the Rai Coast of Papua New Guinea locate "in relationships, and not in things" and therefore do not view abstractions of objects as imbued with value. Jeff Todd Titon's important remarks on issues related to the Royal Ballet of Cambodia and the Chinese *guqin* indicate the ways that UNESCO suspends practice in time and ignores the nuance of local debates concerning practice that sustain it (2009, 126–28).

7. Việt, interview with the author, December 20, 2014.

8. A second festival was organized in Bình Dương in 2017. At the time of this writing, a third festival in Cần Thơ was organized in 2020 but was temporarily postponed due to the COVID-19 pandemic.

9. I did not attend the festival. One friend did try to arrange an invitation to be sent to me, but he later told me that some members of the organizing committee were uncomfortable with the idea of inviting a foreigner. Another friend surmised that this discomfort might have emerged because they could foresee the controversy that would taint the success of the festival, and they did not want an international representative to view this. That said, these are rumors.

10. In the video, Huỳnh Khải (2011b) interviews the singer Văn Hường about the history of "Vọng cổ."

11. The word *miệt vườn* is also sometimes translated as "hick," though it does not have the same connotations as the English word.

12. Vương Duy Biên, transcribed public remarks, August 9, 2013.

13. Anonymous research consultant, personal communication with the author, July 19, 2018.

14. Dustin Ngo is perhaps one of the more well-known producers of "lo-fi" hip-hop in Vietnam, which he posts to YouTube and Bandcamp. One of my favorite tracks is a trap remix of "Võ Đông Sơ- Bạch Thu Hà" (2MORO Music 2016).

REFERENCES

Addiss, Steven. 1971. "Music of the Chăm Peoples." *Asian Music* 2(1): 32–38.

Agawu, Kofi. 1992. "Representing African Music." *Critical Inquiry* 18(2): 245–66.

Alves, Bill. 2001. "Kembangan in the Music of Lou Harrison." *Perspectives of New Music* 39(2): 29–56.

Anderton, Abby. 2019. *Rubble Music: Occupying the Ruins of Postwar Berlin, 1945–1950.* Bloomington: Indiana University Press.

Ang, Claudine. 2013. "Regionalism in Southern Narratives of Vietnamese History: The Case of the 'Southern Advance' [*Nam Tiến*]." *Journal of Vietnamese Studies* 8(3): 1–26.

Anh Thư. 2013. "Lý Nhã Kỳ: 'Ăn cơm Việt Nam và nghe nhạc dân tộc thì không gì bằng'" ["There Is Nothing More Equal than Eating Vietnamese Food and Listening to Traditional Music"]. *Thanh Niên*, August 10, 2013. https://thanhnien.vn/van-hoa /ly-nha-ky-an-com-viet-nam-va-nghe-nhac-dan-toc-thi-khong-gi-bang-804150.html (accessed August 23, 2018).

Anisensel, Aliénor. 2012. "Le Parti et le patrimoine: Le cas de la tradition musicale du *Ca trù*" ["The Party and Heritage: The Case of *Ca trù* Traditional Music"]. *Communisme* 2012: 303–18.

Arana, Miranda. 1999. *Neotraditional Music in Vietnam.* Kent, OH: Nhac Viet, 1999.

Arnold-de Simine, Silke. 2015. "The Ruin as Memorial – The Memorial as Ruin." *Performance Research* 20(3): 94–102.

Bakhtin, Mikhail Mikhailovich. 1981. *The Dialogic Imagination: Four Essays*, trans. Caryl Emerson and Michael Holquist. Austin: University of Texas Press.

Ban biên soạn chuyên từ điển. 2003. *Từ điển tiếng Việt* [*Vietnamese Dictionary*]. Hanoi: HXB Văn hóa Thông tin.

Ban Chấp hành Trung ương Đảng. [1998] 2003. "Nghị quyết Hội nghị lần thứ năm Ban Chấp hành Trung ương Đảng (khóa VIII) về xây dựng và phát triển nền văn hóa Việt Nam tiên tiến, đậm đà bản sắc dân tộc" ["Resolution of the Fifth Conference of the Central Executive Committee (of the Eighth Congress) on Building and Developing an Advanced Vietnamese Culture Imbued with the National Identity"]. *Báo Điện tử*

Đảng Cộng sản Việt Nam. http://dangcongsan.vn/cpv/Modules/News/NewsDetail .aspx?co_id=30579&cn_id=124001 (accessed October 3, 2013).

Barber, Karin. 2007. "Improvisation and the Art of Making Things Stick." *Creativity and Cultural Improvisation*, 25–41. Oxford and New York: Berg.

Barndt, Kerstin. 2010. "'Memory Traces of an Abandoned Set of Futures': Industrial Ruin in the Postindustrial Landscapes of Germany." In *Ruins of Modernity*, edited by Julia Hell and Andreas Schönle, 270–93. Durham, NC: Duke University Press.

Barthes, Roland. 1977. "Death of the Author." In *Image, Music, Text*, trans. Stephen Heath, 142–48. New York: Hill and Wang.

Bateson, Gregory. [1972] 2000. *Steps to an Ecology of Mind*. Chicago and London: University of Chicago Press.

Baudrillard, Jean. 1988. *The Ecstasy of Communication*. Translated from French by Bernard & Caroline Schutze. New York: Semiotext(e).

———. 1989. "The Anorexic Ruins." Translated by from French David Antal. In *Looking Back on the End of the World*, edited by Dietmar Kamper and Christoph Wulf, 29–45. New York: Semiotext(e).

Baym, Nancy K. 2018. *Playing to the Crowd: Musicians, Audiences, and the Intimate Work of Connection*. New York: New York University Press.

Becker, Howard. [1984] 2008. *Art Worlds*. Berkeley and Los Angeles: University of California Press.

Becker, Judith. 1980. "A Southeast Asian Musical Process: Thai *Thǎw* and Javanese *Irama*." *Ethnomusicology* 24(3): 453–64.

———. 2004. *Deep Listeners: Music, Emotion, and Trancing*. Bloomington: Indiana University Press.

Becker, Judith, and Alton Becker. 1981. "A Musical Icon: Power and Meaning in Javanese Gamelan Music." In *The Sign in Music and Literature*, edited by W. Steiner, 203–15. Austin: University of Texas Press.

Bendrups, Dan, Katelyn Barney, and Catherine Grant. 2013. "An Introduction to Sustainability and Ethnomusicology in the Australasian Context." *Musicology Australia* 35(2): 153–58.

Beresford, Melanie. 1988. "Issues in Economic Unification: Overcoming the Legacy of Separation." In *Postwar Vietnam: Dilemmas in Socialist Development*, edited by David G. Marr and Christine B. White, 95–110. Ithaca, NY: Cornell Southeast Asia Program.

Beresford, Melanie, and Tran Ngoc Angie. 2004. "Introduction." In *Reaching for the Dream: Challenges of Sustainable Development in Vietnam*, edited by Melanie Beresford and Tran Ngoc Angie, 1–18. Copenhagen: NIAS Press.

Bergeron, Katherine. 1998. *Decadent Enchantments: The Revival of Gregorian Chant at Solesmes*. Berkeley: University of California Press.

Bithell, Caroline, and Juniper Hill, eds. 2014. *The Oxford Handbook of Music Revival*. New York: Oxford University Press.

Black, Alison Harley. 1989. *Man and Nature in the Philosophical Thought of Wang Fu-chih*. Seattle: University of Washington Press.

Blacking, John. 1977. "Some Problems of Theory and Method in the Study of Musical Change." *Yearbook of the International Folk Music Council* 9: 1–26.

Boas, Franz. [1927] 2010. *Primitive Art*. Mineola, NY: Dover Publications.

Bohlman, Philip V. 1988. *The Study of Folk Music in the Modern World*. Bloomington and Indianapolis: Indiana University Press.

Born, Georgina. 2005. "On Musical Mediation: Ontology, Technology and Creativity." *twentieth-century music* 2(1): 7–36.

Boym, Svetlana. 2001. *The Future of Nostalgia*. New York: Basic Books.

Brinner, Benjamin. 1995. *Knowing Music, Making Music: Javanese Gamelan and the Theory of Musical Competence and Interaction*. Chicago: University of Chicago Press.

Bronner, Simon J. 1992. "Introduction." In *Creativity and Tradition in Folklore: New Directions*, edited by Simon J. Bronner, 1–38. Logan: Utah State University Press.

Buchanan, Donna A. 1995. "Metaphors of Power, Metaphors of Truth: The Politics of Music Professionalism in Bulgarian Folk Orchestras." *Ethnomusicology* 39(3): 381–416.

Buhle, Paul. 1986. Introduction to *State Capitalism and World Revolution*, by C.L.R. James, with Raya Dunayevskaya and Grace Lee, xi–xxiii. Chicago: Charles H. Kerr Publishing Company.

Bui, Long. 2016. "The Refugee Repertoire: Performing and Staging the Postmemories of Violence." *MELUS* 41(3): 112–32.

Burnard, Pamela. 2012. *Musical Creativities in Practice*. Oxford: Oxford University Press.

Cannon, Alexander M. 2012. "Virtually Audible in Diaspora: The Transnational Preservation of Vietnamese Traditional Music." *Journal of Vietnamese Studies* 7(3): 122–56.

———. 2013. "When Charisma Sustains Tradition: Deploying Musical Competence in Southern Vietnam." *Ethnomusicology* 57(1): 87–114.

———. 2016. "From Nameless to Nomenclature: Creating Music Genre in Southern Vietnam." *Asian Music* 47(2): 138–71.

———. 2018. "Laughter, Liquor, and Licentiousness: Preservation through Play in Southern Vietnamese Traditional Music." In *The Routledge Companion to the Study of Local Musicking*, edited by Suzel A. Riley and Katherine Brucher, 321–33. New York and London: Routledge.

de Certeau, Michel. [1980] 1984. *The Practice of Everyday Life*. Translated from French by Steven Rendall. Berkeley: University of California Press.

Chan, Wing-Tsit. 1963. *A Source Book in Chinese Philosophy*. Princeton, NJ: Princeton University Press.

Chew, Valerie. 2008. "South East Asia Cultural Festival." *National Library Board Singapore.* http://eresources.nlb.gov.sg/infopedia/articles/SIP_1374_2008-11-22.html (accessed July 31, 2016).

———. 2009. "Lee Khoon Choy." *National Library Board Singapore.* http://eresources.nlb.gov.sg/infopedia/articles/SIP_1373_2009-01-05.html (accessed July 31, 2016).

Chính phủ Việt Nam. 2012. "Quy định về biểu diễn nghệ thuật, trình diễn thời trang; thi người đẹp và người mẫu; lưu hành, kinh doanh bản ghi âm, ghi hình ca múa nhạc, sân khẩu" ["Government Decision: Rule on Artistic Performance, Fashion Shows; Beauty Contests and Modeling; the Circulation and Business of Recording and Videotaping Singing, Music, Dance and Theater"]. Số 79/2012/NĐ-CP. *Cổng thông tin Điện tử Chính phủ nước Cộng hoà Xã hội chủ nghĩa Việt Nam.* http://www.chinhphu.vn/portal/page/portal/chinhphu/hethongvanban?class_id=1&mode=detail&document_id=163961 (accessed March 6, 2016).

Chumley, Lily. 2016. *Creativity Class: Art School and Culture Work in Post-Socialist China.* Princeton: Princeton University Press.

Clarke, Eric F. 2012. "Creativity in Performance." In *Musical Imaginations: Multidisciplinary Perspectives on Creativity, Performance and Perception,* edited by David J. Hargreaves, Dorothy E. Miell, and Raymond A.R. MacDonald, 17–30. Oxford: Oxford University Press.

Clarke, Eric F., and Mark Doffman, 2017. "Introduction and Overview." In *Distributed Creativity: Collaboration and Improvisation in Contemporary Music,* edited by Eric F. Clarke and Mark Doffman, 1–18. New York: Oxford University Press.

Clarke, Eric F., Mark Doffman, and Liza Lim. 2013. "Distributed Creativity and Ecological Dynamics: A Case Study of Liza Lim's 'Tongue of the Invisible.'" *Music & Letters* 94(4): 628–63.

Cô Kim. 2016. "Chẳng cần hoa lá cành, David Beckham vẫn khiến khối cô chết mê tại show Louis Vuitton" ["One Does Not Need to Be Hoa lá cành, David Beckham Still Is a Lady-Killer in the Louis Vuitton Show"]. *Kenh14.com,* June 23, 2016. http://kenh14.vn/chang-can-hoa-la-canh-david-beckham-van-khien-khoi-co-chet-me-tai-show-louis-vuitton-20160623233814349.chn (accessed August 25, 2018).

Cook, Nicholas. 2006. "Playing God: Creativity, Analysis, and Aesthetic Inclusion." In *Musical Creativity: Multidisciplinary Research in Theory and Practice,* edited by Irène Deliège and Geraint A. Wiggins, 9–24. New York: Psychology Press.

———. 2013. *Beyond the Score: Music as Performance.* Oxford and New York: Oxford University Press.

———. 2018. *Music as Creative Practice.* New York: Oxford University Press.

Conquergood, Dwight. 1989. "Poetics, Play, Process and Power: The Performance Turn in Anthropology." *Text and Performance Quarterly* 9(1): 82–95.

————. 2002. "Performance Studies: Interventions and Radical Research." *The Drama Review* 46(2): 145–56.

Cropley, David H., et al., eds. 2010. *The Dark Side of Creativity*. Cambridge: Cambridge University Press.

Csikszentmihalyi, Mihaly. 1990. *Flow: The Psychology of Optimal Experience*. New York: HarperCollins Publishers.

————. 1996. *Creativity: Flow and the Psychology of Discovery and Invention*. New York: HarperCollins Publishers.

Csordas, Thomas. 1997. *Language, Charisma, and Creativity: The Ritual Life of a Religious Movement*. Berkeley and Los Angeles: University of California Press.

Cù Huy Cận. [1974] 1976. "Về tính dân tộc trong âm nhạc" ["About the National Character in Music"]. In *Về tính dân tộc trong âm nhạc Việt Nam* ["Regarding the National Character in Vietnamese Music"], edited by Tôn Gia Ngân, 122–33. Hà Nội: NXB Văn hóa, 1976.

cuoimim. n.d. "Đơn giản – Hoàng Rapper." *NhacCuaTui.com*. https://www.nhaccuatui .com/bai-hat/don-gian-hoang-rapper.mDQa2mgwsRSK.html (accessed August 19, 2018).

Dương Bích Hà. 1997. *Lý Huế* [*The Lý Songs of Huế*]. Hà Nội: NXB Âm nhạc.

Dương Văn Minh. 1963. "Quyết-Nghị của Hội-Đồng Quân-Nhân Cách Mạng về việc truất-phế Tổng-Thống Ngô-Đình-Diệm và Giải-tán Chánh-Phủ" ["Decision of the Military Revolutionary Council Concerning the Destitution of Former President Ngô Đình Diệm and the Dissolution of His Government"]. *Văn hóa nguyệt san* 12(11): n.p.

Duy Việt. 2013. "Hội nghị tổng kết 15 năm thực hiện Nghị quyết Trung ương 5 (khóa VIII)" ["Conference Summarizing 15 Years Realizing the Fifth Central Resolution of the Eighth Party Congress"]. *Daklak.gov.vn*, January 25, 2013. http://krongnang.daklak .gov.vn/bai-viet/hội-nghị-tổng-kết-15-năm-thực-hiện-nghị-quyết-trung-ương-5 -khóa-vii--195 (accessed August 27, 2018).

Đắc Nhẫn and Ngọc Thới. 1974. *Bài bản cải lương* [*Works of Cải lương*]. Hà Nội: NXB Văn hóa.

Danielson, Virginia. 1997. *The Voice of Egypt: Umm Kulthūm, Arabic Song, and Egyptian Society in the Twentieth Century*. Chicago: University of Chicago Press.

Đảng công sảng đông dương. [1943] 1985. "Đề cương văn hóa Việt Nam" ["Draft of the Fundamentals of Vietnamese Culture"]. In *Một chặng đường văn hóa: Hồi ức và tư liệu về việc tiếp nhận Đề cương văn hóa (1943) của Đảng* [*One Stage in the Direction of Culture: Recollections and Documents of the Work of Implementing the Party's Draft of the Fundamentals of Vietnamese Culture*], edited by Nguyễn Phúc et al., 15–20. Hà Nội: NXB Tác phẩm mới.

Densmore, Frances. 1973. *Chippewa Music*. Minneapolis: Ross & Haines, Inc.

Derrida, Jacques. [1996] 2010. *Athens, Still Remains: The Photographs of Jean-François Bonhomme*. Translated from French by Pascale-Anne Brault and Michael Naas. New York: Fordham University Press.

Devriès, Anik. 1977. "Les musiques d'Extrême-Orient à l'Exposition Universelle de 1889" ["The Music of the Far East at the 1889 Universal Exposition"]. *Cahiers Debussy* (nouvelle serie) 1: 25–37.

Diamond, Catherine. 2003. "Emptying the Sea by the Bucketful: The Dilemma of Cambodian Theatre." *Asian Theatre Journal* 20(2): 147–78.

Do, Thien. 2003. *Vietnamese Supernaturalism: Views from the Southern Region*. London and New York: Routledge.

Đỗ Ngọc Quang. 2003. "Tiến sĩ Nguyễn Đình Thi – Người lữ hành vì hoà bình, huynh đệ . . ." ["Dr Nguyễn Đình Thi: A Traveller for Peace and Brotherhood"]. *VietNamNet*, July 17, 2003. http://vnn.vietnamnet.vn/psks/nhanvat/2003/7/14406/ (accessed July 12, 2020).

Dor, George. 2004. "Communal Creativity and Song Ownership in Anlo Ewe Musical Practice: The Case of Havolu." *Ethnomusicology* 48(1): 26–51.

Đức Huy. 2003. "Hội thảo 60 năm Đề cương văn hóa Việt Nam" ["Conference on Sixty Years of the *Draft of the Fundamentals of Vietnamese Culture*"]. *Hà Nội Mới Online*, June 25, 2003. http://www.hanoimoi.com.vn/forumdetail/Van_hoa/330/h7897i -th78430-60-n259m-2727873-c432417ng-v259n-hoa-vi7879t-nam.htm (accessed September 8, 2010).

Đức Triết. 2013. "Khách du lịch thích thú với đờn ca tài tử đất Bắc" ["Tourists Have an Interest in đờn ca tài tử of the North"]. *Tuổi Trẻ*, August 8, 2013. http://dulich.tuoitre .vn/PrintView.aspx?ArticleID=562631&ChannelID=100 (accessed October 17, 2013).

Dumoutier, Gustave. 1890. *Les chants et les traditions populaires des annamites* [*The Songs and Popular Traditions of the Vietnamese*]. Paris: Ernest Leroux.

Elliott, David W. P. 2012. *Changing Worlds: Vietnam's Transition from Cold War to Globalization*. New York: Oxford University Press.

Felch, Susan M. 2005. "'In the Chorus of Others': M.M. Bakhtin's Sense of Tradition." In *The Force of Tradition: Response and Resistance in Literature, Religion, and Cultural Studies*, edited by Donald G. Marshall, 55–77. Lanham: Rowman & Littlefield Publishers, Inc.

Feld, Steven. 1984. "Communication, Music, and Speech about Music." *Yearbook for Traditional Music* 16: 1–18.

———. 1988. "Aesthetics as Iconicity of Style, or 'Lift-up-over Sounding': Getting into the Kaluli Groove." *Yearbook for Traditional Music* 20: 74–113.

Ferrière, Joseph, et al. 1906. *L'Indo-Chine 1906: Cochinchine, Cambodge, Annam, Tonkin, Laos, Quang-Tchéou-Ouan*. Gouvernement Général de l'Indo-Chine.

Firpo, Christina. 2016. "Sex and Song: Clandestine Prostitution in Tonkin's Ả Đào Music Houses, 1920s–1940s." *Journal of Vietnamese Studies* 11(2): 1–36.

Floyd, Jr., Samuel A. 1980. "Black American Music and Aesthetic Communication." *Black Music Research Journal* 1: 1–17.

———. 1981/1982. "Toward a Philosophy of Black Music Scholarship." *Black Music Research Journal* 2: 72–93.

———. 1983. "On Black Music Research." *Black Music Research Journal* 3: 46–57.

———. 1995. *The Power of Black Music: Interpreting Its History from Africa to the United States*. Oxford and New York: Oxford University Press.

Frith, Simon. 2011. "Creativity as Social Fact." In *Musical Imaginations: Multidisciplinary Perspectives on Creativity, Performance, and Perception*, edited by David J. Hargreaves, Dorothy E. Miell, and Raymond A.R. MacDonald, 62–72. Oxford: Oxford University Press.

Gates, Jr., Henry Louis. 1988. *The Signifying Monkey: A Theory of African-American Literary Criticism*. New York: Oxford University Press.

Gaunt, Kyra D. 2006. *The Games Black Girls Play: Learning the Ropes from Double-Dutch to Hip-Hop*. New York and London: New York University Press.

Gautier, Judith. 1900. *Les musiques bizarres à l'Exposition de 1900* [*The Exotic Music at the 1900 Exposition*]. Paris: Librairie Ollendorff.

Gibbs, Jason. 2003/2004. "The West's Songs, Our Songs: The Introduction and Adaptation of Western Popular Song in Vietnam before 1940." *Asian Music* 35(1): 57–83.

Gilroy, Paul. 1993. *The Black Atlantic: Modernity and Double Consciousness*. Cambridge, MA: Harvard University Press.

Ginsberg, Robert. 2004. *The Aesthetics of Ruins*. Amsterdam and New York: Rodopi.

de Gironcourt, Georges. 1943. "Rescherces de Géographie musical en Indochine" ["Studies of the Indochinese Musical Geography"]. *Bulletin de la Société des Études Indochinoises* XVII No. 4: 7–174.

Goehr, Lydia. 1992. *The Imaginary Museum of Musical Works: An Essay in the Philosophy of Music*. Oxford and New York: Oxford University Press.

Grant, Catherine. 2012. "Rethinking Safeguarding: Objections and Responses to Protecting and Promoting Endangered Musical Heritage." *Ethnomusicology Forum* 21(1): 31–51.

———. 2014. *Music Endangerment: How Language Maintenance Can Help*. New York: Oxford University Press.

Grauer, Victor. 2005. "Cantometrics: Song and Social Culture: A Response." *The Magazine for Traditional Music throughout the World*, http://www.mustrad.org.uk/articles /cantome2.htm (accessed June 23, 2017).

Goffman, Erving. 1981. *Forms of Talk*. Philadelphia: University of Pennsylvania Press, 1981.

H.T. Dũng and C. Quốc. 2014. "Bao nhiêu tỉ đồng phục vụ Festival đờn ca tài tử?" ["How Many Billions of Đồng Were Spent on the Đờn ca tài tử Festival?"]. *Tuổi trẻ*, May 8,

2014. http://tuoitre.vn/tin/chinh-tri-xa-hoi/20140508/bao-nhieu-ti-dong-phuc-vu
-festival-don-ca-tai-tu/606224.html (accessed June 28, 2015).

Hà Đình Nguyên. 2011. "Đờn ca tài tử phô diễn lực lượng" ["Đờn ca tài tử Is Gaining
Strength"]. *Thanh Niên*, September 20, 2011. https://thanhnien.vn/van-hoa/don-ca
-tai-tu-pho-dien-luc-luong-178489.html (accessed August 27, 2018).

———. 2014. "Báu vật đờn ca tài tử - Kỳ 3: Nguyễn Vĩnh Bảo – đệ nhất danh cầm"
["The Treasure of Đờn ca tài tử - No. 3: Nguyễn Vĩnh Bảo – First-order Musician"].
Thanh niên, February 19, 2014. http://www.thanhnien.com.vn/van-hoa-nghe-thuat
/bau-vat-don-ca-tai-tu-ky-3-nguyen-vinh-bao-de-nhat-danh-cam-2927.html (accessed June 12, 2015).

Hà Huy Giáp. [1974] 1976. "Nắm vững vốn dân tộc, học tập tinh hoa thế giới, để xây dựng
một nền âm nhạc hiện thực xã hội chủ nghĩa Việt Nam" ["Thoroughly Grasping the
Nation, to Learn the Quintessence of the World, in order to Build a Vietnamese Musical
Socialist Realism"]. In *Về tính dân tộc trong âm nhạc Việt Nam* [*Regarding the National
Character in Vietnamese Music*], edited by Tôn Gia Ngân, 4–22. Hà Nội: NXB Văn hóa.

Hall, Stuart. [1991] 2019. "Old and New Identities, Old and New Ethnicities." In *Essential
Essays / Stuart Hall: Identity and Diaspora*, edited by David Morley, 63–82. Durham
and London: Duke University Press.

Harms, Erik. 2011. *Saigon's Edge: On the Margins of Ho Chi Minh City*. Minneapolis:
University of Minnesota Press.

———. 2016. *Luxury and Rubble: Civility and Dispossession in the New Saigon*. Oakland:
University of California Press.

Harnish, David. 2007. "'Digging' and 'Upgrading': Government Efforts to 'Develop' Music
and Dance in Lombok, Indonesia." *Asian Music* 38(1): 61–87.

Harris, Rachel. 2012. "Tracks: Temporal Shifts and Transnational Networks of Sentiment
in Uyghur Song." *Ethnomusicology* 56(3): 450–75.

Hesmondhalgh, David. 2013. *The Cultural Industries*. London: SAGE.

Hewison, Robert. 2014. *Cultural Capital: The Rise and Fall of Creative Britain*. London:
Verso.

Hill, Juniper. 2009. "Rebellious Pedagogy, Ideological Transformation, and Creative
Freedom in Finnish Contemporary Folk Music." *Ethnomusicology* 53(1): 86–114.

———. 2012. "Imagining Creativity: An Ethnomusicological Perspective on How Belief
Systems Encourage or Inhibit Creative Activities in Music." In *Musical Imaginations:
Multidisciplinary Perspectives on Creativity, Performance, and Perception*, edited by
David J. Hargreaves, Dorothy E. Miell, and Raymond A.R. MacDonald, 87–104. Ox-
ford: Oxford University Press.

———. 2018. *Becoming Creative: Insights from Musicians in a Diverse World*. New York:
Oxford University Press.

Hoàng Chương et al. 2011. *Qúa trình hình thành phát triển nghệ thuật cải lương* [*The

Processing of Forming and Developing Cải lương]. Hà Nội: Trung tâm nghiên cứu bảo tồn và phát huy văn hóa dân tộc.

Hoàng Đạm. 2003. *Hòa tấu biến hóa lòng bản: Âm nhạc cổ truyền người Việt* [*Ensemble Heterophony in Vietnamese Traditional Music*]. Hà Nội: Viện âm nhạc.

Hoàng Yến. 1919. "La musique a Huế: Đờn Nguyệt et đờn tranh" ["Music in Huế: The Zither and Moon-shaped Lute"]. *Bulletin des amis du vieux Huế* 6(3): 233–387.

Hồng Nhung. 2018. "Tài tử miệt vườn vào top Trending Youtube" ["The Show *Tài tử miệt vườn* is a Top Trend on YouTube"]. *Đài Phát thanh – Truyền hình Đồng Tháp*, July 29, 2018. http://www.thdt.vn/35918/tai-tu-miet-vuon-vao-top-trending-youtube .html (accessed August 25, 2018).

Huỳnh Khải. 2011. "Nhạc sĩ Huỳnh Khải: Âm nhạc dân tộc có sức sống mãnh liệt" ["According to Artist Huỳnh Khải, National Music Has Vitality"]. *Sài Gòn Giải Phóng*, March 19, 2011.

Igwebuike, Ebuka Elias. 2017. "Metaphor, Identity and Ideologies in Igbo Folk Music." *Muziki* 14(1): 62–77.

Jähnichen, Gisa. 2011. "Uniqueness Re-examined: The Vietnamese Lute Đàn Đáy." *Yearbook for Traditional Music* 43: 147–79.

James, C.L.R., with Raya Dunayevskaya and Grace Lee. [1950] 1986. *State Capitalism and World Revolution*. Chicago: Charles H. Kerr Publishing Company.

Jamieson, Neil L. 1993. *Understanding Vietnam*. Berkeley and Los Angeles: University of California Press.

Jandl, Thomas. 2013. *Vietnam in the Global Economy: The Dynamics of Integration, Decentralization, and Contested Politics*. Lanham, MD: Lexington Books.

Kartomi, Margaret. 1981. "The Processes and Results of Musical Culture Contact: A Discussion of Terminology and Concepts." *Ethnomusicology* 25(2): 227–49.

Keyes, Cheryl L. 2004. *Rap Music and Street Consciousness*. Urbana: University of Illinois Press.

Kiều Phong and Đường Loan. 2018. "Bí thư Thành uỷ TPHCM Nguyễn Thiện Nhân: 'Muốn chống bạo loạn, cái gốc là an dân'" ["Municipal Party Secretary for Ho Chi Minh City Nguyễn Thiện Nhân: 'To Repel Violence, the Source is the People'"]. *Sài Gòn Giải Phóng*, July 4, 2018. http://www.sggp.org.vn/bi-thu-thanh-uy-tphcm-nguyen-thien -nhan-muon-chong-bao-loan-cai-goc-la-an-dan-530543.html (accessed July 5, 2018).

Kieu Phong and Duong Loan. 2018. "City Party Chief Urges Residents and Officials to be More Creative." *SGGP English Edition*, July 5, 2018. http://sggpnews.org.vn/hochiminh city/city-party-chief-urges-residents-and-officials-to-be-more-creative-75718.html (accessed July 5, 2018).

Kiều Tấn. 1993. "Tìm hiểu điệu thức trong âm nhạc tài tử Nam Bộ" ["Understanding Modality in *Nhạc tài tử* in the South"]. In *Thang âm điệu thức trong âm nhạc truyền thống một số dân tộc miền Nam Việt Nam* [*Modality in Traditional Music: A Number of Southern Vietnamese Ethnic Groups*], edited by Lư Nhất Vũ, 303–400. Tp. Hồ Chí Minh: Viện văn hóa nghệ thuật.

———. 2002. "Hệ thống bài bản nhạc tài tử" ["The Repertoire of Tài Tử Music"]. In *Bảo tồn và phát huy di sản văn hóa phi vật thể trên địa bàn TP. Hồ Chí Minh* [*The Preservation and Conservation of Intangible Cultural Heritage in the Ho Chi Minh City Area*], edited by Lê Hoàng, 276–86. Tp. Hồ Chí Minh: NXB Trẻ.

Knosp, Gaston. [1907] 1922. "Histoire de la musique dans l'Indochine" ["History of the Music in Indochina"]. In *Encyclopédia de la musique et dictionnaire du conservatoire* [*Encyclopedia of Music and the Dictionary of the Conservatory*], edited by Lionel de la Laurencie, 3100–46. Paris: Librairie Delgrave.

Kondo, Dorinne. 2018. *Worldmaking: Race, Performance, and the Work of Creativity.* Durham and London: Duke University Press.

Kramer, Lawrence. 2011. *Interpreting Music.* Berkeley: University of California Press.

L.T. Ngã. 2013. "Cần sớm có chính sách đào tạo, đầu tư cho Đờn ca tài tử" ["We Quickly Need Training and Investments Policy for Đờn ca tài tử"]. *Tuổi Trẻ*, October 12, 2013. tuoitre.vn/Van-hoa-Giai-tri/574106/can-som-co-chinh-sach-dao-tao-dau-tu-cho-don-ca-tai-tu.html (accessed October 17, 2013).

Lam, Joseph S. C. 1998. *State Sacrifices and Music in Ming China: Orthodoxy, Creativity, and Expressiveness.* Albany: State University of New York Press.

Landry, Charles. 1994. *The Creative City: A Toolkit for Urban Innovators.* London: Comedia.

Lanzara, Giovan Francesco. 2016. *Shifting Practices: Reflections on Technology, Practice, and Innovation.* Cambridge, MA: The MIT Press.

Lão Tử. 2018. *Đạo Đức Kinh* [*Book of Tao*]. Translated from Chinese by Vũ Thế Ngọc. Tp. Hồ Chí Minh: NXB Thế giới.

Laozi. 2005. *Tao Te Ching.* Translated from Chinese by Sam Hamill. Boston: Shambhala.

Le Bris, E. 1922. "Musique Annamite; Airs traditionnels" ["Vietnamese Music, Traditional Songs"]. *Bulletin des amis du vieux Huế* 9(4): 255–309.

Lê Như Giang. 2008. "Đờn ca tài tử nên . . . tài tử?" ["The Music of Talented Amateurs, Therefore . . . Amateurish?"]. *Lao động*, November 21, 2008. http://www.laodong.com.vn/Utilities/PrintView.aspx?ID=115521 (accessed November 23, 2008.)

Lê Tuấn Hùng. 1991. "The Dynamics of Change in Hue and Tai Tu Music of Vietnam between c.1890 and c.1920." *Monash University Center of Southeast Asian Studies Working Paper* 67. Clayton, Victoria: Centre of Southeast Asian Studies, Monash University.

———. 1998. *Đàn Tranh Music of Vietnam: Traditions and Innovations.* Melbourne: Australia Asia Foundation.

Leach, James. 2003. "Owning Creativity: Cultural Property and the Efficacy of Custom on the Rai Coast of Papua New Guinea." *Journal of Material Culture* 8(2): 123–43.

Lee, Yuan-Yuan, and Sin-yan Shen. 1999. *Chinese Musical Instruments.* Chicago: Chinese Music Society of North America.

Li Tana. 1998. *Nguyễn Cochinchina: Southern Vietnam in the Seventeenth and Eighteenth Centuries*. Ithaca: Southeast Asia Program Publications.

Limón, José E. 1992. *Mexican Ballads, Chicano Poems: History and Influence in Mexican-American Social Poetry*. Berkeley and Los Angeles: University of California Press.

Linson, Adam, and Eric F. Clarke. 2017. "Distributed Cognition, Ecological Theory and Group Improvisation." In *Distributed Creativity: Collaboration and Improvisation in Contemporary Music*, edited by Eric F. Clarke and Mark Doffman, 52–69. New York: Oxford University Press.

Liu Jianmei. 2016. *Zhuangzi and Modern Chinese Literature*. New York: Oxford University Press.

Lomax, Alan. 1959. "Folk Song Style." *American Anthropologist* 61: 927–54.

———. [1962] 1971. "Song Structure and Social Structure." In *Readings in Ethnomusicology*, edited by David P. McAllester, 227–52. New York: Johnson Reprint Corp.

Lư Nhất Vũ and Lê Giang. 1981. *Dân ca Bến Tre [Bến Tre Folksongs]*. Tp. Hồ Chí Minh: Ty văn hóa và thông tin Bến Tre xuất bản.

———. 1983. *Tìm hiểu dân ca Nam bộ [Understanding Southern Folksongs]*. Tp. Hồ Chí Minh: NXB Tp. Hồ Chí Minh.

Mahon, Maureen. 2014. "Music, Power, and Practice." *Ethnomusicology* 58(2): 327–33.

Manabe, Noriko. 2006. "Globalization and Japanese Creativity: Adaptations of Japanese Language to Rap." *Ethnomusicology* 50(1): 1–36.

Marr, David G. 1981. *Vietnamese Tradition on Trial, 1920–1945*. Berkeley and Los Angeles: University of California Press.

———. 1995. *Vietnam 1945: The Quest for Power*. Berkeley and Los Angeles: University of California Press.

Masina, Pietro P. 2006. *Vietnam's Development Strategies*. London and New York: Routledge.

McHale, Shawn Frederick. 2004. *Print and Power: Confucianism, Communism, and Buddhism in the Making of Modern Vietnam*. Honolulu: University of Hawai'i Press.

McLeod, Mark W. 1991. *The Vietnamese Response to French Intervention, 1862–1974*. New York: Praeger.

McLeod, Norma. 1974. "Ethnomusicological Research and Anthropology." *Annual Review of Anthropology* 3: 99–115.

McLeod, Kembrew, and Peter DiCola. 2011. *Creative License: The Law and Culture of Digital Sampling*. Durham: Duke University Press.

McPhee, Colin. 1944. *A House in Bali*. New York: The John Day Company.

Meeker, Lauren. 2013. *Sounding Out Heritage: Cultural Politics and the Social Practice of Quan Họ Folk Song in Northern Vietnam*. Honolulu: University of Hawai'i Press.

Merriam, Alan P. 1960. "Ethnomusiscology Discussion and Definition of the Field." *Ethnomusicology* 4(3): 107–14.

———. 1964. *The Anthropology of Music*. Evanston, IL: Northwestern University Press.

Meyer, Leonard B. [1960] 1971. "Universalism and Relativism in the Study of Ethnic Music." In *Readings in Ethnomusicology*, edited by David P. McAllester, 269–76. New York: Johnson Reprint Corp.

Minh Nga. 2014. "Trả lại không gian cho đờn ca tài tử: Còn đâu chất tài tử?" ["Returning to the Space for Đờn ca tài tử: And where is the Tài tử character?"]. *Người lao động*, March 24, 2014. https://nld.com.vn/van-hoa-van-nghe/tra-lai-khong-gian-cho-don -ca-tai-tu-con-dau-chat-tai-tu-20140324224245151.htm (accessed August 28, 2018).

Minh Tân. 2002. "Câu lạc bộ Tiếng Hát Quê Hương" ["Tiếng Hát Quê Hương Ensemble"]. *Người lao động*, August 2: 6.

Mitani, Yoko. 1981. "Some Melodic Features of Chinese Qin Music." In *Music and Tradition: Essays on Asian and Others Musics Presented to Laurence Picken*, edited by D. R. Widdess, 123–42. Cambridge: Cambridge University Press.

Mitchell, II, Ernest Julius, 2010. "'Black Renaissance': A Brief History of the Concept." *Amerikastudien / American Studies* 55(4): 641–65.

Monson, Ingrid. 1996. *Saying Something: Jazz Improvisation and Interaction*. Chicago and London: University of Chicago Press.

Mould, Oliver. 2018. *Against Creativity*. London and New York: Verso.

Narayan, Kirin. 2016. *Everyday Creativity: Singing Goddesses in the Himalayan Foothills*. Chicago: University of Chicago Press.

Naroditskaya, Inna. 2005. "Azerbaijani Mugham and Carpet: Cross-Domain Mapping." *Ethnomusicology Forum* 14(1): 25–55.

Nettl, Bruno. 1954. "Notes on Musical Composition in Primitive Cultures." *Anthropological Quarterly* 27(3): 81–90.

Nguyễn Du. 1983. *Truyện Kiều* [*Tale of Kiều*]. Translated from Vietnamese by Huỳnh Sanh Thông. New Haven, CT: Yale University Press.

Nguyễn Đăng Thục. 1955. "Sứ-Mạng Văn-Hóa phương Nam" ["The Cultural Mission of the South"]. *Văn hóa nguyệt san* 1: 1–15.

Nguyễn Đình Hòa. 1964. "Activities of the Vietnam National Commission for UNESCO." *Văn hóa nguyệt san* 13(2&3): 351–56.

———. 1999. *From the City Inside the Red River: A Cultural Memoir of Mid-Century Vietnam*. Jefferson, NC: McFarland & Company.

Nguyễn Đình Lai. 1956. "Étude sur la musique sino-viêtnamienne et les chants populaires du Việt-Nam" ["Study on Sino-Vietnamese music and the popular songs of Vietnam"]. *Bulletin de la Société des Études Indochinoises* XXXI No. 1: 1–76.

Nguyễn Đình Thi. 1963. "Phát-triển văn-hóa" ["Developing Culture"]. *Văn hóa nguyệt san* 12(11): 1679–89.

———. 1963. "Phát-triển văn-hóa" ["Developing Culture"]. *Văn hóa nguyệt san* 12(12): 1869–83.

———. 1964. "Phát-triển văn-hóa" ["Developing Culture"]. *Văn hóa nguyệt san* 13(1): 7–25.

Nguyen, Khai Thu. 2012. "A Personal Sorrow: 'Cải Lương' and the Politics of North and South Vietnam." *Asian Theatre Journal* 29(1): 255–75.

Nguyễn Lê Tuyên and Nguyễn Đức Hiệp. 2013. *Hát bội, đờn ca tài tử và cải lương: Cuối TK 19 đầu TK 20* [*Hát bội, Đờn ca tài tử and Cải lương at the End of the 19th and the Beginning of the 20th Centuries*]. Tp. Hồ Chí Minh: NXB Văn hóa.

Nguyen Nang Dac and Nguyen Phung. n.d. *La musique Viêt traditionnelle* [*Vietnamese Traditional Music*]. Saigon: Association Vietnamienne pour le développement des relations internationales.

Nguyễn Ngọc Bạch. 2004. *Một đời sân khấu* [*A Performing Life*]. Tp. Hồ Chí Minh: NXB Trẻ.

Nguyễn Phúc An. 2019a. *Cụ phó bảng minh xuyên Hoàng Yến & Tác phẩm Cầm học tầm nguyên* [*Hoàng Yến and His Book Studying Instruments from Their Origins*]. Tp. Hồ Chí Minh: NXB Văn hoá – Văn nghệ.

———. 2019b. *Đờn ca tài tử Nam bộ: Khảo & Luận* [*Southern Vietnam's Đờn Ca Tài Tử: Reference and Commentary*]. Tp. Hồ Chí Minh: NXB Tổng hợp Thành phố Hồ Chí Minh.

Nguyễn Phụng Michel. 1997. *Viện Quốc gia Âm nhạc & Kịch nghệ Saïgon & Trường Quốc gia Âm nhạc địa-phương Huế: Hồi ký của G.S. Nguyễn-Phung Michel, Sáng lập viên nguyên giám đốc Viện Q.G.Â.N.K.N Saïgon & Sáng lập viên trường Q.G.Â.N.Đ.P. Huế* [*National Institute of Music and Drama Sài Gòn and the National School of Music in Huế: Memoir of Professor Nguyễn Phụng Michel, First Director of the National Institute of Music and Drama Sài Gòn and First Principal of the National School of Music in Huế*]. Unpublished manuscript.

Nguyễn Phương. 2011. "Tìm lại dấu xưa (2): Rạp hát Aristo, trước và sau năm 1954" ["Finding the Signs of the Past (2): Aristo Theatre Before and After 1954"]. *Cải Lương Việt Nam.* http://cailuongvietnam.vn/news/Nghe-thuat-cai-luong/Tim-lai-dau-xua -2-Rap-hat-Aristo-truoc-va-sau-nam-1954-6725/ (accessed March 2, 2014).

Nguyễn Phương Thảo. 1994. *Văn hóa dân gian Nam bộ* (*Southern Vietnamese Folk Culture*). Hà Nội: NXB Giáo dục.

Nguyên Thê Anh. 1985. "The Vietnamese Monarchy under French Colonial Rule 1884–1945." *Modern Asian Studies* 19(1): 147–62.

Nguyễn Thị Minh Ngọc and Đỗ Hương. 2007. *Sân khấu cải lương ở Thành phố Hồ Chí Minh* [*Cải lương in Ho Chi Minh City*]. Tp. Hồ Chí Minh: NXB Văn hóa Sài Gòn.

Nguyen T. Phong. 2002. "Music and Movement in Vietnamese Buddhism." *the world of music* 44(2): 57–71.

Nguyễn T. Phong. 1998. "Vietnam." In *The Garland Encyclopedia of World Music*, Vol. 4: Southeast Asia, edited by Terry E. Miller and Sean Williams, 444–517. New York: Garland Publishing.

———. 2003. "Vietnamese Music After the Revolution: Reevaluation and Moderniza-tion." *Journal of Chinese Ritual, Theatre and Folklore* 141: 169–84.

———. 2006. "Considering the Fate of Tài Tử Music: The Last Guardian of Tradition." Paper presented at the annual conference of the Society for Ethnomusicology, Hono-lulu, Hawai'i, United States. November 16–19, 2006.

———. 2018. "The Vietnamese Scholarship at the Turn of the Millennium: A Study of the Pioneering Works of Gustave Emile Dumoutier (1850–1904)." *ASIANetwork Exchange* 25(1): 96–114.

Nguyen Th. Phong. 1986. "Restructuring the Fixed Pitches of the Vietnamese Dan Nguyet Lute: A Modification Necessitated by the Modal System." *Asian Music* 18(1): 56–70.

Nguyen Thuyet Phong. 1982. "La musique bouddhique du Vietnam" ["The Buddhist Music of Vietnam"]. PhD diss., Université de Paris Sorbonne.

———. [1986] 1990. *Textes et chants liturgiques et bouddhiques vietnamiens en France & La rétrospective: Etude sur la tradition musicale bouddhique du Vietnam* [*Texts and Vietnamese Buddhist Liturgical Chants in France & Retrospective: Studies on Buddhist Ritual Music of Vietnam*]. Kent, OH: Association for Research in Vietnamese Music.

Nguyễn Tuấn Khanh. 2014. *Bước đường của cải lương* [*On the Road to Cải Lương*]. West-minster, CA: Viện Việt-Học.

Nguyen Van Huyen. 1934. *Les chants alternés des garçons et des filles en Annam* [*Alternat-ing Singing of Boys and Girls in Vietnam*]. Paris: Librairie Orientaliste Paul Geuthner.

Nguyễn Văn Ngưu. 1995. *Cổ nhạc tổ truyền nguyên lý* [*Principal Traditional Works*]. Tp. Hồ Chí Minh: NXB Văn Nghệ.

Nguyen, Viet Thanh. 1997. "Representing Reconciliation: Le Ly Hayslip and the Victim-ized Body." *positions* 5(2): 605–42.

Nguyễn Vĩnh Bảo. n.d.(a). "Cây đàn ghi-ta lõm phím" ["Vietnamese Guitar with the Scooped Fingerboard"]. Unpublished manuscript.

———. n.d.(b). "Chương trình học nhạc tài tử" ["Program of Studying Đờn ca tài tử"]: A Response to Nguyễn Phụng Michel's History of the Saigon Conservatory. Unpub-lished manuscript.

———. n.d.(c). "Danh sách những nhạc sư, nhạc sĩ mà tôi được dịp tiếp xúc từ năm 1925" ["A List of the Masters and Musicians That I Had the Opportunity to Know from 1925"]. Unpublished manuscript.

———. 2008. "Mes hivers, mon vrai trésor . . ." ["My Winters, My Real Treasure"]. *Vinh Bao, The Only One Forum*. http://vinhbao.theonly1.net/forum/viewtopic.php?t=313 (accessed June 30, 2014).

———. 2010. "Le déserteur" ["The Dissenter"]. Poem received via email, December 28, 2010.

Nguyễn-võ Thu-hương. 2008. *The Ironies of Freedom: Sex, Culture, and Neoliberal Gov-ernance in Vietnam*. Seattle: University of Washington Press.

Ninh, Kim N. B. 2002. *A World Transformed: The Politics of Culture in Revolutionary Vietnam 1945–1965*. Ann Arbor: University of Michigan Press.

Njoku, Raphael Chijioke. 2020. *West African Masking Traditions and Diaspora Masquerade Carnivals: History, Memory, and Transnationalism*. Rochester: University of Rochester Press.

Nooshin, Laudan. 2015. *Iranian Classical Music: The Discourses and Practice of Creativity*. Farnham, Surrey: Ashgate.

Norton, Barley. 2009. *Songs for the Spirits: Music and Mediums in Modern Vietnam*. Urbana: University of Illinois Press.

———. 2014. "Musical Revival, *Ca Trù* Ontologies, and Intangible Cultural Heritage in Vietnam." In *The Oxford Handbook of Music Revival*, edited by Caroline Bithell and Juniper Hill, 160–81. New York: Oxford University Press.

———. 2018. "Orchestrating the Nation: Court Orchestras, Nationalism and Agency in Vietnam." In *Global Perspectives on Orchestras*, edited by Tina K. Ramnarine, 301–23. New York: Oxford University Press.

Nzewi, Meki. 1974. "Melo-Rhythmic Essence and Hot Rhythm in Nigerian Folk Music." *The Black Perspective in Music* 2(1): 23–28.

Ó Briain, Lonán. 2014. "Minorities Onstage: Cultural Tourism, Cosmopolitanism, and Social Harmony in Northwestern Vietnam." *Asian Music* 45(2): 32–57.

———. 2018. *Musical Minorities: The Sounds of Hmong Ethnicity in Northern Vietnam*. New York: Oxford University Press.

Ó Murchadha, Felix. 2002. "Being as Ruination: Heidegger, Simmel, and the Phenomenology of Ruins." *Philosophy Today* 46: 10–18.

Olsen, Dale A. 2008. *Popular Music of Vietnam: The Politics of Remembering, the Economics of Forgetting*. New York: Routledge.

Pang, Laikwan. 2012. *Creativity and Its Discontents: China's Creative Industries and Intellectual Property Rights Offenses*. Durham: Duke University Press.

Park, Gil-Sung. 2013. "Manufacturing Creativity: Production, Performance, and Dissemination of K-pop." *Korea Journal* 53(4): 14–33.

Pasler, Jann. 2004. "The Utility of Musical Instruments in the Racial and Colonial Agendas of Late Nineteenth-Century France." *Journal of the Royal Musical Association* 129(1): 24–76.

———. 2012. "The Music Criticism of Gaston Knosp: From Newspaper Journalism in Tonkin to Comparative Musicology (1898–1912)." *Revue belge de musicologie* 66: 203–22.

Perlman, Marc. 2004. *Unplayed Melodies: Javanese Gamelan and the Genesis of Music Theory*. Berkeley: University of California Press.

Phạm Cao Phong. 2017. "'Đêm vô thức bản địa' và tiếng vọng Trống Đồng" ['Night of the Indigenous Unconscious' and the Hopeful Sound of the Bronze Drum"]. *BBC Tiếng*

Việt, December 7, 2017. https://www.bbc.com/vietnamese/culture-social-42265188 (accessed August 28, 2018).

Phạm Duy. 1972. *Đặc khảo về dân nhạc ở Việt Nam* [*A Condensed Study of People's Music in Vietnam*]. Saigon: Hiện đại.

Phạm Duy and Dale R. Whiteside, ed. 1975. *Musics of Vietnam*. Carbondale and Edwardsville: Southern Illinois University Press.

Phạm Thúy Hoan. 1999. *Phương pháp đàn tranh cuốn 3* [*Đàn tranh Method: Book 3*]. Tp. Hồ Chí Minh: Tiếng Hát Quê Hương.

Phan Kế Bính. [1915] 1973. *Việt Nam phong tục* [*Vietnamese Customs*]. Sài Gòn: Khai-Trí.

Phan Trung Nghĩa. 2007. "Người Hoa ở Bạc Liêu" ["Chinese People in Bạc Liêu"]. In *Nam bộ xưa và nay* [*Southern Vietnam Yesterday and Today*], edited by Trần Đình Việt, 163–67. Tp. Hồ Chí Minh: NXB Tp. Hồ Chí Minh.

Phụng Hoàng Sang. 1909. *Bản Đờn Tranh và Bài Ca* [*Works for the Đàn tranh and Songs*]. Saigon: Phát Toán Libraire-Imprimeur.

Picard, François. 1991. *La musique chinoise* [*Chinese Music*]. Paris: Minerve.

Pope, Rob. 2005. *Creativity: Theory, History, Practice*. London: Routledge.

Puar, Jasbir. 2007. *Terrorist Assemblages: Homonationalism in Queer Times*. Durham: Duke Unversity Press.

Quý Lâm. 2014. "Thủ tướng: Cải thiện đời sống dân nghèo quan trọng hơn xây nhà hát!" ["Prime Minister: Improving the Lives of the Poor is More Important than Building Theaters"]. *Người lao động*, April 26, 2014. https://nld.com.vn/thoi-su -trong-nuoc/thu-tuong-cai-thien-doi-song-dan-ngheo-quan-trong-hon-xay-nha-hat -20140426160515238.htm (accessed August 24, 2018).

Racy, Ali Jihad. 1998. "Improvisation, Ecstasy, and Performance Dynamics in Arabic Music." In *In the Course of Performance: Studies in the World of Musical Improvisation*, edited by Bruno Nettl and Melinda Russell, 95–112. Chicago: University of Chicago Press.

———. 2003. *Making Music in the Arab World: The Culture and Artistry of Ṭarab*. Cambridge: Cambridge University Press.

Ramnarine, Tina K. 2003. *Ilmatar's Inspirations: Nationalism, Globalization, and the Changing Soundscapes of Finnish Folk Music*. Chicago: University of Chicago Press.

———. 2011. "The Orchestration of Civil Society: Community and Conscience in Symphony Orchestras." *Ethnomusicology Forum* 20(3): 327–51.

———, ed. 2018. *Global Perspectives on Orchestras: Collective Creativity and Social Agency*. New York: Oxford University Press.

Rein, Shaun. 2014. *The End of Copycat China: The Rise of Creativity, Innovation, and Individualism in China*. Hoboken, NJ: John Wiley & Sons.

Reyes, Adelaida. 1999. *Songs of the Caged, Songs of the Free: Music of the Vietnamese Refugee Experience*. Philadelphia: Temple University Press.

Rice, Timothy. 1994. *May It Fill Your Soul: Experiencing Bulgarian Music.* Chicago: University of Chicago Press.

———. 2001. "Reflections on Music and Meaning: Metaphor, Signification and Control in the Bulgarian Case." *British Journal of Ethnomusicology* 10(1): 19–38.

———. 2003. "Time, Place, and Metaphor in Musical Experience and Ethnography." *Ethnomusicology* 47(2): 151–79.

———. 2017. *Modeling Ethnomusicology.* New York: Oxford University Press.

Rigg, Jonathan. 2003. "Exclusion and Embeddedness: The Chinese in Thailand and Vietnam." In *The Chinese Diaspora: Space, Place, Mobility, and Identity,* ed. Laurence J.C. Ma and Carolyn Cartier, 97–116. Lanham: Rowman & Littlefield Publishers, Inc.

Roach, Joseph. 1996. *Cities of the Dead: Circum-Atlantic Performance.* New York: Columbia University Press.

Robinson, Dylan. 2020. *Hungry Listening: Resonant Theory for Indigenous Sound Studies.* Minneapolis: University of Minnesota Press.

Roseman, Marina. 1991. *Healing Sounds from the Malaysian Rainforest: Temiar Music and Medicine.* Berkeley: University of California Press.

Rosen, Jody. 2019. "Does 'Creative' Work Free You From Drudgery, or Just Security?" *The New York Times Magazine,* January 31, 2019. https://www.nytimes.com/2019/01/31/magazine/creative-work-corporations.html (accessed December 3, 2020).

Rouget, Gilbert. 1985. *Music and Trance: A Theory of the Relations between Music and Possession.* Chicago and London: University of Chicago Press.

Sarath, Edward W. 2013. *Improvisation, Creativity, and Consciousness: Jazz as Integral Template for Music, Education, and Society.* Albany: State University of New York Press.

Sasagawa Hideo. 2005. "Post/colonial Discourses on the Cambodian Court Dance." *Southeast Asian Studies* 42(4): 418–41.

Schwenkel, Christina. 2012. "Civilizing the City: Socialist Ruins and Urban Renewal in Central Vietnam." *positions: east asia cultures critique* 20(2): 437–70.

Seeger, Charles. 1966. "The Music Process as a Function in a Context of Functions." *Inter-American Institute for Musical Research* 2: 1–36.

Shannon, Jonathan H. 2003. "Sultans of Spin: Syrian Sacred Music on the World Stage." *American Anthropologist* 105(2): 266–77.

Shelemay, Kay Kaufman. 2006. "Ethiopian Musical Invention in Diaspora: A Tale of Three Musicians." *Diaspora: A Journal of Transnational Studies* 15(2/3): 303–20.

Shelemay, Kay Kaufman, and Steven Kaplan. 2006. "Introduction." *Diaspora: A Journal of Transnational Studies* 15(2/3): 191–213.

Shils, Edward. 1981. *Tradition.* Chicago: University of Chicago Press.

Simmel, Georg. [1911] 1959. "The Ruin." In *Georg Simmel, 1858–1918,* edited by Kurt H. Wolff, 259–66. Columbus: Ohio State University Press.

Singh, Julietta. 2018. *Unthinking Mastery: Dehumanism and Decolonial Entanglements.* Durham and London: Duke University Press.

Sơn Nam. [1969] 2006. "Người Việt có dân tộc tính không?" ["Do Vietnamese Have a National Character?"]. In *Đình miễu và lễ hội dân gian miền Nam* [*Temples and Folk Festivals of Southern Vietnam*], 277–381. Tp. Hồ Chí Minh: NXB Trẻ.

Sơn Nghĩa. 2016. "Nhạc sĩ Huỳnh Khải – người hết lòng vì âm nhạc dân tộc" ["Musician Huỳnh Khải: Devoted to National Music"]. *Báo ảnh Việt Nam*, November 14, 2016. https://vietnam.vnanet.vn/vietnamese/nhac-si-huynh-khai-nguoi-het-long-vi-am -nhac-dan-toc/265513.html (accessed August 15, 2018).

Stahl, Matt. 2013. *Unfree Masters: Recording Artists and the Politics of Work.* Durham and London: Duke University Press.

Stamatis, Yona. 2011. "Rebetiko Nation: Hearing Pavlos Vassiliou's Alternative Greekness Through Rebetiko Song." PhD diss., University of Michigan.

Stock, Jonathan P.J. 1996. *Musical Creativity in Twentieth-Century China· Ahing, His Music, and Its Changing Meanings.* Rochester: University of Rochester Press.

Stone, Ruth M. 2008. *Theory for Ethnomusicology.* New York: Routledge.

Stuart-Fox, Martin. 1998. *The Lao Kingdom of Lān Xāng: Rise and Decline.* Bangkok: White Lotus Press.

Sugarman, Jane C. 1997. *Engendering Song: Singing and Subjectivity at Prespa Albanian Weddings.* Chicago and London: University of Chicago Press.

Sutton, R. Anderson. 1991. *Traditions of Gamelan Music in Java: Musical Pluralism and Regional Identity.* Cambridge: Cambridge University Press.

———. 2001/2002. "Individuality and 'Writing' in Javanese Music Learning." *Asian Music* 33(1): 75–103.

———. 2006. "Tradition Serving Modernity? The Musical Lives of a Makassarese Drummer." *Asian Music* 37(1): 1–23.

Sutton-Smith, Brian. 1997. *The Ambiguity of Play.* Cambridge, MA and London: Harvard University Press.

Taberd, AJ.L. [1838] 2004. *Dictionarium Anamitico Latinum.* Hà Nội: NXB Văn học.

Tai, Hue-Tam Ho. 1992. *Radicalism and the Origins of the Vietnamese Revolution.* Cambridge: Harvard University Press.

———. 2001. "Introduction: Situating Memory." In *The Country of Memory: Remaking the Past in Late Socialist Vietnam*, edited by Hue-Tam Ho Tai, 1–17. Berkeley: University of California Press.

Tấn Đức and Chí Quốc. 2014. "Đừng làm đờn ca tài tử biến chất" ["Don't Alter Đờn ca tài tử"]. *Tuổi Trẻ*, April 28, 2014. http://tuoitre.vn/Van-hoa-Giai-tri/604805 /dung-lam-don-ca-tai-tu-bien-chat.html (accessed July 1, 2014).

Taruskin, Richard. 1992. "Tradition and Authority." *Early Music* 20(2): 311–25.

Taylor, Diana. 2009. "Performing Ruins." In *Telling Ruins in Latin America*, edited by

Michael J. Lazzara and Vicky Unruh, 13–26. New York: Palgrave Macmillan.

Taylor, K.W. 2013. *A History of the Vietnamese*. Cambridge: Cambridge University Press.

Taylor, Philip. 2001. *Fragments of the Present: Searching for Modernity in Vietnam's South*. Honolulu: University of Hawai'i Press.

Thái Văn Kiểm. 1950. *La Princesse Huyền-Trân et l'influence sino-chàme sur la musique classique Vietnamienne* [*The Huyền-Trân Princess and the Sino-Champanese Influence on Vietnamese Traditional Music*]. Saigon: Editions "France-Vietnam."

———. 1964. "Panorama de la musique classique vietnamienne: Des origines a nos jours" ["Perspectives on Vietnamese Traditional Music: From the Origins to Today"]. *Bulletin de la Société des Etudes Indochinoises* 39(1): 55–102.

Thanh Hiệp. 2014. "Xứng danh bậc thầy đờn, ca" ["A Worthy Rank of Playing and Singing"]. *Người lao động*, October 18, 2014. http://nld.com.vn/van-hoa-van-nghe/xung -danh-bac-thay-don-ca-20141018085658421.htm (accessed August 25, 2018).

Thanh Nien. 2011. "Save a Folk Music Genre from Crassness." *Thanh Nien Daily*, April 15, 2011. http://www.thanhniennews.com/arts-culture/save-a-folk-music-genre-from -crassness-22478.html (accessed August 8, 2013).

Thế Hạnh. 2013. "Kiên Giang nhiều sân chơi hấp dẫn cho người mộ điệu tài tử" ["Kiên Giang has Many Stages to Engage Tài tử Recruits"]. *Báo Văn hóa Điện tử*, October 16, 2013. http://www.baovanhoa.vn/VANHOAVANNGHE/print-57996.vho (accessed October 17, 2013).

Thrasher, Alan R. 2001. "Yueqin." In *Grove Music Online* (*Oxford Music Online*). https:// doi.org/10.1093/gmo/9781561592630.article.46583 (accessed February 22, 2021).

———. 2008. Sizhu *Instrumental Music of South China: Ethos, Theory and Practice*. Leiden and Boston: Brill.

Thương Tùng. 2005. "Chủ nhiệm câu lạc bộ Tiếng Hát Quê Hương – Nghệ sĩ đàn tranh Phạm Thúy Hoan: Âm nhạc dân tộc đã giữ tôi ở lại" ["Director of the Tiếng Hát Quê Hương Ensemble – Đàn tranh artist Phạm Thúy Hoan: National Music Kept Me Here"]. *Doanh nhân Sài Gòn cuối tuần*, September 30, 2005. http://www.tienghatquehuong .com/Press/PTH_ANDT.htm (accessed February 15, 2011).

Tiersot, Julien. 1889. *Musique pittoresques: Promenades musicales à l'exposition de 1889* [*Picturesque Music: Musical Excursions at the 1889 Exposition*]. Paris: Librairie Fischbacher.

———. 1901a. "Ethnographie musicale, notes prises à l'Exposition (14e article): la musique chinoise et indo-chinoise" ["Musical Ethnography and Notes Taken on the Exposition (14th article): Chinese and Indochinese Music"]. *Le Ménestrel* 67(2): 11–12.

———. 1901b. "Ethnographie musicale, notes prises à l'Exposition (15e article): la musique chinoise et indo-chinoise" ["Musical Ethnography and Notes Taken on the Exposition (15th article): Chinese and Indochinese Music"]. *Le Ménestrel* 67(3): 19–20.

Titon, Jeff Todd. 2009. "Music and Sustainability: An Ecological Viewpoint." *The World of Music* 51(1): 119–37.

Tô Vũ, Chí Vũ, and Thụy Loan. 1977. "Âm nhạc phương Tây đã thâm nhập vào Việt Nam như thế nào?" ["How Did Western Music Infiltrate Vietnam?"] *Nghiên cứu Nghệ thuật* 17: 78–90.

Toynbee, Jason. 2017. "The Labour That Dare Not Speak Its Name." In *Distributed Creativity: Collaboration and Improvisation in Contemporary Music*, edited by Eric F. Clarke and Mark Doffman, 37–51. New York: Oxford University Press.

Trainor, John Paul. 1977. "Modality in the *Nhạc Tài Tử* of South Vietnam." PhD diss., University of Washington.

Trần Quang Hải. 2010. "Đàn tranh được phổ biến, thịnh hành nhất vào thời gian nào thưa chú?" ["When was the Zither Popularized and Made Prevalent?"]. *Vietnamese: From Sea to Sea* http://www.vsscanada.org/vn/culture/art_and_music/the_zither/the_zither_page_4.php (accessed November 18, 2010).

Trần Sanh Lại. 1930. *Bản đờn và bài ca theo điệu cải-lương dễ đờn và dễ ca lắm* [*Pieces to Play and Sing in the Style of Cải Lương: Easy to Play and Really Easy to Sing*]. Saigon: Bao-Ton.

Trần Văn Khải. 1970. *Nghệ thuật sân khấu Việt Nam* [*Vietnamese Theatrical Art*]. Sài Gòn: Nhà sách Khai Trí.

Trần Văn Khê. 1959. "Mises au point de l'étude sur la musique sino-viêtnamienne et les chants populaires du Việt Nam" ["Clarifications of the Study on Sino-Vietnamese Music and the Popular Songs of Vietnam"]. *Bulletin de la Société des Études Indochinoises* XXXIV No. 1: 13–19.

———. 1962. *La musique vietnamienne traditionnelle* [*Vietnamese Traditional Music*]. Paris: Presses Universitaires de France.

———. 1967. *Viêt-Nam (Les Traditions Musicales)* [*Vietnam (The Musical Traditions)*]. Berlin: Buchet/Chastel.

———. 2000. *Văn hóa và âm nhạc dân tộc* [*Culture and National Music*]. Tp. Hồ Chí Minh: NXB Thanh Niên.

———. 2004. *Du ngoạn trong âm nhạc truyền thống Việt Nam* [*Excursions in Vietnamese Traditional Music*]. Tp. Hồ Chí Minh: NXB. Trẻ.

———. 2013. "Đờn ca tài tử Nam bộ được UNESCO vinh danh – Học chân phương mà đờn hoa lá" ["Southern Đờn ca tài tử Inscribed by UNESCO – Learn Through the Basics but Play in the Foliage"]. *Báo Đà Nẵng*, December 16, 2013. http://www.baodanang.vn/channel/5414/201312/don-ca-tai-tu-nam-bo-duoc-unesco-vinh-danh-hoc-chan-phuong-ma-don-hoa-la-2293949/ (accessed June 12, 2015).

Trigg, Dylan. 2009. "The Place of Trauma: Memory, Hauntings, and the Temporality of Ruins." *Memory Studies* 2: 87–101.

Trinh Nguyễn. 2013. "Chính sách văn hóa – quyết nhanh, làm chậm" ["Cultural Policy: Decide Quickly, Implement Slowly"]. *Thanh Niên*, June 13, 2013. https://thanhnien.vn/van-hoa/chinh-sach-van-hoa-quyet-nhanh-lam-cham-25986.html (accessed October 17, 2013).

Trouillet, J.-Paul, ed. 1906. "L'Indo-Chine à l'Exposition de Marseille" ["Indochina at the Marseille Exposition"]. *La Dépêche Coloniale Illustrée* 6(9): 97–108.

Trương Bình Tòng. 1996. *Nhạc tài tử, Nhạc sân khấu cải lương* [*Nhạc tài tử, The Music of Cải lương Theatre*]. Tp. Hồ Chí Minh: NXB Sân khấu.

Trường Chinh. [1944] 1985. "Mấy nguyên tắc lớn của cuộc vận động văn hóa mới Việt Nam lúc này" ["Some Great Principles of Mobilizing a New Vietnamese Culture"]. In *Một chặng đường văn hóa: Hồi ức và tư liệu về việc tiếp nhận Đề cương văn hóa (1943) của Đảng* [*One Stage in the Direction of Culture: Recollections and Documents of the Work of Accepting the Party's Draft of the Fundamentals of Vietnamese Culture*], edited by Nguyễn Phúc et al., 21–26. Hà Nội: NXB Tác phẩm mới.

———. [1948] 1985. "Chủ nghĩa Mắc và văn hóa Việt Nam" ["Marxism and Vietnamese Culture"]. In *Về văn hóa và nghệ thuật Tập I* [*On Culture and Art, Volume I*], edited by Lý Hải Châu, 52–124. Hà Nội: NXB. Văn học.

Turino, Thomas. 1990. "Structure, Context, and Strategy in Musical Ethnography." *Ethnomusicology* 34(3): 399–412.

———. 2008. *Music as Social Life: The Politics of Participation*. Chicago and London: University of Chicago Press.

Turley, William S. 2009. *The Second Indochina War: A Concise Political and Military History*. Lanham: Rowman & Littlefield Publishers, Inc.

Valverde, Kieu-Linh Caroline. 2012. *Transnationalizing Viet Nam: Community, Culture, and Politics in the Diaspora*. Philadelphia: Temple University Press.

Vo, Nghia M. 2011. *Saigon: A History*. Jefferson, NC and London: McFarland & Company, Inc.

Võ Trường Kỳ. 2014. *Đờn ca tài tử Nam bộ*. Hà Nội: NXB Đại học Quốc gia Hà Nội.

Vũ Huy Chân. 1955. "Nước Việt Nam với 5 000 năm lịch sử" ["The Five-thousand-year History of Vietnam"]. *Văn hóa nguyệt san* 1(3): 350–52.

Vũ Nhật Thăng. 1998. *Thang âm Nhạc Cải lương – Tài tử* [*Scales of Cải lương and Tài tử Music*]. Hà Nội: Viện âm nhạc, NXB Âm nhạc.

Vũ Tự Lân. 1997. *Những ảnh hưởng của âm nhạc châu Âu trong ca khúc Việt Nam giai đoạn 1930-1950* [*The Influences of Western Music on Vietnamese Stage Melodies from 1930 to 1950*]. Hà Nội: NXB Thế Giới.

Vương Hồng Sển. [1968] 2007. *Hồi ký 50 năm mê hát: Năm mươi năm Cải lương* [*Memories of 50 Years of Loving to Sing: Fifty Years of Cải lương*]. Tp. Hồ Chí Minh: NXB Trẻ.

Wachsmann, Klaus. 1961. "Criteria for Acculturation." In *International Musicological Society Report of the Eighth Congress, New York 1961*, edited by Jan LaRue, 139–49. Basel: Bärenreiter Kassel.

Waterman, Richard A. [1955] 1971. "Music in Australian Aboriginal Culture—Some Sociological and Psychological Implications." In *Readings in Ethnomusicology*, edited by David P. McAllester, 167–74. New York: Johnson Reprint Corp.

Watts, Alan, with Al Chung-liang Huang. 1975. *Tao: The Watercourse Way*. New York: Pantheon Books.

Wenger, Etienne. 1998. *Communities of Practice: Learning, Meaning, and Identity*. New York: Cambridge University Press.

Whitmore, John K. 2011. "'The Last Great King of Classical Southeast Asia: 'Chế Bồng Nga' and Fourteenth-century Champa." In *The Cham of Vietnam: History, Society and Art*, edited by Trần Kỳ Phương and Bruce M. Lockhart, 168–203. Singapore: NUS Press.

Wilcox, Emily E. 2018. "Dynamic Inheritance: Representative Works and the Authoring of Tradition in Chinese Dance." *Journal of Folklore Research* 55(1): 77–111.

Williamson, John, and Martin Cloonan. 2007. "Rethinking the Music Industry." *Popular Music* 26(2): 305–22.

Winnicott, D. W. [1971] 2005. *Playing and Reality*. London and New York: Routledge.

Witzleben, J. Lawrence. 1995. *"Silk and Bamboo" Music in Shanghai: The Jiangnan Sizhu Instrumental Ensemble Tradition*. Kent, OH: Kent State University Press.

Wolters, O. W. 1967. *Early Indonesian Commerce: A Study of the Origins of Srivijaya*. Ithaca: Cornell University Press.

———. [1982] 1999. *History, Culture, and Region in Southeast Asian Perspectives*. Ithaca: SEAP Publications.

Wong, Deborah. 2001. *Sounding the Center: History and Aesthetics in Thai Buddhist Performance*. Chicago and London: University of Chicago Press.

———. 2004. *Speak It Louder: Asian Americans Making Music*. New York and London: Routledge.

Woodside, Alexander Barton. [1971] 1988. *Vietnam and the Chinese Model: A Comparative Study of Vietnamese and Chinese Government in the First Half of the Nineteenth Century*. Cambridge, MA and London: Harvard University Press.

———. 1983. "The Historical Background." In *The Tale of Kiều*, edited by Huỳnh Sanh Thông, xi–xvii. New Haven, CT: Yale University Press.

Xuân Hạ and Đất Mũi. 2013. "Phó Thủ tướng Vũ Văn Ninh: Phát huy hơn nữa các giá trị của đờn ca tài tử" ["Deputy Prime Minister Vũ Văn Ninh: Encourage the Promotion of the Value of Đờn ca tài tử"]. *Sài Gòn Giải Phóng*, July 5, 2013. http://www.sggp.org.vn/pho -thu-tuong-vu-van-ninh-phat-huy-hon-nua-cac-gia-tri-cua-don-ca-tai-tu-228873. html (accessed August 27, 2018).

Yung, Bell. 2009. "Tsar Teh-yun at Age 100: A Life of Qin Music, Poetry, and Calligraphy." In *Lives in Chinese Music*, edited by Helen Rees, 65–90. Urbana: University of Illinois Press.

Zembylas, Tasos, and Martin Niederauer. 2018. *Composing Processes and Artistic Agency: Tacit Knowledge in Composing*. Oxon and New York: Routledge.

Select Discography

Nguyễn T. Phong. 1989. *Phong Nguyen: Improvisation*. World Music Enterprises WME1007. Cassette.

Nguyễn Thiện Vũ. n.d. *Độc tấu guitar phím lõm 20 bản tổ đờn ca tài tử*. [20 Fundamental Pieces of Đờn ca tài tử for Solo Guitar] https://www.youtube.com/watch?v=hqB _adDFVvI (accessed August 28, 2018).

Nguyên Vinh Bao and Trân Van Khê. [1972] 1992. *Vietnam: Tradition du Sud*. CD. Ocora Radio France C 580043.

Trần Hải Đăng and Đoàn Thanh Tùng. 2014. *Vietnam le Don Ca Tai Tu: Music de Chambre du Mekong du Mékong / Vietnam: The Don Ca Tai Tu: Chamber Music of the Mekong Delta*. CD. INEDIT/Maison des Cultures du Monde W 260148.

Videos and Documentary Films

2MORO Music. 2016. "Võ Đông Sơ Bạch Thu Hà (Trap Remix)" YouTube. https://www .youtube.com/watch?v=XcXP_L3WS-U (accessed August 16, 2020).

BTV. 2015. "Giọng ca nhí Hò Xự Xang Xê Cống: Phần II" ["The Voice of Young People Singing Sol La Do Re Mi"]. YouTube (originally on Bạc Liêu Television). https://www .youtube.com/watch?v=pIwHVmQf3tA (accessed August 25, 2018).

HTV. 2007. *Ngân vang mãi tiếng đàn tranh* [*The Sound of the Zither Resonates Forever*]. DVD. Tp. Hồ Chí Minh: Đài truyền hình thành phố Hồ Chí Minh.

Huỳnh Khải. 2011b. "Huynh Khai – Vong co hai 3 – Van Huong.wmv" ["Huỳnh Khải – Comedy Vọng cổ 3 – Văn Hường"]. YouTube. https://www.youtube.com /watch?v=xLNg8JKx4Vk (accessed July 13, 2021).

Lâm Hải 2013. "Lịch sử Việt Nam 4000 năm" ["4000 Years of Vietnamese History"]. YouTube (originally on Zing TV). https://www.youtube.com/watch?v=ZkHBYz0_yt4 (accessed August 9, 2016).

Truyền Hình Đồng Tháp. 2018. "Chị Chiệp bán vé số hát vọng cổ ngọt như mía cùng nghệ sỹ Thanh Hàng" ["Ms. Chiệp Sells Lottery Tickets and Sweetly Sings Vọng cổ with Thanh Hàng"]. YouTube (originally on Đồng Tháp Television). https://www .youtube.com/watch?v=IDX98voffIQ (accessed July 13, 2021).

INDEX

Page numbers in *italics* indicate figures and maps.

narratives, 59; mastery discourse and, 44; musical practice during, 29, 66–71; neocolonialism, 16, 45; rules based on system of, 26

communal creativity, 34, 37–38

Communist Party, 18–19, 31, 144, 149–50, 161, 176

Confucianism, 5, 63, 143

Conquergood, Dwight, 49–51

Cook, Nicholas, 25

copyright laws, 228–29n7

court music, 62, 69, 163, 203

creativity *(sáng tạo):* Buddhism and, 5, 63; communal, 34, 37–38; conceptualizations of, 20, 24–28; Confucianism and, 5, 63; Daoism and, 5–6, 63–65, 218; discriminatory nature of, 8–9, 26–27, 34, 45, 48, 216; distributed, 47–49, 53; divine elements of, 24–26, 39; ethnocentric views of, 39; in ethnomusicology, 8–9, 15, 34–49, 52–54, 216, 228n6; in folk music, 41, 48, 50; genius and. *See* genius creativity paradigm; global, 15, 19–20, 32–33, 133, 216–17, 219; humanistic approach to, 35, 37, 39; identity formation and, 28–32, 49; improvisation and. *See* improvisation; local, 20, 32, 34, 42–43, 61–65, 199, 217; in Marxist ideology, 29–32; mediators of, 16, 122–28, 200, 215; metaphors of, 5, 16, 24, 112–22; in national music, 42; neoliberal model of, 6, 24, 28, 31, 44, 216–17; objectifying nature of, 8, 44; play and, 49–53; in public discourse, 15, 18–20, 23–24, *24*, 216; reparative, 15, 44, 47–49, 172, 175, 217; social scientific approach to, 35, 37–39; technology in mediation, 16, 200, 215; temporal dimensions of, 25, 26; traditional, 19, 20, 57

Csikszentmihalyi, Mihaly, 26, 128–29

Csordas, Thomas, 5

Cù Huy Cận, 152

cultural development, 20, 139, 142–46, *162*, 162–67, 170

cultural production: in colonial era, 70, 145; drivers of, 43; historical narratives of, 59; models of, 51, 194; musical ruins and, 171; societal imbalance and, 146; state control of, 142, 145, 150–52; unification of, 149

Culture Monthly (journal), 146, 239n7

"Dạ cổ hoài lang," 7, 180, 205

Đắc Nhẫn, 88, 235n31

đàn kìm (lute): embellishment on, 118, 120, 121; features of, *84, 85;* at international expositions, 68, 71, 72; ornamentation and, 85, 101; scales produced by, 88–89, *89;* sound aesthetics and, 93; study of, 6, 13, 14; tuning of, 85, 89, 233n12

đàn sến (lute): embellishment on, 120–21, *121;* features of, 78, 85–87, *87;* origins of, 85–86, 233nn5–6; ornamentation and, 92; scales produced by, 88; study of, 10, 13

đàn tộc tính (also *tính dân tộc;* national character), 147, 152

đàn tranh (zither): Asian Zither Festival, 163–67, *165*, 242n33; embellishment on, *119,* 119–20; features of, 61, 82–85, *84;* improvisation and, 83, 85; at international expositions, 68, 72; ornamentation and, 80, 83, 85, 94, 101; study of, 6, 12; tuning of, 83, 90–91, *170,* 233n12

Daoism: creativity and, 5–6, 63–65, 218; metaphors in, 64, 112, 175; nonaction in, 64, 218; spontaneity in, 64–65, 130, 167, 218

de Certeau, Michel, 1–3

dehumanist approach, 45, 54, 217

Democratic Republic of Vietnam (DRVN): cultural policy in, 145, 150, 152–54, 160; establishment of, 144; musical practice in, 88. *See also* Vietnam

Densmore, Frances, 36

Derrida, Jacques, 183

development *(phát triển):* conceptualizations of, 180; cultural, 20, 139, 142–46, *162,* 162–67, 170; economic, 18–19, 142, 161, 170, 201; failures of, 16, 175–77, 182–85; as metaphor, 16, 142, 169–70, 219; of

Index **273**

lutes. See đàn kìm; đàn sến

national music *(nhạc dân tộc):* creativity in, 42; description of, 10; development of, 154–61, 167; *rao* in, 96; scale utilized in, 88

National School of Music (Saigon), 11, 12, 70, 146–48, 154, 160

nationalism: folk songs and, 55, 151, 156; homogenizing tendencies of, 48; in Huế Festival performances, 140, 141; perceptions of traditional music based on, 190; unity through, 146, 147, 153

neocolonialism, 16, 45

neoliberal model of creativity, 6, 24, 28, 31, 44, 216–17

neotraditional music, 153, 188, 196

Nettl, Bruno, 38

Ngô Đình Diệm, 144, 239n7

Ngọc Thới, 88, 235n31

Nguyễn Đăng Thục, 146

Nguyễn Đình Hòa, 148, 240–41n16

Nguyễn Đình Lai, 60, 61

Nguyễn Đình Thi, 146, 239–40n8

Nguyễn Đức Hiệp, 69

Nguyễn Lê Tuyên, 69

Nguyen Nang Dac, 60

Nguyễn Phúc An, 63

Nguyen Phung, 60

Nguyễn Phụng Michel, 70, 144–45, 147, 152, 240n9

Nguyễn Quang Đại, 71

Nguyễn Tấn Dũng, 203, 206

Nguyễn Thái Hòa, *159*

Nguyễn Thị Chiệp, 210–13, *212*

Nguyễn Thị Minh Ngọc, 71

Nguyễn Thị Trâm Anh, 56

Nguyễn Thiện Nhân, 18–19, 217

Nguyễn Thiện Vũ, 120, 208

Nguyễn Thuyết Phong: background of, 14; on Buddhist influences, 62–63; on *đờn ca tài tử,* 7; on folk music, 156; on frame metaphor, 113; on modes, 88; on "Nam xuân," 123; on Nguyễn Thuyết Phong, 11; on traditional music, 9

Nguyễn Tống Triều, 71, 72

Nguyễn Tuấn Khanh, 72

Nguyễn Văn Ngưu, 235n31

Nguyen Viang, 68–69

Nguyễn Vĩnh Bảo: on *Bắc* mode, 234n31; background of, 10–12, 147, 148; criticisms of, 181–82, 190–91; on development, 180, 182, 184–86, 196; on *đờn ca tài tử,* 6–8, 101, 219; on embellishment, 117–21, *119;* improvisations by, 62, 92; influence of, 104–5, 172; instruments played by, 12, 80, 81, *84;* master status of, 45; on memory and music, 56, 75, 95; metaphors utilized by, 112, 218; on musical ruins, 171–73, 177, 183–84, 187–89; on "Nam xuân," 123, 125, 127; on ornamentation, 92–94; on pitch pairs, 90–91; on preservation of traditional music, 169–70; *rao* as used by, 96, 112, 234n27; on rules of performance, 60, 109; spontaneity in performances of, 75, 76; tuning practices, 90, *170,* 235n41; writings of, 180–83

nhạc dân tộc. See national music

nhạc đỏ (red music), 149

nhạc lễ. See ceremonial music

Nhạc lễ (Hạ) mode, 88, 97, 99, 99–100, 118

nhạc tài tử Nam bộ. See đờn ca tài tử

nhấn. See pitch bending

Njoku, Raphael Chijioke, 109

nonaction: in Daoism, 64, 218; inspiration and, 74; musical ruins and, 174; spontaneity from, 130

Nooshin, Laudan, 35, 39, 40, 43

northern Vietnam: Chinese influence in, 58; ethnomusicological study of, 9; European influence in, 66; historical narratives of, 58. *See also* Democratic Republic of Vietnam

Norton, Barley, 9, 76, 115, 143, 151, 203

Nzewi, Meki, 52

Ó Briain, Lonán, 9

Ó Murchadha, Felix, 174

Oán mode, 88, 97, 100, 103–4, 213, 236n49

objectification, 8, 44

Olsen, Dale A., 214

ornamentation: by *đàn kìm* players, 85, 101; by *đàn sến* players, 92; by *đàn tranh* players, 80, 83, 85, 94, 101; glissandi, 80, 83, 118–19, 158, 166, 184, 186; in improvisation, 92; modes and, 91–93, *99*, 101–4, *102*; musical adaptations through, 7, 186, 187; sound aesthetics and, 94; tapping, 83, 91–92, 94, 134, 166; tremolo, 92, 120, 166. *See also* pitch bending; vibrato

Pang, Laikwan, 28, 31, 35, 43, 51, 171
Park, Gil-Sung, 228n6
Pasler, Jann, 67–68
Perlman, Marc, 110, 112
Phạm Cao Phong, 29
Phạm Duy, 4, 9
Phạm Ngọc Lanh, 3, 14, 141
Phạm Thúy Hoan: background of, 12; influence of, 160, 166–67; international collaborations, 145, 161, 163–64, 219; on seeds of tradition, 55–56, 107, 218; social activism of, 156; as Teacher of Merit, 12, 143; traditional music promoted by, 193–94; on *Việt Cộng*, 229–30n1; youth culture supported by, 215. *See also* Sounds of the Homeland Ensemble
Phan Kế Bính, 143–44
phát triển. See development
Phung Hoàng Sang, 124, 125
pitch bending *(nhấn)*: categories of, 92; emotional expression through, 5; intervallic relationships in, 91–92; modes and, 101, 102, *102*; muscle memory for, 91, 158; overuse of, 121; techniques for, 85, 101
pitch pairs, 90–91, 99
play, 49–53
popular music, 52, 140, 149, 176, 192, 214
Puar, Jasbir, 51
Pure Land Buddhism, 62

Quang Dũng, 125, 127–28
queer theory, 51

Racy, Ali Jihad, 129
Ramnarine, Tina, 36, 40, 43, 48, 50

rao (improvised prelude): functions of, 80, 95–96; length of, 96, 234n27; metaphorical use of, 112; of "Nam xuân," 134–35, *135*; named works following, 83, 85, 97; spontaneity in, 213
refugee communities, 2, 9, 149
Rein, Shaun, 31
reparative creativity, 15, 44, 47–49, 172, 175, 217
Republic of Vietnam (RVN): collapse of, 93, 149; creativity as practiced during, 19; cultural policy in, 143, 145–48, 152–54, 160; establishment of, 144; musical practice in, 88. *See also* Vietnam
Reyes, Adelaida, 9
Rice, Timothy, 108
Roach, Joseph, 179
Robinson, Dylan, 3
Rosen, Jody, 26, 28
ruins. *See* musical ruins
rung. See vibrato
RVN. *See* Republic of Vietnam

Saigon. *See* Ho Chi Minh City
sáng tạo. See creativity
Sarath, Ed, 229n6
Sáu Hóa, 13, 124–25
scales, 88–90, *89*, *99*, 99–104, *101–2*
Schwenkel, Christina, 176
Second Indochina War. *See* Vietnam War
seed metaphor, 55–57, 65, 79
Seeger, Charles, 37
Shelemay, Kay Kaufman, 43
Shils, Edward, 185
Sidney, Philip, 25
Signifyin(g), 51, 110
Simmel, Georg, 173–74
Singh, Julietta, 35, 44, 45, 143, 217
social ecstatic practice, 131–34, *133*
social media: access restrictions, 176; information dissemination with, 14, 20, 209–10; musical ruins and, 173, 179, 189–91
social scientific approach, 35, 37–39

Socialist Republic of Vietnam (SRVN). *See* Vietnam

solo ecstatic practice, 134–36, *135, 137*

song thinh technique, 116, 120–21, *121,* 127, 158

soul of music, 5, 8, 94, 121, 140, 169

sound aesthetics, 93–94

Sounds of the Homeland Ensemble: development initiatives, 143, 154–61, 167; folk music utilized by, 55, 107; history of, 153–54; international collaborations, 145; lack of *rao* in, 96; performances by, 9–10, 96, 158–60, *159,* 165; rehearsals of, 9–10, 55, 107, 143, 153–58, *155, 157*

southern Vietnam: Chinese influence in, 60–61; cultural production in, 59; economic growth in, 200; ethnomusicological study of, 9–10; European influence in, 66–70; historical narratives of, 57–59; international collaborations, 163; map of, *11;* migration to, 59–61, 71, 79, 86, 217; modernization of, 8, 59; rural areas of, 227–28n11; in twenty-first century, 20–24, *21. See also* music; Republic of Vietnam; *specific cities*

spontaneity: containment of, 176; in Daoism, 64–65, 130, 167, 218; ecstatic practice and, 108, 129–30, 134; embellishment and, 16, 118; guided, 76; inspiration and, 74–75; musical ruins and, 174; from nonaction, 130; in pitch production, 127; in *rao,* 213; in youth culture, 215. *See also* improvisation

SRVN (Socialist Republic of Vietnam). *See* Vietnam

Stahl, Matt, 228–29n7

Stock, Jonathan, 41–42

structural melody. *See lòng bản*

Sugarman, Jane, 47

tâm hồn. See soul of music

tapping *(mõ),* 83, 91–92, 94, 134, 166

Taylor, Diana, 172

Taylor, K. W., 59

Taylor, Philip, 179, 180

technology: cultural consumption through, 22;

development and, 141–42; in mediation of creativity, 16, 200, 215. *See also* social media

Thái Văn Kiểm, 173

Thầy Phước Cường, 14, 62, 63, 78–79, 113, 114

Theravada Buddhism, 230n4

Thrasher, Alan, 74, 232n27, 233n5

Thụy Loan, 66–67, 70

Tiếng Hát Quê Hương. *See* Sounds of the Homeland Ensemble

Tiersot, Julien, 68, 69

timbre, 31, 52, 93–94, 120, 198, 211

tính dân tộc (also *dân tộc tính;* national character), 147, 152

Titon, Jeff Todd, 172

Tô Vũ, 66–67, 70

Toynbee, Jason, 39, 228n7

traditional creativity, 19, 20, 57

traditional music. *See đờn ca tài tử;* folk music

Trainor, John Paul, 88, 101, 103, 236n45

Trần Minh Đức: background of, 12–13; in Cần Thơ performance space, 78–79; ecstatic practice by, 108, 128, 130, 132, 134–36; on frame of practice, 114; instruments played by, 10, 13, 78, 86–87, *87;* metaphors utilized by, 112, 218; "Nam xuân" performed by, 134–36, *135, 137;* on ornamentation, 92

Trần Văn Khải, 71–72

Trần Văn Khê: on creativity, 112–13; on *đàn sến,* 233n5; on *đờn ca tài tử,* 179, 208, 244n2; educational background, 12; on embellishment, 117; international collaborations, 163; on modes, 87–88, 103, 236n46; on "Nam xuân," 123; on pitch usage, 236n43; on traditional music, 9, 61

tremolo, 92, 120, 166

Trigg, Dylan, 174, 175

Trương Bình Tòng, 101, 103–4, 236n49

Trường Chinh, 150, 151

Trường Quốc gia Âm nhạc (also Trường Quốc gia Âm nhạc Kịch nghệ). *See* National School of Music

tự nhiên. See spontaneity

Turino, Thomas, 10, 114, 128–29

MUSIC / CULTURE

A series from Wesleyan University Press
Edited by Deborah Wong, Sherrie Tucker, and Jeremy Wallach
Originating editors: George Lipsitz, Susan McClary, and Robert Walser

The Music/Culture series has consistently reshaped and redirected music scholarship. Founded in 1993 by George Lipsitz, Susan McClary, and Robert Walser, the series features outstanding critical work on music. Unconstrained by disciplinary divides, the series addresses music and power through a range of times, places, and approaches. Music/Culture strives to integrate a variety of approaches to the study of music, linking analysis of musical significance to larger issues of power—what is permitted and forbidden, who is included and excluded, who speaks and who gets silenced. From ethnographic classics to cutting-edge studies, Music/Culture zeroes in on how musicians articulate social needs, conflicts, coalitions, and hope. Books in the series investigate the cultural work of music in urgent and sometimes experimental ways, from the radical fringe to the quotidian. Music/Culture asks deep and broad questions about music through the framework of the most restless and rigorous critical theory.

Marié Abe
Resonances of Chindon-ya:
Sounding Space and Sociality
in Contemporary Japan

Frances Aparicio
Listening to Salsa: Gender, Latin Popular
Music, and Puerto Rican Cultures

Paul Austerlitz
Jazz Consciousness: Music, Race,
and Humanity

Christina Baade and Kristin McGee
Beyoncé in the World: Making Meaning
with Queen Bey in Troubled Times

Emma Baulch
Genre Publics: Popular Music, Technologies,
and Class in Indonesia

Harris M. Berger
Metal, Rock, and Jazz: Perception
and the Phenomenology
of Musical Experience

ABOUT THE AUTHOR

Alexander M. Cannon (he/him/his) is an associate professor in the Department of Music at the University of Birmingham in the United Kingdom. He holds an undergraduate degree in music and mathematical economics from Pomona College (California) and an MA and PhD from the University of Michigan. He currently serves as Co-Editor of *Ethnomusicology Forum* and as a member of the British Forum for Ethnomusicology Executive Committee. He has previously published in the journals *Asian Music, Ethnomusicology, Ethnomusicology Forum,* and the *Journal of Vietnamese Studies.*